PLAY, DREAMS

AND IMITATION

DATE			

FIRST PUBLISHED IN THE NORTON LIBRARY 1962

ISBN 0-393-00171-7

W. W. Norton & Company, Inc. is also the publisher of the works of Erik H. Erikson, Otto Fenichel, Karen Horney, Harry Stack Sullivan, and The Standard Edition of the Complete Psychological Works of Sigmund Freud.

W. W. Norton & Company, Inc., 500 Fifth Avenue, New York, NY 10110
W. W. Norton & Company Ltd, 10 Coptic Street, London WC1A 1PU

Printed in the United States of America

1 2 3 4 5 6 7 8 9 0

AUTHOR'S PREFACE
TO THE ENGLISH TRANSLATION

THE publication of the English translation of *La Formation du Symbole* is for me an opportunity to express my indebtedness to English-speaking psychologists, in particular to C. Spearman, S. and N. Issacs, C. Burt and C. W. Valentine, who have contributed so much to the study of the child and of symbolism. It is also a matter of great satisfaction to me that this book is now available to the English reading public.

This volume is the third of a series devoted to the first years of the child's development, the two others being concerned with the beginnings of intelligence and the child's construction of reality (*La naissance de l'intelligence chez l'enfant* and *La construction du réel chez l'enfant*). Although this book contains frequent references to the two other volumes, which deal with the same three children and study the relationships between their mental activities, it nevertheless constitutes in itself an independent and complete study.

I should like to add a word with regard to the translation. A certain author is said to have declared that he understood himself better as a result of reading a French translation of his work. This is probably true of all good translations ; but unfortunately they are very rare ! In the present case I feel that my original somewhat difficult text has become in English more understandable, thanks to the efforts of my translators, to whom I take this opportunity of expressing my appreciation.

JEAN PIAGET.

May, 1951.

TRANSLATORS' NOTE

MOST of the terms used in the text are self-explanatory, or explained as they occur. It is thought advisable, however, to define the following important, recurrent terms at the outset.

Equilibrium. Used here to convey the idea that two changes in opposite directions balance each other without the balance necessarily being permanent. Since it is concerned with changes, it is dynamic.

Group. This is a notion taken from mathematics, and can be illustrated by the following example :—The operation of addition applied to whole numbers is such that (*a*) any two successive additions can be replaced by a third which combines them, and (*b*) each addition can be neutralised by a suitable subtraction called its inverse operation. A *group* is a set of operations such that (*a*) they can be composed so that any two will produce a third belonging to the same set, and (*b*) the set contains the inverse of each of the operations composing it.

Ludic. Used here to qualify behaviours related to play.

Oneiric. Used here to qualify dreams.

Operation. Although this word is taken from arithmetic, it contains a psychological component which is essential to the understanding of it. An operation is an action that has become abstract and has acquired the property of being combined with other operations, in particular in the form of groups.

Reversibility. This notion is taken from thermodynamics. In this branch of physics the processes form pairs, which represent two opposite directions in which a system can evolve. The equilibrium of these pairs is said to be reversible when the system can evolve indifferently in either direction. Reversibility here indicates a psychological situation analogous to that of physics, *i.e.*, the psychological processes involved are at any given moment in reversible equilibrium.

Schema. This word is used to indicate an elementary structure, particularly in the beginnings of psychological life.

CONTENTS

CONTENTS

Page

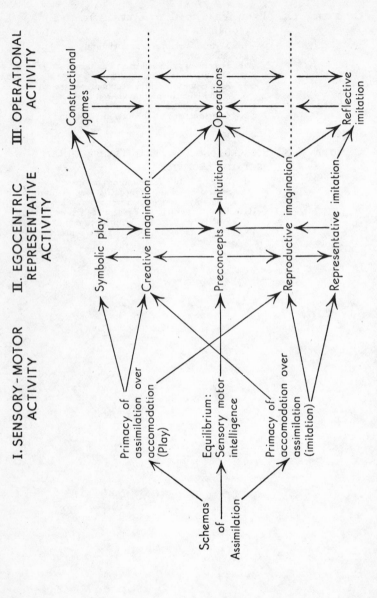

INTRODUCTION

La Genèse du nombre and *Le Développement des Quantités chez l'Enfant* were the last volumes we devoted to the development of rational thought in the child. These dealt with the construction of the various systems of operations involved in logical and mathematical functions when the mind is confronted with the real world. They were thus concerned with intuitive or representational thought only in a somewhat negative way, our main object being to indicate its shortcomings and show the necessity for completing and correcting it by means of operations properly so called. But imaged or intuitive representation as such raises a series of problems which need to be discussed in their own right. We need to consider the function of the development of representation and not only its ultimate inclusion within the framework of operations (or rather, that is to say, we need to consider the progressive articulations which gradually transform representation into operational, reversible thought). It is therefore important to give an account of the beginnings of representation and to attempt to understand its specific method of functioning. Only when this has been done is it possible to clarify the connection between intuition and operations, both in those cases where the first is produced into the second, and in those, which may be equally numerous, where imaged representation retains an existence of its own apart from operations, as in play, imitation, and symbolic thought.

In two previous volumes, *La Naissance de l'Intelligence* and *La Construction du Réel chez l'Enfant*, we studied sensory motor intelligence in the pre-verbal stage, *i.e.*, that aspect of intelligence which is a preparation in the field of elementary activity for what will much later become the operations of reflective thought. What now therefore requires to be done is to bridge the gap between sensory-motor activity prior to representation, and the operational forms of thought. The problem again becomes that of describing the beginnings of representational thought and of placing its evolution with respect to the sensory-motor stage at one end and the operational stage at the other.

Obviously these problems involve the question of the role of language, which has already been much studied. In our first two volumes, *Le Langage et la Pensée chez l'Enfant* and *Le Jugement et le Raisonnement chez l'Enfant*, we considered this question from the point of view of the socialisation of thought. We shall come back to it here only in connection with the first verbal schemas and with " preconcepts," so characteristic of the two to four-year-old stage. We shall rather try to show that the acquisition of language is itself subordinated to the working of a symbolic function which can be seen in the development of imitation and play as well as in that of verbal mechanisms. Our study of the beginnings of representation in the child will mainly be in those fields where the individual processes of mental life dominate the collective factors, and we shall emphasise these individual processes particularly in the case of imitation, which though it leads to inter-individual relationships does not necessarily result from them. We shall confine ourselves to the development of representation in general, only dealing with the description of particular representations in so far as they are related to those already studied in our previous works, *La Représentation du Monde* and *La Causalité Physique chez l'Enfant*.

Even within these limitations, the problems to be discussed are very wide. We shall first study the development of imitation. In *La Naissance de l'Intelligence* we have already made the assumption that representation derives to some extent from imitation. In his important book, *De l'Acte à la Pensée*, concerned with the same problems, Professor Wallon takes the same view, and gives us a further reason for reconsidering the question in the light of facts accumulated in the past from a study of our own children. We must say that, far from accepting all Professor Wallon's theses, we shall often be led to reply to him.

But imitation is but one of the sources of representation, for which it provides the necessary imaged " signifiers." Play also, especially from the point of view of " meanings " can be considered as leading from activity to representation, in so far as it evolves from its initial stage of sensory-motor activity to its second stage of symbolic or imaginative play. We would even say that it is in the evolution of play that the assimilating processes characteristic of the beginnings of individual representation are most clearly evident. The second and longest part of this volume will therefore be devoted to a study of play and related phenomena. We shall start by examining the beginnings of play during the first year, as an introduction to the study of the symbol. The question of games with rules will only be touched on, since one example, marbles, has already been studied at length in *Le Jugement Moral chez l'Enfant*. Hence it is symbolic play that will be our main concern, and discussion of it will inevitably lead us to a consideration of the question of " unconscious " symbolism and symbolic thought in general, in the sense of the psycho-analysts from Freud to Silberer, Adler and Jung.

Only after discussing the problems of imitation, play and unconscious symbolic thought can we then, in the third and last part, place within the whole structure the beginnings of cognitive representation and draw the resulting conclusions as to the mechanism of representational activity or the symbolic function.

We shall develop two main theses. The first is that in the field of play and imitation it is possible to trace the transition from sensory-motor assimilation and accommodation to the mental assimilation and accommodation which characterise the beginnings of representation. Representation begins when there is simultaneous differentiation and co-ordination between "signifiers" and "signified." The first differentiations are provided by imitation and the mental image derived from it, both of which extend accommodation to external objects. The meanings of the symbols, on the other hand, come by way of assimilation, which is the dominating factor in play and plays an equal part with accommodation in adapted representation. Having progressively separated at the sensory-motor level and so developed as to be capable of going beyond the immediate present, assimilation and accommodation finally come together in a combination made necessary by this advance beyond the immediate present. The constitution of the symbolic function is only possible as a result of this union between actual or mental imitation of an absent model and the " meanings " provided by the various forms of assimilation. Then it is that language, a system of collective signs, becomes possible, and through the set of individual symbols and of these signs the sensory-motor schemas can be transformed into concepts or integrate new concepts. Our first thesis, a continuation of that in *La Naissance de l'Intelligence*, will therefore be that there is functional continuity between the sensory-motor and the representational, a continuity which determines the construction of the successive structures. This hypothesis does not appear to be obvious. Professor Wallon objects that " Piaget, in spite of his insistence on the continuity of this progression, has been obliged to introduce two terms not included in the motor schemas: the ego and the symbol." *(De l'Acte à la Pensée*, p. 45.) On the contrary, we shall try to show how the symbol results from the pre-representational schematism. The ego will doubtless follow of itself.

Our second thesis is that the various forms of representation interact. There is representation when an absent model is imitated. There is representation in symbolic play, in imagination and even in dreams. The system of concepts and logical relations, both in their intuitive and operational forms, implies representation. What then are the elements common to these various representations, and is it even possible to maintain that they contain comparable mechanisms?

Classical associationist psychology found an easy solution to the problem by making all representations derive from a single, simple reality: the image, a direct continuation of sensation. But the image itself raises a problem, for far from being an immediate continuation of perception as such, it does not seem to intervene in mental life before the second year. Moreover, it is only a " signifier," or symbol, and to understand the part it plays it is necessary to study the relationship between the various " signifiers " and the various " signified," in short the whole representational activity.

A second means of attempting a solution of these problems is by bringing in social life. Professor Wallon, after attempting to explain the elementary forms of mental life, emotion at the " projective " level and that of " understanding of situations," by the intervention at various stages of physiological systems each integrating those which precede it but without preparing through functional continuity for those which will follow, has recourse to social factors such as ritual, myth, language and the higher forms of imitation in order to account for representation. But the question that then arises is why and how the child is influenced at certain definite moments by this or that social action. Language, for example, is acquired at this age and not at that, in this order and not in that, and therefore only modifies thought in so far as thought is susceptible of being modified. It is therefore not " social life " as a whole that psychology must invoke, but a series of relationships established in all possible combinations between individuals of distinct levels of mental development, and as a consequence of various types of interaction (coercion, co-operation, imitation, discussion, etc.). Though obviously social life plays an essential role in the elaboration of concepts and of the representational schemas related to verbal expression, it does not in itself explain the beginnings of the image or the symbol as they are to be seen in deferred imitation or in the first imaginative games of the one year-old child. Moreover, no sociologist has yet undertaken to prove the social origin of the unconscious " anatomical " symbols to be found in dreams or of the images of the half-sleeping state.

The problem we shall discuss in this volume is therefore that of the symbolic function itself considered as a mechanism common to the various systems of representations and as an individual mechanism whose existence is a prerequisite for interaction of thought between individuals and consequently for the constitution or acquisition of collective meanings. This in no way implies that we dispute the social nature of collective meanings, far from it, since we have constantly tried to show that reason implies co-operation and reciprocity. But the social fact is for us a fact to be explained, not to be invoked as an extra-psychological factor. Hence it seems to us that the study of the symbolic function must cover all the initial forms of representation, from imitation and ludic or oneiric symbols to verbal schemas and elementary pre-conceptual structures. Only then will the functional unity of the development which leads from sensory-motor to operational intelligence be seen through successive individual or social structures. Progressive equilibrium between assimilation of objects to individual activity and accommodation of activity to objects results in the reversibility which characterises the operations of reason, while the primacy of accommodation characterises imitation and the image, and the primacy of assimilation explains play and the " unconscious " symbol.

PART I

IMITATION

IMITATION does not depend on an instinctive or hereditary technique as P. Guillaume shows in a work which has thrown new light on the question. The child learns to imitate, and this learning process, like any other, raises all the problems involved in sensory-motor and mental development. This conclusion would still be true even if in the tendency to imitate there were an element transmitted through heredity, since a distinction must be made between a tendency and the technique which makes its development possible.

We would go further, and consider the pre-verbal imitation of the child as one of the manifestations of his intelligence. In tracing the development of imitation during the first two years, we cannot fail to be struck by its active character. During this period it is in no way " automatic " or " non-intentional." On the contrary, very early we find evidence of intelligent co-ordinations, both in the acquisition of the tools it uses and in its aims. Moreover, as we shall see, the connection between the stages of imitation and the six stages we found in the development of sensory-motor intelligence [1] is so close that in the analysis which follows we shall use the same scale.

This being the case, the facts can at once be interpreted in the following way. Sensory-motor intelligence is, in our view, the development of an assimilating activity which tends to incorporate external objects in its schemas while at the same time accommodating the schemas to the external world. A stable equilibrium between assimilation and accommodation results in properly intelligent adaptation. But if the subject's schemas of action are modified by the external world without his utilising this external world, i.e., if there is primacy of accommodation over assimilation, the activity tends to become imitation. Imitation is thus seen to be merely a continuation of the effort at accommodation, closely connected with the act of intelligence, of which it is one differentiated aspect, a temporarily detached part.

It is clear from the outset that the problem of imitation is linked with that of representation. Since representation involves the image of an object, it can be seen to be a kind of interiorised imitation, and therefore a continuation of accommodation.

[1] See *La naissance de l'intelligence chez l'enfant* and *La construction du réel chez l'enfant* (referred to later as *N.I.* and *C.R.* respectively).

CHAPTER I

AT what stage of development does imitation begin? The varying
opinions of writers with regard to this question are evidence of the
difficulties involved in making a sharp distinction between properly
representative imitation and its preparatory forms. Wallon goes so
far as to say that "imitation does not occur before the second half
of the second year." [1]

Such an opinion is admissible on the hypothesis that mental evolution takes place by discontinuous stages, but it begs the question by
assuming an absolute opposition between the representative and the
sensory-motor. As a matter of fact, even if there were justification
for relating the various stages of mental development to well-defined
neurological levels, the fact remains that, in spite of the relative
discontinuity of the structures, there is a certain functional continuity,
each structure preparing for its successors while utilising its predecessors. It is no explanation to say that there is a succession of
superposed psycho-neurological mechanisms at work, even if it can
be shown exactly how each one integrates those which precede it.
This is the point of view of the medical man, but the attitude of the
psychologist who wishes to profit from the findings of experimental
embryology must be based on a closer comparison between psycho-
genesis and organogenesis. The various stages which embryology shows
to exist in the construction of a living body are characterised not only
by a sequence of quite distinct and discontinuous structurations, but
also by a dynamics involving both continuity and a certain direction,
the latter being a tendency towards equilibrium or state of completion
of growth. [2]

Thus, when we studied the beginnings of intelligence (see *N.I.*),
we were forced to go as far back as the reflex in order to trace the
course of the assimilating activity which finally leads to the construction of adapted schemas, for it is only by a principle of functional
continuity that the indefinite variety of structures can be explained.
In the same way, if we call the act by which a model is reproduced

[1] *De l'Acte à la Pensée*, p. 157.
[2] "In embryology," says Brachet, "the true significance of the word 'development' must always be kept in mind. It means that all forms and all organs are
built up by a slow, progressive series of complications, closely interrelated and ending
only when the adult state is achieved." *La vie créatrice des formes* (Alcan, 1927), p. 171.

imitation (and this does not imply ability to represent the model, which may simply be " perceived "), we again find ourselves obliged to trace step by step, through the same stages as those of sensory-motor activity in general, all the behaviours which may achieve this result, beginning with the reflexes.

§ 1. *Stage I: Preparation through the reflex*

Since the reproduction of a model seems to involve an element acquired by experience, imitation would appear by definition to be excluded from the level of pure reflexes. The matter is, however, worthy of examination, since so many authors have believed in the hereditary character of imitation, not only as a tendency but also as a technique. We will begin with the few observations we have been able to make with regard to our own children:

> OBS. 1. On the very night after his birth, T. was wakened by the babies in the nearby cots and began to cry in chorus with them. At 0 ; 0 (3) he was drowsy, but not actually asleep, when one of the other babies began to wail; he himself thereupon began to cry. At 0 ; 0 (4) and 0 ; 0 (6) he again began to whimper, and started to cry in earnest when I tried to imitate his interrupted whimpering. A mere whistle and other cries failed to produce any reaction.

There are two possible interpretations of these commonplace observations, but neither of them seems to justify the use of the word imitation. On the one hand it may be that the baby was merely unpleasantly affected by being wakened by the cries of his neigh-bours, yet without establishing any relation between the sounds he heard and his own crying, whereas a whistle or other sound left him indifferent. On the other hand, it is possible that the crying occurred as a result of its repetition, owing to a kind of reflex analogous to that we saw in the case of suction (*N.I.*, Chap. I, § 1–2), but in this case with intensification of the sound through the help of the ear. In this second case, the crying of the other babies would increase the vocal reflex through confusion with his own crying.

Thus in neither case is there imitation, but merely the starting off of a reflex by an external stimulus. But although the reflex mechanisms do not give rise to imitation, their functioning involves certain pro-cesses which make imitation possible during the later stages. In so far as the reflex leads to repetition, which continues after the removal of the initial stimulus (*cf.* suction in the void), it is being used for functional assimilation, and although there is not as yet any acquisition through external experience, this will become possible with the first conditioning through accommodation. Indeed the transition is so imperceptible that it is difficult to be sure whether, in the case of obs. 1 there is a beginning of conditioning or not. But if the second interpretation is correct, *i.e.*, if the child's own crying was intensified through his failure to differentiate between it and the crying he heard, we have an illustration of the point at which the simple reflex will give rise to reproductive assimilation through incorporation of external elements in the reflex schema. After this point, imitation becomes possible.

§ 2.   *Stage II: Sporadic imitation*

The second stage is characterised by the fact that the reflex schemas are broadened, by the incorporation of certain external elements as a result of real experience, into " differentiated " circular reactions. In the case of suction, for instance, new gestures such as the systematic putting of the thumb into the mouth are added to the reflex schema. In the same way, reflex crying is differentiated into wailing or vocalisations reproduced for their own sake, and vision is broadened to include accommodation to moving objects. Now the extent to which the schemas integrate new elements determines how far accommodation to these elements can be continued as imitation when the models presented are identical with the original elements. Indeed, during this second stage, accommodation to new data keeps pace with the ability to recapture them through reproductive assimilation. Thus it is in so far as the child can accommodate his hearing and his phonation to new sounds that he is capable of reproducing them through circular reactions. From then onwards, he has only to hear the sound in question, even though he himself has not just made it, for it to be assimilated to the corresponding schema and for accommodation of the schema to the sound to result in imitation.

Two conditions then are necessary before imitation can occur. The schemas must be capable of differentiation when confronted with the data of experience, and the model must be perceived by the child to be analogous to results he has himself obtained, *i.e.*, the model must be assimilated to a circular schema he has already acquired.

In the case of phonation, these two conditions already obtain as early as the second month of life:

OBS. 2. At o ; 1 (4) T. was wide awake, looking straight in front of him, motionless and silent. Three times in succession the crying of L. (four years old) started him crying also. Such a reaction appeared to be quite distinct from those in obs. 1. As soon as L. stopped crying, he too stopped. It therefore seemed to be a clear case of contagion, and no longer a mere starting off of a reflex by an appropriate stimulus.

At o ; 1 (9), for the first time, T. kept up, through circular reaction, a whimpering which usually preceded tears. I imitated him just at the moment when the whimpering turned into crying. He stopped crying, and resumed the earlier sound.[1]

[1] This observation confirms that of C. W. Valentine on B at o ; 1 (1): mutual imitation of whimpering. See *Brit. Journ. of Psychology*, XXI (1930), p. 108.

At 0 ; 1 (22) he spontaneously produced certain sounds such as *eu*, *é*, etc., and seemed to do so more emphatically, with or without a smile, when they were reproduced after he had uttered them himself. Same observation at 0 ; 1 (23) and 0 ; 1 (30).

At 0 ; 2 (11) after he had made the sounds *la*, *le*, etc., I reproduced them. He repeated them seven times out of nine, slowly and distinctly. The same day, I reproduced the sounds he usually made when he himself had not made them for more than half an hour. He smiled silently, then began to babble, and stopped smiling. He did not reproduce each individual sound, but uttered sounds under the influence of my voice when I confined myself to sounds with which he was familiar.

At 0 ; 2 (14) he showed no reaction to the voices of half a dozen little girls, but as soon as I uttered sounds reminiscent of his own, he began to croon.

At 0 ; 2 (17) he imitated me as soon as I uttered sounds identical with his own (such as *arr*), or even when it was merely my intonation which recalled his. He again imitated me even when he had not been crooning himself immediately before. He began by smiling, then made an effort with his mouth open (remaining silent for a moment) and only then produced a sound. Such a behaviour clearly indicates the existence of a definite attempt at imitation.

At 0 ; 2 (25) I made the sound *aa*. There was a long, ineffective effort, with his mouth open, followed by a faint sound. Then a broad smile and regular imitation.

To sum up, in T.'s case, from 0 ; 1 (4) onwards, there was a sort of vocal contagion which developed into a general mutual stimulation, and then at 0 ; 2 (17) and 0 ; 2 (25) into an attempt at differentiated imitation. But from then until the end of the stage there was no further development of differentiated imitation. Mutual imitation alone persisted, with sporadic attempts to reproduce specific sounds uttered spontaneously shortly before the experiment.

obs. 3. In the case of J., vocal contagion seemed to begin only during the second half of the second month. At 0 ; 1 (20) and 0 ; 1 (27), for instance, I noted vocal responses to her mother's voice. At 0 ; 2 (3) she replied a score of times in similar circumstances, stopping after each one, and at 0 ; 2 (4) she reproduced certain specific sounds which she had uttered spontaneously a short time before.

Then, even more so than in the case of T., there occurred a kind of period of latency, during which J. continued to show signs of vocal contagion and sometimes of mutual imitation, but without any attempt to imitate specific sounds. Even at 0 ; 5 (5) I noted that J. reacted to a voice without imitating the specific sound she heard.

At 0 ; 5 (12) J. had been silent for some time when I said *rra* two or three times. She gazed at me attentively and suddenly began to croon without imitating the exact sound. Same observations at 0 ; 6 (0), 0 ; 6 (6), 0 ; 6 (16), etc.

At o ; 6 (25), however, there began a phase of much more systematic imitation characteristic of the third stage. (J. developed more slowly than her brother and sister. See *N.I.*)

OBS. 4.   At o ; 1 (21) L. spontaneously uttered the sound *rra*, but did not react at once when I reproduced it. At o ; 1 (24), however, when I made a prolonged *âa*, she twice uttered a similar sound, although she had previously been silent for a quarter of an hour.

At o ; 1 (25) she was watching me while I said " a, ha, ha, rra," etc. I noticed certain movements of her mouth, movements not of suction but of vocalisation. She succeeded once or twice in producing some rather vague sounds, and although there was no imitation in the strict sense, there was obvious vocal contagion.

At o ; 1 (26) when I made the sound " rra " she replied by a kind of rolled " rr " eight times out of eleven. During the intervals she said nothing. Same observation the following day, and again at o ; 2 (2), etc.

At o ; 3 (5) I noted a differentiation in the sounds of her laughter. I imitated them. She reacted by reproducing them quite clearly, but only when she had already uttered them immediately before.

At o ; 3 (24) she imitated *aa*, and vaguely *arr* in similar conditions, *i.e.*, when there was mutual imitation.

There were no further developments until about o ; 5.

This beginning of vocal imitation, belonging to the second stage, appears to us to be characterised in three ways. Firstly, there is obvious vocal contagion as soon as the child becomes capable of circular reactions with respect to phonation. In other words, the voices of others stimulate the child's voice, whether it be a case of crying or some other sound. When it is a case of crying, the contagion is almost automatic, probably as a result of the emotion which accompanies the utterance. In the second case, however, the contagion is subject to two kinds of restrictive conditions. In order to stimulate the baby's voice, the other voices must either reproduce certain familiar sounds already uttered by the child, or certain intonations known to him. Moreover, the child must be interested in the sounds he hears, in which case the contagion is in no way automatic, but is a kind of spontaneous circular reaction. In a word, vocal contagion is merely stimulation of the child's voice by another voice, without exact imitation of the sounds he hears.

Secondly, there is mutual imitation, which is apparently exact imitation, when the experimenter imitates the child at the very moment when he is uttering this or that particular sound. The child then redoubles his efforts and, stimulated by the other voice, imitates in his turn the sound his partner is imitating. Obviously, in such a case (*e.g.*, when T. at o ; 2 (11) repeated *la* and *le* after he had made these sounds of his own accord at the beginning of the experiment), the imitation is exact only in so far as the experimenter exactly imitates the child. The child makes no effort to adapt himself to the sound he hears, but merely has to retain the sound he himself was making a moment earlier, and his imitation is only a continuation of the circular reaction.

Thirdly, the child may sporadically imitate with relative precision a known sound (*i.e.*, a sound he has already discovered for himself) without having uttered it immediately before. For instance, T. at 0 ; 2 (17) imitated the sound *arr* without preliminary practice, and attempted to adapt himself to it. But during this period, such a behaviour is very exceptional, and of course at this stage a child will never attempt to imitate a new sound in order to learn it.

What are the conclusions to be drawn from these facts? Guillaume, who gives examples of observations analogous to ours from the end of the second month onwards, says that " in the first five months there is no evidence of imitation except in cases of a quite unusual character," as, for example, when for two weeks, from 0 ; 2 (11) to 0 ; 2 (26), one of his children imitated the chief sounds with which he was familiar (*gue, pou, re*). Stern quotes a similar case at the age of two months, Ferretti one at three months, ten at three and four months, etc. We are clearly justified in refusing to call mere stimulation of the child's voice by that of another imitation, but the question which arises is whether, as Guillaume seems to suggest, there is discontinuity between this behaviour and imitation in the strict sense, or whether there is relative continuity. An explanation based on the mechanisms of transfer, such as was first given by Guillaume, makes it legitimate to accept the idea of discontinuity. But if imitation is merely a continuation of reproductive assimilation, through further development of the element of accommodation inherent in the circular reactions, vocal contagion is clearly the beginning of phonic imitation, and in our view all the intermediary stages between these facts and those of the later levels are to be found.

We now come to the question of *vision*, and here also there seems to be evidence of a beginning of imitation at this stage. It is to be found in the behaviours by means of which the child accommodates himself to the displacement of other faces.

OBS. 5. At 0 ; 1 (26) L. turned her head spontaneously from side to side. At 0 ; 1 (27) she watched my face when I quickly moved my head from left to right. She then immediately reproduced this movement three times in succession. After a pause, I did it again. She began again, and it was noticeable that she reproduced the movement much more definitely when I had finished mine than she did while she was watching me.

I resumed the experiment on the following days and the result was always the same. At 0 ; 2 (2) in particular, each time she definitely continued the movement she had observed. The evening of the same day, she reacted in a similar way to a different movement. I nodded my head up and down and she watched me, with a slight movement of her head. As soon as I stopped, she reproduced my movement, making it much more clearly defined. It thus seemed as though, while she was watching, she was confining herself to accommodating the movements of her eyes and head to the movement she was observing, and as though after observation, her accommodation became definite imitation.

But it was not merely a matter of perceptive-motor accommodation, for immediately afterwards L. continued to nod her head up and down when I again began to move mine from side to side. She watched me without moving as long as my sideways movement continued, and as soon as I stopped, moved her own head up and down.

At 0 ; 2 (16), however, L. differentiated clearly between the two movements. She was upright in her mother's arms, opposite me. I began to nod my head up and down. While she was watching, L. kept quite still except for slight movements in order to watch what I was doing. As soon as I stopped, she distinctly reproduced the up and down movement. I then moved my head from left to right and vice versa. L. moved her head slightly as she watched, and as soon as I stopped, reproduced the sideways movement. Her mother, who was holding her, clearly felt the difference in the movements of the spine and muscles.

There were similar differentiated reactions at 0 ; 2 (20), 0 ; 2 (24), etc. The same observation was made at 0 ; 3 (18), 0 ; 3 (30), and during the following stage.

OBS. 6. T.'s reactions seemed to me vaguer at the outset, but became definite from about 0 ; 3 onwards.

At 0 ; 1 (30) I moved my head from left to right in front of him, saying " ta, ta, ta, ta " (twice to the left and twice to the right). He gazed at me and followed my movements. When I stopped, he made a few sounds, smiling as he did so, then seemed to make some movements of the head to continue the accommodation. It is not certain that this was so, however, because whenever he stopped looking at an object, he usually made similar spontaneous movements. All that can be said (and I resumed the experiment on the following days) is that he seemed to move his head more after I had moved mine.

At 0 ; 2 (7) imitation of the sideways movements seemed clearer. He followed me with his eyes, smiled, then moved his head quite distinctly. Same reaction at 0 ; 2 (23).

At 0 ; 3 (1) I moved my hand horizontally in front of T.'s eyes. He followed it with his eyes, and when it stopped, he continued the movement, moving his head sideways. Same reaction with a rattle.

At 0 ; 3 (4) T. was in his mother's arms, upright and motionless. I bent my head to left and right. He followed me with his eyes, making slight movements, and when I stopped, clearly imitated me. On the following days, there was the same reaction. From o ; 3 (21) onwards, more especially, T. moved his head when I moved mine or moved my hands. Subsequently this movement, which became gradually more frequent, came to be used in the case of the rattles which hung from his cot (third stage).

A behaviour of this kind, so clearly displayed in the case of L., well illustrates the nature of the first stage of imitation. It is a continuation of accommodation within the circular reactions that are already in use, *i.e.*, within activities which are a compound of assimilation and accommodation.

To our mind, as we have already said (*N.I.*, Chap. II), no initial perceptive behaviour, visual, auditory, etc., is a simple act. Each is an assimilating activity, susceptible of practice or repetition, and therefore of recognition and generalisation. Accommodation of the sense organs to an objective, and of the movements of these organs to the movements of objects cannot in that case be a primary fact, and must always be relative to assimilation of objects to the child's activity.[1] It is for this reason that in the beginning subject and object are one, and primitive consciousness cannot distinguish the part played by the one from that played by the other.

Consequently, all accommodation to external data tends to be repeated, since it is not differentiated from reproductive assimilation, and as soon as accommodation passes the purely reflex level and takes experience into account, this repetition of the whole act constitutes a primary circular reaction. In normal circumstances, *i.e.*, when the activity of the object does not unduly engage that of the subject, this tendency to repetition shows itself merely as a need to prolong perception, but it ceases with, or shortly after the disappearance of the perceived object. When, however, the object provides an external stimulus to the subject's assimilating activity, accommodation to the object continues beyond perception, and it is this phenomenon which constitutes the beginning of imitation. This is the position when, as we have just seen, the child's phonation is stimulated by the convergence between his own voice and the voice of another.

While in the case of phonation only the existence of the fact was observable, in the case of vision involving movements of others' faces, we are in a position to analyse the mechanism. Here, indeed, the child is forced, in order to follow the movements of the person he is watching, to make exactly the same head movements as the model (and this, of course, long before he is aware of any resemblance between his own face and those of others). Thus, in order to retain

---

[1] A mechanism of this kind has since been called by V. Weizsäcker " Der Gestaltkreis " (1941).

his perception of another person's movements (*i.e.*, in order to continue
to see another face moving), all the child has to do is to reproduce his
own movements of accommodation. As soon as he moves his head,
the other head again seems to him to be moving. This imitation is
in no way peculiar to other faces; the same reaction is produced in the
case of moving hands, toys, etc. It is visually perceived movement
as such which is imitated, and not only movements of the head.

An example such as this shows the beginnings of imitation to be
simply a continuation of movements of accommodation, when these
movements are part of an already formed circular reaction or of a
general assimilating activity. In the case of phonation, which we
examined earlier, the phenomenon is exactly the same, except for the
content of the perception to be preserved. As he cries or crows,
the child perceives a sound which he wishes to keep up or to repeat.
As this perception forms part of a general schema of assimilation,
which is both phonic and auditory, the child merely contrives to
reproduce the sound, auditory accommodation to his own voice
thus depending on reproductive vocal assimilation, since it is when the
voice and the ear are co-ordinated that the primary circular reaction
resulting from experience becomes something more than a mere
vocal reflex. When the child now hears others making sounds
similar to those he himself makes, accommodation to these sounds
is inseparable from a schema of assimilation already formed, and
thus at once sets the schema in motion, the result being imitation.
In the case of phonation, as of vision, the model to which the child is
accommodating himself is assimilated to a known schema, and this
makes it possible for the accommodation to be continued as imitation.
In fact, at this stage there is so little distinction between accommodation
and assimilation that imitation might as easily be considered to derive
from the one as from the other. But as we shall see later, imitation of
new models furthers the development of accommodation, and it is only
when imitation is restricted to the reproduction of sounds and gestures
already made spontaneously by the child that the distinction is
difficult.

A third example will confirm these first hypotheses: that of *prehension*. If the above interpretations are correct, we must expect that
each new co-ordination or recently acquired circular reaction will
give rise to imitation of some kind, in so far as the movements of
others can be assimilated by general analogy with those perceived
by the child on himself. And this is exactly what occurs in the field
of prehension. When the child, during the third of the five stages
we distinguished in his mastery of prehension (*N.I.*, Chap. II, § 4),
becomes capable of co-ordinating the movements of his hands with his
vision, he acquires simultaneously the power of imitating certain
movements of other hands, by assimilating them to his own.

OBS. 7. We have seen (*N.I.*, obs. 74) how T. began, at 0 ; 3 (3) to seize my hand, to the exclusion of any other visible object, probably because he assimilated it to his own and was in the habit of clasping his hands when they came into his field of vision (obs. 73). This may have seemed a somewhat bold interpretation in view of the disproportion between the visual appearance of an adult's hand and that of a child of three months. I was able, however, at 0 ; 3 (4) to establish the existence, in T.'s case, of imitation of movements of the hand. The simultaneous appearance of these two behaviours is difficult to explain except by such assimilation.

At 0 ; 3 (4), indeed, I only had to bring my hand close to him for him to seize it, and to let him see it at a distance for him to clasp his own hands, whereas there was no such reaction in the case of other objects. An hour after making this observation, I stood in front of him, a certain distance away, and instead of keeping my hand still, I alternately separated my hands and brought them together. T. who was sucking his thumb, took his hand out of his mouth, watching me carefully, and then distinctly reproduced my movement three times.

The evening of the same day, he woke after a long nap and while he was still dazed with sleep, looked first at someone standing by his cot and then examined my hands which were moving to and fro. He gazed at them steadily, but did not move his own for a minute or two. His arms were outstretched on his pillow. I stopped; there was still no reaction. I began again. He continued to watch me attentively, moved his hands where they were, slowly brought them together and suddenly clasped them in a sweeping movement. I again stopped, and he let his hands fall, one on each side of him. When I began again, he immediately clasped his hands. The same reactions occurred a third and fourth time, after which he stopped looking at my hands and gazed at his own and sucked them.

At 0 ; 3 (5) he looked at my hands for a long time without moving, then moved his own, at first gently, then more vigorously. He finally brought them to within 2 inches of one another (without seeing them). The same reaction occurred an hour later, but as my hands were near him, he seized them, interest in prehension prevailing over the tendency to imitation.

At 0 ; 3 (6) there was the same reaction. But during the fourth and fifth stages of prehension he again began to imitate distinctly the movement of separating and bringing together the hands. This was most noticeable at 0 ; 3 (8) and 0 ; 3 (23) as well as throughout the third stage.

OBS. 8. At 0 ; 5 (5) J. was still at the third stage of prehension (see *N.I.*, obs. 70), and looked several times at her clasped hands. I then tried the experiment of alternately separating and bringing together my hands as I stood in front of her. She watched me attentively and reproduced the movement three times. She stopped when I stopped and began again when I did, never looking at her own hands, but keeping her eyes fixed on mine.

At 0 ; 5 (6) and 0 ; 5 (7) she failed to react, perhaps because I was at the side and not in front of her. At 0 ; 5 (8), however, when I resumed my movement in front of her, she imitated me fourteen times in just under two minutes. I myself only did it about forty times. After I stopped, she only did it three times in five minutes. It was thus a clear case of imitation.

We find in these examples confirmation of the interpretation suggested earlier in the case of vision. Before imitating the movement of my hands, J. and T. were in possession of a definite schema which was both manual and visual: separating and bringing together their hands, and watching them move. Consequently, when the child watched my hands making the same movement, she both accommodated her eyes to the movement and assimilated the movement to the familiar schema. There is nothing mysterious in this assimilation, which is merely recognitive, and analogous to that which enables the child to recognise his parents at a distance in spite of apparent change of dimensions, or to that which allows him to react with a smile to certain strangers who resemble those with whom he is familiar, while showing anxiety in front of others (*N.I.*, obs. 37). Since the child thus assimilates other hands to his own, without confusing them with, or necessarily distinguishing them from, his own (having at this stage no conception of individual objects or classes of objects), he reacts in accordance with the corresponding familiar schema, recognitive and reproductive assimilation being indissociable during this second stage. Like the earlier imitations, that of the movement of the hands is thus merely a continuation of accommodation, the model being assimilated to a schema already constituted. It is as yet scarcely distinguishable from the combined assimilation and accommodation of the primary circular reactions.

But this interpretation of the beginnings of imitation as being a combination of assimilation and accommodation raises a difficulty. Does imitation presuppose an act of assimilation, or is the assimilation of the model and of the imitative gesture a result of the imitation, as some authors maintain?

In his profound analysis of the various theories, Guillaume concludes that imitation is the result of a definite training, determined by a series of " transfers." In his view, in order to copy the gestures or the voices of others, the child does not need to assimilate them to his own. He only has to follow certain signals, without being aware of what he is doing, consciousness of assimilation coming only after the event, as a result of the involuntary convergence of his actions with those of others. Moreover, when it is a case of imitation being bound up with an already existing circular reaction, the position is the same, since, according to Guillaume, in a circular reaction, perception is not motor from the outset, but acquires this character through transfer.

The extension of transfer to new signals then accounts for the transition from the circular reaction (self-imitation) to imitation of others, and here again assimilation is not a prerequisite for imitation but the consequence of it.

There are two difficulties inherent in this thesis which prevent us from accepting it as it stands, in spite of the fact that later on we shall have to recognise, in view of Guillaume's observations, that imitation through training does occur.

If we consider first of all the circular reaction, how are we to explain the fact that perception " combines " with a movement and acquires a motor power which is not inherent in it? It cannot be a question of passive association, otherwise the child's activity would be the plaything of the most haphazard occurrences. He would, for instance, always cough when confronted with a rattle if he had once looked at one during a fit of coughing, and so on. The explanation is not to be found either in the repetition of associations, for repetition takes place only in relation to a purpose: association is therefore not a primary fact, but the result of a complex set of elements characterised by the pursuit of an aim. Guillaume himself recognised this when at a later stage he accepted the Gestalt psychology. He admitted that a perception, in order to give rise to an effort at repetition and thus acquire a motor efficacy, must have " significance " or " interest." Obviously neither of these terms can have any meaning except in relation to a pattern of action, of which the significance is the intellectual aspect and the interest the affective aspect. It is not that a perception *begins* by being interesting or meaningful and *later* acquires a motor power through association with a movement: it is interesting or meaningful *just because* it intervenes in the performance of an action and is thus assimilated to a sensory-motor schema. The first datum is therefore neither the perception, nor the movement, nor the association of the two, but the assimilation of the perceived object to a schema of action, which is *at the same time* motor reproduction and perceptive recognition, *i.e.*, reproductive and recognitive assimilation. Hence it is the assimilation which provides significance and interest and thus gives rise to repetition. Seen thus, the circular reaction is merely an assimilation by which new objects are directly incorporated in known schemas, these schemas being at the same time differentiated (sounds, movements of the head, prehension, etc.), while the " transfer " is merely an indirect or mediate assimilation depending on the existence of a sanction operating from without, *i.e.*, again depending on a schema of assimilation.

The transition from the circular reaction (active repetition of an interesting result) to imitation of an external model corresponding to the circular schemas, such as we described in obs. 2 to 8, then presents no difficulties. Owing to its actual convergence with the movement or the sound already known, the model is directly assimilated to the child's own activity, and the circular character of this action allows of its immediate repetition. There is thus no imitation of what is new, since accommodation to the model, which is continued through the imitation, is already included in the circular schema, and the motor property of the perception of the model results merely from the assimilation of the model to an already existing schema. In this direct imitation through a combination of assimilation and accommodation, the interest of the model is therefore immanent in its repetition, since objects interest the child only in so far as they can be used for a purpose, and when perception of them creates as it were a demand for immediate reproduction of the schema. This is very clearly seen in the case of phonation, when the baby is stimulated by a familiar sound but remains indifferent to other phonemes which are very similar to it.

There is, however, justification for distinguishing, side by side with this imitation which is an immediate continuation of the circular schemas, an " imitation through training," in which there is differentiation of acquired schemas and no direct assimilation of the model to the child's own activity. Guillaume gives an excellent example of a child who as early as 0 ; 2, when he was playing with his tongue through circular reaction, learnt to put it out in response to the same movement made by his mother. Another example of the same kind is the apparent imitation of smiling as early as the fifth or sixth week. All that we would say is that these are examples of " pseudo-imitation," quite distinct from the imitation seen in obs. 2–8 and offering no explanation for it. Pseudo-imitation does not last, except under the influence of continual stimulation (as in the case of smiling, for instance), whereas true imitation, even when it is only sporadic, as at this stage, does last because it is a result of assimilation.

Later on we shall come to other cases, of which we have made a special study, of this acquired pseudo-imitation (obs. 17 and 18). For the present, all that need be said is that in view of Guillaume's findings we took great care from the outset to eliminate as far as possible the influence of training when making our observations. It was for this reason that our three subjects showed much slower but more regular progress in imitation than babies who are continually subjected to adult influence, and more especially to the pedagogical mania of nurses.

§ 3. *Stage III: Systematic imitation of sounds already belonging to the phonation of the child and of movements he has already made and seen*

With the co-ordination of vision and prehension, which occurs on an average at 0 ; 4 (15), new circular reactions through which influence can be exerted on objects make their appearance. These " secondary reactions " (*N.I.*, Chap. III), gradually integrate the " primary " circular reactions of the preceding stage. Obviously this progress must have its effect on imitation, since with the broadening of the schemas involving activities visible to the child, new models become susceptible of assimilation to the schemas.

But in comparison with that of the following stages, the imitation at this third stage, although becoming more systematic, is still limited by the very nature of the secondary circular reaction. There is as yet no co-ordination of the secondary schemas one with another, nor does accommodation take precedence over assimilation in the pursuit of novelty for its own sake (as will be the case in the " investigations " of the fourth stage and more particularly in the " tertiary circular reactions " of the fifth). Thus the imitation of the third stage is still essentially conservative, showing no indication of efforts at accommodation to new models such as will be observable in the following stages. Moreover, the " signals " inherent in the secondary reactions are still linked with the immediate action, and do not give rise, like the mobile " indices " of the fourth stage, to anticipations or reconstructions going beyond the immediate perception (*N.I.*, Chap III, § 3, and Chap. IV, § 4). This being so, the intellectual mechanism of the child will not allow him to imitate movements he sees made by others when the corresponding movements of his own body are known to him only tactually or kinesthetically, and not visually (as, for instance, putting out his tongue). To be able to make the connection between his own body and those of others, the child would require mobile indices which are not yet at his disposal. Thus since the child cannot see his own face, there will be no imitation of movements of the face at this stage, provided that training, and therefore pseudo-imitation, is avoided.

I. We shall begin with a few examples of vocal imitation. As far as the first group is concerned, we are justified in saying that the vocal contagion and sporadic imitation of the first stage are now replaced by deliberate, systematic imitation of each of the sounds known to the child. But there is little indication, before the fourth stage, of any ability to imitate new sounds suggested as models:

OBS. 9. At 0 ; 6 (25) J. invented a new sound by putting her tongue between her teeth. It was something like *pfs*. Her mother then made the same sound. J. was delighted and laughed as she repeated it in her turn. Then came a long period of mutual imitation. J. said *pfs*, her mother imitated her, and J. watched her without moving her lips. Then when her mother stopped, J. began again, and so it went on. Later on, after remaining silent for some time, I myself said *pfs*. J. laughed and at once imitated me. There was the same reaction the next day, beginning in the morning (before she had herself spontaneously made the sound in question) and lasting throughout the day.

At o ; 7 (11) and on the following days, I only had to say *pfs* for her to imitate me correctly at once.

At o ; 7 (13) she imitated this sound without seeing me or realising where it was coming from.

OBS. 10. At o ; 6 (26) J. frequently made, during the day, the sounds *bva, bve* and also *va* and *ve* without anyone imitating her. On the next day, however, at o ; 6 (27), when I said " *bva, bve*," etc., to her, she looked at me, smiled, and said: " *pfs, pfs . . . bva*." Thus instead of at once imitating the model given to her, J. began by reproducing the sound she had become used to imitating two days earlier. Was it the similarity of the situation which made her go back to that sound ? Or had the earlier sound become a " device for making something interesting continue to happen " (see *N.I.*, Chap. III, § 4) ? Or was it merely automatism ? The answer is to be found in the observations that follow.

The evening of the same day, every time I said *bva*, J. said *pfs*, without any attempt at imitation. Afterwards I heard her saying " *abou, abou* " (a new sound derived from *bva* which she was trying out on that day). I thereupon said *pfs* a number of times, she smiled, and each time said *abou*.

At o ; 7 (13) I said *hha*, a sound with which she was familiar. She smiled, and as soon as I stopped, opened her mouth as if to make me go on, but without trying to make any sound. When I stopped saying *hha* altogether, however, she herself uttered the sound correctly.

At o ; 7 (15) she was in her cot saying *mam, mam*, etc., and could not see me. When I said *bva*, she was silent for a moment, and then, although she still could not see me, softly said *bva, bva*, as though she were trying it out. When I again said it, she said *bva mam, bva mam*, etc.

Such behaviours seem to us instructive. Obviously the child's only aim is to make the sound he hears continue. Just as, during the whole of this stage, he tries to make the interesting things he sees last, and to that end uses a series of devices drawn from his secondary circular reactions, so in the vocal field he wants the sounds he hears to continue, and sets about achieving this in the following way. Sometimes, to influence others, he uses sounds that have already been used in imitations, or those he has just repeated himself (which constitutes the vocal equivalent of " devices to make interesting things seen continue "). At other times, either spontaneously or when the first method fails, he actually imitates sounds made by someone else. In both cases there is evident interest in repetition, and repetition of phonemes which have no significance as such.

OBS. 11. At o ; 7 (17) J. at once imitated the sounds *pfs, bva, mam, abou, hha* and a new phoneme *pff* which she had been trying out for several days, differentiating between them, and without

having made them herself immediately before.   She was enjoying
the imitation, and no longer producing one sound instead of another.

At 0 ; 7 (20) she heard a goatherd's horn with a sound like an
âa.   She at once imitated it, almost at the right pitch, with a single
continuous note.

At 0 ; 8 (2) and 0 ; 8 (9) she again imitated all the phonemes
she knew, including the new sounds *papa* and *baba* which had no
meaning for her.

At 0 ; 8 (11) she also imitated *apf* or *apfen* and the sound of
coughing.

At 0 ; 8 (16) she reproduced a complex action: tapping on the
quilt and saying *apf*.

At 0 ; 8 (20) she imitated *arr* and the sound of deep breathing.

At 0 ; 8 (14) and 0 ; 8 (19), on the other hand, she did not
again try to imitate the new sounds.   As soon as a phoneme unknown to her was inserted in the series of models given to her, she
was silent, or if the sound interested her (probably by analogy with
those she made herself) she tried to make it go on by making other
sounds (see obs. 10).

It will be seen that during this stage the child becomes capable of
imitating almost all the sounds he can utter spontaneously, provided
that he can isolate them from the sound group.   As Guillaume has
said, in order to be reproduced a sound must be as it were a recog-
nisable object, irrespective of differences of quality and pitch.   We
cannot, however, agree that the child at this stage imitates only those
phonemes which are meaningful, and that progress in understanding
of the meaning of sounds keeps pace with progress in utterance of
them.   One of Guillaume's subjects, L., did indeed react as early as
0 ; 5 to words such as " Goodbye," " One, two, three, dance ! ",
" Kiss," " Pull his hair," " Scold him," etc., and it is obvious that a
child influenced to this extent by an adult environment will certainly
attribute to all sounds some meaning, direct or indirect.   But in our
view these facts do not prove that there is any correlation between the
imitability of phonemes and their meaning.   In the first place, this
same subject, L., at 0 ; 6, only imitated "papa," " tata," " tété " and
" man," four phonemes uttered by most children of that age, irrespective of any meaning (at least this was so in the case of our children).
In the second place, all of our three children, who were never trained
during this stage to associate words or sounds with actions or objects,
clearly imitated the spontaneous phonemes, which could only have an
auditory-motor significance.   Moreover, when they failed to imitate
them, the children tried to get others to repeat them, even making
use of other known phonemes as " devices " to make the adult produce
the required result (obs. 10).   It might perhaps be objected that
since our children had no verbal signals at their disposal they gave to
these spontaneous sounds some general meaning inherent in the

repetition, but in that case the position would be the same for all vocal utterances, and imitation would not then imply the desire to reproduce meaningful sounds as distinct from any others.

As for the mechanism of this vocal imitation, the explanation we suggested in § 2 seems to apply here also. It is a recognitive and reproductive " assimilation " rather than a series of " transfers." It can of course be said that mutual imitation (obs. 9) takes place through " transfer " and that we also were " training " our children by conditioning them to react in that way. But the reply to this is to be found in obs. 10, which shows clearly that the child, far from passively associating a signal with an action, actively tried to make the sound she heard go on, and to that end used by turns any vocal " device " chosen at random, as well as imitation. Thus in such cases, imitation does not appear to be an association, but an active process, *i.e.*, intentional assimilation.

II. The child learns at this stage to imitate other people's movements which are analogous to the familiar, visible movements he himself makes. He thus imitates all gestures except those which are new to him and those which he cannot see himself make. In other words, his imitation is determined by the content of his primary and secondary circular reactions in so far as the movements they involve give rise to visual perception. It is therefore in relation to the circular reactions of this stage (which we studied in *N.I.*, Chap. III) that the significance of the following examples will be understood.

The simplest case is that of movements of the hand, such as grasping visible objects, etc. (circular schemas related to the activity of the hand alone, and not yet involving movements of objects). Attempts at imitation of these movements immediately make clear the fundamental fact that at first it is only as entities that the schemas are imitated, specific movements which form part of the schemas but which are not yet isolated by the child being no better imitated than new movements. For instance, the actions of grasping, waving the hand, moving the fingers, etc., are imitated without difficulty, whereas the action of opening and closing the hand is not imitated before it has given rise to a separate circular reaction.

OBS. 12. At o ; 6 (22) J. did not imitate the gesture of opening and closing a hand, but she did imitate that of bringing together and separating two hands (see second stage, obs. 7–8) and that of moving one hand within the field of vision.

At o ; 7 (16), while she was watching, I took hold of a cord hanging from the top of her cot, without shaking or pulling it, and she immediately imitated the movement five times.

At o ; 7 (22) she imitated a general movement of the fingers with the hand kept still, but she neither imitated a new individual movement of the fingers, such as raising the forefinger, nor the action of opening and closing the hand.   The reason appears to be that she often moved her fingers spontaneously (see *C.R.*, obs. 130) whereas she only opened and closed her hands as part of more complex activities such as grasping.   Similar reactions at 0 ; 8 (1).

At 0 ; 8 (13) I observed that she alternately opened and closed her right hand, watching it with great attention as if this movement, as an isolated schema, was new for her (see *C.R.*, obs. 130). I made no experiment at that point, but the same evening I showed her my hand as I opened and closed it rhythmically.   She thereupon imitated the movement, rather awkwardly but quite distinctly. She was lying on her stomach and not looking at her hand, but there was a clear correlation between her movements and mine (she was not making this movement just before).

OBS. 13.   In the case of L. there was the same continuity between the primary and secondary reactions, but the phenomena appeared in a different order.   As we saw elsewhere (*N.I.*, obs. 67), as early as 0 ; 3 (13) L. watched her hands opening and closing (which J. did not do before 0 ; 8, as we have just seen).   On the other hand, she did not study simple movements of her own hands as J. did between 0 ; 4 and 0 ; 6 (*N.I.*, obs. 70).

At 0 ; 4 (23), without any previous practice, I showed L. my hand which I was slowly opening and closing.   She seemed to be imitating me.   All the time my suggestion lasted she kept up a similar movement and either stopped or did something else as soon as I stopped.

There was the same reaction when I repeated the experiment at 0 ; 4 (26).   But was this response of L. merely due to an attempt at prehension?   To test this, I then showed her some other object. She again opened and closed her hand, but only twice, then immediately tried to seize the object and suck it.   I resumed the experiment with my hand, and she clearly imitated it, her gesture being quite different from the one she made on seeing the toy.

At 0 ; 5 (6) I resumed my observation, with my arm raised in front of her.   She alternately opened and closed her hand, without even bringing her arm nearer.   She was therefore not attempting to grasp it.   When, however, in order to check this I put a carrot in the same place, there was an immediate attempt at prehension. There was thus no doubt that in the first case she had been imitating.

L. on the contrary, at 0 ; 5 (6) made no attempt to imitate the movement of bringing together and separating the hands, nor that of moving one hand within the field of vision.

At 0 ; 5 (7) and 0 ; 5 (10), etc., same reactions.   She imitated the gesture of opening and closing a hand, but not that of separating the hands and bringing them together.   The same thing occurred at 0 ; 5 (12), but when I kept my hand closed, she examined my fist with interest, without being capable of imitating the gesture. Same observations at 0 ; 5 (18) and 0 ; 5 (23).

At 0 ; 6 (2), however, L. was watching her own hands which she was spontaneously separating and bringing together.   I repeated the movement about ten minutes after she stopped. She gave a distinct imitation of it, whereas three days before there had been no reaction to such a suggestion. I then opened and closed my hand without moving my arm, then made a movement with my arm without moving my hand and finally again began to separate and bring together my hands. She imitated all three movements correctly. The same evening, the same experiments produced similar reactions.

The next day, at 0 ; 6 (3), and also at 0 ; 6 (4) and 0 ; 6 (5), L. did not again imitate the movement of separating and bringing together the hands because she was not herself doing so before the experiment. At 0 ; 6 (19), however, she succeeded in imitating the movement without having made it just before. Same reaction at 0 ; 6 (21) and on the following days: again at 0 ; 6 (30), 0 ; 7 (8), etc.

As regards the gesture of merely moving an arm about, she also stopped imitating it between 0 ; 6 (3) and the end of that month, except when she herself had made the movement just before. After 0 ; 7 (4), however, she copied it correctly.

I also tried to differentiate the schema of opening and closing the hand by merely moving my fingers, and she imitated this movement from 0 ; 6 (5) onwards. It was, naturally, only a general movement of all the fingers, and she could not yet imitate a new, specific gesture such as raising the forefinger.

OBS. 14. From 0 ; 3 (23) onwards, T. imitated the gesture of waving goodbye, which he used (without having learnt it from those around him) as a " device " for making the top of his cot shake, thus repeating a known circular reaction. But precisely because the gesture in question could be used as a " device for making interesting things go on happening," the question arises whether T. was aware that he was imitating or whether he merely wanted to make me continue my movement. I therefore swung my hand sideways (the movement of separating and bringing the hands together). T. imitated this last gesture, and began to wave goodbye again when I also did so.

There were the same reactions at 0 ; 3 (27), 0 ; 4 (18), 0 ; 5 (8) and 0 ; 5 (24).

At 0 ; 4 (5) T. looked at his thumb, which was upright, and moved it about. I reproduced the gesture, and he imitated me. He laughed and compared our two hands several times. At 0 ; 4 (6) his hands were still when I showed him my clenched fist with the thumb on the outside, and gently moved my whole hand. He looked at it, then at his own, turning his head to do so, then again at mine, and only then slowly moved his own and raised his thumb. Same reaction the next day.

At 0 ; 4 (30), when I opened and closed my hand in front of him, he moved his fingers and spontaneously looked at his right hand as if to compare them. Same reaction at 0 ; 5 (0). At 0 ; 5 (8) he seemed definitely to imitate the gesture of opening and closing the hand, but the following days he again only moved his fingers. This continued to be his reaction at o ; 7 (12) and at o ; 8 (6). I had never seen T. merely open and close his hand as a circular reaction, whereas he was accustomed to study the movement of his fingers.

During this stage T. therefore imitated four schemas related to the movement of hands: waving goodbye, separating and bringing the hands together, raising the thumb, and moving the fingers, and he himself discovered and practised these four schemas.

Thus it seems that the child at this stage is capable of imitating all movements of the hands that he can make spontaneously, but is unable to imitate those movements which are part of a more complex whole and which must first be differentiated as independent schemas. As for new movements we shall find later on that he does not imitate them.

Imitation of simple secondary circular reactions such as hitting, scratching, etc., provides us with a second group of facts:

OBS. 15. At o ; 7 (5) and on the following days, J. imitated the action of scratching material, *e.g.*, her sheet, a pillow, etc. She often did this herself as a circular reaction. I observed this imitation again at o ; 7 (15), o ; 8 (6), etc.

At o ; 7 (27), *i.e.*, a few days after she first began to hit things (see *N.I.*, obs. 103) she imitated her mother beating an eiderdown. She looked only at the hands of the model, never at her own.

At o ; 7 (30) she watched me when I tapped my thigh, a yard and a half away from her. She at once tapped the cheek of her mother who was holding her in her arms.

At o ; 8 (5) she immediately hit a celluloid duck that I had just struck in front of her. Same reaction with a doll. A moment later she was lying on her stomach, screaming with hunger. To distract her, her mother took a brush and hit a porcelain soap-dish with it. J. at once imitated this somewhat complicated movement, being able to do so because she had just learnt to rub things against the sides of her cot. Same reaction at o ; 8 (8), with a comb against the sides of the bed.

At o ; 8 (13) she hit her mother's knee as she watched me hitting mine.

L. also imitated the following gestures: scratching (from o ; 6), shaking objects that had been grasped (from o ; 7), striking an object (after the end of the sixth month). Same reactions in the case of T., but somewhat earlier in consequence of his general precocity.

We still have to consider the case of complex circular reactions such as those related to hanging objects, reactions which are complex as a result of physical circumstances, and not psychologically. Such schemas, like the preceding ones, give rise to imitation. However, since the child's interest is here focussed on the final result of his action and not on the movements he has to make to achieve it, imitation in such cases is not distinguishable from reproduction of the total schema.

Does it then follow, as Guillaume suggests, that the identity between the movements of the model and those of the subject is due to mere convergence, and that there is no true imitation, imitation only occurring as a succession of transfers? In order to decide let us note the following reactions:

OBS. 16. At 0 ; 7 (20) J. shook the canopy of her cot by pulling the hanging cord every time I myself did so by way of example.

At 0 ; 8 (1) she was sitting in front of the French window. I moved one side of it to and fro; she at once seized it and did the same thing.

At 0 ; 8 (13) she was looking at a hanging doll that I was swinging. As soon as I stopped, she began to swing it, reproducing my movement.

T. reacted in this way as early as 0 ; 3 (23). For example, as soon as I shook a rattle in front of him, he used to look for the string to which it was attached and seize hold of it to shake it.

There are three possible interpretations of these examples.

Firstly, it is quite possible that the child was merely trying to reproduce a result that had been observed, and in so doing, without being aware of it, imitated the movements of the model simply through convergence. Secondly, it is possible on the other hand that the child was interested in the movements as such, irrespective of their results. If these two explanations were the only ones, obviously the first would be the more likely, but in our opinion there is a third possible interpretation, which is that the action and its result constitute a single schema, recognised as such by the child and giving rise as such to repetition. The first explanation would not imply previous assimilation of the action of the model to those of the child. The second would imply assimilation which was not only immediate but also to some extent analytic, all perception being continued automatically as imitation. The third would imply assimilation, but a general assimilation depending on the previous existence of schemas.

It is not easy to find a solution to the problem if we merely consider obs. 16. A comparison with obs. 12–14 and obs. 15, however, seems to entail two general conclusions, which enable us to discard both the classic conception of imitation as being merely a continuation of perception, and the somewhat narrow interpretation of imitation as being the result of a series of transfers.

The first conclusion is that, during this stage, a model is imitated only if it can be assimilated to a schema already formed, *i.e.*, to a sensory-motor whole practised as such. For instance, in obs. 12–14, J. did not imitate the action of opening and closing the hands until she had practised it as a separate action, in spite of the fact that prehension constantly involved this action. On the other hand, she very quickly imitated the action of separating the hands and bringing them together again, because she often made this movement herself within her field of vision. L., on the contrary, imitated the first of these actions earlier, and the second later, because her circular reactions were formed in that order. Even in the case of movements of one hand alone, the child therefore does not at this stage imitate parts of whole movements with which he is familiar; he only imitates whole movements which he has observed and practised as separate schemas. With regard to actions related to objects the position is obviously the same. At this stage, perception of a model corresponding to known movements is not of itself sufficient to give rise to imitation. The model must be assimilated to a spontaneous schema, since it is only by way of schemas of assimilation that the child can recognise the subsequent accommodation and continue it as imitation.

Conversely, however—and this is the second conclusion—any schema practised as such can give rise to imitation provided that the movements the child has to make are within his field of vision. This is true both of the simplest and the most complex schemas, irrespective of the external results of the action. When they have been practised spontaneously through differentiated circular reactions, pure movements which have no obvious result catch the child's attention and give rise to imitative reproduction in just the same way as do actions which have complex results. In our opinion everything depends on the baby's education. Left to himself, he gives to the study of his own actions the time that he would otherwise give to learning all kinds of tricks.

This brings us to a consideration of imitation through training, or pseudo-imitation. We do not deny its existence, and as we shall now show we have even tried to bring it about on certain specific occasions. Nevertheless we believe that this behaviour is distinct from imitation through direct assimilation and accommodation. It cannot explain true imitation, because it never lasts unless the training is prolonged and constantly kept up. We indicated earlier, in connection with the second stage, that smiling, which can obviously be kept up indefinitely, is a good example of this pseudo-imitation with non-intentional convergence between the action of the model and that of the subject. To understand the nature of the behaviours that can be developed by training during this third stage, it will be useful first of all to list the actions which the child does not imitate spontaneously. The following observations provide us with some examples of temporary pseudo-imitation:

OBS. 17. At 0 ; 5 (2) J. put out her tongue several times in succession. I put mine out in front of her, keeping time with her gesture, and she seemed to repeat the action all the better. But it was only a temporary association. A quarter of an hour later, no suggestion on my part could induce her to begin again. There was the same negative reaction the next few days.

At 0 ; 6 (1) I waved goodbye, then put out my tongue, then opened my mouth and put my thumb into it. There was no reaction, since the first movement did not correspond to a known schema, and the others involved parts of her face which she could not see. Same reactions at 0 ; 6 (22), 0 ; 6 (25), etc.

At 0 ; 7 (21), when she yawned several times in succession, I seized the opportunity to yawn in front of her, but she did not imitate me. Same observation with regard to the schema of putting out the tongue and opening the mouth without yawning.

From 0 ; 7 (15) to 0 ; 8 (3) I systematically tried to get her to imitate the " marionette " movement (turning the wrist with the hand open), the action of clapping, putting out the tongue, putting fingers in the mouth, but all to no avail.

From 0 ; 8 (4) onwards, however, she began to imitate certain movements of the mouth, but as we shall see in the following stage, she succeeded in doing so by following certain clues, instead of by passively associating the movements with permanent signs.

OBS. 18. L., at 0 ; 5 (9), put out her tongue several times. Each time, I also did so. She then showed great interest, put out her own as soon as I pulled mine back, and so on. She behaved as though her action (of which she was aware through the sensations of her lips and tongue) constituted an " effective device " for making my action, of which she was only aware visually, continue. It was thus a case of pseudo-imitation based on the perception of a connection between her action and mine. Unlike J. at 0 ; 5 (2), L. again began putting out her tongue after a moment's interruption when I resumed my suggestion. The next day, however, at 0 ; 5 (10), and on the following days, 0 ; 5 (11), 0 ; 5 (12), 0 ; 5 (14) and 0 ; 5 (16), my stimulus produced no reaction whatever.

At 0 ; 5 (21) she made a noise with her saliva as she put out her tongue. I imitated the noise, and she imitated me in her turn, again putting out her tongue. Her behaviour thus became similar to what it was at 0 ; 5 (9), but an hour later, as well as on the following days, nothing remained of this association. At 0 ; 6 (2) I made a special effort to make her put out her tongue or merely open her mouth, but without success.

At 0 ; 6 (19), when she put out her tongue I imitated her, and mutual imitation followed, lasting at least five minutes. L. carefully watched my tongue and seemed to find a connection between her gesture and mine. But shortly afterwards, and on the following days, she failed to react to the stimulus.

At 0 ; 7 (1) she did not imitate any movement connected with the mouth, opening it, yawning, moving the lips, putting out the tongue, and so on. But for several days, her mother had been opening and closing her mouth at the same time as she did during meals in order to get her to swallow some soup she was not fond of. This device seemed to be successful in that L. ate better when she was enjoying watching her mother's mouth move, but it did not give rise to any imitation outside meal times. There was thus pseudo-imitation, linked with a specific situation, but not well enough established to be generalised.

At 0 ; 8 (2), 0 ; 8 (5) and 0 ; 8 (10) there was still no progress. At 0 ; 8 (14) she put her forefinger in her mouth and made a noise which amused her. When I imitated her, she laughed. This was followed by prolonged mutual imitation, but the same evening my suggestion was no longer effective.

It was only between 0 ; 9 and 0 ; 10 that movements relating to the mouth were really imitated.[1]

These observations confirm the conclusion, which we owe to Guillaume, that at this stage there is no spontaneous imitation of movements which the child cannot see himself make. For instance, the child perceives visually movements related to the mouth when they are made by others, but is only aware of them in himself through kinesthetic and gustative sensations. Consequently they do not give rise to any immediate, direct imitation and some training is necessary before they can be acquired.

This result can be achieved in two different ways: by progressive accommodation and assimilation or by training under suggestion. But the first of these assumes the use of intelligent " indices " and mediate assimilation, which only develop from the fourth stage onwards. The second alternative, training, leads to pseudo-imitation which can be produced much more easily and therefore takes place earlier, tending, since it is kept up by practice, to overshadow the manifestations of spontaneous assimilation. Obs. 17 and 18, for instance, show that by merely repeating in front of a child an action he himself makes spontaneously a temporary association is formed which makes him continue the action, the model then serving simply as a stimulating signal. The association can obviously be strengthened by a continual show of approval of the action, until assimilation becomes possible with the progress of intelligence. This is what occurs when adults constantly play with the child and the gestures he makes come to have an affective content as a result of adult approval of them. When it is merely a case of mutual imitation, however, the association is labile and disappears after the experiment.

We can therefore conclude that in obs. 10–16, since the technique used in each case was the same, there was true imitation. Imitation of known sounds and visible movements proved to be lasting after a few mutual imitations, whereas imitation of non-visible movements would have required, for its consolidation, a succession of sanctions alien to immediate assimilation.

[1] C. W. Valentine (*op. cit.*, p. 110) records imitation of protrusion of the tongue at 0 ; 6 in the case of C. (182 days), and at 0 ; 8 in the case of Y., but we do not know whether this imitation lasted.

CHAPTER II

DIRECT imitation, through progressive differentiation between accommodation and assimilation, is fully developed in stages IV and V, but we are still only on the threshold of deferred imitation or imitation involving a beginning of representation, which belong to stage VI.

§ 1. *Stage IV. I. Imitation of movements already made by the child but which are not visible to him*

From the point of view of the general evolution of intelligence, stage IV, which begins between 0 ; 8 and 0 ; 9, is characterised by co-ordination of schemas one with another, resulting in increased mobility and in the constitution of a system of " indices " relatively detached from actual perception (see *N.I.*, chap. IV). In the child's construction of space, objects, and causality, the global relationships which characterise mere secondary circular reactions (see *C.R.*) are replaced by rapid elaboration of differentiated relationships between things.

This two-fold progress has its impact on imitation in the following way. The co-ordination of schemas, and the system of " indices," enable the child to assimilate the movements of others to those of his own body, even when his own movements are not visible to him. On the other hand, the association of relationships facilitates accommodation to new models. We shall first proceed to analyse the former of these two acquisitions, since it affords a better illustration than any other of the close connection between the development of imitation and that of intelligence in general. Provided that the interference of the observer is restricted to the minimum, it is possible to follow every step of the gradual assimilation of the visible movements of the faces of others to the invisible movements of the child's own face:

OBS. 19. At 0 ; 8 (4) J. was moving her lips as she bit on her jaws. I did the same thing, and she stopped and watched me attentively. When I stopped, she began again, I imitated her, she again stopped, and so it went on. In contrast to what occurred earlier (obs. 17) J. again began to imitate me an hour later, and on the next day, without having made the movement immediately before (but of course only when I again provided her with the same model).

In order to understand this new development, two circumstances must be noted. Firstly, for some days she had not merely imitated sounds for their own sake, but had watched the mouth of the model with great attention. Thus at 0 ; 8 (2) (see obs. 11) she had imitated the sounds *pfs, bva, hha, mam mam, bva, papa, baba,* etc., but paying great attention to my mouth, as though she were interested in the mechanism of speech (in the same way as she examined a rattle when she shook it). Secondly, as she moved her lips, at 0 ; 8 (4), J. began by making a slight noise with her saliva as a result of the friction of her lips against her teeth, and I had imitated this sound at the outset. Her interest in the movements of the mouth was thus clearly due to interest in the production of the sound.

At 0 ; 8 (7) I resumed the experiment without making any sound, and without J. herself having made the movement beforehand. She watched my lips moving, and then distinctly imitated me three times, keeping her eyes fixed on my mouth. The same evening there was a similar reaction. She showed the same interest and was obviously " trying to see what would happen." She moved her lips, at first slowly and timidly, then more boldly, as if she were testing the efficacy of the procedure.

On the following days the suggestion of the model continued to be effective, the schema apparently being definitely acquired.

OBS. 20. At 0 ; 8 (9) I put out my tongue in front of J., thus resuming the experiment interrupted at 0 ; 8 (3) which up till then had given only negative results (obs. 17). At first J. watched me without reacting, but at about the eighth attempt she began to bite her lips as before, and at the ninth and tenth she grew bolder, and thereafter reacted each time in the same way.

The same evening her reaction was immediate: as soon as I put out my tongue she bit her lips.

At 0 ; 8 (12) same reaction. At 0 ; 8 (13) she put out her tongue, biting it as she did so. When I imitated her she seemed to imitate me in return, watching my tongue very carefully. But from the next day onwards until 0 ; 9 (1) she again began to bite only her lips when I put out my tongue at her without her having done so. Biting the lips thus seemed to her the adequate response to every movement of someone else's mouth (as we shall again see in the course of the following observations).

At 0 ; 9 (2), however, J. put out her tongue and said *ba . . . ba* at the same time. I quickly imitated her, and she began again, laughing. After only three or four repetitions, I put out my tongue without making any sound. J. looked at it attentively, moved her lips and bit them for a moment, then put out her tongue several times in succession without making any sound. After a quarter of an hour I began again, and then about half an hour later. Each time she again began to bite her lips, but a moment later distinctly put out her tongue.

At o ; 9 (3) she again began to bite her lips without putting out her tongue, but at o ; 9 (8) she did both together.

At o ; 9 (11) she finally succeeded in definitely distinguishing between the two schemas. I put out my tongue at her when she had not been doing it just before. Her first reaction was to bite her lips at once, and then after a moment, to put out her tongue several times. I interrupted the experiment, and then again put out my tongue. She watched me attentively, biting her lips, but she put her tongue out more quickly and more distinctly. After a second pause, I put out my tongue, and she then put hers out very definitely without biting her lips, after having watched me very carefully. This must obviously have been conscious imitation.

The next day at o ; 9 (12) I put out my tongue, and she at once put hers out, with a little smile. Three hours later I began again. She put hers out four times in succession, laughing with pleasure. Same reaction at o ; 9 (13), with the same show of satisfaction. At o ; 9 (14), as soon as I showed her my tongue, she put hers out as far as it would go, with a mischievous look.

It is thus clear how the model of someone else's tongue was first assimilated to the schema of moving the lips, and how, by means of an auditory index, the *ba . . . ba* of o ; 9 (2), J. succeeded in distinguishing this schema from that of putting out the tongue.

OBS. 21. The action of putting a finger in the mouth gave rise to a process of acquisition which was exactly similar except for the stimulus used.

At o ; 8 (3), as we saw in obs. 17, J. still did not imitate the gesture of putting a finger in the mouth. This was still the case at o ; 8 (11). She watched me sucking my thumb, then my forefinger, without any reaction. Similarly at o ; 8 (13).

At o ; 8 (28), however, she seized the finger I took out of my mouth, felt it, and drew it towards her own mouth to suck it. I then put it back into my own mouth. She drew herself up when I stopped (to make me go on), then put her own hand in her mouth, watching mine as she did so. The second and third times she again sucked her hand. Was this imitation, or was she merely trying to replace my finger, which she had not succeeded in sucking, by her own? What followed seemed to show that it was something between the two.

At o ; 9 (o) she watched me very attentively while I sucked my forefinger, and began to bite her lips. This had been her reaction for about three weeks when I put out my tongue, and it was now occurring for the first time in response to my biting a finger. In other words, J. was beginning to assimilate this sight to her schemas of mouth movements, probably under the influence of the experiment she made two days earlier, when she tried to transfer my finger from my mouth to her own.

At o ; 9 (1) she again began to suck her lips as soon as she saw me put my finger in my mouth, but she did not move her hand.

At o ; 9 (2) she gazed attentively at my fingers as they went in and out of my mouth and at once began to bite her lips. She then brought her thumb towards her mouth, and it slowly went nearer as she watched me. It stopped on her lower lip and she did not put it into her mouth.

At o ; 9 (3) she only bit her lips. She did suck her thumb from time to time, but at such long intervals that it did not seem to be imitation.

At o ; 9 (8) she did no more than bite her lips.

At o ; 9 (11), however, there was definite imitation. After showing her my finger, I put it in my mouth at regular intervals. At first there was no reaction, then I saw her raise her right fore-finger four times in succession while the other fingers remained bent. The whole hand was resting on the sheet, outside her field of vision. She then ended by putting her forefinger into her mouth three times, slowly and as if she were carefully following what she was doing.

At o ; 9 (12) she watched me sucking my finger and a moment later put her forefinger into her mouth. Three hours later I tried the experiment again: she then clearly raised her forefinger, keeping the other fingers bent, but did nothing more. On the evening of the same day, she reacted in a similar way, and then suddenly put her finger between her lips.

At o ; 9 (13) I put my finger into my mouth (without having previously put out my tongue at her). She watched my movement attentively, and then put out her tongue at me. I then showed her my finger, moved it towards her, and only then put it into my mouth. She then raised her right forefinger, twice in succession, then her left one. Then very slowly she brought her right fore-finger up to her mouth, and finally put it in, without taking her eyes off my own movement.

At o ; 9 (16) she began by raising her forefinger, without seeing it, and then suddenly put it in her mouth. Same reaction at o ; 9 (17), o ; 9 (21), etc. From then on, imitation was immediate.

OBS. 22. An action similar to those described above, but one which of itself does not constitute a schema (which gives rise to independent circular reactions) is that of opening and closing the mouth. This movement is of course involved in the last two. It is therefore worth while to find out whether it was imitated through transfer or through assimilating differentiation.

At o ; 8 (11) J. watched me carefully when I opened my mouth and slowly closed it again. Her reaction was to bite her lips, which thus constituted the general, undifferentiated schema with which all the earlier imitations had started. There were no further reactions that day.

At o ; 8 (21) she was watching her mother who was eating, opening and closing her mouth distinctly. J. again reacted by biting her lips. Moreover, from o ; 8 (10) to about o ; 9 (15) I frequently yawned in front of her, but without producing any evidence of contagion. When I did so very slowly, she either bit her lips or gazed at me indifferently.

From 0 ; 9 (15) to 0 ; 10 (11) there was no noticeable progress. But at 0 ; 10 (12) she amused herself by pressing her gums together so that the two lower middle incisors were pressed against the upper jaw. After she had made this movement several times, I alternately opened and closed my mouth. She laughed, and at once imitated me, without bothering any more about her gums or teeth. When I began again a moment later, there was the same reaction.

An hour later, she was finishing her meal, and had not been pressing her gums together. I opened and closed my mouth, and she at once imitated me, laughing, and with a show of satisfaction. Her mother then opened her mouth to see if J. would imitate her also. J. laughed and turned round to gaze at my mouth. Then came the imitation. The evening of the same day, when she woke at 10 o'clock, she immediately imitated the same movement. Her reaction was the same on the following day, several times.

At 0 ; 10 (16) I opened my mouth in front of her. She opened and closed hers, but began by pressing her gums together, as at 0 ; 10 (12). After that she merely imitated me. Same reactions the next day, at 0 ; 10 (17).

On the following days J. no longer needed this reminder in order to imitate correctly the movement of opening the mouth. It thus seems clear that her action of pressing her gums together served as a stimulus for the transition from the general schema of biting her lips to comprehension of the specific movement of opening and closing the mouth. But this stimulus, far from producing an automatic transfer, at once served as an instrument for assimilation.

From 0 ; 11 (15) onwards J. imitated yawning, but she deliberately reproduced the movement and the sound (the sound serving as an index) instead of yawning through contagion.

OBS. 23. A few further examples of imitation related to the mouth.

At about 0 ; 10 (0) J. began to blow bubbles of saliva filled with air between her lips, saying *méhê, méhê*. At 0 ; 10 (6) her mother did the same thing, and made the same sound. J. at once imitated her. I then made only bubbles, and she copied me without making any sound. At 0 ; 10 (14) she at once imitated the same gesture, without the help of any sound. Same reaction at 0 ; 10 (17) and 0 ; 10 (21). Thus it was the sound *méhê* which at the beginning served as an index for assimilating the making of bubbles by other people to the corresponding action done by the child herself.

At 0 ; 10 (18) J. invented a new schema, which consisted of pressing her lips together and making her lower lip stick out by putting her tongue against it. While she was doing it of her own accord, I did the same thing three times, and she watched my mouth as she went on doing it. The same evening she began to do it again. When I did it five minutes after she had stopped, she imitated me twice in succession. When on the following days I reproduced the same movement without her having made it beforehand, she did not react, and I concluded that it had been a case of pseudo-imitation. But at o ; 11 (23) I repeated the experiment when J. had not done it more than twice, and as soon as I imitated her, she imitated me in return. The next day I did it without her having done it. She imitated me immediately, then smiled and touched her lips with her right forefinger, as if to verify the connection between what she saw happening to me and what she herself felt.

At o ; 11 (20) J. watched me when I had some bread in my mouth and was making it come and go between my lips (without showing my tongue). She laughed, then put out her tongue, slowly and quite deliberately.

obs. 24. Having dealt with imitation of movements of the mouth, we shall now come to imitation of movements connected with the nose.

At about o ; 9 (6) J. acquired the habit of pressing her face against her mother's cheek and blowing through her nose or sniffing loudly in that position. At o ; 9 (11) she began to make the same sound, but out of its context: she breathed loudly without moving either her head or her nose. An hour or two afterwards I began to do the same thing. She at once imitated me and seemed to be exploring my face to see where the sound came from. She first looked at my mouth, and then seemed to be examining my nose. But she did not as yet imitate either the gesture of touching the nose with the forefinger or the whole hand, or that of moving the nose.

At about o ; 10, however, J. amused herself by blowing and breathing loudly as she puckered her nose and almost closed her eyes. I had only to repeat the same thing, either immediately, or without any connection with her own gestures, for her to imitate immediately the whole movement. Then, from o ; 10 (6) onwards, I tried dissociating the nose movements from the other elements of the schema. I looked at J. and puckered my nose without making any sound. At first J. looked at me without reacting, then she silently contracted her nose. At o ; 10 (8) the same thing happened. At o ; 10 (9), however, as soon as she saw my nose move, she responded by breathing loudly, laughing as she did so, but then applied herself to puckering her nose in silence. At o ; 10 (17) her response was to move her nose without making any sound. The same thing occurred at o ; 10 (20), etc.

At o ; 10 (6), after the imitation just described, I tried a new combination by making use of a momentary circular reaction of the child. What happened was that J. began of her own accord to sniff loudly as she touched her nose with her right forefinger. I imitated her, shortly after she had stopped. She then began to blow, and looked attentively at my finger, slightly moving her own, but she did not succeed in reproducing the schema. A few days later, the same experiment yielded no further result (J. had not done it again of her own accord). At o ; 11 (1), however, I only had to put my finger against my nose and blow, for J. to make the same movement correctly three times, after a few moments of observation.

At o ; 11 (16) J. put her finger in her nose several times. When I did the same thing in front of her, she looked at me carefully, but without reacting. At o ; 11 (25), however, when I imitated her, she imitated me, laughing. At o ; 11 (26) she at once imitated the gesture, without having made it of her own accord before I did.

OBS. 25. Now we have a few examples of imitation related to the eyes.

At o ; 8 (28) I put my face very close to that of J. and then alternately opened and closed my eyes. J. showed great interest and felt my eyes in an attempt to prolong what she saw. The same thing occurred at o ; 9 (1) and during the following weeks. I noted a completely negative reaction at o ; 11 (11).

At o ; 11 (14), however, she tried to imitate me, and made a mistake which is of interest for the theory of imitation. She watched me, laughed, and then, while continuing to look at my eyes, slowly opened and closed her mouth. She reacted to my stimulus eight times more in the same way.

Meanwhile, at o ; 11 (2), when she was rubbing her eyes with the back of her hand (as she often did), I did the same thing in front of her. She was unable to repeat the movement, and merely looked at the back of her hand after raising it once in the direction of her head (with the intention of imitating me). At o ; 11 (11) she again failed completely.

At o ; 11 (16), however, I rubbed my eyes in front of her just after she had rubbed her right eye. She laughed, as if she had understood, then, watching with great interest what I was doing, she passed the back of her hand to and fro in front of her mouth. There was thus confusion between the eye and the mouth, as there had been two days earlier, when J. opened and closed her mouth instead of her eyes. But this time J. seemed to be dissatisfied with her assimilation, for she next slowly moved the back of her hand against her cheek, still rubbing and watching me all the time, as if looking for the equivalent of my eyes on her own person. She found her ear, rubbed it, then came back to her cheeks and gave up the attempt. Five minutes later she again spontaneously rubbed her right eye, but for a longer time than before. I immediately rubbed my eyes and she again watched me with keen interest. She then again began to rub her mouth, then her cheek, as if she were investigating, keeping her eyes on me all the time.

At o ; 11 (20) she rubbed her eyes when she woke. I did the same, and she laughed. When she stopped, I began again, but she did not imitate me. Ten minutes later, however, as soon as I rubbed my eye she distinctly imitated me twice, watching me as she did so, although she had not made the movement in the meantime. A moment later I began again, and she again imitated me. That this was a genuine case of imitation of the movement as such is

proved by the fact that she only once really rubbed her eye as
though it were itching. The other times she merely passed her
hand over the corner of her eyebrow. The same evening there was
further imitation of the same type, without any previous activity
on her part.

The next day, at o ; 11 (21), I rubbed my eyes in front of her at
8 o'clock in the morning. She at once imitated me. At 6 in the
evening, I opened and closed my eyes, and she replied by rubbing
her eye. Same reaction on the following days.

From 1 ; 0 (2) onwards she imitated the movement of opening
and closing the eyes, without first rubbing them.

OBS. 26. At o ; 11 (8) J. had her left forefinger in her ear, which
she was exploring tactually. I then put my finger in my ear as I
stood in front of her. She watched me closely and stopped what she
was doing. I too stopped. When I did it again, she looked at me
with interest and then put her finger back into her ear. The same
thing occurred five or six times, but it was not certain that there
was real imitation. However, after an interval of several minutes,
during which J. was doing something quite different (crumpling a
newspaper), I raised my finger to my ear. Then, with her eyes on
me, she distinctly put her finger up to her ear and put hers in
shortly after I put in mine.

At o ; 11 (11) she immediately imitated the same movement
when she had not made it previously. There was the same reaction
at o ; 11 (22), o ; 11 (23), etc. I again noted it at 1 ; 0 (7) and
during the following weeks.

OBS. 27. Finally, at about o ; 11, when J. was being dried after
her bath she acquired the habit of humming so as to hear her voice
quavering, especially while her face was being rubbed. At o ; 11 (9)
when her mother was singing to her, she patted her cheeks to make
her voice quaver. J. smiled, and a moment later put her hand to
her cheek and began to hum. She did not succeed in reproducing
her mother's movement, but she found her cheek without difficulty
and touched it with her finger.

At o ; 11 (11) J. watched me while I was rubbing my cheeks
with the back of my hand. She distinctly imitated me, after going
through the movements of touching her ear and putting her forefinger against her nose.

At o ; 11 (12) the same thing occurred.

At 1 ; 0 (13) she successfully imitated the action of patting a
cheek, touching the lips and putting a hand in front of the mouth.

These observations show how J., starting from imitation of movements of the mouth, finally succeeded in establishing a correspondence
between parts of other faces and her own nose, eyes, ears and cheeks.

OBS. 28. As we have already seen (obs. 18) it was not until the
end of o ; 8 that L. imitated any movement of the mouth, and the

position was of course the same with regard to movements connected with the nose, eyes, etc.

At 0 ; 9 (4), when I put out my tongue, L. raised her forefinger. She did the same thing on the following days so systematically that there was no doubt as to the connection. But this movement of her finger was neither a " device " commonly used by L. nor a schema that I had developed in her by mutual imitation on the preceding days. It would therefore seem that the child's reaction can only be explained by the analogy between the protruded tongue and the raised finger (cf. the assimilation of the eyes to the mouth in the case of J.: obs. 25). After that I was away from home for three weeks, and at 0 ; 9 (25) L. showed no reaction either to movements of the tongue or to the action of opening and closing the mouth. She also failed to react when I sucked my thumb.

At 0 ; 10 (3), however, when I put my forefinger into my mouth (without making any sound), she looked at me attentively, then examined her own finger, as if she had never seen it before. This happened five times in succession. She only once put her finger into her mouth after examining it, and it is not possible to conclude from this one instance that it was a case of imitation. Afterwards, when I put out my tongue at her, there was no reaction.

The same day, however, when I silently opened and closed my mouth in front of L., she looked at me with great interest and said " *Atata*." She had imitated various sounds during the last few days, watching my mouth carefully, but on that particular day I had made no experiment with vocal imitation. The explanation therefore seems to be that she recognised a movement she had already observed and reacted by producing the sound which usually accompanied the movement.

At 0 ; 10 (5) the same thing occurred: L. said " *atata* " as soon as I opened and closed my mouth without making any sound. When I again did so, making a noise with my saliva, she imitated the sound without appearing to show any interest in the movement.

At 0 ; 10 (6) I put out my tongue. L. immediately replied " *tata* " and then silently opened and closed her mouth. I then did the same thing, and she again began to open and close her mouth, sometimes without making any sound, sometimes saying " *tata*."

At 0 ; 10 (7) when I put out my tongue she said " *tata*," but when I opened and closed my mouth she definitely imitated me, without making any sound. There was the same reaction at 0 ; 10 (8) and again at 0 ; 10 (14).

At 0 ; 10 (16) when I opened and closed my mouth she either imitated me clearly or merely moved her lips as if she were chewing. Moreover, when I put out my tongue just after she had put out hers, she laughed with delight, as though she grasped the connection. Suddenly she began to say *bla, bla*, continuing to put out her tongue. When I imitated her she laughed still more.

The next day she did not react when I put out my tongue, even when I said *bla* at the same time, but she did imitate the action of opening and closing the mouth. At 0 ; 10 (18), however, she again succeeded very well in imitating me when I put out my tongue (both with and without the sound as an index). She also continued to imitate the movement of opening and closing the mouth, as well as that of moving the lips.

On the following days her reactions seemed to be confused. Whether I put out my tongue (with or without the sound *bla*), or opened and closed my mouth, or moved my lips, she reacted indiscriminately with the five following schemas: opening and closing her mouth without making any sound, saying " *atata*," moving her lips, smacking her lips (for the sound) and putting out her tongue.

From 0 ; 10 (27) onwards, however, she again differentiated between the different movements, and even better than before. She put out her tongue silently when I did so, and even succeeded in moving it from right to left and vice versa when I did so in front of her. This differentiation took place suddenly, without further practice.

At 0 ; 10 (26), when I sucked my thumb, she opened and closed her mouth. From 0 ; 11 (4) onwards she at once imitated the gesture correctly.

OBS. 29. From 0 ; 10 to 0 ; 11 (0) the action of opening and closing the eyes produced no reaction in the case of L. At 0 ; 11 (5), however, when I opened and closed my eyes, she first opened and closed her hands, very slowly and systematically. Then, equally slowly, she opened and closed her mouth, saying *tata*.

At 1 ; 0 (14), however, the same stimulus gave rise to two consecutive reactions. First she blinked, opening and closing her mouth at the same time, as if she were unable to distinguish the two schemas from the motor and kinesthetic point of view, then she covered her face with a pillow, then removed it and began again as soon as I shut my eyes again.

At 1 ; 0 (16) she again opened and closed her mouth when I opened and closed my eyes, and then covered her face with the pillow.

It was not until 1 ; 2 (7), *i.e.*, during the fifth stage, that L. clearly imitated this gesture, without covering her face. This last reaction, which was her systematic response to my eye movements between 1 ; 0 (14) and 1 ; 2, evidently delayed the correct imitation.

Movements connected with the nose, ears, etc., were not imitated during this stage for want of spontaneous circular reactions which could have been differentiated in real imitation.

OBS. 30. In the case of T. there was no reaction to movements of the mouth and eyes until about 0 ; 9. At 0 ; 9 (21), however, he looked at me attentively when I opened and closed my mouth (without making a sound), and then said *tata* and *papa*.[1] Obviously the reason for this reaction was that he recognised the movement I made when I myself said *papa* (he had imitated the sound on the preceding days) and thus assimilated this movement of my lips to the familiar vocal schema.

At 0 ; 9 (28) he did not imitate me when I put out my tongue or sucked my thumb, but when I opened my mouth he said *papa*.

At 0 ; 9 (29), when I opened my mouth (still without making any sound), T. again said *papa*, but this time in a whisper. He did not, however, imitate any movement related to the tongue, eyes or nose.

At 0 ; 9 (30) he again said *papa* or *tata* in a whisper when I opened my mouth, but when I put out my tongue he opened his mouth without making any sound. The same day, when I again began to open and close my mouth, he imitated me correctly, no longer making any sound.

At 0 ; 10 (7) he succeeded in putting out his tongue when I did so to the accompaniment of a kind of click, but could not imitate me when the movement was made silently.

At 0 ; 10 (10), however, he put out his tongue when I did so (without any sound). When I chewed in front of him (making no sound), he said *papa*, but when I put some bread in my mouth he did not react. He also did not imitate me when I put a finger in my mouth.

At 0 ; 10 (21) he correctly imitated the following movements: opening the mouth (silently), putting out the tongue (also silently), and putting a finger in the mouth. He imitated the last of these at the first attempt, without any sound as index and without any previous spontaneous reaction.

At 1 ; 0 (5) I observed that yawning was contagious for him.

OBS. 31. Until 0 ; 9 (29) T. did not imitate any movement of the eyes or any movement of the hand related either to the eyes or nose.

At 0 ; 9 (30), however, when I opened and closed my eyes (as I had done for several weeks in succession), he reacted in the following way. He began by opening and closing his hands, like L. at 0 ; 11 (5), then opened and closed his mouth, like L. at the same age and J. at 0 ; 11 (14). It should be noted that it was this same day, 0 ; 9 (30), that T. first succeeded in opening and closing his mouth without saying *papa* or *tata* in response to my movements. It could not, however, have been a question of perseveration, since T. had not imitated the mouth movements immediately before those of the eyes.

At 0 ; 10 (16), when I resumed the same experiment, T. again began by opening and closing his mouth, then stopped for a moment and suddenly began to blink. This schema, which he often practised spontaneously, had never given rise to mutual imitation. It was therefore achieved by an act of assimilation, because he applied

---

[1] For T. papa had no meaning: it was merely a sound.

it here for the imitation of eye movements. On the following days he reacted immediately in this way.

At 0 ; 10 (21), when I blew through my nose (a thing he often used to do, but was not doing just then), he at once imitated me. When, however, I put my finger on my nose, he blinked his eyes and puckered his nose. At 0 ; 10 (25) he at once imitated me when I puckered my nose, but at 0 ; 11 (5) he did not do so when I put my finger against my nose (for this last movement, see obs. 50b).

We have given these somewhat lengthy observations in full so that our readers may be in possession of all the required material. They confirm Guillaume's thesis that training in imitation is necessary, especially when it is a case of imitation of movements which the child cannot see himself make. A striking example is that of yawning, which, although later on it is very contagious and gives rise to auto-matic imitation, does not produce any immediate imitative reaction during the first year since there is no direct correspondence between the child's visual perception of the mouths of others and the tactilo-kinesthetic perception of his own mouth. It is true, then, that imitation is acquired, but to what end and by what means?

With regard to the end, the facts provided by these observations confirm what we discovered from the observations of the earlier stages. The child takes a spontaneous interest in movements as such for no other reason than that they correspond to schemas he is practising, *i.e.*, to sensory-motor patterns which are an end in themselves. For instance, moving one's lips, putting out one's tongue, putting a finger on one's mouth, pushing out one's lower lip, puckering one's nose, etc., gave rise to systematic imitation on the part of our children much earlier than certain movements of the same organs which had an obvious meaning, such as eating, putting a spoon up to one's mouth, smelling flowers (actions which Guillaume's subjects imitated between 0 ; 7 and 0 ; 9 but which ours only imitated after 1 ; 0). It is true that all the movements quoted in obs. 19–31 are " meaning-ful " in that there is mutual imitation and that they are related to the child's spontaneous schemas. There is, however, no justification for concluding from these observations that imitation begins with the movements which have most significance and is later transferred to those which have no special function. The reason for the order observed is to be found in the mechanism of the spontaneous schemas: imitation begins with patterns which are an end in themselves and is only later applied to specific actions which are integrated in these schemas. In other words, the progress of imitation keeps pace with that of the formation of schemas of assimilation, both of them pro-ceeding by gradual differentiation, *i.e.*, by accommodations depending on co-ordinations.

This brings us to the question of the means. It is obvious that

obs. 19–31 cannot, like the earlier ones, be interpreted as direct
assimilation of a model to the child's schema. Are we then compelled
to have recourse to " transfers " based on " signals " as in the case of
conditioned associations, or is the explanation to be found in mediate
assimilation dependent on " indices " grasped by intelligence? For
instance, when J. (obs. 19) learnt to imitate a certain movement of
the lips as a result of the sound of saliva, was this sound a " signal "
which gave rise to the same action as that of the model through mere
association and without identification, or was it an " index " which
enabled the child to assimilate the visible movement of the model to
her own movement which was not visible, but which she could hear?
The difference between the two interpretations is the following: the
" signal " (in the sense in which it is understood in the case of conditioned behaviours) is embodied firmly and finally in a schema and
produces its effect more or less automatically, whereas the " index "
is a mobile sign, detached from the action taking place, and making
possible both anticipation of an immediate future and reconstruction
of a recent past (see *N.I.*, Chap. IV, § 4).

In the case of obs. 19–31, there seem to be certain reasons for
accepting the interpretation of mediate assimilation based on intelligent
" indices." This does not of course exclude the possibility of the
associative " signal " sometimes existing alongside the " index."
What is of primary importance is the mobility shown in the signs used
by the child in his understanding of the model. It is interesting to
examine, in this connection, the number of possible combinations of
these signs, in accordance with the principles of co-ordination of
schemas at this stage (*cf. N.I.*, Chap. IV, § 3). Four main combinations can be distinguished:

1. First of all there is the case in which a sound serves as an index
to enable the child to assimilate a movement he has seen others make
to a non-visible movement of his own (see obs. 19, 20, 23, 24, 27, 28
and 30). What is striking in all these examples is the very transitory
part played by the sound. It is just sufficient to enable the child to
give a meaning to the visual data he perceives on others. In obs.
19, for instance, the sound of saliva was necessary the first day as a
lead to imitation of the movement of the lips, but after the second
experiment it became unnecessary. It thus seems as though the
sound was merely used as a mean term, which is precisely the function
of the index as opposed to the signal. Although the child cannot
picture his own mouth (and does not need to do so) he understands
through the sound he hears that the movements he sees made by the
mouths of others are concomitant with a certain tactilo-kinesthetic
impression in his own mouth. In other words, thanks to the index,
the child assimilates the visual and auditory model to the auditory
motor schema with which he is familiar in himself, and imitation

becomes possible through accommodation to this schema. The sound then becomes unnecessary, whereas if it were a signal it would have to persist as a stimulus, or, in case of transfer, itself be produced as a result of visual perception. When a silent, visual suggestion does in fact produce a vocal motor response (obs. 30) it is only transitory, and the sound very soon disappears.

2. Secondly there is the case in which the child assimilates the model to a schema involving the same organ but not identical with the one suggested. In obs. 20, 21 and 22, for instance, when I put out my tongue, sucked my fingers and opened my mouth, J. reacted by biting her lips, and in obs. 28, L. opened her mouth when I put out my tongue. In such cases the meaning of the suggestion is partially understood, since it is similar to an existing schema, but there is no exact correspondence. It is possible to consider that there is a transfer, but transfer through similarity. The meaning of the model itself then depends on an act of assimilation, and the visual perceptions, far from being mere signals, are indices resulting from the similarity.

3. The same thing occurs in a third case, that in which there is assimilation of the model to the child's schema through progressive differentiations based on indices of mere resemblance. For instance, in obs. 22, J., after first reacting to my suggestion of opening and closing my mouth by simply biting her lips, later spontaneously pressed her gums together. After that, I only had to repeat my action for her to open and close her mouth (*cf.* also obs. 23, pushing out the lower lip with the tongue ; obs. 24, finger in the nose ; and obs. 26, finger in the ear). Is this a case merely of connection through contiguity, *i.e.*, a signal with motor transfer, or of assimilation through intelligent " indices " ? The child's behaviour seems to indicate understanding. When J. pressed her gums together, it was not this action that she was reproducing, but what she saw in the model. It was as though she had suddenly grasped the relationship between what she saw happening to my mouth and the motor impression of her own mouth making a similar movement, and as though this understanding enabled her to copy successfully what she had hitherto failed to imitate. Similarly, when at o ; 10 (18) she pushed out her lower lip with her tongue when I did so (obs. 23), it was as though she suddenly grasped the connection between what she saw and what she was doing, which was quite natural since she could already imitate movements of the mouth and tongue. When it came to putting her finger in her nose and ear, she was able to find analogous relationships.

In short, through mutual assimilation, it is quite possible for there to be a progressive translation from the visual into the tactilo-kinesthetic, and the converse. All the learning of prehension, which is completed at the beginning of the third stage, implies a gradual co-ordination in the body of the child between, on the one hand,

visual data (sight of the hand and of its movements) and on the other,
tactile and kinesthetic data. It is therefore perfectly normal for this
co-ordination, which during the third stage is kept up through the
activity of the secondary circular reactions, to result, in the fourth
stage (*i.e.*, at the level of mutual assimilation of these secondary
schemas), in correspondence between the visual data seen on others
and the tactilo-kinesthetic schemas connected with the non-visible
movements of the child's own body. Moreover, since the child does
not only imitate actions of complex significance but is interested in
movements for their own sake, it is clear that this correspondence
will lead him to investigations which will be a continuation of all his
earlier sensory-motor behaviours.

4. A fourth and last case is that of the analogical understanding
of the significance of the model, not as in case 2 through confusion of
movements connected with the same organ, but through confusion of
organs which bear some resemblance to one another. This is the
most interesting and the most decisive case. The mistakes the child
makes in his interpretations reveal the inner mechanism of his imitative
technique and provide clear confirmation of the findings we gave
earlier. The most typical example is that of the eyes. In response
to my movement of opening and closing my eyes, J. at o ; 11 (14)
opened and closed her mouth (obs. 25), L. at o ; 11 (5) opened and
closed her hands, then her mouth (obs. 29), and T. at o ; 9 (30)
did likewise with his hands and mouth (obs. 31). Furthermore, L.
and T. continued for some days to confuse the eyes and mouth, and
J. at o ; 11 (16) still put her hand in front of her mouth in response
to my gesture of rubbing my eyes. It is also worth noting that at
o ; 9 (4) L. raised her forefinger when I put out my tongue (obs. 28).
In our view, mistakes such as these are extremely illuminating. It
certainly cannot be a question of considering the visual perception
of the movement of someone else's eyes as a signal which sets in motion
the child's schemas of the hand or mouth, for no bond of contiguity
in space or time has caused him to make a connection between them.
The child's mistake must therefore be due entirely to analogy. When
the child sees other people's eyes opening and closing, he assimilates
what he sees, not to the visual schema related to other people's mouths,
but to a general schema, partly visual but mainly tactilo-kinesthetic,
of opening and closing something. This motor schema is essentially
connected, as far as the child's own movements are concerned, with
movements of the hand and mouth, those of the mouth not being visible
to him but already familiar through imitation. These therefore are
the organs that the child will use in response to movements of other
people's eyes. His mistake is due to confusion, it is true, but it is
intelligent confusion: the model is assimilated to an analogous schema
susceptible of translating the visual into the kinesthetic.

To sum up, in these four cases assimilation precedes imitative accommodation and takes place mediately by means of intelligent indices. But there is still another argument to be added to those we have already examined. If imitation took place through associative transfers, we should expect to find the learning process obeying the classic law of such acquisitions, *i.e.*, its curve would be an exponential. A good example studied by Guillaume is that of progressive adaptation to a bicycle. But although the imitations described in obs. 19–31 may sometimes show only slow gradation, there always comes a moment when the child " grasps " the relationship between the model and the corresponding gesture and suddenly imitates. It is as though he first tried out various hypotheses and then finally decided on one of them. Thus imitation of movements already made by the child but not visible to him, fits into the general development of the intelligent activities of this stage ; the co-ordination of primary and secondary schemas, and the application of tools which are familiar to situations which are new. For imitation of such movements to be possible, there must be co-ordination of visual schemas with tactilo-kinesthetic schemas, all of them primary, it is true, but serving, with the help of mobile indices, as means to an end, that end being imitation. Moreover, the intelligent co-ordinations of this fourth stage lead to the construction of the first characteristics of the " object " and to the beginning of objectivation of space and causality. This general progress will obviously have repercussions on imitation, in that it gives rise to investigation into the correspondence between the bodies of others, viewed as autonomous sources of causality, and the child's own body, which he perceives to be similar to other bodies.

§ 2. *Stage IV: II. Beginning of imitation of new auditory and visual models*

The study of imitation reveals the striking fact that when the child becomes capable of imitating movements he has already made, but which he cannot see on his own body, he also tries to copy sounds and gestures that are new to him and which hitherto left him indifferent. In our view, this correlation is to be explained by the general progress of intelligence. The fact that up to the third stage imitation proceeds by way of simple, rigid, unco-ordinated schemas accounts for the child's failure to attempt to imitate new models before that stage, accommodation to a new model requiring a certain flexibility in the schemas which essentially depends on their co-ordination. Conversely, the fact that at the fourth stage the schemas at the child's disposal become susceptible of mobile accommodation exactly in so far as they begin to be co-ordinated one with another, accounts for the beginning of imitation of new models at this stage. As we have seen, before this stage, accommodation and assimilation were undifferentiated. From stage V onwards, the differentiation becomes such that active experimentation is possible (tertiary circular reactions) and therefore we find imitation of new models of all kinds. During stage IV the reactions are intermediary: accommodation, which is beginning to be differentiated from assimilation through co-ordination of schemas, gives rise only to " investigations " (*N.I.*, p. 256), and therefore to a beginning of imitation of new models.

We give here a few observations, the first of which are attempts at imitation of new sounds and phonemes.

OBS. 32a. At 0 ; 8 (8), *i.e.*, a few days after she first imitated movements not visible on herself, J. reacted for the first time to a sound which was new to her. When I said to her: " Vou vou, vou vou," she at once replied " *Bou bou, bou bou*," whereas hitherto the sound " vou vou " had produced no reaction. Her reply " bou bou " can be seen to be a phoneme analogous to the one she had earlier uttered of her own accord (" abou " in obs. 11).

At 0 ; 8 (28) the sound " poupou " evoked the response " *pou . . . ou.*"

At 0 ; 9 (16) the sound " gaga " gave rise to a sustained effort. J. said " *mama*," then " *aha*," then " *baba*," " *vava*," and finally " *papa*." The sound " pipi " (which had no meaning for her) produced " *vv*," then " *pp . . . pp* " and finally " *pff*." When I said " poupou " as at 0 ; 8 (28), J. replied " *bvv*," " *abou*," then " *bvou*," " *bou*," and finally in a whisper, " *pou* " and " *pou . . . ou.*"

At 0 ; 9 (26) " toutou " produced " *ou . . . ou* " and " tititi " produced first " *i . . . i . . . i*," and then " *tetete*."

At 0 ; 10 (25) she at once imitated the noise of smacking the lips and at 0 ; 11 (20) the sound " papa " (which had no meaning for her).

OBS. 32b. During this stage, L. also made quite definite efforts, but with little success, to reproduce sounds new to her. At 0 ; 9 (28) for instance, she reacted to the phoneme " papa " with the following sounds: " *aha . . . dada . . . gaga . . . tata*." She needed many tentative efforts in order to arrive at " *papa*."

On the following days her reaction to the same model was almost always " *atata*." It was only at about 0 ; 10 (8) that she made a serious effort to react correctly.

OBS. 33. At 0 ; 8 (19) J. watched my hand with interest when I pressed my forefinger against my thumb. When I stopped, she first touched either my finger or my thumb to make me go on. I then showed her my raised forefinger. She imitated the movement and finally put the tip of her finger against mine.

At 0 ; 9 (12) I alternately bent and straightened my finger, and she opened and closed her hand. At 0 ; 9 (16) she reacted to the same model several times in succession by waving her hand, but as soon as she stopped trying to imitate me she raised her finger correctly. When I resumed, she again began to wave goodbye.

At o ; 9 (19) I tried the same experiment. She imitated me, but used her whole hand, which she straightened and bent, without taking her eyes off my finger.

At o ; 9 (21) there was the same reaction. Finally, at o ; 9 (22), she succeeded in isolating and imitating correctly the movement of the forefinger.

From o ; 9 (22) onwards, I resumed the first experiment of touching the tip of my thumb with my forefinger or middle finger. I also snapped my middle finger against the base of the thumb to rouse her interest. At o ; 9 (24) she reacted by moving her fingers, which she bent and straightened quite quickly, but without differentiating between them. From o ; 10 to 1 ; 0 she abandoned any attempt at imitation. At last, at 1 ; 0 (25), she put her forefinger against the tip of her thumb, in response to the first model. When I snapped my middle finger against the base of the thumb, she merely rubbed her forefinger against her thumb in an attempt to produce a sound. Same reaction at 1 ; 0 (26) and on the following days. Only at the beginning of the fifth stage, therefore, was she able to imitate touching the thumb with the forefinger.

OBS. 34. This is how J. learnt to imitate the well-known " marionette " movement (the open hand held vertically and pivoting on the wrist).

From o ; 9 to o ; 10 I frequently showed J. this movement without the tune usually associated with it, and of course without giving her any help by holding her hands. Throughout the period J. showed a lively interest in what she saw, frequently looked at her own hands after seeing mine pivoting, but never attempted to imitate me.

At o ; 10 (9) she watched me with great attention, then suddenly raised her right hand with the palm towards her, and gazed at it, and then three times alternately examined my hand and her own. Her hand remained still, however, which seems to indicate that there was an attempt at understanding without any effort at realisation.

At o ; 10 (18) she smiled when I made the movement, and then waved goodbye. Her reaction was the same several times in succession.

At o ; 11 (16) and o ; 11 (18) there was no reaction. At o ; 11 (19), however, she watched my movement carefully, without moving. But about five minutes later, she raised her right arm, with her fist clenched, and swung her hand round on the wrist several times without looking at it (a suggestion of the correct movement). When I resumed the experiment, she made no further attempt to imitate it!

At o ; 11 (28), after ten days with no reaction, she again began to raise her arm, clench her fist and make faint rotatory movements interspersed with waves of the hand. At o ; 11 (29) I surprised her in the act of spontaneously making the marionette movement, with her hand clenched. A quarter of an hour later I repeated the movement and she imitated me.

At 1 ; 0 (0) there was mutual imitation, which she began. From 1 ; 0 (3) onwards she at once imitated the movement.

OBS. 35. At 0 ; 11 (0) J. was sitting in front of me, her feet free. I alternately bent forward and straightened my head and trunk. J. reacted three times in succession with a wave of the hand, and then imitated my movement correctly.

At 0 ; 11 (1) she was seated and I was half-lying in front of her. I raised my right leg and swung it up and down. She first reacted by bending and straightening her whole trunk (as she had done the day before), and then by waving her hand. This goodbye gesture was roughly similar to that of my leg, but was made with the arm and the hand.

At 0 ; 11 (11) the same model produced the following reactions. J. began by waving goodbye, as before (this had been her response to my action during the preceding days). Then, a few moments later, she moved her feet, slightly raising her leg. Finally she definitely raised her right foot, keeping her eyes on mine.

At 1 ; 0 (2), when I resumed the experiment, she immediately imitated me.

OBS. 36. Here are a few further examples of imitation of new movements by J., imitation which was immediate:

At 0 ; 11 (6) I struck the back of one hand with the other, and J. immediately imitated me.

At 0 ; 11 (9) her mother hit a duck with the end of a comb and J. reproduced the movement without any hesitation.

Same success at 0 ; 11 (19) when I struck the notes of a xylophone with the head of a little hammer.

At 0 ; 11 (27) she drummed on the table in response to this stimulus, and there was the same reaction with various objects one after the other.

OBS. 37. We have already seen (obs. 13) that L., as early as 0 ; 6 (5), succeeded in imitating moving fingers (a general movement of all the fingers) but without as yet being able to copy a new, specific movement such as raising her forefinger.

At 0 ; 7 (27) I again showed her my raised forefinger. She replied by opening and closing her hand, but without reproducing the movement of the finger, except by chance.

At 0 ; 8 (30) her reaction was still to move all her fingers. At 0 ; 9 (4), as we have already seen (obs. 28), she raised her finger when I put out my tongue. A few hours later, I showed her my raised finger: she imitated the gesture, but then moved all her fingers at once.

At 0 ; 9 (25) she was sitting in her pram. I began by moving my hand and then moved it out of sight behind one of the sides. L. looked for a long time at the place where it disappeared, then, with a smile, raised her hand and imitated my movement, following the line taken by my hand up to the point of its disappearance.

I then moved my forefinger. L. first shook her foot hard, then moved her hands about, and only finally moved her fingers. She did not raise her forefinger by itself. The same evening, however, she began by moving all her fingers and then moved only her forefinger.

On the following days her imitation was correct from the start.

OBS. 38. At o ; 10 (o) L. watched me hitting my stomach. She hit her knees (she was sitting down). At o ; 11 (26) she tried to imitate me when I was holding a ball with my arm erect. She seized the ball, then raised her hand, and after several attempts, succeeded in raising the ball above the level of her head, though without fully extending her arm.

At o ; 11 (28) she at once imitated me when I covered an object with a handkerchief. Here we have the schema of looking for things. L. knew how to find something hidden under a screen, but had not yet herself put a screen over anything. She had, however, at o ; 11 (3) and o ; 11 (15) hidden her feet and a rattle under a blanket or a rug (cf. C.R., obs. 85).

As usual two questions arise in connection with these examples. What is the aim of such imitations, and what is the technique used by the child?

Why indeed does the child, who up to the third stage imitated in others only those movements which he himself could make, now begin to attempt to reproduce new models? Is this new progress in imitation a development of the earlier imitation, or is there discontinuity? We have accepted the fact that up till now there has been functional continuity in the succession of imitative structures, although authors as authoritative as Guillaume and Wallon are opposed to this view. For example, for Guillaume there is no direct relation between the initial imitation, which is merely a continuation of the circular reaction, and true imitation, since the latter is the intentional reproduction of models which have complex significance. In his view, it is only by way of successive transfers that the child begins to imitate movements as such, and thus it is only after going through a long process that he comes to the elementary imitation of actions which have no significance. We have been able to show that it is possible to find all the gradations between the reproductive assimilation of the circular reaction or self-imitation, the recognitive and reproductive assimilation of the beginnings of imitation of others through incorporation of the model in the circular schema, and the mediate assimilation, through intelligently co-ordinated indices, of the imitation of movements known to the child but which he cannot see himself make. In all these cases the imitation is determined by the extent to which the child tends to preserve and repeat each of the actions of which he is capable, and it is thus both accommodation and assimilation. During the first stages, the model and the child's own action are more or less undifferentiated since the assimilating and accommodating tendencies are not yet dissociated. Even in the third stage, neither persons nor objects are viewed as having autonomous activity, and the child always considers what he sees as a kind of continuation of his own activity. Whether he imitates through recognitive and reproductive assimilation, or endeavours, by his imitative response, to prolong what he sees or hears, the imitation is not essentially different from the circular reaction, and it is for this reason that up to that stage there is no imitation of new elements. When confronted with new models, the child either remains indifferent or tries to prolong the situation by a random use of schemas, in a kind of " causality through efficacy " (*cf. C.R.*, Chap. III, § 2). In the fourth stage, however, the progress of intelligence and the beginning of differentiation between accommodation and assimilation enable the child to imitate movements with which he is familiar but which he cannot see himself make. A certain opposition then arises, within the general similarities, between what is suggested from outside and the habitual movements of the child, and from then onwards imitation becomes a specific function, which continues accommodation and begins to be distinct from mere reproductive assimilation, of which it nevertheless makes use. Now since in the fourth stage there is the beginning of dissociation between subject and object, the assimilating schemas through which the child adapts himself to things and persons must necessarily be gradually further and further differentiated. The way in which the child then views the situations with which he is confronted is quite different from that of the earlier stages. Instead of appearing to be the continuation of his own activity, they are now partially independent realities which are analogous to what he himself can do and yet distinct from it. Then and only then do new models have interest for the child and imitation follows accommodation.

There is thus nothing mysterious about the interest in new models which makes its appearance at this stage. It is, more than would at first appear, a continuation of earlier interests mainly concerned with the preservation of habitual behaviours. In all " circular " activities, and hence in all imitation of what is already known, the interest of the desired result resides in the fact that this result provides support for the activity, and hence for its reproduction. Interest is merely the affective aspect of assimilation. When the subject sees objects as distinct from himself and sees models as objects, models can no longer be assimilated wholesale: they are seen to be both different from and similar to the child himself. It is no longer only identity, but also similarity which becomes a source of interest. It is true that as yet it is only those models which have some analogy with the child's schemas which give rise to imitation. Those which are too remote from the child's experience leave him indifferent, as for instance unfamiliar movements which would have to be made without being seen. But sounds and movements which are new to the child, and yet comparable to those he has already made, give rise to an immediate effort at reproduction. The interest thus appears to come from a kind of conflict between the partial resemblance which makes the child want to assimilate, and the partial difference which attracts his attention the more because it is an obstacle to immediate reproduction. It is therefore this two-fold character of resemblance and opposition which seems to be the incentive for imitation. In this sense, imitation of new situations is a continuation of imitation of what is familiar, both involving previous assimilation, which is of course obvious, since accommodation is only possible when there are schemas capable of being accommodated, and the use of these schemas implies assimilation.

If, however, the suggested models are closely enough related to the child's own activity to provoke the tendency to reproduce, and yet at the same time distinct from his existing schemas, it only remains to accommodate the schemas to the models. All circular reactions follow the same pattern: interest in a new result discovered by chance, when it is reminiscent of others which are already familiar, followed by attempts to reproduce this result. For this reason the circular reaction has rightly been compared to self-imitation. In the case of new models, however, the result is extrinsic to the child's action but is connected with it by some analogy and therefore gives rise to the same desire for reproduction. The necessary accommodation is then more complex, and is further dissociated from assimilation, and therefore imitation begins to be an independent function. It must, however, be clearly understood that from the beginning its function is the same, but less differentiated. What the child does in the case of all models is to accommodate to them the schemas at his disposal. If the models are familiar, the schemas will be already formed (and in that case accommodation is not differentiated from assimilation). If the models are partially new, the schemas will be modified as a result of the new element (and in this case accommodation is differentiated and becomes imitation).

Having discussed the question of the aim, we now come to that of the technique. It is obvious that, precisely because of their novelty, there cannot be direct assimilation of new models to the analogous schemas, nor can there be sudden accommodation of the schemas to the models. What first takes place is a tentative investigation comparable to what we called "investigation of new objects" (*N.I.*, Chap. IV, § 5) at the same stage in general evolution. Various schemas are tried out one after the other to see whether one of them will fit the model. For instance, in obs. 32 the new sound " gaga "

gave rise to " mama," " aha," " baba," " vava " and finally " papa."
Then, when it is possible, the child co-ordinates the schemas one with
another in order to find a combination which accords with the model.
Again in obs. 32 the sound " poupou " thus produced " bv," then
" abou," then, by a kind of blending of the two, " bvou " and " bou,"
sounds which finally led to the correct imitation " pou " and " pou
. . . ou." There is only one step between this and true accommodation: instead of trying out several schemas or combining them, the
child will simply change the one nearest to the required result until
he achieves convergence with the model. For instance, in obs. 33
the action of bending and straightening the forefinger gave rise
first to a wave of the arm and hand, then of the hand alone, and
finally of the finger in question isolated from the others. Finally,
through the combination of co-ordination and differentiation, the
desired result is achieved immediately, as for instance in obs. 36, when
J. succeeded in striking the back of one hand with the other and in
hitting the notes of a key-board with a hammer, and in obs. 38, when
L. immediately imitated the action of covering something with a
handkerchief. We would point out, in conclusion, that all these
methods are in accordance with the intelligent behaviours of stage IV:
the application of known means to new situations as a result of co-
ordination of schemas, and further investigation. It is only in the
fifth stage that a general method of imitation of what is new can be
developed.

§ 3. *Stage V: Systematic imitation of new models including those involving
movements invisible to the child*

In the method characteristic of the preceding stage there are two
kinds of limitations. It can be applied only to models which are to
some extent analogous to the child's spontaneous actions, and the
accommodation of the known schemas to the new models is often only
roughly approximate. Imitation of new models becomes systematic
and exact only in the fifth stage, showing a striking parallel with the
progress of intelligence itself, with which it appears to be closely
related. It will be remembered that during this stage there is progressive differentiation between accommodation and assimilation.
On the one hand, the " tertiary circular reaction " takes the place of
mere investigation, that is to say the child becomes capable of experimenting in order to discover new properties of objects. On the other
hand, " the discovery of new tools through active experimentation "
extends these tertiary reactions within the co-ordination of the schemas.
These same characteristics influence the imitation of new models by
enabling the child to go beyond mere application and accommodation
of existing schemas to accommodation through systematic and controlled trial and error. We shall first give some examples showing

how children learnt, through active experiment, to imitate certain visible movements which produced definite results:

OBS. 39. At 1 ; 0 (20) J. watched me removing and replacing the top of my tobacco jar. It was within her reach and she could have tried to achieve the same result. She merely raised and lowered her hand, however, thus imitating the movement of my hand but not its external effect.

At 1 ; 0 (21), however, she imitated the action of drawing. I put a sheet of paper in front of her and made a few pencil strokes on it. I then put down the pencil: she at once seized it and imitated my movement with her right hand. She did not succeed at first in writing, but by a chance movement of the pencil she made a few marks and promptly went on doing so. She then transferred the pencil to her left hand, but turned it the other way up in doing so. She then tried to draw with the wrong end. Finding that nothing happened, she did not turn it round, but put it back into her right hand and waited. To make her write again, I went through the motion of making marks with my finger. She at once imitated me, but with her finger.

At 1 ; 0 (28) she rubbed her arm to imitate the action of washing with soap.

On the same day, 1 ; 0 (28), I put a cork on the edge of her cot and knocked it off with a stick. I then put it back and held out the stick to J. She at once took hold of it and hit the cork until it fell down (cf. N.I., obs. 159).

OBS. 40. Now we have some examples of movements connected with parts of the child's body which he can see, but with which he is not very familiar.

At 1 ; 1 (10), when J. was in front of me, I rubbed my thigh with my right hand. She watched me, laughed, and then rubbed first her cheek and then her chest.

At 1 ; 2 (12), when I struck my abdomen, she hit the table, then her own knees (she was sitting down). At 1 ; 3 (30) when I did it she at once hit her knees, and then when I rubbed my stomach, she hit first her knees and then her thigh. It was only at 1 ; 4 (15) that she went straight to her stomach.

Also at 1 ; 3 (30) I lifted my waistcoat and put my finger underneath, at waist level. She then put her forefinger on her knee, felt round about, and finally put it into her sock.

At 1 ; 4 (21) she saw her mother putting on a bracelet. As soon as it was available, she took it, and after a few tentative efforts, put it on her arm.

OBS. 41. It seems appropriate to examine the counterpart in the field of verbal imitation of this trial and error imitation of new movements. It was, as a matter of fact, during this fifth stage that J., L. and T. began to make their first clumsy efforts to reproduce the words of adults. An analysis of these efforts would take us too far afield, and we shall merely give one or two quite commonplace examples, just to indicate the synchronisms.

It was only at about 1 ; 3 (15) that J. began actively to imitate meaningful sounds that were new to her, *i.e.*, words in adult speech not identical with the spontaneous phonemes of the child (such as " papa," " maman," " vouvou," etc.). Before the sixth stage, during which the child becomes capable of deferred reproductions which are correct at the first attempt, imitation naturally takes place through controlled trial and error.

At 1 ; 3 (18), for instance, in response to the word " parti," J. said " *papeu*," doubtless through analogy with " papa." Afterwards, of her own accord, she said " *papeu* " when people went out of the room or when things came to an end, and she gradually corrected it to " *pati*."

At 1 ; 3 (25) she said " *bou* " for " bouche," " *mou* " for " mouche," " *menou* " for " minou " and " *sa* " for " chat," etc. On the following days " *bou* " became " *bousse*," etc.

At 1 ; 3 (29) she said " *bagba* " and " *bagam* " indiscriminately for " bague " and " boîte," and only gradually came to distinguish the two meanings and the two sound patterns. These distinctions were made, in correlation with one another, during the course of the following weeks.

On the same day, " canard " produced " *caca* " and " lapin " became " *papin*," but at 1 ; 4 (0) " canard " produced " *cacain* " by analogy with " lapin."

At 1 ; 4 (2) " oiseau " became " *aieu*," etc.

These few examples suffice to show that imitation of new sounds, like that of unfamiliar movements, proceeds by way of simultaneous co-ordination of familiar schemas and progressive accommodation of these schemas to the model through trial and error.

OBS. 42. At 1 ; 1 (23) L. carefully watched me swinging my watch which I held by the end of the chain. As soon as I put it down, she imitated me, but held the chain at a point close to the watch. When her hand was too near the watch to allow it to swing properly, she put it down in front of her and then picked up the chain again, taking care to increase the distance.

When L. was 1 ; 2 (7) I hit myself in the stomach. She reacted by first clapping her hands (through assimilation to the familiar schema of applauding), and then by hitting the lower part of her stomach. The next day there were the same two reactions. At 1 ; 2 (18), however, she succeeded straightaway in hitting the same part of her stomach as I did.

At 1 ; 3 (1) she succeeded after several attempts in imitating J. who was digging with a little spade.

At 1 ; 3 (19) she succeeded in rubbing both her chest and legs with a sponge, in imitation of these models.

At 1 ; 4 (0) she reproduced the action of scribbling, gradually correcting the position of the pencil until she succeeded in making a few lines on the paper.

And now we have some examples of imitation of new movements connected with parts of the body not visible to the child:

OBS. 43.   We saw in obs. 19–27 how J. succeeded, during the preceding stage, in imitating certain familiar movements connected with the mouth, nose, eyes and ears, because she had a tactual knowledge of these organs, and was thus able, by means of a system of indices, to make her own movements correspond with those of the model. During the same period, I tried to make her imitate some new models. The simplest movement I attempted, was to make her put her hand on her forehead, either anywhere, or at certain precise spots. This does not seem to be one of the actions the child makes spontaneously. He may have acquired a tactual knowledge of his hair, but he still has to find the relationship of his forehead to his hair, and his forehead is obviously the least interesting part of his face, and therefore the least familiar to him. Up to o ; 11 (11) there was no attempt to imitate any movement connected with the hair or the forehead. On that day, however, when I put my hand on my hair, J. raised hers, and seemed to be feeling in the right direction. There was no reaction as far as the forehead was concerned.

At o ; 11 (20) she watched me with interest when I touched my forehead with my forefinger. She then put her right forefinger on her left eye, moved it over her eyebrow, then rubbed the left side of her forehead with the back of her hand, but as if she were looking for something else. She reached her ear, but came back towards her eye.

At o ; 11 (23), when I touched my forehead she rubbed her right eye doubtfully, watching me carefully as she did so. Once or twice her hand went a little above her eyebrow, but then came back to her eye. Same reaction at o ; 11 (24). At o ; 11 (26) she three times touched the sides of her forehead above her eyes, but never the centre. The rest of the time she merely rubbed her eye.

At o ; 11 (28), J., confronted with the same model, continued merely to rub her eye and eyebrow. But afterwards, when I seized a lock of my hair and moved it about on my temple, she succeeded for the first time in imitating me. She suddenly took her hand from her eyebrow, which she was touching, felt above it, found her hair and took hold of it, quite deliberately.

At o ; 11 (30) she at once pulled her hair when I pulled mine. She also touched her head when I did so, but when I rubbed my forehead she gave up. It is noteworthy that when she pulled her hair she sometimes turned her head suddenly in an attempt to see it. This movement is a clear indication of an effort to discover the connection between tactual and visual perceptions.

At 1 ; o (16) J. discovered her forehead. When I touched the middle of mine, she first rubbed her eye, then felt above it and touched her hair, after which she brought her hand down a little and finally put her finger on her forehead. On the following days she at once succeeded in imitating this gesture, and even found approximately the right spots indicated by the model.

OBS. 44. In connection with this discovery of the hair and forehead, through which the child's grasp of the correspondence between his own face and that of others is completed, it is appropriate to quote a somewhat different experiment, but one which is equally relevant to the question of imitation, namely that with a mirror.

From 1 ; 0 (10) onwards, J. was put from time to time in front of a large mirror set up at the end of the cot in which she was sitting. After a few moments of surprise, she showed great pleasure at the sight of her reflection. She waved at it, waved harder when she saw her double repeating her gesture, smiled, held out her arms, etc. This is not the place to discuss what her conception of the reflection was, nor what she made of other people's reflections when she saw them in the mirror. The only question which interests us for the moment is that of imitation, and it is obvious that between the reflection and the child's own gestures there is a connection analogous to that between the model and the child herself.

At 1 ; 0 (13) J. was in front of the mirror. Without her being aware of my presence (I was hidden behind a curtain and made no sound whatever), I put a toy above her head, and she suddenly saw in the mirror its reflection above the reflection of her hair. She gazed at it in amazement and suddenly turned her head to look at the real toy. It would seem that there must be a connection between this reaction and J.'s behaviour at 0 ; 11 (30) when she turned her head to see her own hair (obs. 43).

At 1 ; 0 (19) I resumed the experiment, making a toy monkey appear above her head. This time she did not turn round, but keeping her eyes on the reflection in the mirror, she raised her arm and felt about for the monkey above her hair. She then extended her arm further and with her eyes still fixed on the mirror, reached the monkey. Same reaction with other objects.

Subsequently I made the same toys appear first on the right, then on the left, without making a sound, and in such a way that she could only see them in the mirror. She at once looked for them on the right side, first with her hand, then turning her head. Same reactions at 1 ; 0 (20) and on the following days.

OBS. 45. At 1 ; 1 (15) J. watched me when I made a long nose at her. She first put her fingers on her nose, then her forefinger only. A series of repetitions produced no new reaction.

Later on, in the evening of the same day, I put my thumb in my mouth, at the same time raising my fingers. J. at once put her thumb in her mouth and moved her fingers until they reached a fairly correct position. I then took my thumb out of my mouth, and put it to my nose without changing the position of the fingers, thus again making a long nose. J. succeeded in doing the same thing. Thus by merely separating the operations involved in making a long nose, I had made it possible for her to imitate it correctly.

At 1 ; 3 (7) I again put my thumb in my mouth, with the fingers raised, but this time I sucked my thumb noisily. J., who had in the meantime forgotten the model and how to imitate it, broke up the movement in the following way. She began by blowing a kiss (to produce the sound), then she put her thumb in her mouth, with her forefinger on her nose (without making any sound), and finally raised her other fingers. She thus perceived the model in terms of various schemas of assimilation (the sound of a kiss, the action of sucking her thumb, and that of raising her finger) and then accommodated these schemas to the model.

There was also the following tentative effort at imitation related to the nose. At 1 ; 3 (30) J. watched me touching the top of my nose with my forefinger, and then touched the corner of her eye (also with her forefinger). Then, hesitantly, after wandering off in the direction of her forehead, her finger reached the right spot. She kept it there for a moment, then touched the top of my nose and went back to her own, satisfied.

OBS. 46. We now give some examples of imitation of new movements connected with the mouth.

At 1 ; 1 (19) J. was in front of me when I touched the tip of my tongue with my forefinger. She at once tried to imitate me, doing so in three stages. She first touched her lip with her forefinger (a schema with which she was familiar). She then put out her tongue without moving her finger (another schema she already knew), and finally she again brought her finger towards her mouth, obviously felt for her tongue, and succeeded in touching the tip.

The same day I put my tongue against the left commissure of my mouth. J. at once put out her tongue, moved it about and finally pushed it against the right commissure (which was natural, since I was opposite her).

At 1 ; 1 (23) she tried to imitate me when I touched my chin. She began by feeling in the direction of her ear, which she found, then she took hold of her nose. She then touched her eyes, and, with her eyes on me, brought her hand down towards her mouth. She then took hold of her lips, and stopped there. At 1 ; 2 (3), however, she started from her mouth and, carefully moving her hand downwards, finally reached her chin.

OBS. 47. It will be seen that in each of the preceding examples the child proceeded by active experimentation, basing his investigation on what he already knew. It should be noted, in this connection, that throughout this stage the child is all the time concerned with parts of the face familiar so him (eyes, ears, nose, mouth, etc.) and is organising in relation to them true " tertiary circular reactions " which will enable him to become gradually more fully aware of the connection between tactual and visual perceptions.

Thus at 1 ; 1 (15) J. touched my eyes and gently felt them with her finger. She tried to open and close them, then suddenly, without any hesitation, touched her own, as if to compare them.

At 1 ; 1 (19) she carefully explored my left ear: she touched the outer ear, made it move about, pushed her finger into the opening, etc. Then, just as she did in the case of my eyes, she at once put her hand to her own right ear, and felt it.

At 1 ; 1 (21), when I was carrying her, she happened to knock her right hand against my nose, and she at once touched her own.

At 1 ; 2 (3) and 1 ; 3 (30) she did the same with my mouth and teeth.

OBS. 48.   Here are a few more examples of attempts at imitation of new movements, movements more complex than the earlier ones.

At 1 ; 1 (23) J. was sitting opposite me. I puffed out my cheeks and then pressed each of them with a forefinger, letting the air escape through my mouth. J. then put the palm of her right hand over her mouth and made a sound like a kiss. She then touched her cheeks but did not succeed in reproducing the complete action.

At 1 ; 2 (30) I hit both my knees with my hands and then put my palms together (as in the gesture of applause, but without making any sound). She touched her knees and then put her palms over her eyes (the peekaboo gesture). She then again put her hands on her knees.

At 1 ; 4 (0) I touched my cheeks one after the other with my forefinger. She first patted the two corners of her mouth, then laid her forefinger on her right cheek. It was only after doing this that she managed to touch her cheeks alternately.

The same day I described a circle round my face with my forefinger. J. showed great interest in this, and first touched the right side of her nose, then described a vague curve in the void, after which she touched her mouth. She observed me for a moment, stopped moving, then again made a vague curve and touched her mouth. I continued my suggestion, following the same path all the time (forehead, right ear, chin, left ear, and forehead, without touching anything, but keeping close to the outline of the face). This time J. made a semi-circle round her nose, then with her forefinger described a vague, very elongated oval in space.

OBS. 49.   At 1 ; 0 (5) L. hit her head with a box. I did the same thing and she imitated me in return. This achievement, which belongs to the preceding stage, gave rise on the following days to controlled tentative efforts characteristic of the fifth period. At 1 ; 0 (11), for instance, she tried to imitate me when I put a piece of cardboard flat on my head. At first she watched me without reacting, then when I put my empty hand on my hair she took the cardboard and moved it towards her forehead. The same

day, when I just hit my head with my left palm, she raised her right
hand and touched her ear.

At 1 ; 0 (12) she was playing with a chain. I hit my head with
my hand (without touching the chain). She then put the chain on
her hair.

At 1 ; 1 (18), however, when I hit my head with her doll, she
hit her nose and eyes with it as soon as I gave it back to her.

At 1 ; 1 (23) she laughed loudly when I pulled my hair. She
then felt for the corresponding part of her own face (on her nose and
near her eyes; *cf.* the above observation). Then she gradually
went backwards towards her ear, which she pulled. (It should be
remembered, as we noted in obs. 28, that L. did not discover
during the fourth stage either her eyes, ears or nose, since she had
no spontaneous circular reactions related to these organs, and
therefore no appropriate indices.) The next time, as soon as I
took hold of my hair, she went straight to her ear, but let go of it,
felt further back, and discovered a lock of hair which she pulled
hard.

L. only discovered her forehead after she had found her nose and
eyes (see the following observation).

OBS. 50a. At 1 ; 1 (25) L. watched me carefully when I touched
my nose with my forefinger (this movement, which she had never
made spontaneously, had not previously been used experimentally
by me). She at once raised her forefinger and felt in the direction
of her mouth (which she knew). She touched her lips, then
moved her hand above her mouth. She first explored the area
at the side of her nose, then found her nose and at once took hold
of it.

I then touched my ears. She felt round the side of her nose and
then put her finger on her right cheek bone.

I then put my finger on my forehead and L. felt round her mouth.
When I opened and closed my eyes, she again opened and closed
her mouth as she did during the preceding stage, but when I
touched my eyes she did not react.

When I rubbed the back of my hand under my nose she imitated
me immediately.

At 1 ; 2 (6) L. looked for my tongue of her own accord, opening
my mouth (which was closed) with her fingers. She touched my
tongue and then at once touched hers, definitely making a long and
careful comparison. She did so again the next day. I then tried
opening and closing my eyes. She immediately reproduced the
movement, keeping her eyes half closed and puckering her nose, as
if she had just understood the difference between the eyes and the
mouth as a result of the preceding imitation.

At 1 ; 2 (10) she again imitated me when I closed my eyes,
but could not touch either her ears or forehead.

At 1 ; 3 (3), however, she succeeded without much difficulty in
finding her ear, starting from her eye and feeling backwards. To
find her forehead, she felt on her temple, just behind her eye, and

then succeeded in moving her finger up and pointing to the side of her forehead.

OBS. 50b. At 0 ; 11 (29) T. tried to imitate the movement I made when I put my forefinger on my nose (see obs. 31), and put his finger in his mouth. When I put my hand on my head, he brought his hand up to the level of his eyes in an attempt to imitate me.

At 1 ; 1 (8), when I touched my nose, he put his hand up to his ear (a schema familiar to him).

At 1 ; 3 (4) he put his forefinger into his nostril, took it out, and then tried to put it in again, without success. He put it on his right eye, touched his nose half-way up, then at the top, and finally put his finger in his mouth.

At 1 ; 4 (0), however, he imitated me when I put my hand against my nose and on my head.

The main interest of these reactions lies in their relationship to the intelligent behaviours of the same age. Whereas previously there was merely co-ordination of two schemas, the one serving as a tool and the other giving an aim to the action, and accommodation of both to the new situation, at the fifth stage intelligence is capable of co-ordinating a greater number of schemas and of differentiating them in the process in order to accommodate them to the objective. This directed investigation then leads to the discovery of new tools, such as, for example, schemas of " support " (pulling an object towards one in order to reach an objective placed on it, etc.) (*cf. N.I.*, Chap. V).

The imitation of the fifth stage, compared with that of the previous stage, shows analogous differences. The child's experimental investigation is now much more flexible and better directed through a series of auxiliary schemas which give meaning to the various elements met with in the course of the process (*cf. N.I.*, Chap. V, § 4). It is true that the imitation of sounds and of new visible movements (obs. 39–42) differs only in degree from that of stage IV, but the reproduction of unknown movements related to non-visible parts of the body presupposes systematic experiment and a set of meaningful auxiliary schemas which make this behaviour comparable to the " discovery of new tools." For instance, when J. (obs. 43) succeeded in locating her forehead with her hand by making use of visual perception of my forehead, she not only solved a problem which was new to her, but also used new tools. She started from her eye, which she knew, and then groped about, touching first her ear, then her hair, realising that she had not reached her objective, and then was finally satisfied when she succeeded in touching her forehead. How did she direct herself, and more particularly how did she decide what was right and what was not? In the case of her forehead it was a tactual acquaintance with her cheeks (obs. 27) which gave her a milestone for the recognition. In the case of her hair it was an acquaintance with silky and woolly objects, and the proof that this correspondence between the visual and the tactual was deliberate and controlled by the child is to be found in the very characteristic gesture of suddenly turning her head in order to see her hair (obs. 43).

To sum up, in the case of invisible movements of his body, the child no longer confines himself, as in stage IV, to trying out various known schemas, but differentiates them and experiments with them. He was already doing this in stage IV when it was a case of visible movements, but he now proceeds with much greater perseverance and assurance. Imitation has thus become a kind of systematic accommodation tending to modify the schemas with respect to the object, as distinct from the accommodations inherent in the act of intelligence, which, although they too apply the schemas to the object, incorporate the object in a system of varied usages.

CHAPTER III

DURING the sixth stage of the development of sensory-motor intelligence
the schemas become sufficiently independent of immediate perception
and experiment to give rise to mental combinations. In other words,
the experimentation is interiorised and co-ordination takes place
before there is external adjustment.

Exactly the same thing occurs in the case of imitation, the only
difference being that it is the accommodation that is interiorised,
and is differentiated from the general system of combined assimilations
and accommodations which constitute the act of intelligence. On
the one hand, the child is immediately able to imitate new models,
external experimental accommodation being replaced by an internal
combination of movements. On the other, and this is the main
point, " deferred imitation " makes its appearance, *i.e.*, the first
reproduction of the model does not necessarily occur when the model
is present, but may do so when it has been absent for some considerable
time. In other words, imitation is no longer dependent on the actual
action, and the child becomes capable of imitating internally a series
of models in the form of images or suggestions of actions. Imitation
thus begins to reach the level of representation.

All our analyses of the earlier stages have been a preparation for
the solution of the great problem with which we are now faced. Does
this representative capacity come to the support of imitation from
outside, as a new factor, or can we consider that the representative
image is itself only the interiorised product of imitation in its final
state?

§ 1. *Stage VI: Deferred imitation*

We shall begin with a few examples related to imitation of real
people and images.

OBS. 51. At 1 ; 4 (0) J. watched me quickly crossing and un-
crossing my arms and hitting my shoulders with my hands (the
movement one uses to get warm). She had never before tried to
imitate this action, which I had recently suggested to her two or
three times. She succeeded, however, in giving a correct imitation
at the first attempt. Her movement was rather short, but was
perfectly reproduced.

The same thing occurred later with various complicated movements of the arms and hands, such as making a cross, putting her
arms above and behind her head, etc.

OBS. 52. At 1 ; 4 (3) J. had a visit from a little boy of 1 ; 6,
whom she used to see from time to time, and who, in the course
of the afternoon got into a terrible temper. He screamed as he
tried to get out of a play-pen and pushed it backwards, stamping his
feet. J. stood watching him in amazement, never having witnessed
such a scene before. The next day, she herself screamed in her
play-pen and tried to move it, stamping her foot lightly several
times in succession. The imitation of the whole scene was most
striking. Had it been immediate, it would naturally not have
involved representation, but coming as it did after an interval of
more than twelve hours, it must have involved some representative
or pre-representative element.

At 1 ; 4 (17), after a visit from the same boy, she again gave a
clear imitation of him, but in another position. She was standing
up, and drew herself up with her head and shoulders thrown back,
and laughed loudly (like the model).

OBS. 53. At 1 ; 6 (23) J. was looking at an illustrated paper and
her attention was caught by the photograph (much reduced in size)
of a little boy with his mouth wide open, gaping with amazement.
She thereupon attempted to reproduce the action and at once
managed to do so most successfully. The observation is interesting,
because the situation was one in which there was no suggestion of
imitation: J. was merely looking at pictures. It was as though she
felt the need to mime what she saw in order to grasp it.

OBS. 54. With regard to her deferred imitations of the behaviours
of her little friend (obs. 52), it is useful to note that at the same
period J. began to reproduce certain words, not at the time they were
uttered, but in similar situations, and without having previously
imitated them.

Thus at 1 ; 4 (8) J. said " *in step* " as she was walking, although
she had never uttered these words and they had not been said in
her presence immediately before. It was thus a case of virtual
imitation becoming real imitation in an active context.

At 1 ; 4 (10) she pointed to her mother's nose, and said " *nose*,"
again without having uttered the word before and without hearing
it immediately before.

At 1 ; 4 (14) she said " *Flop* " to a dog she knew, in similar
circumstances.

Subsequently, this phenomenon naturally becomes more and
more frequent. The child tends less and less to use for the first
time a word or a group of words when he has just heard them.
What was important from our point of view was to note the beginning of this type of vocal imitation and to relate it to the preceding
observations.

OBS. 55. We were able to observe the first signs of representation in the imitative behaviours of L. at 1 ; 4 (5) in the following circumstances. I showed her my nose. She immediately tried to find her own, found the side of it, then pointed it out correctly with her forefinger. She then went and got her doll, which was about a foot long, from a sofa some distance away, and tried to find its nose. Although it was so small, she succeeded in touching it. This example shows that L. was no longer satisfied with merely imitating an actual model, but was trying, through immediate generalisation, to find the equivalent of her own organs on someone she had not yet imitated and who could not easily be imitated (being a doll).

On the following days this pre-representative capacity gave rise to deferred imitations which were quasi-symbolic. At 1 ; 4 (23), for instance, L. imitated in her bath J. who was not there. She took a towel, rolled it up into a ball, wiped her mouth with it and put it under her chin, as her sister often did.

At 1 ; 5 (7) she rocked her doll in her arms, as her sister did, without the model being present.

We now have some interesting examples of imitation of objects. In order to be brief, we have not hitherto insisted on imitation of objects, since during the earlier stages it is not distinguishable from imitation of movements made by persons (swinging, etc.). At the level of deferred imitation, however, curious reactions are observable, through the movements of the child's body, of reproduction of physical situations interesting to the child, such as hanging objects, openings which can be made wider, etc. In the few observations that follow, we shall begin by referring, in the case of each of our three subjects, to some characteristic examples of imitation of objects during stages IV and V, in order to show more clearly both the continuity and the novelty of the reactions of stage VI with respect to those of the earlier levels.

OBS. 56. J. mainly provided examples, during stage IV, of imitation of material objects, probably related to " causality through imitation " (cf. C.R., Chap. III). At 0 ; 9 (9), for instance, she was looking at a celluloid parrot when, without showing myself, my hand being covered with a blanket, I made it swing vertically. She at once imitated this movement, probably to make the parrot go on swinging. Similarly, at 0 ; 10 (7) she watched a brush and a cardboard box swinging in the same way. She reacted by waving her hand. During stage V her imitation of objects was mainly perceptive. At 1 ; 2 (25), for instance, she saw a lamp which hung from the ceiling swaying. She at once swayed her body, saying " bim bam." J. was probably thus trying to express what was happening and to classify it by means of a word and a motor schema combined.

During the sixth stage, imitation of objects acquires a definitely representative function. At 1 ; 3 (8) J. was playing with a clown with long feet and happened to catch the feet in the low neck of her dress. She had difficulty in getting them out, but as soon as she had done so, she tried to put them back in the same position. There can be no doubt that this was an effort to understand what had happened: otherwise the child's behaviour would be pointless. As she did not succeed, she put out her hand in front of her, bent her forefinger at a right angle to reproduce the shape of the clown's feet, described exactly the same trajectory as the clown and thus succeeded in putting her finger into the neck of her dress. She looked at the motionless finger for a moment, then pulled at her dress, without of course being able to see what she was doing. Then, satisfied, she removed her finger and went on to something else.

In imitating in this way with her finger and her hand the shape and movement of the clown, J. was doubtless merely trying to construct a kind of active representation of the thing that had just happened and that she did not understand.

OBS. 57. L. also provided examples of imitation of objects with an essentially representative aim.

At 1 ; 1 (25), for instance, she was sitting in her cot. I was holding my bicycle, and pushed it forwards and backwards parallel to the side of the cot. L. showed great interest in its movement, and first made it continue by herself pushing the saddle (I was of course holding the handle-bars and thus helping her to move the machine). She then bent forward to see what was happening, looked at the ground as if seeking to understand the movement, and finally swayed slowly backward and forwards with the same rhythm as that of the bicycle (which was then motionless).

The child's whole behaviour seemed to indicate clearly that this imitation, like that of J., took place merely for the purpose of representation.

We have already noted (*N.I.*, obs. 180) a striking example of intelligent investigation during which L. tried to depict the solution she sought by imitating with her mouth the opening of a match-box. At 1 ; 4 (0) L. tried to get a watch chain out of a match-box when the box was not more than an eighth of an inch open. She gazed at the box with great attention, then opened and closed her mouth several times in succession, at first only slightly and then wider and wider. It was clear that the child, in her effort to picture to herself the means of enlarging the opening, was using as " signifier " her own mouth, with the movements of which she was familiar tactually and kinesthetically as well as by analogy with the visual image of the mouths of others. It is possible that there may also have been an element of " causality through imitation," L. perhaps still trying, in spite of her age, to act on the box through her miming. But the essential thing for her, as the context of the behaviour clearly showed, was to grasp the situation, and to picture it to herself actively in order to do so.

OBS. 58. T. imitated material objects as well as persons at every stage.

I. Stages II–V. As early as o ; 3 (1) T. moved his head from side to side when I did so or when I moved my hand to and fro in front of him, and he made the same movement when I swung a rattle horizontally (obs. 6). At o ; 3 (24), when I moved a bag of beads up and down he did not react, but as soon as I swung it horizontally he moved his head from side to side.

At o ; 7 (5) he reacted by waving his hand when I moved a pillow up and down, thus imitating with his hand the movement of the object. At o ; 10 (20) there was a pillow with a watch chain on it in front of him. He could not see me, and I alternately raised and lowered the pillow, whereupon he reacted by alternately raising his trunk and letting it fall back. The same day, horizontal movements of a tin box produced sideways movements of his head.

II. Stage VI. At 1 ; 0 (10) T. was looking at a box of matches which I was holding on its end and alternately opening and closing. Showing great delight, he watched with great attention, and imitated the box in three ways. 1. He opened and closed his right hand, keeping his eyes on the box. 2. He said " *tff, tff* " to reproduce the sound the box made. 3. He reacted like L. at 1 ; 4 (0) by opening and closing his mouth. It seemed to me that these reactions were much more concomitants of perception than attempts to act on the object, since the child's movements were unobtrusive, not deliberate " devices " varying in intensity as a result of success or failure.

At 1 ; 0 (11) he imitated the sound of a rattling window and swayed to the same rhythm.

At 1 ; 0 (23) I moved a notebook like a fan in front of T.'s face, without making any sound. He reacted either by moving his head from side to side or by gently blowing through his nose or mouth. It was not a question of " devices " to make the movement continue, but of straightforward perception or representation.

In these observations we find three new elements as compared with those of the previous stage: immediate imitation of complex new models (obs. 51), deferred imitation (obs. 52–55) and imitation of material objects resulting in representation (obs. 56–58).

Hitherto, the child has only been able to imitate immediately movements and sounds already known to him, or those which could be reproduced merely through co-ordination of earlier simple schemas. When the model was quite new, the child only succeeded in imitating it after considerable trial and error. In obs. 51, however, J. at once imitated a new and complex movement, as if accommodation had taken place internally and without external experimentation.

This interiorisation of imitation is still clearer in the second group of examples. Although earlier the child often reproduced models without actually perceiving them, this only happened in the case of models which he had already imitated. What is peculiar to the reactions in obs. 52–55, however, is that the child was able to reproduce for the first time in the absence of the model a movement or a sound never before imitated, the imitation being apparently based merely on a memory unaccompanied by actual perception.[1] Here again, therefore, it seems as if the accommodation of the schemas of assimilation to the model, which hitherto has been external and empirical, has through long use become sufficiently independent of the immediate action to function internally by itself.

At this point the problem we indicated at the beginning of this section becomes of vital importance. Is deferred imitation in continuity with that of the earlier stages, of which it is the interiorisation—as " interior language " is the interiorisation of speech—or must we recognise that at this sixth stage there is a new faculty (evocative memory, representation, etc.) which accounts for what occurs: deferred imitation of an absent model, or immediate direct imitation of new models? More especially when the child imitates for the first time a model which he has not seen for hours or days, it certainly seems as if the model perceived externally has been replaced by an " internal model." Is this then the product of imitation or the product of a general " representation " which makes its appearance at this level and produces this transformation of imitation as well as many other new reactions (appearance of speech and transformation of sensory-motor intelligence into representative and conceptual intelligence)?

Let us first clearly define our terms. We use the word " representation " in two different senses. In its broad sense, representation is identical with thought, *i.e.*, with all intelligence which is based on a system of concepts or mental schemas and not merely on perceptions and actions. In its narrow sense, representation is restricted to the mental or memory image, *i.e.*, the symbolic evocation of absent realities. It is obvious that these two kinds of representation are related. The concept is an abstract schema and the image a concrete symbol, and in spite of the fact that we no longer consider thought to be merely a system of images, it is possible that all thought is accompanied by images, for if thinking consists in relating meanings, the image would be a " signifier " and the concept a " signified." [2] Moreover, it is very probable that both representations develop concurrently. In *N.I.* and *C.R.* we found that representation in the broad sense made its appearance at this same sixth stage in the child's sensory-motor intelligence, and we now find in the same children the simultaneous beginning of deferred imitation which at least implies representation in the narrow sense (internal model or memory).

---

[1] C. W. Valentine (*op. cit.*, p. 115) also only observed this deferred imitation in the second year of development.

[2] *Cf.* the interesting chapter by I. Meyerson on *Les Images*, in the 2nd edition of the *Traité de psychologie*, by Dumas.

In order to make a clear distinction between the two notions, we shall from now on call representation in the broad sense " conceptual representation," and representation in the narrow sense " symbolic or imaged representation," or merely " symbols " and " images." In accordance with the terminology of the linguists, we shall reserve the term " symbol " for " motivated " signifiers, *i.e.*, those which are related to the signified by some resemblance, as distinct from " signs " which are " arbitrary " (*i.e.*, conventional or socially determined). At this same stage we find that in addition to concepts and symbols, signs begin to be used, since at approximately the same time as sensory-motor intelligence develops into conceptual representation and imitation becomes symbolic representation, the system of social signs makes its appearance in the form of speech. The problem therefore involves three terms: concepts, symbols or images, and verbal signs.

A first solution might be to consider these three terms as inter-dependent since they all depend on social life, and this, if we under-stand it aright, is Wallon's solution. Not only are concepts related to signs, but also the " transition " made through imitation between " perceptive-motor " or " perceptive-postural constellations " and their " equivalent in images, symbols and propositions " depends on language. This accounts for the radical distinction made by this author between the apparently imitative reactions of the first eighteen months and true imitation, which " does not occur before the second half of the second year." But this conception, which is theoretical rather than experimental, is of little assistance in providing an explanation of the facts in detail. We are of course entirely in agreement that thought cannot be explained without recourse to social factors, but the general concept of " social life " seems to us inadmissible in psychology. " Society " is neither a thing nor a cause, but a system of relationships, and it is for the psychologist to classify these relation-ships and analyse separately their respective effects. This we attempted to do in our earlier study of the contrary effects of con-straint and co-operation on the formation of logic, and now, in this very complicated question of the first beginnings of symbolism, we must proceed to a methodical analysis of all the possible factors instead of suddenly leaping from neurology to sociology.

When at the fourth stage the child is capable, with the help of obviously intelligent " indices," of discovering the correspondence between the face of the model and his own invisible movements, are we to agree with the theorist who says that this is not yet imitation, whereas the deferred imitation of the gait of a friend a few months later really is imitation? Are we to make the hypothesis of dis-continuity between the reactions of the fourth and fifth stages and those of the sixth? Assuredly there has been a shift from the sensory-motor to the representative, but does this represent the attainment of an end or must it be imputed to factors peculiar to human " society "? A comparison with what occurs in the case of the anthropoids is helpful at this point. It might well be that in the child the acquisition of articulate language begins at the same time as certain symbolic representations appear as the culminating point in the evolution of sensory-motor intelligence, without this convergence providing an explanation for the fact, if in the anthropoids we find an analogous symbolic capacity without any system of signs. This actually is the case. As Guillaume says: [1] " human speech is the principal manifestation, but not the only one, of a very general *symbolic function*." The ape, though incapable of speech, shows interest in " symbolic objects comparable to our monetary signs." Young chimpanzees were trained, first to get grapes out of a machine by putting tokens into a slot, and then to obtain these tokens by working another machine. " In spite of the fact that they had to wait from three to twenty-four hours before being able to use the tokens, the apes were ready to work for an hour to provide themselves with a supply." In 1936 Wolff succeeded in training apes to " distinguish several kinds of tokens according to the arbitrary significance he attached to them. Some were worthless, others represented one grape, others two, and others, which entitled the holder either to water or to dried fruits, were used with discernment by animals which had been deprived for twenty-four hours of one or the other." Nyssen and Crawford (1936), by putting apes in two adjacent cages, in only one of which there was a distributing machine, succeeded in getting them to make gifts and exchanges, the symbolic value of the useful or worthless tokens being perfectly recognised.

These facts should be considered in relation to Kœhler's experiments [2] concerning the representative memory of the chimpanzee. He found that this animal could remember very well after an hour that some fruit had been buried in some sand and also the exact spot, and as soon as it obtained a stick it tried to unearth it at a distance of 4 feet from the bars of its cage. It is therefore clear that, prior to any language, more or less complex systems of representations can be formed which imply something more than the mere perceptive " index." It is a case of " signifiers " which are differentiated from the " signified " to which they refer, whether it be a matter of " symbolic objects " like the tokens, which must be considered to be half-way between the index and the symbol proper, or of " representations," to use Kœhler's term, *i.e.*, of memory-images.[3]

Deferred and representative imitation does not therefore necessarily

---

[1] *La psychologie des singes*, in *Nouveau traité de psychologie*, by Dumas, Vol. VIII, pp. 325–6.

[2] *Intelligence of the Higher Apes.*

[3] Kœhler's caution with regard to this very point is well known.

require the intervention of conceptual representations nor of " signs,"
since symbols such as images, memories, symbolic objects, etc., are
inherent in the individual mechanisms of thought. We can therefore consider a second solution to our problem, which is that once
sensory-motor imitation has reached the level characteristic of the
fifth stage, the mental image comes to its support as a new factor,
which has no connection with its mechanisms but is integrated in
them once their development is completed. But two difficulties
immediately arise, the first being the question of the origin of the
image. The image is not implied in any of the reactions of the
preceding stages. Why then does it appear at the sixth stage, and
how is this sudden appearance to be explained? The second difficulty
is even greater. Does deferred imitation imply the existence of a
mental image from the start, or does it lead to it? We ourselves,
and many others also, have frequently been able through intro-
spection to observe what occurs. We are sometimes conscious of
imitating someone, but without knowing whom (*e.g.*, smiling in a
way different from our own), and discover later, but only later, the
image of the model (*e.g.*, someone seen on a railway journey, smiling
as he read). There is therefore no proof that imaged representation,
the memory-image, etc., precede deferred imitation, since it is possible
for them to follow it and depend on it.

This brings us to the third solution of our problem. May it not
be that the mental image, *i.e.*, the symbol when it is the interior copy
or reproduction of the object, is merely the product of the interiorisation of imitation? We now know that the image is not, as was long
believed, a mere continuation of perception. It is the result of a
construction akin to that which produces the schemas of intelligence
but which takes its materials from " the world of sensation." But
we must add that this material is motor as well as sensorial. The
ability to reproduce a tune which has been heard makes the inner
hearing of it infinitely more precise, and the visual image remains
vague if it cannot be drawn or mimed. The image is as it were the
draft of potential imitation. Why should it therefore not be the
product of the interiorisation of imitation once this has reached its
full development, just as interior language is both the draft of words
to come and the interiorisation of acquired exterior language? When
the accommodation of sensory-motor schemas takes the form of visible
gestures, it constitutes imitation proper, but when, sufficiently developed
to need no external experiment, it remains virtual and interior, would
it not lead to interiorised imitation, which would be the image?

An examination of the imitation of objects in obs. 56–58 will be of
help to us in deciding between these solutions. It should first be
observed that things, much more than people, give rise to utilitarian
movements on the part of the child, *i.e.*, to assimilation to the usual

practical schemas. Up to the fourth stage, *i.e.*, as long as accommodation and assimilation are undifferentiated, imitation of objects therefore is still part of the circular reactions. But from then onwards, *i.e.*, when there is progressive dissociation of the two tendencies, imitation of objects becomes distinct from their use, though it is rarer than that of people since utilitarian reactions still predominate. It should, however, be noted that in every " investigation " (stage IV) and in every " tertiary circular reaction " (stage V), the pursuit of novelties and their reproduction as such involve a certain imitation. When, for instance, the child uses his hand to make a hanging object swing, he is, in a sense, imitating by the movement of his hand that of the object. Later, when accommodation is sufficiently freed, this imitation of inert objects acquires a quasi-representative role. When, for instance, in obs. 58, T. imitated with his hand and mouth the opening of a match-box, he was obviously not attempting to act on the box, but merely adding a kind of plastic representation which would help him to understand what he was perceiving. Moreover, in obs. 57, when L. wanted to open the box which was almost closed and tried to anticipate through representation the future development of the situation, it was precisely to this imitative representation that she resorted, opening and closing her mouth.

The extent to which imitation itself plays the part of the interior image and almost of " mental experience " is quite clear from these last examples. But what is most obvious—and we have been leading up to this—is that the image used by L. was precisely not mental, since it was still exterior. It is therefore clear that in such a reaction representative imitation does not follow the image, but precedes it, the interior symbol thus being a product of interiorisation and not a new factor from some other source.

If we pursue the comparison between the image and interior language, it is interesting to note a certain parallelism between the behaviours of L. and T. and the verbal reactions of children between the ages of two and four or five (the time lag being due to the slower acquisition of language). The child is for a long time incapable of interior language, hence the soliloquies, the " monologues " and even the " collective monologues " of very young children, which we described earlier (*Language and Thought of the Child*), whereas later on interiorisation becomes gradually more and more complete. The mental image, which is still not interiorised at the beginning of the sixth stage, shows a similar line of development.

We must, however, point out an essential difference between the symbol as represented by the image and the social signs of language. The mental image remains individual, and it is precisely for that reason and because it is only a translation of personal experiences that it plays a unique role alongside the system of collective signs.

That is why interiorised language, in spite of being interiorised, is much more socialised than the image and always retains a tendency to exteriorisation. At all its stages it is the draft of potential exterior language. The transformation of imitation into images, on the contrary, involves a larger part of true interiorisation. Even in imaginative day-dreaming and in dreams themselves, the imitation of experienced situations and of people and things, often strikingly exact even to the minutest detail, is translated into images.

This is one of the two poles towards which the symbol will move. At the other pole, the image may, like interior language, constitute a draft for new exteriorisations. It may again display itself in imitation, both of people and things, in drawing and plastic techniques, in rhythms and sounds, dances and rituals, in language itself, where, in the form of the " affective language " discovered and analysed by Bally, the power of expression is enhanced by resorting to the image and the symbol.

But in order to understand the future destinies of the image and of symbolic representation, which as we have seen are provided by imitation with the wherewithal to make more or less accurate copies of reality, it will be necessary to study the counterpart of imitation, *i.e.*, play and imaginative construction, which will make use of these copies in very varying ways, endowing them with meanings ever more remote from their imitative point of departure.

§ 2. *Further evolution of imitation,*[1] *imitation and the image*

We shall first examine the forms taken by imitation after the acquisition of language. We shall be brief on this point, for the evolution of imitation between the ages of two and seven or eight is well known, and the observations we have been able to make add little that is new. From two to seven, representative imitation develops spontaneously, often being unconscious because of its ease and egocentrism, whereas at about seven or eight it becomes deliberate and takes its place in intelligence as a whole.

In our study of the development of imitation we have proceeded in two different ways. On the one hand we noted the different imitations of J., L. and T. and the way in which they imitated their parents. On the other, at a school in Geneva, La Maison des Petits, we made the following very simple experiment. Children of from four to seven, who were examined one at a time, watched building being done with bricks and were then given similar material to see what they would do with it. The suggested model was built either by an adult or another child who was sometimes older, sometimes the same age and sometimes younger. The results of the experiment were so

[1] With the collaboration of Elizabeth Sontag.

commonplace that it is useless to give a systematic analysis of them. We shall therefore confine ourselves to two general observations, one concerning the incentives and the other the technique of the imitation.

With regard to the incentives, it is a striking fact that imitation is never a behaviour which is an end in itself (and this is equally true at this age as at the pre-verbal stage). It does of course always result from special accommodation to a given model, but it is through being assimilated directly or indirectly to a schema which is identical or analogous that the model gives rise to this imitative accommodation. In other words, imitation is always a continuation of understanding, but in the direction of differentiation with respect to new models. The child imitates an aeroplane or a tower because he understands their significance, and he is only interested in them when they have some bearing on his own activities. But in addition to the factors already present at the sensory-motor level, a new incentive for imitation now intervenes, and this is the child's estimate of the person he imitates. There is evidence of the influence of this factor even after the first few months, in the sense that the baby will more readily imitate a familiar figure than a stranger, but with the broadening of his social contacts and the development of his thought, new shades of various kinds make their appearance. For instance, the esteem in which the model is held becomes a most important element. An adult who has personal authority or an older child who is admired will be imitated on that account, whereas a child of the same age, and more particularly a younger child suggesting the same models will often meet with no success. Tarde, in spite of having so carefully studied these factors of prestige, failed to understand, in suggesting that imitation is the consolidating factor of social life, that it is never anything more than a vehicle, and not a motive, for inter-individual relations. To our mind the dynamic link is to be found either in compulsion, authority and unilateral respect, which give rise to imitation of the superior by the subordinate, or in mutual respect and intellectual and moral equality, which are the origin of imitation between equals.

At the two to seven year-old level, when co-operation is still sporadic, imitation between equals, and sometimes even between younger and older children when the latter have no special authority, gives rise to an interesting situation. The same thing occurs in relation to language, as we saw in *Language and Thought of the Child*, Chap. I, and we found it occurring again in our observations of J., L. and T., and of the children at the Maison des Petits. The child often imitates without being aware of it, merely through confusion of his activity or his point of view with those of others. If our definition of infantile egocentrism is accepted, we have here a typical manifestation of it. The child's egocentrism is essentially a phenomenon of indifferentiation, *i.e.*, confusion of his own point of view with that of others or of the activity of things and persons with his own activity. Defined thus, it is both suggestibility and unconscious projection of the ego into the group, and lack of awareness of the point of view of others and unconscious absorption of the group into the ego. In both cases it is essentially unconscious, precisely because it is the expression of a failure to differentiate. What happens in the case of imitation is the following. A child will often say that he does not wish to copy a suggested model, a plane or a house, for instance. He says he does not like it, it is not pretty, he wants to do " something quite different," and he then proceeds to reproduce exactly the model he has before him ! We even found the case of a boy of six who accused a boy of seven of imitating him when the position was exactly the reverse. Another boy of six, who had the choice between a car, a house and a church which were already finished, and a plane in process of construction, declared that he did not like planes and " wouldn't make that," and then proceeded to copy it, completely forgetting his earlier intentions. In the same way, L. at the age of three continually copied the games of J. who was five and a half, thinking that she was inventing them.

The interest of this imitation through confusion between the ego and others lies in the fact that in a sense it reproduces, with a " vertical lag," what we saw in Chap. I with regard to the beginnings of sensory-motor imitation. At the sensory-motor level also, the first models (movements of the hand and of the whole head) are integrated only because they are directly assimilated to the schemas of the child's own activity. The imitation is unconscious, arising merely through confusion between external movements and those of the ego. The fact that we now again find the same phenomenon at a higher level means that the representative activity in question is again in its early stages and involves the same process of co-ordination of points of view and of differentiation between what is internal and external. Hence the lag, which is once again due to the continuity of the functional situations, although the structures involved are entirely different.

This brings us to the question of the technique, the structural mechanism of these new types of imitation, and we are again faced by the problem of the relationship between imitation and the mental image.

Properly representative imitation at the two to seven year-old level, as distinct from sensory-motor imitation, is characterised by the fact that imaged representation of the model now always precedes the reproduction of it. During stages I to V of sensory-motor imitation there are no mental images. In stage VI of this first period, imaged representation makes its appearance, but remains as it were immanent in the imitation. Since the imitation is already " deferred," it implies the image, but in our view the image consists of interiorised imitation.

Now, however, the image acquires a life of its own, and the child who imitates is often unaware that he is doing so. His response to the model seems to him to come from within himself, which means that his imitation is a continuation of his interior images and not that it gives rise to them.

Can we then once more, at this new stage of the development of imitation, consider the mental image as interiorised imitation? And if so, what view are we to take of the relationship between the external act of imitation and the representative schema, i.e., the image? And finally, if now it is the image which provokes imitation, whereas earlier it was direct perception, how are we to interpret the relationship between the image and perception?

The solution at which we have so far arrived is that on the one hand imitation is merely the continuation of the accommodations of sensory-motor intelligence, and on the other the first mental images are interiorised imitation. At the level of verbal and representative intelligence, which we are now considering, we must therefore first discover what has become of sensory-motor intelligence. Has it been entirely transformed into conceptual thought under the influence of language and social intercourse, or does it persist independently, still having something of its original form, on a lower level of behaviour, like the reflexes, perceptions and habits, all of which appeared long before verbal intelligence and which persist throughout life at the base of the hierarchy of activities?

Sensory-motor intelligence, which during the first two years co-ordinates perceptions and actions, and thus makes possible the construction of the notions of permanent objects, practical space and perceptive constancy of form and dimensions, continues to play a fundamental role throughout the rest of the period of mental development and even in the adult stage. Although it is outstripped, as far as the general control of behaviours is concerned, by conceptual intelligence, which develops the initial schemas into rational operations, sensory-motor intelligence nevertheless remains, all through life, and in a form very similar to its characteristic structure in stages V and VI (from ten to eighteen months), the essential tool for perceptive activity and the indispensable intermediary between the perceptions and conceptual intelligence. " Geometrical intuition " depends at all its tages on the continuity of perceptive constructions, thereby clearly indicating the essential part played by the image as the link between perception and the representative concept. The image, however, is not the product of pure perception, but of imitative accommodation, which itself bears witness to the existence of an activity which is above perception and action but below reflective thought. It is this activity which is the continuation of sensory-motor intelligence prior to the acquisition of language. After the appearance of language, we shall term it perceptive intelligence, or more simply " perceptive activity."

The investigations we have been able to carry out as to the development of perception from infancy to the adult stage, have shown the existence of two quite distinct levels in the mechanisms of perception. On the one hand there is direct apprehension of perceptive relationships, which gives rise to structures that are relatively independent of age. Geometrical illusions, for instance, are common to the adult, the child, and even animals of very varying levels (the Delbeuf illusion was found to work with minnows). On the other hand, there is a " perceptive activity " consisting of comparisons, analyses, anticipations, etc., which is the source of corrections and regulations and which grows regularly with age.[1] For instance, a subject is shown three vertical rods, one (A) 10 cm. long, fixed, 1 metre from the subject; a second (C) variable, 4 metres away in the frontal plane; and a third (B) between A and C but slightly to one side. B is equal to A and is also fixed. The following results have been found: 1. When the rods are shown two at a time, their ratios are on the whole judged equally well at all ages: when C is 10 cm., it is seen as different from A because of the effect of distance; B is seen as equal to A (the two having been put side by side at the beginning of the experiment), and C is seen as equal to B (B being nearer to C than to A). 2. When the rods are shown at the same time, C being 10 cm., they are at once seen as equal by adults and by children of about seven or eight, whereas younger children see A = B, B = C and A > C ! In this particular case, therefore, there is transposition of ratios after a certain age, but inability to transpose before that age. Experiments requiring anticipations show similar results. There is an obvious, progressive improvement in these mechanisms with age, as was shown by the experiments of Auersperg and Buhrmester involving the movement of a white square on a black disc, and that of Usnadze on the apparent inequality of two equal circles when seen after two unequal circles. And finally, in spite of the Gestalt dogma of constancy of depth perception, there is evidence of definite progress up to the age of ten, provided that certain systematic errors are avoided, such as, for example, the " standard " error (systematic over-estimation of the most frequently seen element), and in the case of Burzlaff's experiments, the special importance given to the median element of the series. This constancy is due to regulations whose evolution can be traced, and in no sense to an invariable organisation.[2] In trying to determine the nature of this perceptive activity, we find that it is, in fact, a continuation of the sensory-motor intelligence which precedes the appearance of language and conceptual intelligence. This

[1] See *Arch. de psychol.*, 1945: " Recherches sur le développement des perceptions," V and VIII.

[2] *Ibid. Recherches*, III and VI to VIII.

continuity is in no way surprising, since it is precisely the sensory-motor schemas evolved during the first year of life which ensure the gradual organisation of the object, of space, and of constancy of form and dimensions. When conceptual intelligence makes its appearance, the sensory-motor schemas which constitute its sub-structure, while continuing to be specially devoted to the regulation of motor habits and perception, are at the same time gradually integrated to some extent in conceptual and operational schemas.

It thus becomes possible to view the image, even at the highest levels of representation, as interior imitation resulting from the ever-present sensory-motor schemas. The image is therefore not the continuation of perception as such, but of perceptive activity which is an elementary form of intelligence deriving from the sensory-motor intelligence characteristic of the first eighteen months of life. And just as the accommodations of this initial intelligence form sensory-motor imitation, so the accommodations of the perceptive activity form the image, which is thus interiorised imitation. That is why, at the level of the sixth stage of sensory-motor intelligence, deferred imitation, which is due to interiorised activity of the schemas, is already continued as the image. When perceptive activity is integrated in conceptual forms of intelligence, the image is *ipso facto* also integrated and finds its connection with the higher forms of imitation.

What is the process which takes place when we form a mental image of a visual scene perceived earlier? We analyse, compare and transform, using an activity which starts in perceptive regulation and comparison, but is integrated in a system of concepts enabling us to give meanings to the elements and relationships thus analysed. Now it is this perceptive activity, and not perception as such, which produces the image, which is a kind of schema or summary of the perceived object. Moreover, the image is immediately integrated in conceptual intelligence as a " signifier," in the same way as the perceptive activity was integrated earlier at the very moment of perception, since perception may involve an intellectual as well as a sensory-motor significance.

We can thus see how, at the representative levels, interiorised imitation leads to the formation of images which may in their turn give rise to new exterior imitations.[1]

It must be added that as far as children of from two to seven are concerned there is little attempt to imitate the details of a model, and the imitation is of a very general character. For instance, in copying a plane, a house or a tower, although they follow a general plan related to the perceived object they are easily satisfied as regards detail. In this respect imitation can be compared to drawing at the same level,

---

[1] H. Delacroix considered imitation to be the continuation of the movements necessary for perception.

drawing also being imitation and thus constituting a special case of the behaviours we are attempting to analyse. We are familiar, through the interesting works of Luquet, with the essential characteristics of the " image " which is the starting point of drawing-imitation, the " internal model " which leads to intellectual realism, to incapacity to synthesise, and to the devices used by children in their drawings. What is interesting to us here is that both the syncretic character of the first representative imitations and the various characteristics of imitative drawing, are the expression of the essential laws of perceptive activity at this level. It has been emphasised that children's perceptions are syncretic and general, but it is not perception as such which has this characteristic between the ages of two and seven, but rather perceptive activity, which being incapable of analysis and comparison, of anticipation and transposition, leaves the child passive in the presence of what he perceives. This syncretism of perceptive activity explains both the relative rigidity of children's imagery and the essential aspects of imitation and drawing.

At about seven or eight there is a three-fold progress. Firstly, there is imitation of detail, with analysis and reconstitution of the model. Secondly, there is consciousness of imitation, *i.e.*, clear dissociation of external elements from what belongs to the ego; and thirdly and most important, there is discrimination, since imitation is used only as an aid to the fulfilment of the needs inherent in the child's activity. At this level imitation can thus be called reflective, *i.e.*, it is controlled by intelligence as a whole. To put it more exactly, it is reintegrated in intelligence, since imitation always has been the continuation of the accommodation of the schemas of intelligence, and it is when the progress of this accommodating mechanism is in equilibrium with that of mental assimilation that the interaction of these two processes replaces imitation in the general framework of intelligent activity.

§ 3.   *Theories of imitation*

Having reached the end of our study of the origin and evolution of imitation, we shall now examine the main known theories of this important function, in order to see the value of the conclusions at which we have arrived.

First of all, is the idea of an " imitative instinct " admissible? Every instinct has two aspects: the tendency (which the Germans call " Trieb ") and the technique, or way of expression. As regards the latter, Guillaume has proved conclusively that there is nothing innate in imitation. The child learns to imitate, and this learning process is particularly obvious in the field of movements he cannot see himself make. As we saw in the case of J., L. and T., yawning, for instance, though it may be a reflex, becomes contagious only during the second year because before that stage the correspondence between the visual model and the child's own movements has not been grasped. As for the " tendency " to imitate, the hypothesis of instinctive components has been made. For Claparède there is an " instinct of conformity " which makes the child copy those around him. In our view it is very rash to call a " tendency " which does not correspond to reflex-" techniques " like those of nutrition and sex, an instinct, for then intelligence itself would be the most essential of all instincts. In order to trace the beginnings of imitation, we should have to consider as instinctive the mechanism of assimilation itself, *i.e.*, the tendency to reproduce what has been experienced. And even this would not explain imitation as such, since imitation is gradually differentiated from assimilation in the form of accommodation of the assimilating schemas. In particular, imitation of new elements, seen in terms of instinct, presents an insoluble problem.

Is imitation then to be explained by means of the perceptive behaviours or conditioned reactions which follow the reflexes in the hierarchy of behaviours? Classic associationism interpreted imitation as being the product of association between perception of the model and auditory or visual memory-images, and between the latter and motor images. We are familiar with all the difficulties involved in this interpretation. G. Finnbogason (*L'intelligence sympathique*) tried to reduce imitation to perception, which he considered as being motor from the start and therefore entailing a tendency to reproduce the perceived object. H. Delacroix developed this hypothesis in a subtle analysis [1] to which we are indebted for many ideas. Pure, automatic imitation copies things as well as persons, but imitation of things is rarely translated into external actions ; it remains in the form of a draft, as when we follow with our eyes the outline of a perceived figure. It is these descriptive movements which are the germ of imitation, and imitation makes its appearance when they spread throughout the body, as when the billiard player mimes the trajectory of the ball he has followed with his eyes. In every day life, these descriptive movements are inhibited by the movements in which they are used, but they have free expression in the case of the young child and the artist, both of whom are less utilitarian than we are.

Objections have been raised to this theory, particularly by Guillaume, who believes the association between perception and movement to be acquired. It is clear, for instance, in imitation related to invisible parts of the child's body, how many co-ordinations are necessary for its achievement. In spite of this objection, it seems to us that there is something in the idea of an essential connection between perception and motricity. The neurologist von Weizsäcker and his school have

---

[1] H. Delacroix. *De L'automatisme dans l'imitation. Journ. de Psychol.* (1921).

shown that the notion of an essentially motor reflex and of a sensitivity independent of it is the product of abstractions as unjustified as those which governed the theory of the reflex arc for so long before Sherrington brought to light the natural motor totalities. Von Weizsäcker's solution is to blend the notions of reflex totality and perceptive " Gestalt " in a single concept which he calls " Gestalt-kreis," in which reflexes and sensations are interdependent.[1] This corresponds almost exactly with what we maintained concerning " sensory-motor schemas of assimilation," and our explanation of the formation of elementary spatial structures by means of such schemas is in general agreement with the work of A. Auersperg on the motor anticipations and reconstitutions inherent in the perception of moving objects.[2] Nevertheless, as Guillaume says, the sensory-motor schemas of a given level are not merely continued as such in those of a higher level. The transition from one stage to the next presupposes that the schemas of the first integrate new elements, and therefore it remains true that imitation is learnt. It is the product of a " perceptive activity " (§ 2) and not of the original perceptions. The learning process is, however, not necessarily the result of training, but takes place through actively combined assimilations and accommodations.[3]

The question with which we are faced is whether the evolution that leads to imitation depends on a succession of acts of sensory-

[1] V. von Weizsäcker, *Der Gestaltkreis*, Leipzig, 1941.

[2] Auersperg and Buhrmark, *Exper. Beitrag zur Frage d. Bewegstehens, Zeitschr. f. Sinnesphysiol.*, Vol. 66, p. 274.

[3] It seems advisable here to make an observation essential to the comprehension of the idea of assimilation, which Wallon, for instance, appears to have misunderstood. The fundamental fact which necessitates the idea of assimilation is that no new external element ever gives rise to perceptive, motor or intelligent adaptation without being related to earlier activities. We do not perceive an object, move it, move with respect to it or understand it, except in relation to other objects or to earlier actions involving the same object. No new behaviours therefore ever arise out of the blue, without any link with the immediate or distant past. In order to explain this fact, common sense (including that of many a neurologist) merely argues as follows: when a behaviour A characteristic of a given stage becomes a higher behaviour B, the new elements b, characteristic of B, in merging with the behaviour A, produce B. For example, a perception A, associated with a movement b, will form a new whole B of which A will be an integral part. In our view, and this is the main significance of our hypothesis of assimilation, the merging of the new elements in the earlier behaviour is one aspect only of the whole mechanism. There is as it were reciprocal integration, *i.e.*, the behaviour A was already a whole (whether it be called a " schema " or a " Gestaltkreis ") and this whole has integrated the new elements b and has thus become B. In other words, the integration of A by B is due not only to the fact that b has been added to A, but also, and more particularly, to the fact that the schema A has assimilated b. This explains why there is continuity in mental life in spite of the qualitative differences between the successive structures, and shows that the heterogeneous levels superposed one on the other, to which Wallon wishes to reduce the whole development, are but one of the two aspects of this evolution. [Trans. note: This footnote forms part of the body of the original text and is followed by a polemic between the two authors which has been omitted here since it adds nothing to the subject.]

motor assimilation using nested entities, or whether the sensory elements are associated with the motor elements only from without. In the first case, the schemas of assimilation imply from the outset an accommodation which will become imitative. This does not mean that any model may be imitated at any time, but that the progress of imitation and that of construction of schemas keep pace with one another (starting at the level of perception, which begins with the construction of sensory-motor schemas). In the second case, however, imitation is the result of association between perceptions and movements, the former constituting " signals " for the latter.

The second of these interpretations was the one developed by Guillaume in his interesting work *L'Imitation*. In his view, since imitation is not an instinctive technique, and does not result from perception as such, the only possible explanation for the incentive which makes the child imitate is to be found in interests external to the imitation. In other words, it is at first only significant movements or the effects of these movements on objects that are imitated, to the exclusion of movements which have no extrinsic significance. The similarity between the movements of the model and those of the subject is at first the result of mere convergence, due to the similarity of their somatic apparatus, and the transition from this overall imitation to that of specific movements is the result of training, which, through a series of associative transfers, gives to the perceptions associated with the movements the value of signals. Finally, once the child has acquired through transfer the capacity to imitate the detail of movements, he becomes aware of similarities and is then able to assimilate the model to himself.

We have already paid tribute to this analysis which by its close examination of earlier theories has transformed the whole question of imitation. We find it difficult, however, to follow Guillaume on two important points; the role of the external significance, and that of the associative transfer. As regards the first of these, observation of my own children suggests that there is no foundation for the belief that movements which have extrinsic significance are imitated before those which have not. If all that is meant is that the baby is interested in actions as a whole before he analyses them, then Guillaume is certainly right, but in that case, all the movements the child imitates would be significant for him, including those with no external results. To our mind, all movements (and sounds) that are susceptible of repetition are from the earliest stages significant, which means that significance depends on sensory-motor assimilation. Whether the child is taught various little tricks, as in the cases quoted by Guillaume, or merely sees movements made in front of him, as in the case of my own children, the result is the same. It is the possibility of reproduction which interests the child, *i.e.*, the interest is not external to the action but immanent in it, and is identical with recognitive and reproductive assimilation.

As for the technique of imitation, we have already discussed at length the inadequacy of the mechanism of associative transfer as an explanation for the progress of imitation, since this progress is parallel to that of the construction of intelligence itself. Guillaume does not deny that there is a connection between imitative behaviours and intelligence, since imitation implies intentional investigation. But it is in the pursuit of the end, *i.e.*, the external result of the imitated action, that he sees the working of intelligence, whereas the copying of the means to that end, *i.e.*, the movements as such, is the result of a secondary derivation consisting of transfers. If, however, less stress is laid on the opposition between the end and the means, the role of intelligence is thereby enhanced, and in actual fact the successive steps in the learning process we have described are much more comparable to a series of assimilations and accommodations, *i.e.*, to reactions akin to sensory-motor intelligence, than to a system of mere transfers. In particular, the mistakes in imitation which we emphasised earlier, are indicative of false hypotheses rather than of wrong associations. When the child opens and closes his mouth in response to movements of the eye-lids, rubs his lips when the model rubs his eyes, raises his hand and looks at the palm in response to the " marionette " movement, reacts with his trunk and hands when the model uses his legs, and so on, it is obvious that these are efforts at direct assimilation and not merely interference of automatisms. It is not denied that certain signals occur in the course of the child's investigations, but their function is not that of the trigger which sets off the conditioned reflexes, it is that of the index used in intelligent experimentation.

In a word, imitation is acquired through constant assimilation of models to schemas which are capable of being accommodated to them. We need not, however, wholly reject Guillaume's idea of associative transfer. The only defect in his interpretation is that it is too narrow. Although it is inadequate as an explanation of the beginnings of imitation, it accounts very well for the fact that imitation becomes automatic. Almost from the outset, there is in the imitative behaviours a kind of " will to overcome " which we underestimate in resorting to transfer as the only explanation, but as soon as imitation comes into its own, with a skilled technique, it becomes automatic, and the end in view becomes more important than the actions which are a means to it, the action then being adjusted to the end through immediate association. Thus in the case of imitation, as no doubt in all others, associative transfer is only a derived mechanism which appears during the secondary stages of the activity, and not a primary mechanism capable of explaining the actual formation of the behaviours.

We shall attempt, in conclusion, to summarise the findings of our analysis. Sensory-motor activity is essentially assimilatory. Amid the chaos of impressions by which he is beset, the baby's main concern is to preserve and recognise those which accompany the functioning of his organs. This effort at repetition creates " schemas," *i.e.*, aggregates which are both motor and perceptive, and which are themselves maintained through assimilation which is both reproductive and recognitive. These schemas, merely reflex at first (stage I), later integrate an indefinite series of external elements, the assimilation thereby becoming capable of generalisation. But this process is never completed. Those parts of reality which are again encountered are fraught with a multitude of new shades and elements which can at first be ignored in assimilating occurrences to the habitual schemas, but which in the long run must be taken into account. Every behaviour then has two poles: assimilation to earlier schemas and accommodation of these schemas to new situations. Assimilation keeps its original function of preserving and consolidating through use what is of interest to the child's activity. But when, in the course of the process, objects similar to those being investigated, but sufficiently distinct from them to require a special effort of accommodation, are met, the tendency is for the schema thus differentiated to retain the new elements as such. It is this gradual differentiation of the schemas through combined assimilation and accommodation which is characteristic of the circular reactions of stages II and III. But at these levels, although assimilation and accommodation are moving in opposite directions, they are not as yet actively differentiated. Although the one tends to preserve and the other to modify the schemas, this modification is still dictated by what has so far been assimilated and is not deliberately sought. For this reason, at these stages, imitation, which is a continuation of accommodation, is never more than the reproduction of familiar models, imitation of others being identified with the self-imitation of the circular reaction.

From the fourth stage onwards, assimilation becomes mediate, *i.e.*, the mutually assimilating schemas are so co-ordinated that some of them serve as tools in the assimilating activity of others. Intelligence makes its appearance at this point, since there is subordination of means to ends, and application of known means to new situations. From now on, through the interplay of this mutual assimilation of schemas and the accommodation to which it gives rise, an ever-widening universe becomes assimilable, each new conquest enlarging the field still to be conquered. At this level there are the beginnings of active differentiation between assimilation and accommodation, the former increasing in mobility as its range widens, and the latter leading to an " investigation " of the various individual components which offer resistance to general integration in the child's schemas.

Then and then only does imitation acquire its specific function of reproduction of new models (including those which are only indirectly familiar, since they correspond to movements the child cannot see himself making). Hitherto, imitation tended to be restricted to reproduction of those models which could be assimilated to the child's activity by accommodation of the activity to the models. But as the child cannot assimilate the whole universe to his activity, now that accommodation of the schemas has become actively differentiated he identifies himself with the new models. Imitation proper is thus seen to be a continuation of the accommodation of assimilating schemas. This it has been from the outset, but it becomes specifically so with the active differentiation of stage IV. During stage V imitation of new models becomes systematic, thanks to the progress of accommodation in the direction of active experimentation, and in the course of stage VI it reaches the level of deferred imitation, through the interiorisation of accommodation.

Imitation then, and this is our essential conclusion, fits into the general framework of the sensory-motor adaptations which characterise the construction of intelligence. As we have constantly seen (*N.I.* and *C.R.*), intelligent adaptation is the equilibrium between assimilation and accommodation. Without assimilation, accommodation would fail to produce co-ordination or comprehension, while without accommodation, mere assimilation would distort the object to suit the subject. Sensory-motor intelligence is therefore always both accommodation of the old schema to the new object, and assimilation of the new object to the old schema. But accommodation is essentially inconstant, being in fact only the " negative " of the objective data which are an obstacle to the integral assimilation of reality to the child's activity. Continually at the mercy of the new circumstances which give assimilation scope for development, it only attains equilibrium by envisaging reality as a series of " positives," *i.e.*, stable copies or reproductions, the forerunners of representation proper. The function of imitation seems to be to produce this set of " positives," which correspond to the " negatives " of accommodation and which, at each new " printing," [1] make new reconstitutions and anticipations possible. The mental image or symbolic representation thus comes into being, as the product of the function of more or less exact imitation.

The " technique " of imitation, and the explanation for the fact that it keeps pace with the progress of intelligence, of which it merely develops the accommodating mechanisms, can now be understood. As early as stage II we can see the process beginning in connection with the construction of the first acquired schemas. A good example

[1] This " printing," by which the " negative " of accommodation is transferred to the " positive " of imitation, is of course the result of reproductive assimilation.

is that of L. (obs. 5) who in order to perceive the movements of my head had to follow them with her eyes and head, and when my movement stopped, went on with hers in a kind of imitative continuation. In this sense Delacroix is right when he says that imitation is the continuation of the descriptive movements involved in perception. This example also shows that a movement is not " associated " with a perception, but is inherent in the perceptive schema itself. The Gestalt theory has shown that factors of symmetry in the visual field occasion a movement of the body when an object on which the gaze is concentrated is moved from the centre to the border of the field, thus producing asymmetry. But from the beginning of stage III, these elementary schemas no longer suffice as an explanation of imitative accommodation and new elements must be added to them. With the co-ordination of vision and prehension, new schemas are formed which in no way result from " association " of earlier perceptive schemas with movements hitherto independent of them, but from mutual assimilation of these two kinds of schemas giving rise to a new whole. The accommodation of this whole to the models it is capable of assimilating gives rise to the motor imitation of stage IV. As regards the imitation of stages IV to VI, we have already shown that it keeps pace with the progress of intelligence itself. Thus at all levels imitation is the continuation of the accommodation of the schemas of sensory-motor intelligence, from perception and habits to interiorised co-ordinations.

This accounts for the fact that at all levels (and in the case of the anthropoids as well as in the child) there is imitation of visual models only in so far as they are understood. In this connection, it could be shown, in particular, that the various levels of imitation correspond to those of the schemas of the object and of causality. So long as the object-notion has not been formed, imitation rests on a kind of lack of differentiation between the model and the self, and is accompanied by a " causality through imitation " (cf. C.R., p. 251) which is itself merely a " device for making what looks interesting continue." Once the object-notion is formed, however, and causality is objectified, the bodies of others become realities, comparable to, but not identical with, the child's own body. This accounts for the child's remarkable efforts to find a correspondence between the organs of the model and his own, leading to representation of the latter, particularly the face. It is unnecessary to emphasise the connection between imitation and space-construction.

It is, however, essential to emphasise, in conclusion, that although imitation always depends on intelligence it is in no way identical with it. As we have just reminded our readers, intelligence tends towards permanent equilibrium between assimilation and accommodation. For instance, in order to draw an objective towards him by means of a stick, the child must assimilate both stick and objective to the schema of prehension and that of movement through contact, and he must also accommodate these schemas to the objects, their length, distance, etc., in accordance with the causal order hand-stick-objective. Imitation, on the contrary, is the continuation of accommodation, of which it is the " positive " and to which it therefore subordinates assimilation. For instance, imitation will reproduce the motion made by the stick in reaching the objective, the movement of the hand thus being determined by those of the stick and the objective (which is by definition accommodation), without the hand actually affecting the objects (which would be assimilation). There is, however, a third possibility, that of assimilation *per se*. Let us assume, for instance, that the stick does not reach its objective and that the child consoles himself by hitting something else, or that he suddenly becomes interested in moving the stick for its own sake, or that when he has no stick he takes a piece of paper and applies the schema of the stick to it for fun. In such cases there is a kind of free assimilation, without accommodation to spatial conditions or to the significance of the objects. This is simply play, in which reality is subordinated to assimilation which is distorting, since there is no accommodation. Intelligent adaptation, imitation and play are thus the three possibilities, and they result according as there is stable equilibrium between assimilation and accommodation or primacy of one of these two tendencies over the other.

PART II

PLAY

If every act of intelligence is an equilibrium between assimilation and accommodation, while imitation is a continuation of accommodation for its own sake, it may be said conversely that play is essentially assimilation, or the primacy of assimilation over accommodation.

Play is primarily mere functional or reproductive assimilation. The phenomenon of " pre-exercise," which K. Groos considered the characteristic of all play, can only be explained by the biological process according to which every organ develops through use. Just as for its growth an organ needs nourishment in proportion to its functioning, so each mental activity, from the most elementary to the highest, needs for its development to be fed from without by a continuous flow, which in this case is purely functional, not material. Primitive play begins by being almost identical with the set of sensory-motor behaviours, of which it is only one pole: that of those behaviours which no longer need new accommodation and are reproduced purely for " functional pleasure " (K. Bühler's " Funktionslust "). But with the interiorisation of schemas, play becomes more distinct from the adaptive behaviours properly so-called (intelligence), and tends towards assimilation as such. Unlike objective thought, which seeks to adapt itself to the requirements of external reality, imaginative play is a symbolic transposition which subjects things to the child's activity, without rules or limitations. It is therefore almost pure assimilation, *i.e.*, thought polarised by preoccupation with individual satisfaction. Since it is a mere expansion of tendencies, it freely assimilates things to one another and everything to the ego. While therefore in the initial stages of representation the aspect of copy which is inherent in the symbol as " signifier " is a continuation of imitation, what the symbol signifies, *i.e.*, the " signified " may vary between the adequate adaptation characteristic of intelligence (assimilation and accommodation in equilibrium) and free satisfaction (assimilation subordinating accommodation). Finally, with the socialisation of the child, play acquires rules or gradually adapts symbolic imagination to reality in the form of constructions which are still spontaneous but which imitate reality. In these two forms, the individual symbol yields either to the collective rule, or to the objective or representational symbol, or to both.

Thus the evolution of play, which continually interferes with that of imitation and representation in general, makes it possible to differentiate between the various types of symbols, from those which by their mechanism of mere egocentric assimilation are farthest removed from " signs," to those which, by the accommodating and assimilating character of their representation, converge on the conceptual sign, though without being identified with it.

CHAPTER IV

THE BEGINNINGS OF PLAY

PLAY in its initial stages being merely the pole of the behaviours defined by assimilation, almost all the behaviours we studied in relation to intelligence (*N.I.* and *C.R.*) are susceptible of becoming play as soon as they are repeated for mere assimilation, *i.e.*, purely for functional pleasure.

Just as accommodation continually spreads beyond the framework of adaptation, so also does assimilation, and the reason for this is simple. Schemas temporarily out of use cannot just disappear, threatened with atrophy for lack of use, but will become active for their own sake, for no other end than the functional pleasure of use. Such is play in its beginnings, the converse and complement of imitation. Imitation makes use of the schemas when these are adjustable to a model which corresponds with habitual activities, or when they can be differentiated by comparison with models which though new are related to these activities. Imitation is therefore, or at least becomes, a kind of hyperadaptation, through accommodation to models which are virtually though not actually usable. Play, on the contrary, proceeds by relaxation of the effort at adaptation and by maintenance or exercise of activities for the mere pleasure of mastering them and acquiring thereby a feeling of virtuosity or power. Imitation and play will of course combine, but only at the level of representation, and will become the set of what might be called " inactive " adaptations, in contrast to intelligence in action. During the sensory-motor stages, they are separate, even to some extent antithetic, and therefore they must be studied separately.

When does play begin? The question arises at the *first stage*, that of purely reflex adaptations. For an interpretation of play like that of K. Groos, for whom play is pre-exercise of essential instincts, the origin of play must be found in this initial stage since sucking gives rise to exercises in the void, apart from meals (*N.I.*, Chap. I, § 2). But it seems very difficult to consider reflex exercises as real games when they merely continue the pleasure of feeding-time and consolidate the functioning of the hereditary set-up, thus being evidence of real adaptation.

During the *second stage*, on the other hand, play already seems to assume part of the adaptive behaviours, but the continuity between it and them is such that it would be difficult to say where it begins, and this question of boundary raises a problem which concerns the whole interpretation of later play. " Games " with the voice at the time of the first lallations, movements of the head and hands accompanied by smiles and pleasure, are these already part of play, or do they belong to a different order? Are " primary circular reactions " generally speaking ludic, adaptive, or both? If we merely apply the classical criteria, from the " pre-exercise " of Groos to the " disinterested " (or as Baldwin calls it) the " autotelic " character of play, we should have to say (and Claparède went almost so far) that everything during the first months of life, except feeding and emotions like fear and anger, is play. Indeed, when the child looks for the sake of looking, handles for the sake of handling, moves his arms and hands (and in the next stage shakes hanging objects and his toys) he is doing actions which are an end in themselves, as are all practice games, and which do not form part of any series of actions imposed by someone else or from outside. They no more have an external aim than the later motor exercises such as throwing stones into a pond, making water spirt from a tap, jumping, and so on, which are always considered to be games. But all autotelic activities are certainly not games. Science has this characteristic, and particularly pure mathematics, whose object is immanent in thought itself, but if it is compared to a " superior " game, it is clear that it differs from a mere game by its forced adaptation to an internal or external reality. In a general way, all adaptation is autotelic, but a distinction must be made between assimilation with actual accommodation and pure assimilation or assimilation which subordinates to itself earlier accommodations and assimilates the real to the activity itself without effort or limitation. Only the latter seems to be characteristic of play; otherwise the attempt to identify play with " pre-exercise " in general would involve the inclusion in it of practically all the child's activity.

But although the circular reactions have not in themselves this ludic character, it can be said that most of them are continued as games. We find, indeed, though naturally without being able to trace any definite boundary, that the child, after showing by his seriousness that he is making a real effort at accommodation, later reproduces these behaviours merely for pleasure, accompanied by smiles and even laughter, and without the expectation of results characteristic of the circular reactions through which the child learns. It can be maintained that at this stage the reaction ceases to be an act of complete adaptation and merely gives rise to the pleasure of pure assimilation, assimilation which is simply functional: the " Funktionslust " of K. Bühler. Of course, the schemas due to circular reaction do not only result in games. Once acquired, they may equally well become parts of more complete adaptations. In other words, a schema is never essentially ludic or non-ludic, and its character as play depends on its context and on its actual functioning. But all schemas are capable of giving rise to pure assimilation, whose extreme form is play. The phenomenon is clear in the case of schemas such as those of phonation, prehension (watching moving fingers, etc.) and certain visual schemas (looking at things upside down, etc.).

OBS. 59. It will be remembered that T., at 0 ; 2 (21), adopted the habit of throwing his head back to look at familiar things from this new position (see *N.I.*, obs. 36). At 0 ; 2 (23 or 24) he seemed to repeat this movement with ever-increasing enjoyment and ever-decreasing interest in the external result : he brought his head back to the upright position and then threw it back again time after time, laughing loudly. In other words, the circular reaction ceased to be " serious " or instructive, if such expressions can be applied to a baby of less than three months, and became a game.

At 0 ; 3 T. played with his voice, not only through interest in the sound, but for " functional pleasure," laughing at his own power.

At 0 ; 2 (19 and 20) he smiled at his hands and at 0 ; 2 (25) at objects that he shook with his hand, while at other times he gazed at them with deep seriousness.

In short, during this second stage, play only appears as yet as a slight differentiation from adaptive assimilation. It is only in virtue of its later development that we can speak of two distinct facts. But the later evolution of play enables us to note the duality even at this stage, just as the evolution of imitation compels us to see the birth of imitation in the self-imitation of the circular reaction.

During the *third stage*, that of secondary circular reactions, the process remains the same, but the differentiation between play and intellectual assimilation is rather more advanced. Indeed, as soon as the circular reactions no longer involve only the child's own body or the perceptive canvas of elementary sensorial activity, but also objects manipulated with increasing deliberation, the " pleasure of being the cause " emphasised by K. Groos is added to the mere " functional pleasure " of K. Bühler. The action on things, which begins with each new secondary reaction, in a context of objective interest and intentional accommodation, often even of anxiety (as when the child sways new hanging objects or shakes new toys which produce sound) will thus unfailingly become a game as soon as the new phenomenon is grasped by the child and offers no further scope for investigation properly so called.

OBS. 60. One need only re-read obs. 94–104 of the volume *N.I.* to find all the examples needed of the transition from assimilation proper to secondary reactions, to the pure assimilation which characterises play properly so called. For example, in obs. 94, L. discovered the possibility of making objects hanging from the top of her cot swing. At first, between 0 ; 3 (6) and 0 ; 3 (16), she studied the phenomenon without smiling, or smiling only a little, but with an appearance of intense interest, as though she was studying it. Subsequently, however, from about 0 ; 4, she never indulged in this activity, which lasted up to about 0 ; 8 and even beyond, without a show of great joy and power. In other words assimilation was no longer accompanied by accommodation and therefore was no longer an effort at comprehension : there was merely assimilation to the activity itself, *i.e.*, use of the phenomenon for the pleasure of the activity, and that is play.

These observations might be repeated in the case of each of the secondary reactions. But it is more curious to note that even the " procedures for prolonging an interesting spectacle," *i.e.*, the behaviours resulting from a generalisation of the secondary schemas (*N.I.*, obs. 110–118) give rise to an activity which is real play. Movements such as drawing oneself up so as not to lose a visual picture or a sound, carried out at first with great seriousness and almost with anxiety as to the result, are subsequently used on all occasions and almost " for fun." When the procedure is successful, the child uses it with the same " pleasure of being the cause " as in simple circular reactions, and moreover, even when the child himself sees it to be unsuccessful, he ends by repeating the movement without expecting anything from it, merely for amusement. This action must not be confused with the sensory-motor gestures of recognition, of which we spoke earlier (*N.I.*, obs. 107) : the attitude of the child shows whether he is playing or striving to recognise the object.

During the *fourth stage*, that of co-ordination of the secondary schemas, two new elements related to play make their appearance. Firstly, the behaviours most characteristic of this period, or " the application of known schemas to new situations " (see *N.I.*, obs. 120–130) are capable, like the earlier ones, of being continued in ludic manifestations in so far as they are carried out for mere assimilation, *i.e.*, for the pleasure of the activity and without any effort at adaptation to achieve a definite end.

OBS. 61. At 0 ; 7 (13), after learning to remove an obstacle to gain his objective, T. began to enjoy this kind of exercise. When several times in succession I put my hand or a piece of cardboard between him and the toy he desired, he reached the stage of momentarily forgetting the toy and pushed aside the obstacle, bursting into laughter. What had been intelligent adaptation had thus become play, through transfer of interest to the action itself, regardless of its aim.

Secondly, the mobility of the schemas (see *N.I.* 5, etc.) allows of the formation of real ludic combinations, the child going from one schema to another, no longer to try them out successively but merely to master them, without any effort at adaptation.

OBS. 62. At o ; 9 (3) J. was sitting in her cot and I hung her celluloid duck above her. She pulled a string hanging from the top of the cot and in this way shook the duck for a moment, laughing. Her involuntary movements left an impression on her eiderdown : she then forgot the duck, pulled the eiderdown towards her and moved the whole of it with her feet and arms. As the top of the cot was also being shaken, she looked at it, stretched up then fell back heavily, shaking the whole cot. After doing this some ten times, J. again noticed her duck : she then grasped a doll also hanging from the top of the cot and went on shaking it, which made the duck swing. Then noticing the movement of her hands she let everything go, so as to clasp and shake them (continuing the preceding movement). Then she pulled her pillow from under her head, and having shaken it, struck it hard and struck the sides of the cot and the doll with it. As she was holding the pillow, she noticed the fringe, which she began to suck. This action, which reminded her of what she did every day before going to sleep, caused her to lie down on her side, in the position for sleep, holding a corner of the fringe and sucking her thumb. This, however, did not last for half a minute and J. resumed her earlier activity.

A comparison between this sequence of behaviours and that of obs. 136 of *N.I.* at once makes plain the difference between play and strictly intelligent activity. In the case of the schemas successively tried out with new objects (obs. 136) J. merely sought to assimilate the objects, and, as it were, to " define them by use." Since there was adaptation of the schemas to an external reality which constituted a problem, there was intelligence properly so called. In the present case, on the contrary, although the process is the same, the schemas follow one after the other without any external aim. The objects to which they are applied are no longer a problem, but merely serve as an opportunity for activity. This activity is no longer an effort to learn, it is only a happy display of known actions.

But there is more in such behaviours than a mere sequence of aimless combinations with no attempt at accommodation. There is what might be called a " ritualisation " of the schemas, which, no longer in their adaptive context, are as it were imitated or " played " plasti-cally. It is specially worth noting how J. goes through the ritual of all the actions she usually does when she is about to go to sleep (lies down, sucks her thumb, holds the fringe), merely because this schema is evoked by the circumstances. It is clear that this " ritualisation " is a preparation for symbolic games. All that is needed for the ludic ritual to become a symbol is that the child, instead of merely following the cycle of his habitual movements, should be aware of the make-believe, *i.e.*, that he should " pretend " to sleep.   In the sixth stage, we shall find just this.

During the *fifth stage* certain new elements will ensure the transition from the behaviours of stage IV to the ludic symbol of stage VI, and for that very reason will accentuate the ritualisation we have just noted.   In relation to the " tertiary circular reactions " or " experiments in order to see the result," it often happens that by chance, the child combines unrelated gestures without really trying to experiment, and subsequently repeats these gestures as a ritual and makes a motor game of them.   But, in contrast to the combinations of stage IV, which are borrowed from the adapted schemas, these combinations are new and almost immediately have the character of play.

OBS. 63.   At o ; 10 (3) J. put her nose close to her mother's cheek and then pressed it against it, which forced her to breathe much more loudly.   This phenomenon at once interested her, but instead of merely repeating it or varying it so as to investigate it, she quickly complicated it for the fun of it: she drew back an inch or two, screwed up her nose, sniffed and breathed out alternately very hard (as if she were blowing her nose), then again thrust her nose against her mother's cheek, laughing heartily.   These actions were repeated at least once a day for more than a month, as a ritual.

At 1 ; 0 (5) she was holding her hair with her right hand during her bath.   The hand, which was wet, slipped and struck the water. J. immediately repeated the action, first carefully putting her hand on her hair then quickly bringing it down on to the water.   She varied the height and position, and one might have thought it was a tertiary circular reaction but for the fact that the child's attitude showed that it was merely a question of ludic combinations.   On the following days, every time she was bathed, the game was repeated with the regularity of a ritual.   For instance, at 1 ; 0 (11) she struck the water as soon as she was in the bath, but stopped as if something was missing ; she then put her hands up to her hair and found her game again.

At 1 ; 3 (19), with one hand, she put a pin as far away as possible and picked it up with the other.   This behaviour, related to the working out of spatial groups, became a ritual game, started by the mere sight of the pin.   Similarly, at 1 ; 4 (0), she had her leg through the handle of a basket.   She pulled it out, put it back at once and examined the position.   But once the geometrical interest was exhausted, the schema became one of play and gave rise to a series of combinations during which J. took the liveliest pleasure in using her new power.

At 1 ; 3 (11) J. asked for her pot and laughed a lot when it was given to her.   She indulged in a certain number of ritual movements, playfully, and the game stopped there, to be taken up again the following days.

At 1 ; 1 (21) she amused herself by making an orange skin on a table sway from side to side. But as she had looked under the skin just before setting it in motion, she did it again as a ritual, at least twenty times ; she took the peel, turned it over, put it down again, made it sway and then began all over again.

These behaviours are curious in that they are combinations not adapted to external circumstances. Obviously there is no necessity to screw up one's nose before wiping it on mother's cheek, to touch one's hair before hitting the water, or to look under a piece of orange peel (already well known) before making it move to and fro. But does the connection seem necessary to the child? We do not think so, although later on similar rituals may be accompanied by a certain feeling of efficacy, under the influence of emotion (as we are familiar with it in the game of avoiding walking on the lines between the stones in the pavement). In the present case, there is only adaptation at the starting point of such behaviours, secondary or tertiary circular reactions. But while in the normal circular reaction the child tends to repeat or vary the phenomenon, the better to adjust himself to it and master it, in this case the child complicates the situation and then repeats exactly all the actions, whether useful or useless, for the mere pleasure of using his activity as completely as possible. In short, during this stage, as before, play is seen to be the function of assimilation extended beyond the limits of adaptation.

The rituals of this stage are then a continuation of those of the previous one, with the difference that those of stage IV consist merely in repeating and combining schemas already established for a non-ludic end, while at this stage they become games almost immediately, and show a greater variety of combinations (a variety due no doubt to the habits following tertiary circular reaction). This progress in ludic ritualisation of schemas entails a corresponding development towards symbolism. Indeed, in so far as the ritual includes " serious " schemas or elements borrowed from such schemas (like the action of wiping one's nose, of asking for a pot, etc.), its effect is to abstract them from their context and consequently to evoke them symbolically. Of course, in such behaviours there is not necessarily as yet the consciousness of " make-believe," since the child confines himself to reproducing the schemas as they stand, without applying them symbolically to new objects. But although what occurs may not be symbolic representation, it is already almost the symbol in action.

With the *sixth stage*, owing to definite progress in the direction of representation, the ludic symbol is dissociated from ritual and takes the form of symbolic schemas. This progress is achieved when empirical intelligence becomes mental association, and external imitation becomes internal or " deferred " imitation, and this at once raises a whole set of problems. Here are some examples:

OBS. 64 (a). In the case of J., who has been our main example in the preceding observations, the true ludic symbol, with every appearance of awareness of "make-believe" first appeared at 1 ; 3 (12) in the following circumstances. She saw a cloth whose fringed edges vaguely recalled those of her pillow; she seized it, held a fold of it in her right hand, sucked the thumb of the same hand and lay down on her side, laughing hard. She kept her eyes open, but blinked from time to time as if she were alluding to closed eyes. Finally, laughing more and more, she cried " Néné " (Nono). The same cloth started the same game on the following days. At 1 ; 3 (13) she treated the collar of her mother's coat in the same way. At 1 ; 3 (30) it was the tail of her rubber donkey which represented the pillow ! And from 1 ; 5 onwards she made her animals, a bear and a plush dog also do " nono."

Similarly, at 1 ; 6 (28) she said " avon " (savon = soap), rubbing her hands together and pretending to wash them (without any water).

At 1 ; 8 (15) and the following days she pretended she was eating various things, e.g., a piece of paper, saying " Very nice."

OBS. 64 (b). The development of these symbols which involve representation does not, of course, exclude that of purely sensory-motor rituals. Thus J., at 1 ; 6 (19), went the round of a balcony hitting the railings at each step with a rhythmical movement, stopping and starting again ; a step, a pause ; a blow, a step, a pause ; a blow, etc.

Frequent relationships are formed between rituals and symbolism, the latter arising from the former as a result of progressive abstraction of the action. For instance, at about 1 ; 3 J. learnt to balance on a curved piece of wood which she rocked with her feet, in a standing position. But at 1 ; 4 she adopted the habit of walking on the ground with her legs apart, pretending to lose her balance, as if she were on the board. She laughed heartily and said " Bimbam."

At 1 ; 6 she herself swayed bits of wood or leaves and kept saying Bimbam and this term finally became a half generic, half symbolic schema referring to branches, hanging objects and even grasses.

OBS. 65. In the case of L. "make believe" or the ludic symbol made its appearance at 1 ; 0 (0), arising, as in the case of J., from the motor ritual. She was sitting in her cot when she unintention-ally fell backwards. Then seeing a pillow, she got into the position for sleeping on her side, seizing the pillow with one hand and pressing it against her face (her ritual was different from J.'s). But instead of miming the action half seriously, like J. in obs. 62, she smiled broadly (she did not know she was being watched) ; her behaviour was then that of J. in obs. 64. She remained in this position for a moment, then sat up delightedly. During the day she went through the process again a number of times, although she was no longer in her cot; first she smiled (this indication of the representational symbol is to be noted), then threw herself back, turned on her side, put her hands over her face as if she held a pillow (though there wasn't one) and remained motionless, with her eyes open, smiling quietly. The symbol was therefore established.

At 1 ; 3 (6) she pretended to put a napkin-ring in her mouth, laughed, shook her head as if saying " no " and removed it. This behaviour was an intermediate stage between ritual and symbol, but at 1 ; 6 (28) she pretended to eat and drink without having anything in her hand. At 1 ; 7 she pretended to drink out of a box and then held it to the mouths of all who were present. These last symbols had been prepared for during the preceding month or two by a progressive ritualisation, the principal stages of which consisted in playing at drinking out of empty glasses and then repeating the action making noises with lips and throat.

These examples show the nature of the behaviours in which we have seen for the first time pretence or the feeling of " make believe " characteristic of the ludic symbol as opposed to simple motor games. The child is using schemas which are familiar, and for the most part already ritualised in games of the previous types: but (1) instead of using them in the presence of the objects to which they are usually applied, he assimilates to them new objectives unrelated to them from the point of view of effective adaptation; (2) these new objects, instead of resulting merely in an extension of the schema (as is the case in the generalisation proper to intelligence), are used with no other purpose than that of allowing the subject to mime or evoke the schemas in question. It is the union of these two conditions—application of the schema to inadequate objects and evocation for pleasure—which in our opinion characterises the beginning of pretence. For instance, as early as the IVth stage, the schema of going to sleep is already giving rise to ludic ritualisations, since in obs. 62 J. reproduces it at the sight of her pillow. But there is then neither symbol nor consciousness of make-believe, since the child merely applies her usual movements to the pillow itself, *i.e.*, to the normal stimulus of the behaviour. There certainly is play, in so far as the schema is only used for pleasure, but there is no symbolism. On the contrary, in obs. 64 J. mimes sleep while she is holding a cloth, a coat collar, or even a donkey's tail, instead of a pillow, and in obs. 65 L. does the same thing, pretending to be holding a pillow when her hands are empty. It can therefore no longer be said that the schema has been evoked by its usual stimulus, and we are forced to recognise that these objects merely serve as substitutes for the pillow, substitutes which become symbolic through the actions simulating sleep (actions which in L.'s case go so far as pretence without any material aid). In a word, there is symbolism, and not only motor play, since there is pretence of assimilating object to a schema and use of a schema without accommodation.

The connection between these "symbolic schemas" or first ludic symbols and the deferred, representational imitation of this same VIth stage is clear. In both types of behaviour we find a representational element whose existence is proved by the deferred character of the reaction. Deferred imitation of a new model takes place after the model has disappeared, and symbolic play reproduces a situation not directly related to the object which gives rise to it, the present object merely serving to evoke an absent one. As regards imitation, on the other hand, we find in the behaviours of 64 and 65 an element which might be considered imitative. In obs. 64 J. imitates the actions she herself makes before going to sleep, or the actions of washing, eating and so on, and in obs. 65 L. does the same. And yet, apart from the fact that this is only self-imitation, it is not purely imitative behaviour, since the objects which are present (the fringes of the cloth, the coat collar, the donkey's tail used as the pillow, and L.'s box used as a plate, etc.) are merely assimilated, regardless of their objective character, to the objects which the imitated action usually accompanies (the pillow, the plate, etc.). There is therefore, and this is characteristic of symbolic play as opposed to mere motor play, both apparent imitation and ludic assimilation. This raises a question to which we shall return presently, but before doing so we must examine the connection between the ludic symbol and the index, the sign, the concept and the development of sensory-motor games.

It is clear, first of all, that the symbolic schemas in question in obs. 64 and 65 are more complex than the sensory-motor index, which has, however, been used by intelligence in the previous stages. The index is only a part or one aspect of the object or of the causal process whose assimilation it makes possible. Being an attribute of the object, it enables it to be anticipated without mental representation, by mere activation of the corresponding schema. For instance, a child of eight or nine months can find a toy under a blanket when its presence is indicated by the rounded outline of the blanket. The symbol, on the other hand, depends on resemblance between the present object, which is the "signifier" and the absent object symbolically "signified" and this constitutes representation. A situation is mentally evoked, not merely anticipated as a whole from the datum of one of its parts.

The symbolic schema of play, therefore, almost reaches the level of the "sign," since in contrast to indices, where the "signifier" is a part or an aspect of the "signified," there is now a sharp distinction between the two. But, as we know, the "sign" is "arbitrary" or conventional, while the symbol is "motivated," i.e., there is resemblance between "signifier" and "signified." Being arbitrary, the sign involves a social relationship, as is obvious in language, a system of verbal signs, while the motivation of the symbol (the resemblance between signifier and signified) may be the product of individual thought.

This is the same problem as that of deferred imitation. It so happens that at the level at which the first ludic symbols appear the child becomes capable of learning to speak, so that the first " signs " seem to be contemporary with these symbols. We see, for instance, that J. says " Néné " or " Nono," which are verbal signs, while she is pretending to sleep, using the fringe of a cloth like that of her pillow. She uses similarly the signs " (s)avon " and " bimbam." Might we not then conclude that the symbol, even in its ludic form, implies the sign and language, since like them it depends on a representational factor? This representational factor would then have to be conceived as a product of social intercourse, the result of intellectual exchange and communication. But in this case, as in the case of imitation, this explanation can be discarded if we consider the continuity between the behaviours of the sixth and the preceding stages, and also the behaviour of the Anthropoids.

Firstly, the formation of such symbolism is not always accompanied by speech or contact with others. For instance, L. (obs. 65), unlike J., pretends to be sleeping while smiling broadly, without saying a word and unaware that she is being watched. This by itself would of course prove nothing, since interiorised verbo-social behaviours might already exist. In conjunction with other arguments, however, it has its value.

Secondly, we find the chimpanzee playing certain symbolic games such as taking " one of its legs in its hands," and treating it " as something extraneous to itself, a real object, perhaps a doll, rocking it in its arms, stroking it and so on " (Kœhler, loc cit.).

Thirdly, the most characteristic effect of the system of verbal signs on the development of intelligence is certainly that it allows of the transformation of sensory-motor schemas into concepts. The normal end of a schema is a concept, since schemas, being instruments for adaptation to ever varying situations, are systems of relationships susceptible of progressive abstraction and generalisation. But in order to acquire the fixity of meaning of concepts, and in particular their degree of generality, which is broader than that of individual experience, schemas must result in inter-individual communication and therefore be expressed by signs. It is thus legitimate to consider the intervention of the social sign as a decisive turning-point in the direction of representation even though the schema at stage VI is already of itself representational. But the symbolic schema of play is in no way a concept, either by its form, " the signifier," or by its content, " the signified." In its form it does not go beyond the level of the imitative image or deferred imitation, i.e., the level of representational imitation characteristic of the sixth stage independently of language. In its content, it is not adapted generalisation but distorting assimilation, *i.e.*, there is no accommodation of the schemas to objective reality, but distortion of the latter for the purpose of the schema. For example, when a donkey's tail serves as a pillow (obs. 64), or a box is used as a plate (obs. 65) it cannot be called adapted generalisation, but merely subjective, and therefore ludic, assimilation. When, however, the same child uses a spoon to pull something towards him, the spoon cannot be considered as the ludic symbol for a stick, and the behaviour must be seen as generalising assimilation. It is only generalising assimilation which leads to concepts, by way of the sign, *i.e.*, through social intercourse, while the ludic symbol continues to be egocentric assimilation, even long after the appearance of language and the most social concepts of which the child is capable.

If, then, the formation of the ludic symbol is not due to the influence of the sign or of verbal socialisation, it must be explained by the previous work of assimilation. It is clear that this type of symbol, like representational imitation, cannot emerge *ex abrupto* at a given moment in mental development. Here, as in the imitative behaviours, there is functional continuity between the successive stages, even when the structures (as opposed to the functions) differ one from another as much as do those of strictly sensory-motor schemas from those of partly interiorised and partly representational schemas. From this point of view, the ludic symbol is in germ (we do not say preformed as a structure, but functionally prepared) in the generalising assimilation of the second stage. When a schema is applied to objectives more and more remote from its initial object, there may be progressive separation between the action and the initial object in that both old and new objectives will be put on the same plane. There is then generalisation of the schema, with a balance between assimilation and accommodation. But in so far as the new objective is considered as a substitute for the initial object, there is emphasis on assimilation, which if it were conscious or mentally interiorised, would constitute a symbolic relationship. It is, of course, not so as yet, since interiorisation is not possible, but from a functional point of view, such a relationship is the forerunner of the symbol. For instance, when a baby sucks his thumb instead of the breast (far be it from us to say that this substitution takes place every time he sucks his thumb!) it would suffice that the thumb served to evoke the breast for there to be a symbol. If this evocation one day takes place, it merely continues the assimilation of the thumb to the schema of sucking, by making the thumb the " signifier " and the breast the " signified." The impossibility of differentiating clearly between signifier and signified prevents us from speaking of the symbol in the second stage, and we cannot therefore accept the idea of preformation held by certain psychoanalysts who already see symbolism, conscious or unconscious, in this sensory-motor assimilation. We do, however, recognise that, functionally, the starting point of the symbol is the ludic assimilation of stages II and III.

In stages IV and V there is progress towards symbolisation to the extent that the development of ludic assimilation leads to a sharper differentiation between signifier and signified. In the course of ludic ritualisation of schemas, the child sometimes reproduces a set of actions that he usually does in quite a different context, *e.g.*, lies down to sleep on seeing his pillow (but only for a second, and without going to sleep), or wipes his nose against his mother's cheek (without really doing it). Such actions are certainly not yet properly symbolic, since the action is only a reproduction of itself and is therefore still both signifier and signified. But as the action is unfinished, and moreover, only done for fun, it is clear that there is a beginning of differentiation between the signifier—the movements actually made, and which are only an attempt at play—and the signified, the whole schema as it would develop if completed " seriously." In other words, there is a kind of symbolic allusion comparable to the so-called " fictions " or " feelings of make-believe " which K. Groos attributed rather too generously to animals, and which are merely patterns of behaviour begun but not carried through. Kittens which fight with their mother and bite without hurting her are not " pretending " to fight, since they do not know what real fighting is, any more than J. miming the actions of going to sleep or blowing her nose has reached the stage of representation or the symbol, since there is no interiorised fiction. But we should certainly be adopting a very prejudiced attitude if we refused to admit that these symbols, which are as it were " played," are a preparation for representational symbols.

When, therefore, during the sixth stage, the properly symbolic schema appears by assimilation of additional objects to the played schema and its initial objective (*e.g.*, assimilation of a donkey's tail to a pillow and to the schema of going to sleep), the new situation can be summed up as the end of the sensory-motor aspect of the progressive differentiation between " signifier " and " signified." The object (the donkey's tail) chosen to represent the initial objective of the schema, and the make-believe actions done to it, then constitute the " signifier," while the " signified " is both the schema as it would develop if completed seriously (really going to sleep) and the object to which it is usually applied (the pillow). The actions accompanying preparation for sleep are thus not only taken out of their ordinary context and left uncompleted merely as an allusion, as in the ludic ritualisations of stages IV and V. They are now applied to new and inadequate objects and are carried out with strict attention to detail although they are entirely make-believe. There is therefore representation, since the " signifier " is dissociated from the " signified," which is a situation which is non-perceptible and only evoked by means of available objects and actions. But this symbolic representation, like deferred imitation, is nothing but a continuation of the whole existing sensory-motor edifice.

We have already observed that, like the deferred imitation with which it is contemporary, it is related to transformations in intelligence itself, which at the sixth stage, becomes capable of using interiorised and therefore representational schemas, as opposed to external or empirical schemas. We must recall here, as we did when dealing with intelligence (*N.I.*, Chap. VI), the progress of the schemas in mobility and speed to a stage at which their co-ordinations and differentiations no longer depend on external trial and error but take place before the actions themselves. This interiorisation of the schemas of intelligence thus makes deferred imitation possible, since imitation is accommodation of schemas, and its deferred character comes from its interiorisation. But deferred imitation in its turn has the effect of making representation possible by facilitating the interior accommodation of schemas to the situations to be anticipated. In exactly the same way, ludic assimilation, which becomes more mobile and deferred in the sixth stage for the same general reasons, is provided by imitation with the representational elements necessary for real symbolic play.

When a donkey's tail is assimilated to a pillow, or a cardboard box to a plate (obs. 64 and 65), this symbolism involves both ludic assimilation, which distorts objects and uses them at will, and a kind of imitation, since the child does the actions of going to sleep or having a meal. It is even clear that it is just by virtue of this particular kind of self-imitation that ludic symbolism becomes possible, for without it there would be neither representation of absent objects nor pretence or feeling of " make-believe." Generally speaking, we find in every ludic symbol this *sui generis* combination of distorting assimilation, which is the basis of play, and a kind of representational imitation, the first providing what is " signified " and the second being the " signifier " of the symbol. But so far we have characterised play and imitation by two somewhat antithetic functions, one being assimilation of things to the ego or to one another in the interests of the ego, and the other accommodation of schemas to things or to external models. How, then, can the two processes, from being opposed, become united in the symbol from stage VI onwards, *i.e.*, when thought and intuitive or representational intelligence begin?

The fact that imitation and play go through the same stages of development, including the representational phase, is easily explained, since both of them proceed, although in opposite directions, from the same differentiation of the original complexus of assimilation and accommodation combined. The first sensory-motor adaptations, as well as real acts of intelligence, presuppose both processes, but with a difference of balance. It is therefore natural that intelligence, which brings them into equilibrium and imitation and play, which emphasise one or the other, should evolve concurrently stage by stage. But how can we explain the fact that imitation and play, from being antithetic at first, can become complementary?

We must first point out that no schema is ever, once and for all, adaptive, imitative or ludic, even when its initial function has made it tend in one of these three directions. Therefore an imitative schema can as easily become ludic as can an adaptive schema. Moreover, it must be remembered that every schema always includes both assimilation and accommodation, since each of these two processes is essentially inseparable from the other. It is therefore only their ratio which determines the adaptive, imitative or ludic character of the schema. This being so, we can describe the various relations as follows.

In the act of intelligent adaptation, each given object or action is assimilated to a previous schema which in return is accommodated to it, assimilation and accommodation thus following step by step the sequence of events, being capable on the one hand of anticipating them and on the other of going back over them. In sensory-motor play the object is merely assimilated to an earlier known schema, without new accommodation or anticipation of later causal sequences. In imitation, on the other hand, the earlier schema is transformed by accommodation to the present model, thus becoming susceptible of immediate or subsequent reconstruction. But though assimilation is thus subordinated to accommodation, the model does not merely become part of complete acts of intelligence, since it is assimilation alone which eventually gives it its generalised meaning. And this meaning may be adaptive in character if the imitative reproduction is later incorporated in acts of assimilation accompanied by new accommodations, for which imitation provides assistance and support. But this meaning may also be ludic in character, if the subsequent assimilation is nothing but a distorting incorporation of the perceived object in earlier schemas originally related to a different object.

The essential difference, therefore, between the ludic symbol and adapted representation is the following. In the act of intelligence assimilation and accommodation are constantly synchronised, and consequently in equilibrium. In the ludic symbol, however, the present object is assimilated to an earlier schema having no objective relation to it, and it is to evoke this schema and the absent objects related to it that imitation comes in and provides the " signifier." To sum up, in the ludic symbol, imitation is not related to the present object but to the absent object required, and therefore imitative accommodation remains subordinated to assimilation. In deferred imitation, on the contrary, imitative accommodation is the aim, and subordinates reproductive assimilation. In the act of intelligence, then, imitation is concerned with the object to be assimilated, and accommodation, even when it continues as representational imitation, still remains in equilibrium with assimilation.

In conclusion, in so far as intelligence, imitation and play are considered, all three, exclusively as sensory-motor, imitation is a continuation of accommodation, play a continuation of assimilation, and intelligence a harmonious combination of the two. In the deferred and interiorised behaviours which characterise the beginnings of representation, imitation, which then extends accommodation to absent as well as to present objects, thereby acquires a function which produces " signifiers " related to the " signified," which are adapted or ludic according as they result from accommodated assimilation or from distorting assimilation, the former characteristic of intelligence and the latter of play.

CHAPTER V

HAVING analysed the genesis of play during the first two years of life,
we must now follow its subsequent development, particularly at the
levels of verbal and intuitive thought (from two to seven) and of
operational intelligence, which is concrete from seven to eleven, and
abstract after eleven. But though in the pre-verbal stage play appears
in a relatively simple form, being essentially sensory-motor, this is no
longer so later on. The first thing to be done, therefore, is to find an
adequate classification, since every methodical analysis involves three
distinct, successive stages: classification, discovery of laws, and causal
explanation. In the field of play, the usual classifications do not seem
to be adequate, because they are the result of preconceived theories,
and not of purely structural analysis independent of interpretations.
We shall begin, then, by examining their practical value.

§ 1. *Critical study of the usual classifications of ludic behaviours*

We have tried to make as complete a collection as possible of
children's games, both by watching our own children day by day in
their spontaneous games, and by observing, with the help of various
collaborators, games in schools (particularly the " Maison des Petits "
in Geneva) and in the street. With about a thousand such observations at our disposal, we attempted to apply to them the recognised
classifications. It immediately became obvious that most authors had
in mind only certain typical games, in particular those which corresponded to their own explanations, and that they ignored the vast
majority of intermediary cases because they could not be classified
according to their preconceived ideas.[1] If, on the other hand, we
decide to take into account all cases, whether typical or not, we are
forced into a classification according to mere structures, since no other
criterion can be found which is at the same time general and yet
capable of application to the detail of particular cases.

One well-known point of view, for example, has been to classify
games according to the tendencies which they put into action, *i.e.*,
according to their *content*. This classification was attempted by K.
Groos, followed by Claparède. Sensorial games (with whistle,
trumpet, etc.), motor games (ball games, running, etc.), intellectual

---

[1] The interesting classification of J. O. Grandjouan *Le qui vive, Jeux d'observations*
(*Éclaireurs de France*, 1942), should, however, be noted.

games (using imagination and curiosity), affective games and exercises of will-power (games needing powers of resistance such as maintaining a difficult position for as long as possible), these are grouped in a first category called " experimental games " or " games of general functions." A second category, " games of special functions," comprises games which involve fighting, chasing, courting, social and family games, and imitative games. This method of grouping clearly depends on the theory of pre-exercise, so that any exception to the classification tends to reveal certain weaknesses in the theory.

The great difficulty encountered in the use of this classification is that it is almost impossible to put under one and the same heading not only the many intermediary cases discovered from daily observation, but even certain standard games. Marbles, for instance, is certainly sensory-motor, since it involves aiming and throwing. But from the age of seven or eight onwards it is also a competitive game, since the players then divide into competing teams (while at the earlier stage each child plays on his own).

As Claparède has said (*Psychologie de l'enfant*, 8th ed., p. 467), " the instinct to compete comes into most games, if not as the main incentive, at least as an additional one." But besides these factors, the essential element is the existence of rules (*cf. Moral Judgment of the Child*, Chap. 1) ; the game of marbles is therefore eminently social. Finally, one cannot fail to be struck by the intellectual complexity of the rules, and since a code cannot be worked out and applied without an effort of reasoning, all the " general functions " are involved here. Where, then, is the game of marbles to be placed in K. Groos's classification?

This multi-polarity of a complex game is, of course, recognised by all authors, but it must surely invalidate a classification based on content. It would not do so if one part of the content overshadowed the others, but in the case of marbles, the predominating element depends on the age of the players, on individual types, and almost on the stages of the game. These difficulties are to be found in varying degrees in all games after a certain level of development. There are, however, some elementary games which do not involve either symbolic imagination or rules, and in which the tendency being exercised is clearly seen, and these will enable us to define the limits within which Groos's theory is valid. Such are all the games of animals (except for a few rare examples of symbolic play among chimpanzees), the sensory-motor games of stages I to V described in the preceding chapter, and the few analogous games which persist after the appearance of language (jumping, throwing stones, etc.). But as soon as symbolic imagination and social rules appear, classification according to content becomes more and more unreliable. We have just seen that this is so in the case of a game with rules. Let us take games with dolls as an example of symbolic play.

At first glance these games might be viewed as typical examples of the exercise of family tendencies, more especially of the maternal instinct. But in the little girl loving her doll like a young mother, fondling it, controlling and training it, how much is "instinct" (assuming instinct to exist as a simple entity in the human species), and how much imitation of what the child appreciates in its own mother? Even if we admit that an instinct is involved, it could only give rise to a vague, general interest, all the detail of the attitudes obviously being inspired by the environment. And that is not all. Systematic observation of a game with dolls immediately shows that the purely maternal attitudes of the child (which are partly acquired through imitation), are but a fraction of the whole game. In most cases, indeed, the doll only serves as an opportunity for the child to re-live symbolically her own life in order to assimilate more easily its various aspects as well as to resolve daily conflicts and realise unsatisfied desires. We can be sure that all the happenings, pleasant or unpleasant, in the child's life will have repercussions on her dolls. In this broad sense the hypothesis that games with dolls have a specific content becomes meaningless. They are a symbolic construction with multiple functions which borrows its means of expression from the family but is by its content related to the whole life of the child.

These observations with regard to marbles and dolls clearly apply to all other games which involve thought. As soon as it is a question of symbols or rules, classification by content becomes impossible, and this brings us to a consideration of what Quérat [1] calls the *origin of games*. Quérat distinguishes three categories: hereditary games (fighting, hunting, chasing); imitative games, which he subdivides into games of social survival (games with bow and arrow, in imitation of a weapon no longer in use) and games of direct imitation; and finally imaginative games, subdivided into metamorphoses of things, animation of toys, creation of imaginary toys, transformation of people, and dramatisation of tales. We are again concerned here with the psychic motor which determines the appearance of games, but since only their starting point is being considered, the question might seem easier of solution. But such a classification is inadmissible in principle and inapplicable in detail. What is meant by hereditary games? If they are the free expression of instinctive tendencies, we meet again all the difficulties of K. Groos's theory. If, on the other hand, we consider hunting games, cultural games and even games of chance as hereditary remains of the activities of primitive societies, we enter the realm of fantasy and there is nowadays no justification for so rash a hypothesis. In any case, it is not a mere classification, but an interpretation, allied to Stanley Hall's famous theory of play, to which we shall return in Chapter VI. Moreover, even if it were possible

[1] *Les jeux des enfants*, Paris, 1905.

to determine the origin of certain games, the result would not necessarily be decisive as regards their functional or even their structural relationships. Marbles and hide-and-seek, for instance, are closely related. In both cases symbolism is either non-existent or quite unimportant, and in both cases there are rules which have been handed down by the social tradition of children and which change a sensory-motor situation into an organised competition. It is possible, however, as certain ethnographers think, that the game of marbles originated in ancient divinatory practices, while games of pursuit are only spontaneous motor games which have acquired rules in the process of socialisation. It is clear that the principle of the " origin " of the games to be classified is extremely debatable. As to the application of the classification in detail, how, for example, are imitative and imaginative games to be clearly differentiated? As we saw at the conclusion of the previous chapter, every symbolic game is both imitative and imaginative. To play at having a meal is both to imitate a real situation and to imagine a new one. A " transformation of things " such as a box becoming a carriage (Quérat's example) involves both imitation of the carriage and imaginative creation, and so on.

We are left then, with a third possible principle of classification. If neither the content, *i.e.*, the function of the game, nor its origin provides univocal classifications, it is because these classifications depend on preconceived interpretations. In order to classify games without being tied beforehand by a theory which explains them, in other words so that the classification shall serve as an explanation instead of assuming one, we must confine ourselves to an analysis of the *structures* presented by each game: the degree of mental complexity, from the elementary sensory-motor game to the advanced social game.

Without claiming to be exhaustive, Stern has given us a good example of this type of classification.[1] He divides games into two large classes: individual and social. In the first, he distinguishes several categories of increasing complexity: mastery of the body (motor games using the body as instrument), mastery of things (destructive and constructive games), and impersonation (transformation of people and things). In the social group are games of pure imitation, games with more than one participant (teacher and pupils, etc.), and fighting games. This time we certainly seem to be moving in the direction of objective classification: analysis of structural qualities only, with the minimum of theoretical assumptions. But certain difficulties of detail prevent us from accepting Stern's classification without reservation. In our opinion, the broad division into individual and social games is unacceptable in the over-simplified

[1] *Psychol. d. fruh. Kindheit*, 4th ed., p. 278 *seq.*

form suggested by its author. On the one hand, the difference between the individual symbolic game (Rollenspiel) and the symbolic game with several characters is only one of degree. Children very often play to, rather than with, one another, and it is extremely difficult to define the exact boundary between the individual and the social. It might even be said that every symbolic game, even if it is an individual game, sooner or later becomes a performance given by the child to an imaginary companion, and that every collective symbolic game, even the most highly organised, retains something of the ineffable which characterises the individual symbol. On the other hand, the most characteristic product of social life, for the child as for the adult, is the existence of rules, and if games which are exclusively social are to be included in a special category, games with rules, rather than symbolism, must be our concern. And lastly, with regard to individual games, it seems to us that there is a relatively clear dividing line between sensory-motor and symbolic games, since the latter involve make-believe and imagination and the former do not.

Another interesting structural classification is that of Charlotte Bühler.[1] Children's games are divided into five groups: (I) functional games (or sensory-motor), (II) games of make-believe or illusion, (III) passive games (looking at pictures, listening to stories, etc.), (IV) constructional games, and (V) collective games. But it is obvious that category III is on a different plane from the others, and Charlotte Bühler herself puts passive games and games of illusion together in her statistical table of the evolution of a child's games (p. 135). As to collective games, we merely repeat that from a structural point of view, it is only the presence of rules which distinguishes them from individual games.

There remains the useful distinction between games of make-believe and constructional games. It is, however, clear that extreme cases are connected by a whole series of intermediary cases: *e.g.*, between a game of make-believe in which a house is symbolically represented by a stone or a piece of wood, and a constructional game in which the child aims at reproducing the house as faithfully and objectively as possible by modelling, using bricks, or even carpentry, every shade of intermediary stage is to be found. Generally speaking —and Mrs. Bühler, like Claparède before her, insists on this point— there is continuity between the child's play and work. Does this not suggest, then, that constructional games form a special category, to be placed both between sensory-motor and symbolic games and also between these two and adapted activity (adaptation which is at the same time practical and representational)? Making a house with plasticine or bricks involves both sensory-motor skill and symbolic

[1] *Kindheit u. Jugend.*, 3rd ed., pp. 129–146 and pp. 229–231.

representation, and, like drawing a house, is a move away from play in the strict sense, towards work, or at least towards spontaneous intelligent activity. The word "occupations" has sometimes been used for these transitional behaviours. For the moment we will confine ourselves to observing that constructional games do not form a category of the same kind as the others, but are a boundary class between games and non-ludic behaviours.

§ 2. *Practice, symbol, and rule*

The conclusion to be drawn from the preceding discussion is that there are three main types of structure which characterise children's games and determine their detailed classification. There are practice games, symbolic games, and games with rules, while constructional games constitute the transition from all three to adapted behaviours.

Some games do not involve any particular technique. Being mere "exercises" they put into action a varied group of behaviours without modification of their structure at that stage of adaptation. The function alone, therefore, differentiates these games. They exercise the structures for no other purpose than the pleasure of functioning. For instance, when a child jumps over a stream for the fun of jumping, jumps back and begins again, he goes through the same actions as when he jumps because he wants to get to the other side, but he does so for pleasure, not of necessity or in order to learn a new behaviour. But when a child pretends to eat a green leaf and calls it spinach, in addition to the sensory-motor portrayal of the action of eating, there is a symbolic evocation which is characteristic of a structure other than that of the adapted representational image, since it is the result of distorting assimilation, and not, like the concept, of generalisation. Similarly, rules for games are not just moral or legal rules which have been borrowed, but rules specially made for the purpose of the game, though they may lead to moral values beyond the game itself.

The mere *practice game*, without symbols, make-believe or rules, is especially characteristic of animal behaviours. When a kitten runs after a dead leaf or a ball of wool, we have no reason to suppose that these objects represent mice for it. When a cat plays with her kitten, using claws and teeth, she knows, of course, that the fight is not in earnest, but there is no need to explain it by saying that the cat imagines what the fight would be if it were real. It is enough that the actions which usually serve the cat for this adaptation are controlled by maternal love and therefore are carried out "uncharged," not as they would be in the presence of a dangerous enemy. The situation in which the schema is then put into action itself provides a reason for the game, and we do not need to see in it, like Groos, awareness of "playing a part" or "make-believe."[1] For Groos, only

[1] K. Groos, *Le jeu des animaux*, Paris, 1902.

the fact that animals cannot speak prevents us from proving the existence of " make-believe," and he does not hesitate to see in the action of the kitten pushing a ball that has stopped moving, " a beginning of the deliberate, conscious illusion which is the most deeply rooted and most advanced element of play " (p. 130). Again, " the animal which knows that it is engaged in a pseudo-activity and continues to play, reaches the level of deliberate make-believe, ' *enjoyment of pretence*,' and is on the verge of artistic creation " (pp. 317–318). But a comparison of these animal games with those of the baby in the pre-verbal stage, bearing in mind the fact that almost all the sensory-motor schemas give rise to ludic exercises, shows the assumption of representational make-believe to be pointless. The ball that the kitten runs after is merely an objective, and when he pushes it he is merely giving himself the opportunity to go on running, and nothing more. It is only in the case of Kœhler's chimpanzee, mentioned earlier, rocking and stroking its leg, that we can speak of make-believe, but this example, which is on a level with the most elementary ludic symbols of the child, is the highest level of animal play, and no conclusions as to the play of the lower species can be drawn from it.

In the case of children, practice games are the first to appear, and characterise stages II to V of preverbal development, in contrast to stage VI when symbolic games begin. But there is a noticeable difference between the child's initial sensory-motor games and the majority of those of animals. In the latter, the motor schemas carried out in the void are frequently reflex or instinctive (fighting, hunting, etc.). Hence the idea of " pre-exercise " used by Groos, which relates these activities to the stage of adult maturity. In the higher species such as the chimpanzee, which plays at turning on water, collecting or destroying things, turning somersaults, mimicking the actions of walking, and so on, and in the child, ludic activity extends far beyond the reflex schemas and is a continuation of almost all actions. Hence our broader conception of functional " exercise." The practice game may be, in our opinion, " post-exercise " and " marginal exercise " as easily as " pre-exercise." Finally, although the practice game is essentially sensory-motor it may be used in the case of the higher functions: *e.g.*, the game of asking questions for the fun of asking, without interest in the problem or the answer.

A second category of children's games is the one we shall call *symbolic games*. In contrast to practice games, which involve neither thought nor any specifically ludic representational structure, symbolic games imply representation of an absent object, since there is comparison between a given and an imagined element. They also imply make-believe representation, since the comparison is distorting assimilation. For instance, a child pushing a box and imagining it as a car, is symbolically representing the car by the box, and is

satisfied with the pretence because the link between " signifier " and
" signified " is entirely subjective. In so far as it implies representation, the symbolic game does not exist among animals (except in the
limit case mentioned earlier) and only appears during the second
year of the child's development. We have seen, however, that
between the symbol properly so-called and the practice game, there
is a third term, the symbol in action without representation. For
instance, the ritual of the actions done when going to sleep is at first
merely taken out of its context and reproduced as a game at the sight
of the pillow (stages IV and V of the preceding chapter), and afterwards mimed with other objects (stage VI), and this marks the
beginning of representation. This continuity does not, of course,
prove that the symbol is already present in sensory-motor ludic
assimilation, as we emphasised in Chapter III. It does, however,
show that when the symbol becomes a part of sensory-motor practice,
it does not replace the sensory-motor element, but merely subordinates
it. Most symbolic games, with the exception of those which are purely
fanciful, make use of complicated actions. They are therefore both
sensory-motor and symbolic, but we call them symbolic when the
symbolism integrates the other elements. Moreover, their functions
deviate more and more from mere practice. Compensation, fulfilment
of wishes, liquidation of conflicts, etc., are continually added to the mere
pleasure of mastering reality, which is a continuation of the pleasure
" of being the cause " inherent in sensory-motor practice.

We shall not make an essential distinction between individual
symbolic games and those involving two or more persons. Symbolism
begins, indeed, with individual behaviours which enable imitation to
be interiorised (imitation of things as well as people), and symbolism
involving more than one makes little change in the structure of the
first symbols. No doubt, when older children play real parts, as for
instance in scenes representing school life, weddings and so on, the
symbolism is greatly improved as compared with that which satisfies
the younger child. It is then that the ludic symbol gradually becomes
adapted representation, in the same way as the small child's crude
effort at building later becomes a skilled construction of wood or stone.
Parts acted in a play are thus only a special case of those creative games
which, while they partly derive from symbolic play, develop in the
direction of constructive activity or work.

Lastly, in the course of development, a third main category is
added to symbolic games, that of *games with rules*. Unlike symbols,
rules necessarily imply social or inter-individual relationships. In a
mere sensory-motor ritual such as touching every pale of a fence as
one goes along, there are no rules, since there is no compulsion. At
the most it implies a sense of regularity, a " Regelbewusstsein," to
use K. Bühler's expression. Rules are a regulation imposed by the

group, and their violation carries a sanction. Although several games with rules are common to children and adults, many are specifically children's, handed down from one generation to the next without adult influence.

Just as symbolic games frequently contain sensory-motor elements, so games with rules may have the same content as the earlier games: *e.g.*, marbles is sensory-motor practice, and charades make use of symbolic imagination. But a new element is added, rules, which are as different from symbols as symbols are from mere practice, and which result from collective organisation of ludic activities.

Practice, symbol and rule then seem to be the three successive stages which characterise the main classes of games from the point of view of their mental structure. What then is the position of constructional or creative games? If we require a genetic classification based on evolution of structures, these games do not constitute a stage like the others, but rather indicate an internal transformation of the symbolic notion towards adapted representation. When the child, instead of using a piece of wood for a boat, really makes a boat by hollowing out the wood, putting in masts, sails and seats, the " signifier " merges into the " signified," and the symbolic game into a real imitation of the boat. The question then is, whether this construction is a game, imitation or spontaneous work. This problem is not specific to such cases, but arises generally with regard to drawing, modelling and all the techniques of representation using materials. Similarly, when a game with " parts " becomes part of a play or a whole drama, we are leaving the realm of play for that of imitation and work. If, therefore, we see the three classes of games as corresponding to three stages, which are also characterised by the three successive forms of intelligence (sensory-motor, representational and reflective), it is evident that constructional games are not a definite stage like the others, but occupy, at the second, and more particularly at the third level, a position half-way between play and intelligent work, or between play and imitation.

§ 3. *Classification and evolution of mere practice games*

In analysing the beginnings of play in the previous chapter, we found that during the first eighteen months almost all the sensory-motor schemas acquired by the child gave rise to functional assimilation on the fringe of the process of adaptation, *i.e.*, a kind of functioning for pleasure. These ludic exercises, which are the child's first form of play, do not belong specifically to the first two years or to the pre-verbal period. They are to be found throughout childhood, whenever a new skill is acquired. As each behaviour is in process of construction and adaptation, there is functional assimilation, or practice for the sake of practice, accompanied by the pleasure of

" being the cause " or the feeling of power. The same thing often happens in the case of the adult. Having just acquired for the first time a wireless set or a car, it is difficult to resist the temptation to use them merely for the fun of using one's new powers. Even in a new academic post one tends to find a certain pleasure at first in the new gestures one makes in public. In every practice game, of course, there comes a time when interest flags, because saturation point has been reached and the objective offers no further opportunity for training. But since this type of play can reappear with each new acquisition, it lasts far beyond early childhood. This does not, of course, mean that practice games are as numerous, either absolutely or relatively, at all ages. On the contrary, as new acquisitions become less and less, and other types of game appear, those with symbols and rules, the frequency of practice games diminishes as time goes on after the appearance of language. Nevertheless, since new ones constantly come into existence, they need to be classified, and their evolution studied.

They can be divided into two categories, according to whether they remain purely sensory-motor or have some bearing on thought itself. There are games involving thought which are not symbolic, and which merely consist in exercising certain functions: *e.g.*, combining words, asking questions for the sake of asking, and so on (we exclude jokes or puns, which do not really come under the heading of play, since their aim is to provoke laughter). Purely sensory-motor practice games can themselves be classified under the following three headings. Their most primitive forms have already been studied in the previous chapter, and we shall come later to the more advanced forms.

To the first class belong *mere practice* games, *i.e.*, those which are nothing more than the reproduction, in its entirety, of a behaviour adapted to a useful function, but which the child repeats out of its usual context just for the pleasure of exercising his power. Almost all the sensory-motor games of stages II to V, except the " rituals " of which we shall speak later, are to be found in this class. But as we have just seen, games or amusements of this type recur at all ages, and the following are a few examples after the age of two: [1]

OBS. 66. At 2 ; 2 (25) J. picked up pebbles and threw them into a pond, laughing a lot as she did so. At 2 ; 6 (3) she set her cot in motion by giving it a push. At the same age she pulled her cot along by string, threw her ball various distances, etc. These were actions she had known from the point of view of intelligence since the beginning of her second year (see *N.I.*) and they were performed here as games.

[1] From now on we shall not use only our own three children J., L. and T., as examples, but shall also give examples of the behaviour of other children.

At 2 ; 8 (2) she filled a pail with sand, overturned it, demolished the sand-pie with her spade and began again, and she did this for more than an hour.

At 3 ; 6 (2) she stuck pine-needles into some tar and then pulled them out again.

At 3 ; 8 (0) she laced and unlaced her shoes, looking very pleased, having just learnt how to do it.

OBS. 67.   At 3 ; 6 Y. made some insects run over the back of his hand and laughed when it tickled.   At 3 ; 7 he scraped the ground, made little heaps of dust and moved them about.   He collected as much dust as he could in his hand and let it trickle out, enjoyed the sensation it produced as it flowed through his fingers, and then began again.

At 3 ; 11 G. took a big piece of modelling clay and broke it into small pieces.   Then he put them all together and began again. To begin with he was experimenting in dividing a whole and putting it together again, but once the adaptation was completed the behaviour became a game.

The nature of the ludic element in these activities is clear.   Each behaviour, whether it be throwing, pulling, pushing, filling and empty-ing, or later on breaking up and putting together again, led to really intelligent acquisition.   In the simplest cases (throwing, pulling etc.), we are concerned with sensory-motor schemas built up through tertiary circular reactions or " experiments to see the result " in stages V and VI of sensory-motor intelligence.   In the more complex cases (breaking up and putting together again), it is a question of practical, intuitive intelligence.   But in all cases the schema used presents no problem of adaptation for the child.   It has been mastered and is used (obs. 66 and 67) merely for functional practice, and for pleasure.

The transition from this first class to the second, that of *fortuitous combinations*, is imperceptible.   The only distinction between these new behaviours and the earlier ones lies in the fact that the child is no longer merely using acquired activities, but building up new combinations which are ludic from the start.   But since these com-binations are fortuitous, they are only an extension of the functional practice typical of the first class.   The most usual source of such games is contact with new toys (ninepins, marbles, etc.), or instruc-tional material (games for teaching areas and volume, blocks, counting frames, etc.).   They may, however, result from contact with objects of any kind.   Here are a few examples:

OBS. 68.   At 3 ; 2 J. arranged ninepins in a line two at a time and finally (by accident) had one row perpendicular to another ; she then made single rows with no apparent purpose.   At 3 ; 6 she put some pebbles in a pail, took them out one by one, put them back, transferred them from one pail to another, etc. Then the game became symbolic (she pretended to be drinking tea, with the pail full of pebbles).

At 3 ; 6 she walked along some railings, touching one after the other, then scratched on the glass panes of a door, and began all over again with the same ritual. About the same date she went through a copse, each time taking the same path and saying: " *I'm playing a game. I'm trying not to let the bracken touch me.*"

OBS. 69. The educational games at the " Maison des Petits " always produce among the three- to four-year-olds play activities without any specific aim, before the appearance of constructions properly so called.

At 3 ; 11 P. spent a long time threading the beads on to the rods of a counting-frame, mixing the colours without rhyme or reason. He also moulded and broke up the modelling clay without making or portraying anything. He aimlessly piled up the blocks of a game of volumes and knocked them down again.

At 4 ; 2 Y. began by emptying a box of bricks on to the floor and putting them back again. Then he amused himself by pushing one brick against another, thus moving as many as possible at once. Then he put one on top of the other and pushed them all.

At 4 ; 3 N. mixed up the different coloured beads the first time she played with the counting-frame. Similarly, with a game of lotto she piled the counters on the cards without bothering to make the colours correspond, and then spread the counters on the table and began to make little heaps of them again.

These sensory-motor games are essentially of short duration. Their starting point is frequently the " ludic ritual " described earlier, with the difference that at the age of one or two they are fortuitous combinations presented by the external world and repeated by the child as games, while in the case of obs. 68 (the fence and the bracken) it was the child herself who made the combination. At a later stage (obs. 68, part 1, and obs. 69) it was a case of trial and error, but was ludic and not adaptive. At their highest, these combinations give rise to symbolism (drinking tea) or to real constructions, as we shall see. Before going any further, we would point out that it is in this second class that we must include games involving *destruction of objects*, of which no examples are needed. It has sometimes been thought that such games are manifestations of instinctive curiosity, but this seems to us exaggerated. When there is real curiosity, we are no longer in the realm of play but in that of intelligent experimentation. In most of these cases, it is merely a matter of trying out for the fun of the activity, or in order to discover new and amusing combinations, and since it is easier to break down than to build up, the game becomes destructive.

The third class is that of *intentional combinations*, the aim being, of course, ludic from the beginning. Here are two ordinary instances, which we give merely for the sake of clarification:

OBS. 70. At 5 ; 2 V. amused himself by jumping up and down on the stairs. At first he carried out his movements aimlessly, but later he tried to jump from the ground on to a seat, increasing the distance he jumped each time. K. (5 ; 6) then did the same, but from the other side. They were eventually jumping at opposite ends, running along the bench to meet one another, one being pushed backwards by the collision. This game, having become social, then became a game with rules (obs. 93).

OBS. 71. P., Y. and N. quickly passed the stage of fortuitous combinations (obs. 69) and amused themselves by arranging bricks, sheets of cardboard and beads in different ways: they threaded the beads on to a frame in order of size, or picked out colours; they arranged the bricks horizontally, or built towers, etc. But these combinations, made up purely as a game, always develop in one of two distinct directions: either the play element triumphs and they become symbolic (" *It's a bridge !* " " *I've made a house !* " etc.), or else interest in constructing prevails and the child's attitude is no longer that of play. He experiments or sets himself tasks which involve practical intelligence and real adaptation.

We see from these examples that sensory-motor practice games do not lead to independent and constructive ludic systems as do symbolic games and games with rules. Their specific function is to practise the behaviour merely for functional pleasure, or for the pleasure obtained from awareness of new powers. As soon as combinations are involved, the games either remain incoherent and even destructive, or else take on a purpose, in which case they develop sooner or later in one of the three following ways: (1) they become symbolic through the addition of representational imagination (obs. 71); (2) they become socialised and tend to become games with rules (obs. 70 brings us to the verge of this); (3) they lead to real adaptation and leave the realm of play for that of practical intelligence or for the field intermediate between these two extremes.

In the case of games of *mental exercise* we find the same three categories, mere practice, fortuitous combinations, and intentional combinations, and within each of these classes we can find instances of the transition from sensory-motor practice to practical intelligence and to verbal intelligence. It is clear, for instance, that having learned to ask questions, especially " why," which is an act of reflective intelligence, the child may amuse himself by asking questions for fun, *i.e.*, his questioning is mere practice. He may also tell a story without head or tail merely for the pleasure of combining chance words and concepts, or he may make up a story just for the pleasure of making it, which constitutes a mental, ludic combination which is intentional.

But it is equally clear that these combinations will be even more labile than those of the sensory-motor practice games, because story-making rarely remains at this level and develops into symbolic imagination all the more easily in that it is in itself an act of thought. It is therefore useless to consider further these residual forms of practice games, which rapidly become less and less important with age, and give place to the essential ludic system which we shall now study. We shall merely give one instance of each of the three categories:

OBS. 72. At 3 ; 8 J. at the sight of a picture asked: " *What's that?*—It's a cowshed.—*Why?*—It's a house for cows.—*Why?*—Because there are cows in it, there, do you see?—*Why are they cows?*—Don't you see? They've got horns.—*Why have they horns? . . .*" etc. As a matter of fact, though in such cases the first question may be serious, the others become more and more just questions asked for the sake of asking and to see how long answers will be forthcoming.

OBS. 73. At 3 ; 9 J. often made up stories merely to contradict or to put ideas together as she pleased. She was not at all concerned with what she was saying, but merely with the combination as such: " *Are those wings?* (an elephant's ear).—No, elephants don't fly.—*Yes they do, I've seen them.*—You're joking.—*No, I'm not. It's true. I've seen them.*" Or again, when her drink was too hot: " *I shall drink it all the same* (she takes good care not to !). *I shall take the hotness out of my stomach.*" And another day: " *I saw a pig washing itself. I'm not joking, I saw it. It was doing like this . . .*" etc.

Some of her inventions turned into real stories (fortuitous ludic combination): " *I was in a cupboard, someone locked it, but I managed to get out. I could see through the glass what was happening,*" etc.

We would again point out that these aimless exercises are basically labile in that they involve no real interest in the thought itself. As soon as this interest is present, they become symbolic games.

§ 4. *Classification and evolution of symbolic games*

The question as to where to draw the line between symbolic and practice games is more than a mere matter of classification, and involves the main problems of the interpretation of play in general. Hence the importance of the preceding classifications. It might be thought (and this is the originality of K. Groos's point of view), that the symbolic game as a whole is again a practice game, but a practice game which exercises (and more particularly " pre-exercises ") the specific form of thought which is imagination.[1] This is not the place to discuss Groos's general theory, especially as the interpretation

[1] K. Groos (*Die Spiele des Menschens*) classifies symbolic games as games which pre-exercise the intellectual functions (Part I, Chap. III, Phantasie).

which we shall develop in the next chapter was born of the difficulty we find in accepting his treatment of symbolic imagination. To confine ourselves for the moment to the problem of mere classification, there is an obvious distinction between intellectual practice games and symbolic games. When the child asks questions for the fun of asking, or makes up a story he knows to be untrue for the fun of telling it, the questions or the imagination are the content of the game, but they take the form of practice. We can therefore say that the game practises questioning or imagination. When, on the other hand, the child changes one object into another, or ascribes to her doll actions analogous to her own, symbolic imagination becomes the instrument for the game, and is no longer the content, the content in this case being the group of persons or happenings represented by the symbol. In other words the content is the object of the child's activities, particularly of its affective life, these being evoked and considered through the medium of the symbol. Just as in non-symbolic games practice is functional assimilation which enables the child to consolidate his sensory-motor powers (use of things), or his intellectual powers (questions, imagination, etc.), so the symbol provides him with the means whereby he can assimilate reality to his desires or interests. In so far as it is a ludic structure, the symbol is thus a continuation of practice, and not a content to be practised like imagination in story-making. In practice, the criterion for classification is simple. In intellectual practice games, the child has no interest in what he is asking or asserting, and enjoys the mere fact of asking or imagining, while in symbolic games he is interested in the things symbolised, and the symbol merely serves to evoke them.

Symbolic games must therefore be classified on the same principle as practice games, *i.e.*, according to the structure of the symbols, viewed as tools for ludic assimilation. In this respect, the most elementary form of the ludic symbol is one of the most interesting, since it indicates the transition and the continuity between sensory-motor practice and symbolism. It is the form which in the previous chapter we called the *symbolic schema*, the reproduction of a sensory-motor schema outside its context and in the absence of its usual objective. In obs. 64 and 65 we have already analysed such examples as pretending to go to sleep. In the pages that follow we shall find many others.

OBS. 74. At 1 ; 1 (20) J. scratched at the wall-paper in the bedroom where there was the design of a bird, then shut her hand as if it held the bird and went to her mother: " *Look* (she opened her hand and pretended to be giving something).—What have you brought me?—*A birdie*." At 2 ; 0 (8) there was the same game with a flower on the wall-paper, then with a sunbeam that she pretended to bring; she then gave her mother " *a bit of light*."

Also at 2 ; 0 (8) she opened the window and shouted, laughing: "*Hi, boy!*" (a boy she met on her walks and who was never in the garden). Then, still laughing, she added: "*Over there!*"

At 2 ; 0 (16) she laughed as she pretended to make a seagull, painted on a box, fly: "*Come*" (opening her arms). Then she pretended to follow it about the room, and added, "*Not come.*"

It is obvious, as we already observed in the previous chapter, that these "symbolic schemas" mark the transition between practice play and symbolic play proper. As in the former, there is still the possibility of practising a behaviour out of its context of present adaptation, merely for functional pleasure, but there is also, as in the latter, the capacity for evoking the behaviour when its usual objective is absent, either in the presence of new objects which are treated as substitutes (obs. 64 and 65) or without any material support (as in obs. 74 and even in obs. 65).

But although the "symbolic schema" is already symbolic play, it is only a primitive form and has the following limitation: it only puts into action a schema associated with the child's own behaviour. In other words, the child does no more than pretend to be doing one of his usual actions, without as yet ascribing these actions to others or assimilating objects one to another as though the function of one could be transferred to another. So the child pretends to sleep (obs. 64 and 65), wash (obs. 64), sway on a board (obs. 64, *b*), eat (obs. 65) offer and demand (obs. 74). All these schemas are practised, not only without present adaptation but also using symbolism, since the child acts in the absence of the usual objectives of the actions and even in the absence of any object whatsoever. Later on, the child will pretend to make objects other than himself eat, sleep or walk and will thus begin symbolically to change one object into another. He does, of course, already use the fringe of a cloth, a coat-collar or a donkey's tail as a pillow (obs. 64), but this ludic assimilation of one object to another is still within the framework of the child's behaviour (pretence of sleeping) and cannot be taken out of it, as in the next stage, and related to things and beings other than himself.

This, then, is the most advanced stage that the ludic symbol can reach in sensory-motor development (stage VI of the preceding chapter). It is still only a matter of schemas related to the child's own actions, but they are practised symbolically, and not in the real situation (as in stages II to V). The symbol is not yet freed as an instrument of thought. It is the behaviour, or the sensory-motor schema, which is the symbol, and not this or that individual object or image. But even so, this beginning of symbolism has considerable significance for the subsequent development of play. When it can be taken out of its context, the symbolic schema will ensure that representation shall take precedence over mere action, thus enabling the child, through play, to assimilate the external world to his ego with infinitely more effective tools than those of mere practice. With the appearance of the symbolic schema, the function which will be that of all symbolic play begins to take shape. Why, indeed, does the child enjoy pretending to sleep, wash, swing, bring a bird? Sleeping and washing are certainly not games, but when practised symbolically they become so. It is clearly impossible to explain this symbolic practice as being pre-exercise: the child certainly does not play like this in order to learn to wash or to sleep. All that he is trying to do is to use freely his individual powers, to reproduce his own actions for the pleasure of seeing himself do them and showing them off to others, in a word to express himself, to assimilate without being hampered by the need to accommodate at the same time.

Symbolic play will therefore consolidate, through representational assimilation of the whole of reality to the ego, what practice play has already achieved through functional assimilation. The " symbolic schema " is the transitional stage, since although the child's own behaviours are still practised, the practice is already symbolic. With the systematic acquisition of language (1 ; 6 to 7 ; 0), a whole series of new ludic symbols appears. These must be classified and analysed, since it is only by a detailed study of their construction that we can test the validity of the explanation we have just suggested of the meaning of symbolic play in general.

STAGE I. TYPES IA and IB. In the first category, which we shall call type IA and which follows the symbolic schema, we find *projection of symbolic schemas on to new objects*. Once a symbolic schema has been constituted, and reproduced on himself by the child, there comes a point at which, through the mechanism of imitation and the relationships established between himself and others, he will apply the now familiar schema to other people and objects. There is already a beginning of this at the end of obs. 64 (*a*) and (*b*), and 65. Having played for two months at pretending to sleep, J. made her bear and her dog do it (64). After herself miming the action she called " bimbam," she made bits of wood and leaves swing (64 (*b*)), and L., after pretending to eat and drink herself, went on to put her box up to the mouths of the other members of the family (65). The " projection of symbolic schemas on to new objects " is merely the generalisation of these behaviours.

> OBS. 75 (*a*). At 1 ; 6 (30) J. said "*cry, cry*" to her dog and herself imitated the sound of crying. On the following days she made her bear, a duck, etc., cry. At 1 ; 7 (1) she made her hat cry.
>
> At 1 ; 7 (25), instead of biting her mother's cheek herself as she usually did, she pressed her bear's face to the same spot and said: "*Oh! Oh!* "

At 1 ; 8 (25) she took a spoon and fed her doll, digging the spoon into an empty bowl. The same day she used a shell, which she put to her mother's mouth and to her doll's. At 1 ; 9 (28) she put a shell on the table and said " *sitting*," then she put it on top of another, adding delightedly: " *Sitting on pot.*"

At 1 ; 11 (0) she made a giraffe drink out of a little pan: " *You've finished, Muoom* " (the mushroom painted on the bottom of her own bowl). She put a doll to bed in a pan, then covered it with a postcard: " *Baby blanket . . . cold.*"

After 2 ; 0 this type of play continued for some considerable time.

OBS. 75 (*b*). At 1 ; 6 (2) L. fed her doll and put it to bed. At 1 ; 6 (4) she laughed as she dandled a spoon as if it were a doll. At 1 ; 6 (22) she put her arm through a doll's dress and moved it forward vertically, laughing heartily as she did so. At 1 ; 8 (0) she laid her doll down, covered it with a blanket, put a ribbon into its hands (she herself had one at this stage when going to sleep) and pretended to sleep as she stood laughing.

The difference between these games and those of obs. 64–65 and 74 is that while the simple symbolic schema is merely a make-believe reproduction of the child's own action, the games in obs. 75 (*a*) and (*b*) ascribe this action to others, thereby completely dissociating the symbol from sensory-motor practice by projecting it as an independent representation. At the same level of development there appears another form of play, superficially different from the preceding games, but complementary to them. We shall call them Type IB, *projection of imitative schemas on to new objects*. In these games there is again projection of symbolic schemas, but schemas borrowed from models which have been imitated, and no longer from the child's own activity.

OBS. 76 (*a*). At 1 ; 9 (20) J. rubbed the floor with a shell, then with a cardboard lid, saying: " *Brush Abebert* " (like the charwoman). The same day she pulled her hair back as she looked at herself in the mirror, and said, laughing: " *Daddy.*" At 2 ; 4 (13) she pretended to be sewing and pulling a thread through, as she looked at a shell and said " *torn.*"

At 1 ; 7 (12) L. pretended to be reading a newspaper, pointed with her finger at certain parts of the sheet of paper she was holding, and muttered to herself. At 1 ; 8 (2) she pretended to be telephoning, then made her doll telephone (assuming a head-voice). On the following days she telephoned with all kinds of things (a leaf, instead of a receiver).

OBS. 76 (*b*). At 1 ; 3 (20), a quarter of an hour after I blew a hunting-horn in his presence, T. picked up a doll's chair a couple of inches high, put it to his mouth and pretended to sound it: " *Tantara.*" He was unaware that he was being watched. This was the first example of symbolic play observed in T., but it is, of course, quite possible that certain symbolic schemas analogous to those of obs. 64 and 65 preceded it when we were not there to observe them.

The structure of these games can be seen to be similar to that of the earlier ones. We are still dealing with schemas applied symbolically to new objects which have replaced the original objective, but in this case the schemas are acquired by imitation and do not form part of the child's own activity. The examples given in obs. 18 (a) and (b), in conjunction with those of 75 (a) and (b), are most significant and enable us to characterise this first form of purely symbolic game as distinct from the transitional "symbolic schemas" of the preceding level.

It will be remembered that when ludic exercises and "rituals" become "symbolic schemas" by being dissociated from the usual activity and applied to new objects, the separation of "signifier" from "signified" which then occurs constitutes symbolism. Both the action which is played and the object to which it is applied are "symbolisers" and the action represented is "symbolised." We also observed (Chap. III, stage VI) that the symboliser was always a kind of imitation, but as the "symbolic schemas" reproduce only the child's own actions, at that stage it was self-imitation. Each of these two characteristics is developed in the "projection of symbolic schemas and imitative schemas." In each of the examples, in obs. 75 (a) and (b) as well as in obs. 76 (a) and (b), we find that imitation takes place as well as assimilation. In obs. 75 (a) and (b), there is complex imitation. In projecting his own behaviours on to others (making animals and dolls cry, eat, drink or sleep) the child himself is imitating the actions they do when they reproduce his own actions ! In obs. 76 (a) and (b) he is imitating other people (the charwoman sweeping, the father telephoning, reading his paper or sounding a horn, etc.). In both cases the imitation is the symboliser, but while in the first case the "symbolised" is the child's own previous activity, in the second it is the model. Nevertheless, the second is play and not pure imitation, because instead of imitating the model directly, which would be easy, the child does so through the medium of adequate objects, which are therefore also symbolisers. To sum up, in both cases ludic assimilation involves a greater number of intermediaries the more it is dissociated from the child's own activity. Hence we shall find in the next two categories of ludic symbols complete dissociation of "symboliser" from "symbolised."

STAGE I. TYPES IIA AND IIB. We shall divide the symbolic games of the second level into two types: type IIA, characterised by *simple identification of one object with another* (the word "simple" being used to distinguish these from the following types in which there is reproduction of whole scenes or new symbolic combinations), and type IIB, *identification of the child's body with that of other people or with things.*

We must first observe that identification of one object with another is implicit in the preceding types, but there the identification is inseparable from the set of actions which gives rise to it, while in the examples which follow, it occurs spontaneously and gives rise to the game:

OBS. 77. At 1 ; 8 (30) J. stroked her mother's hair, saying, "*Pussy, pussy.*" At 1 ; 9 (0) she saw a shell and said "*cup.*" After saying it she picked it up and pretended to drink (*cf.* obs. 65, but here the thought preceded the action). The next day, seeing the same shell, she said "*glass*," then "*cup,*" then "*hat*" and finally "*boat in the water.*"

At 1 ; 9 (3) she took an empty box and moved it to and fro saying "*motycar.*" At 1 ; 9 (20) she filled her hand with shells and said "*flowers.*"

At 1 ; 10 (30) she put a shell on the edge of a big box and made it slide down saying: "*Cat on the wall.*" Then (without any further action) "*tree,*" and then (putting the shell on her head) "*right at the top*" (*i.e.*, of the tree: the day before she had seen the cat climbing a pine tree). At 2 ; 1 (7) she put a shell on the end of her first finger and said "*Thimble,*" then rubbed it against another shell as if she were sewing and said "*mended.*"

At 2 ; 0 (22) she moved her finger along the table and said: "*Finger walking . . . horse trotting.*" Similarly, at 2 ; 1 (4), she slid a postcard along the table and said "*car.*" At 2 ; 3 (8) she made a quick circular movement with her fingers and said: "*Bicycle spoilt.*" Then she began again: "*Bicycle mended.*"

At 2 ; 3 (9) she pointed to a big rough pebble: "*It's a dog.—Where's its head?—There* (a lump on the stone).*—And its eyes?—They've gone.—*But isn't it a stone?*—Yes* (she put it up to my mouth). *Good for dog. It's a boat, it's swimming.*" The next day, eating a biscuit: "*It's a dog. Now it's a lion.*" Her shoe-trees became "*irons,*" etc. At 2 ; 3 (10), holding a brush over her head : "*It's an umbrella,*" then "*a coat,*" etc., etc.

At 3 ; 4 (0), talking to a safety-pin: "*She's going into her house: she's a grandmother.*" But already at this stage the symbols, apart from a few residual exceptions, tended more and more to be used in varied combinations. For instance, at 3 ; 11 (24): "*I've seen a dead frog.—Where?—Here, you can see its eyes and its mouth. Look, there's a big hole in its back.—No, I can't see anything. I was only joking: it's a basket.*"

OBS. 78. In the case of L. it was only at 2 ; 1 (26) that I first observed assimilation of one object to another independently of symbolic schemas in action. The peel of an orange was first assimilated to a potato, then to noodles (which she then gave to her doll to eat).

At 2 ; 1 (27) she let some gravel trickle through her fingers and said: " *It's raining.*"   At 2 ; 3 (22), holding a piece of sugar between her fingers: " *Oh, I can't open the door.*"   At 2 ; 5 (7) two brushes were " *a little house.*"

At 3 ; 0 (22) a small piece of material was " *grandmother, very ill, her legs hurt.*"   But at this age, her symbols tended more and more to become complex combinations.

The games of type IIB are to those of type IIA as those of Type IB were to those of type IA, and are usually called *games of imitation* :

obs. 79.   In the case of J. the assimilation of the ego to others was achieved directly through games of type IB (obs. 76).   At 1 ; 10 (30) she pretended to be playing hide and seek with a cousin who had been away for two months.   Then she herself became her cousin: " *Clive running, Clive jumping, Clive laughing,*" and she imitated him, strutting up and down.   At 2 ; 2 (23) she pretended to be ironing like the washerwoman (just as in obs. 18 she polished the floor like the charwoman), but a moment later she became the washerwoman: " *It's Mrs. Séchaud ironing.*"

At 2 ; 4 (8) she was her mother, " *it's mummy,*" and said to me, " *Come kiss mummy,*" and kissed me.

At 2 ; 6 (3) she was her little sister and mimed the action of sucking the breast, a game which often recurred.   At 2 ; 8 (27) she imitated her sister's movements, then again pretended to suck.

At 2 ; 7 (4), having seen a little boy who said " I'm going home," she went in the same direction, said " *I'm going home,*" and imitated his gait.   The same day she was a lady whom we know.   At 2 ; 7 (23) she was a cousin of her own age (several times during the day, but without imitating either his way of talking or his gait).

At 2 ; 8 (5) she crawled into my room on all fours, saying, " *miaow.*"

At 2 ; 8 (27) she was her nurse.

Subsequently this kind of game merged, like type IIA, into more complex symbolic combinations.

obs. 80.   Although in the case of J. there seemed to be a slight lag between these games of type IIB and those of IIA, in L.'s case, on the contrary, they were exactly contemporaneous.   At 2 ; 1 (27) she came to her mother imitating J.'s gestures and saying: "*Me Jacqueline.*"

At 2 ; 3 (22) she was the postman, and at 2 ; 4 (7) she said (when she was all alone in a corner of my study): " *I'm Chouquette* " (a little friend she had seen recently, but not on the days just before).

At 2 ; 5 (2) " *I'm Suzanne* " (her godmother) and at 3 ; 0 (15) she was " *Thérèse with her velvet hat.*"

Again at 4 ; 3, L., standing at my side, quite still, imitated the sound of bells.   I asked her to stop, but she went on.   I then put my hand over her mouth.   She pushed me away, angrily, but still keeping very straight and said: " *Don't.   I'm a church* " (the belfry).

It is at once obvious that the games of types IIA and IIB are even more closely related than those of types IA and IB, and that in the behaviours of both IIA and IIB there is imitation as well as symbolic assimilation.

In obs. 77 and 78 the child starts with a behaviour similar to those of the " symbolic schemas " in stage VI of the preceding period. J. strokes her mother's hair as though it were a cat, she drinks out of a shell as if it were a glass, and L. gives her doll orange peel to eat as if it were macaroni. As in the games of the previous stages, the child is here merely imitating its own earlier actions, but with new objects, the only difference being (and this is the novelty of the situation) that symbolic identification (hair = cat, shell = glass, peel = macaroni) precedes the imitative action and is indicated by speech before any action takes place, instead of following the action as before. What is more, from now on the imitative action is dissociated from the child's own activity and consists in copying the object which is symbolically evoked. So J. imitates a moving car with an empty box, she imitates a bunch of flowers, a cat walking and climbing a tree, a horse trotting, etc., and L. imitates rain with gravel, a closed door with a piece of sugar, etc. In the symbols of type IIA, therefore, there is an element of imitation properly so called, and this, with the object which is present, constitutes the symboliser (or " signifier "), while the symbolised (or " signified ") is the absent object, purely representational in character, which is evoked both by the action and by the present object. For instance, in the case of the car, both the box and the movement it makes in imitation of a car are the symbols or symbolisers, while the car with which the box is identified, and also the imagined movement of the car, constitute what is symbolised (or signified) by the symbol. Thus the fusion of symbolising imitation and ludic assimilation begun in stage VI of the sensory-motor period is completed.

It is obvious that in behaviours of type IIB (obs. 79 and 80) there is imitation, since the child identifies himself with others. But it is equally obvious that there is something more, and that imitation is subordinated to ludic assimilation, since the child does not merely copy others while continuing to be himself. He identifies himself completely with others just as in obs. 77 and 78 he identified one object with another. Here again, therefore, the imitative action is the symboliser, and the person evoked the symbolised, and the symbol is seen, as in the behaviours of type IIA, as the product of generalisable co-operation between ludic assimilation and imitation, whereas previously imitation went no further than reproduction of the child's own earlier behaviours (symbolic schemas) or application of behaviours observed in others to new objects (type IB).

STAGE I. TYPE III. Once constituted in its generality, the

symbol immediately develops in a variety of *symbolic combinations*. The first of these are almost contemporary with type II, sometimes even with type I, but in a rudimentary form. True symbolic combinations, capable of unlimited development, are characteristic of a third level which is only clearly apparent after the age of three or four, *i.e.*, in the second half of stage I.

At this level, which we shall now examine, it becomes impossible to subdivide the games according to the predominance of assimilation (type A) or imitation of others (type B). In every complex ludic combination like those of games with dolls, or with imaginary characters invented by the child to act with him, the imitative and assimilating elements are so inextricably bound up with one another, or follow one another so closely, that any attempt to find a dominating factor in the game as a whole becomes artificial. The types A, B, C and D, therefore, which we shall distinguish at this third level, are rather types of increasing complexity than types corresponding to those of the previous levels.

The first of these, type IIIA, is that of *simple combinations*, beginning with the transposition of real scenes and gradually developing more widely. These games are a continuation of those of IIA and IIB, but they involve the construction of whole scenes, instead of isolated imitations or mere assimilation of one object to another. The most elementary forms of type IIIA are thus contemporary with type II and only diverge from it gradually, as will be seen from the following examples:

OBS. 81. At 2 ; 1 (9) J. put her doll's head through the balcony railings with its face turned towards the street, and began to tell it what she saw: " *You see the lake and the trees. You see a carriage, a horse,*" etc. The same day she seated her doll on a sofa and told it what she herself had seen in the garden.

At 2 ; 1 (13) she fed it, talking to it for a long time in the way used to encourage her to eat her own meals: " *A little drop more. To please Jacqueline. Just eat this little bit.*" At 2 ; 3 (25) she set it astride a gate and pulled its hair back from its ears to make it listen to a musical box. At 2 ; 7 (15) she explained her own games to it: " *You see, I'm throwing the ball,*" etc.

At 2 ; 5 (25) she prepared a bath for L. A blade of grass represented the thermometer, the bath was a big box and she merely stated that the water was there. J. then plunged the thermometer into the bath and found the water too hot. She waited a moment and then put the grass in again: " *That's all right, thank goodness.*" She then went up to L. (she actually did so) and pretended to take off her apron, her dress, her vest, making the movements but not touching the clothes. At 2 ; 8 (0) she played the same game.

At 2 ; 6 (22) she walked to and fro pretending to be holding a baby in her arms. She carefully put it down on an imaginary bed, made it go to sleep, " *Go to sleep, baby*," then woke it and picked it up. The same day she pretended to be carrying her mother: "*Mummy's very heavy*," then imitated the farmer's wife feeding her hens, with her apron turned up (but without anything in it). Already the detail of all these scenes was quite well developed, but there was no symbolic object; the words were only accompanied by gestures. The game with the imaginary baby recurred at 2 ; 7 (1) with new details, but J. stopped talking when anyone came near. From a distance she was heard saying: " *Now we're going for a walk*," etc. The same day she was carrying in her arms a young lady she had recently seen. At 2 ; 7 (1) she added a new subject, the postman, and reading a letter.

It was at about 2 ; 7 and 2 ; 8 that the complex combinations became quite distinct from games of type IIA and IIB, the transition from these to the later types being made possible by activities such as we have just quoted. At about 2 ; 8, for instance, behaviours such as the following made their appearance. A fortnight earlier J. had met, when she was away, a cousin whom she had not mentioned since. Suddenly everything became " Cousin Andrée " : the cat, a lid, herself, her mother, her dolls, etc. She talked about her all day long and made her do everything: go for walks, have meals, etc., down to the most intimate details, without in the least troubling about resemblances.

At about 2 ; 9 the same cycles were followed with " Marceline," another cousin, but one whom she had only heard talked about and had never seen; then with " Miss Jerli " whom she pretended to imitate and whom she associated with everything. Miss Jerli was her grandmother's greengrocer, and J. had never met her either. It was only her sister L. who was imitated (she cried and didn't speak), when J. pretended Miss Jerli was a character in her games. Marceline and Miss Jerli were simply evoked in imagination or represented by leaves, sticks, etc. The private nature of these cycles is noteworthy. One day when I saw her lying down and went up to her, J. called out: " *Go away, I'm Marceline.*" On other occasions she wanted to be heard, as when she enacted conversations between her parents: " *Yes, my dear . . . No, John.*"

A word-for-word transcription, amounting to several pages, of what she said when playing with her doll at about 2 ; 11 (15) is an inextricable medley of scenes from real life and imaginary episodes, put together without any sequence or definite purpose.

At 3 ; 6 (9) she collected small handfuls of pine-needles to make an ants' nest. There was the pillow, the blanket, the quilt, the sheets, a hole for the baby, a table, a chair, then the mother and a cousin; there was some macaroni in the cellar. " *The ants* (there weren't any) *sit down here* (she sat down herself). *Granny comes.*" Then an imaginary character came in. The next day the game was played again, but it all became a cats' house.

At 4 ; 5 (16) there was a similar game with a boat (a board with spades for oars). After the lake, the waves and the ducks had been arranged, the boat came to a place where negroes lived and here some little friends from the neighbourhood met. This led to imaginary village scenes, scenes of school life, etc.

obs. 82. From the end of her second year, L. also reproduced whole scenes with her dolls. She dressed them up, made them walk, and talked to them; she gave them food and drink, took part in their meals, then put everything away in the cupboard. The earlier appearance of these games in the case of L. and their rapid development during the following months are explained by the fact that L. borrowed from J.'s games.

At 2 ; 7 (22) she made up by herself a long game of washing, drying and ironing her dolls' sheets, then gave all the dolls a bath, which was very well imitated in detail.

At 3 ; 0 (17) there was a long scene in which L. remembered and reproduced episodes she had experienced two months before with some little village children. At 3 ; 0 (22) the same scenes came into a game with the lake, waves, ducks and a boat on which the village children met again.

At 3 ; 1 (0) her father had died, her mother and J. had been run over by a car, and an aunt was in charge. At about 3 ; 1 (17) everybody in the games was naughty, which led to a distortion of the usual scenes.

At 3 ; 3 (29) her stick became various people in turn, a pony she was riding, a lady she was dressing, who went for walks with her and to whom she told stories. After this her spade became a shorter lady whose hair had been washed, etc. Later on she turned into a negress.

After 3 ; 7 her pillow " Ali " became the essential character who was the centre of everything (like Cousin Andrée in the case of J.). " *Ali is very rough* (like a real friend of hers). *He's got lots of faults, you know. I shall keep my Ali until I'm married.*" Sometimes he is the husband helping to look after his two or three children: " *My husband is helping me, but he's rather clumsy, you know* " (an allusion to her father). At 4 ; 2 (22) Ali appeared again, as " *Ali-Baudi, a shepherd at Pive* " (L.'s imaginary village). But here we come to games on a higher level.

obs. 83. One form of symbolic combinations, somewhat superior to the preceding ones, but connected to them by all the intermediate stages, consists of cycles of episodes relating to a character who is imaginary from the start (unlike Ali, who was a pillow, or Marceline and the others, of whom the child had heard though she had not seen them). It was only J. who played this type of game systematically. At 3 ; 11 (20) she invented a creature which she called the " *aseau,*" and which she deliberately distinguished from " oiseau " (bird) which she pronounced correctly at this age. J. imitated it and took its place. She ran about the room flapping her wings (her outstretched arms) to suggest flight. But she also crawled on all fours, growling: " *It's a kind of dog* " and at the same time it was "*like a big bird.*" Its form varied from day to day: it had wings, legs, it was "*huge*," it had long hair (J. said to her mother: "*You've got hair like the aseau* "). It had moral authority: "*You mustn't do that* (tear a piece of paper): *Aseau will scold you.*" Two days later J. tried to eat nicely so that Aseau should not scold her.

At 3 ; 11 (22) J. was looking at a plucked duck: "*It's dead, 'cos it hasn't any feathers.—Yes.—I think the aseaux have eaten them.*" At 3 ; 11 (24), after seeing some climbing boots: "*Aseaux have nails in their feet. They stamp their feet like this, in the stable.*" At 3 ; 11 (6) J. was watching a vein throbbing after a cut: "*What's the little red juice in my skin playing at? It must be doing what the aseau does, look, like this* (jumping every two or three steps).

At 4 ; 0 (7) her aseau had died. At 4 ; 0 (17) "*he turned into a dog, and then afterwards he turned back into an aseau.*" As J. made more and more discoveries about zoology, Aseau acquired all the possible attributes: he was an insect, etc.

In a general way, this strange creature which engaged her attention for about two months was a help in all that she learned or desired, gave her moral encouragement in obeying orders, and consoled her when she was unhappy. Then it disappeared.

Subsequently, at about 4 ; 1 (15), Aseau was replaced by a girl who was a dwarf (*cf.* obs. 84), then by a negress to whom she gave the name "Cadile." Cadile turned into "Marécage," a symbolic companion, and she also was associated with everything new, amusing or difficult.[1] Although Marécage was a negress, she was usually represented by a walking stick, a spade, etc.

Games of this kind are the most interesting we have observed in the field of deliberate symbolic construction. Ranging from mere transposition of real life to the creation of imaginary beings for which no model can be found, all of them involve varying degrees of imitation and distorting assimilation. When real scenes are reproduced in games with dolls, imitation is at its maximum, but there is also transposition for subjective ends, not copying with a view to accommodation. In the story of the "aseau" there is maximal transposition, but each attribute of the "aseau" is imitated from the real world, only the completed picture being imaginary. The imitative and assimilating series which have until now run parallel, merge completely at this level, which constitutes as it were the climax of the isolated symbolic constructions analysed earlier.

What is the function of such games? It would require a large dose of theoretical belief to see in them a continuous tendency to pre-exercise. The child is exercising his present life far more than pre-exercising future activities. Can he be said to be pre-exercising his "imagination," imagination being viewed as a faculty to be developed like intelligence itself? Hardly, since the subsequent

[1] *Cf.* "Judas" quoted by H. Delacroix in the chapter on play in his *Psychology of Art.*

evolution of symbolic imagination will consist in its decrease in favour of representational tools more adapted to the real world. Moreover, the striking feature of these symbolic combinations is the extent to which the child reproduces or continues the real world, the imaginative symbol being only a means of expression to increase his range, not an end in itself. In reality, the child has no imagination, and what we ascribe to him as such is no more than a lack of coherence, and still more, subjective assimilation, as is shown by his transpositions. The imitative element in his games (*i.e.*, the symbolising aspect of his symbols) is comparable to his drawings at that age: a copy of reality, but by juxtaposition of allusions without adequate representation. As regards the content (the symbolised), it is only the child's own life. Just as practice play reproduces through functional assimilation each new acquisition of the child, so " imaginative " play reproduces what he has lived through, but by means of symbolic representation. In both cases the reproduction is primarily self-assertion for the pleasure of exercising his powers and recapturing fleeting experience.

It is noteworthy that the fictitious characters that the child creates in his play as companions for himself acquire existence only in so far as they provide a sympathetic audience or a mirror for the ego. Just as the monologues of children at this age correspond to what will later be interiorised speech, so these imaginary characters are a substitute for the egocentric forms of the adult's interiorised thought (day dreams). These mythical characters no doubt also acquire some of the moral authority of the parents, but only in so far as it thus becomes easier of acceptance than in reality. The character " Aseau " (obs. 83) who goes so far as to scold, is particularly interesting in this connection, and recalls the examples given by Wulf, Ferenczi and Freud of what they call " infantile totemism " or invention of animals which dispense justice.

The assimilation of reality by means of symbolic make-believe is continued in the *compensatory combinations* of type IIIB, where it is a question of correcting reality rather than reproducing it for pleasure. Ludic compensation begins well before games of type III, whenever a forbidden action is done as make-believe for example, but obviously the preceding symbolic combinations develop it still further.

OBS. 84. At 2 ; 4 (8) J., not being allowed to play with the water being used for washing, took an empty cup, went and stood by the forbidden tub and went through the actions, saying: " *I'm pouring out water.*" At 2 ; 6 (28) she wanted to carry Nonette (*i.e.*, L. who had been born shortly before). Her mother told her she could try later on. J. folded her arms and said: " *Nonette's in there. There are two Nonettes.*" She then talked to the imaginary Nonette, rocked her, etc. The same day the game was played again, but became more and more secret. J. stopped talking when

I went up to her, and whispered to Nonette. At 2 ; 7 (28) J. was screaming with temper, and as she was not given her own way she then said she was Nonette, and went on crying, but imitating the crying of L., which consoled her.

At 2 ; 8 (6) J. was angry with her father, tried to hit him, etc., and since this seemed likely to have unfortunate consequences she suddenly cried: " *It was much nicer when Caroline* (a friend of her god-father) *was cross with Godfather.*" She then related, drawing entirely on her imagination, how Caroline had struck Godfather and she began to mime the scene in detail. When later on her mother spoke to her about her original anger, J. would have none of it: " *No, it was Caroline.*" At 2 ; 8 (7), when she was on a diet, she made up a whole scene about a meal.

At 3 ; 11 (15) she was told not to go into the kitchen because of the pails of hot water prepared for a bath: " *Then I'll go into a pretend kitchen. I once saw a little boy who went into a kitchen, and when Odette went past with the hot water he got out of the way.*" The story continued on this theme, by way of compensation. Then it ended with a symbol acceptance: " *After that he didn't go to the kitchen any more.*"

At 4 ; 1 (16) a whole cycle of symbolic combinations was started through the need for compensation. Expecting to see again a dwarf whom she had seen several times before in a village, J. learned that she was dead. She immediately told a story about a little girl dwarf who met a boy dwarf: " *Then he died, but she looked after him so well that he got better and went back home.*" During the next few days the girl dwarf was associated with everything in her life. At 4 ; 3 (0) the snow shovel was her dwarf, and went for walks with her, etc.

The " Marécage " cycle (obs. 83) which was not compensatory in origin, frequently became so when occasion arose.

At 4 ; 7 (20) J. was jealous of her father and said: " *Marécage has a horrid father. He calls her in when she's playing,*" and " *her mother chose badly,*" etc. At 4 ; 8 (1), having to go to bed, she discovered that " *Marécage never lies down in the afternoon, she plays all the time.*" At 4 ; 8 (3), having failed to " tame a grasshopper," she consoled herself: " *Marécage tamed a grasshopper. She had one that followed her everywhere; it went for walks with her and came home with her,*" etc.

A form allied to the preceding one consists in neutralising a fear through play, or in doing in play what one would not dare do in reality. Compensation here becomes *catharsis*.

OBS. 85. At 2 ; 9 (14) L. was afraid of a tractor in a field next to the garden. She then told her doll that " *Dolly told me she would like to ride on a machine like that.*" At 3 ; 0 (0) the same thing happened with aeroplanes. At 3 ; 4 (0): " *You know, when Christian* (a doll) *was a baby they gave him a little steam-roller and a tiny tractor,*" etc. At 4 ; 2 (10) she did not dare, like J., to go alone to a neighbouring barn where some children were making a theatre. She then organised with her dolls a big theatre game, both as compensation and to " purge " her fear.

Type IIIC, which is interesting from the point of view of the theory of symbolic play, is characterised by *liquidating combinations*. Faced with a difficult or unpleasant situation, the child may either compensate for it, as we have seen, or accept it, but in the latter case he tries to re-live it by transposing it symbolically. When the situation is dissociated from the unpleasantness of its context, it is gradually assimilated by being incorporated in other behaviours. We give here a few examples, ranging from the most elementary forms of symbolism to those of the present level:

obs. 86. J., at 2 ; 1 (7), was afraid when sitting on a new chair at table. In the afternoon, she put her dolls in uncomfortable positions and said to them: " *It doesn't matter. It will be all right*," repeating what had been said to her. At 2 ; 3 (0) there was a similar scene with some medicine, which she afterwards gave to a sheep.

At 2 ; 7 (2) she had fallen down and cut her lip. After the usual scene, she consoled herself by projecting it all on to " Cousin Andrée," who took the form of a doll: " *Oh! it's Cousin Andrée. They're washing her because she fell down and hurt her lip. She made a little hole in it. She cried.*" The next day again she played at falling down, pretending to be with her Cousin François, and the " juice from her lip " made a stain on to the wall.

At 2 ; 7 (15) a friend of her mother went for a walk with them. J. who did not care for the presence of a third person, expressed frankly what she felt: " *She's naughty . . . she can't talk. . . . I don't like people to laugh,*" and especially, " *I don't understand what they're saying.*" Then, as soon as the walk was over, J. accepted her, put her beside her in the bath, then in her bed, talked to her, and went for the walk again with her (all in imagination).

At 3 ; 11 (21) she was impressed by the sight of a dead duck which had been plucked and put on the kitchen table. The next day I found J. lying motionless on the sofa in my study, her arms pressed against her body and her legs bent: " What are you doing, J.?—Have you a pain?—Are you ill?—*No, I'm the dead duck.*"

At 4 ; 6 the " Marécage " cycle helped J. not to mind being laughed at, and being frightened when she thought she was lost. The two scenes were reproduced in detail, with Marécage as character.

On the same day I knocked against J.'s hands with a rake and made her cry. I said how sorry I was, and blamed my clumsiness. At first she didn't believe me, and went on being angry as though I had done it deliberately. Then she suddenly said, half appeased: " *You're Jacqueline and I'm daddy. There!* (she hit my fingers). *Now say*: " *You've hurt me.*—(I said it.) *I'm sorry, darling. I didn't do it on purpose. You know how clumsy I am,"* etc. In short, she merely reversed the parts and repeated my exact words.

These forms of play, which consist in liquidating a disagreeable situation by re-living it in make-believe, clearly illustrate the function of symbolic play, which is to assimilate reality to the ego while freeing the ego from the demands of accommodation. In the ordinary cases it is only a matter of intensifying the awareness of newly acquired powers, or of extending them through make-believe. In the case of type IIIB the ego is enabled to take its revenge on reality, *i.e.*, to compensate for it. In the case of type IIIC the proper function of the game is to reproduce in their entirety scenes in which the ego ran the risk of failure, thereby enabling it to assimilate them and emerge victorious. From the point of view of structure, then, there is exact imitation, but imitation with intent to subordinate the model imitated, and not to yield to it.

In the case of the dead duck, it was merely the unpleasantness of a disturbing sight that was liquidated in this way. This particular case brings us to an imperceptible transition to type IVD, one of the extreme forms of ludic symbolism when it is tending towards adapted thought, and which we shall call *anticipatory symbolic combinations.* The three preceding forms are either pure reconstructions (IIIC), reconstructions combined with imaginary elements (IIIA), or reconstructions with compensatory transpositions (IIIB). In the following forms, on the contrary, it is a question of accepting an order or advice (and this is again a kind of liquidation as in IIIC), but there is also symbolic anticipation of the consequences which would ensue should the advice be rejected or the order disobeyed. There is again, therefore, ludic assimilation, but accompanied by anticipation which performs the same function as representation adapted to reality.

OBS. 87 (*a*). J., at 4 ; 6 (23), was walking on a steep mountain-road: " Mind that loose stone."—" *Marécage (obs. 83) once trod on a stone, you know, and didn't take care, and she slipped and hurt herself badly.*" At 4 ; 6 (26), on another rather precipitous path, I pointed out to J. the rushing stream at the foot of the mountain and told her to be careful: " *Do you know what my little negress friend did?.* (Obs. 84.) *She rolled right to the bottom of the mountain into the lake. She rolled for four nights. She scraped her knee and her leg terribly. She did not even cry. They picked her up afterwards. She was in the lake, she couldn't swim and was nearly drowned. At first they couldn't find her and then they did.*—How do you know all that?—*She told me on the boat* (the boat on which J. first saw a negress who gave rise to this cycle)."

At 4 ; 7 (2) we were walking close to some nettles and I told her to be careful. She then pretended to be a little girl who had been stung. The same day she played at scything with a thin, pointed stick. She then said to me of her own accord: " *Daddy, say: You won't cut yourself, Jacqueline, will you?*" Then she told a story similar to the preceding ones.

OBS. 87 (*b*). In the case of L. this kind of game appeared more than a year earlier, a fact which proves that they already belong to the types of the third level (it is also possible that we failed to notice them before 4 ; 6 in the case of J.). At 3 ; 4 (16) L. was playing in the garden and I suggested a walk. She refused firmly. To persuade her, J. told her that she herself always refused at first but afterwards enjoyed it. L. promptly replied: "*My little Christian* (her doll) *once went for a walk and he met a big animal that frightened him. I had to comfort him. And there was such a lot of sun* (this was the real reason, which L. knew would affect me) *that he came home very hot and I couldn't touch him!*"

At 3 ; 5 (3) L. was reluctant to walk round the garden in the evening because owls were hooting in the trees: "*You know there was an owl in the garden and Ali* (her pillow) *went out with big nailed boots. The owl was afraid and went away.*" So we agreed to stamp our shoes on the gravel to clear the way.

Like their predecessors, these games involve straightforward reproduction of reality, but with the addition of exact or slightly exaggerated anticipation of the consequences of the action. But although this anticipation is in conformity with experience, and is evidence of an activity which is almost deductive, it is clear that it is still ludic, since it is presented as a reconstruction ascribed to an imaginary companion, and not as anticipation. In this way, the symbol of the game fulfils its function of assimilation to the ego. J. is not concerned by the thought that stepping on a stone will make her slip, since this represents an unreal future which she finds it difficult to imagine, but it is a vivid, tangible reality for her that " Marécage " fell to the bottom of the slope and was carried into the lake by the mountain stream.

STAGE II. From the age of four to seven, in general, symbolic games, of which we have just described the main forms at the peak period, begin to lose their importance. It is not that they are less numerous, or less intensely felt, but rather that the symbol, by closer adaptation to reality, loses its distorting ludic character and approximates to a straightforward imitative representation of reality.

Three new characteristics distinguish the symbolic games of this stage (4–7) from those of the previous one. The first is the relative *orderliness* of the ludic constructions as opposed to the incoherence of the symbolic combinations of type III (*e.g.*, obs. 82 and 83). The second is that in these new games there is an increasing desire for verisimilitude and *exact imitation of reality*, the third being the appearance of *collective symbolism* properly so-called, *i.e.*, with differentiation and adjustment of roles.

It is, of course, difficult to trace the progress of coherence and order in play, which is by definition free activity, and it is all the more so because at this stage they are relatively undeveloped in comparison with the systematisations of the period after the age of seven or eight. There are, however, good reasons for believing that we are not mistaken in assuming such progress. We know, from experience gained from the clinical method of free conversation, that it is almost impossible to question children of three, because of their lack of coherence of thought in following a conversation. After the age of four, on the other hand, it is possible to pursue an enquiry (this does not of course mean that it can be as fruitful as after the age of seven or eight). It seems clear that this coherence of thought in conversation must be reflected both in the spontaneous speech of play and in the games with roles which we are about to consider. Moreover, research into the notion of order shows that the child of four to six, although unable to tell a story verbally in the right order, or reconstruct at will a sequence of events, can intuitively arrange in order a set of coloured beads,[1] which the child of three cannot do. It is therefore natural that in symbolic play we should find progress in coherence after the age of four or five. It can already be seen in the examples of obs. 87, which is a transition to the games of the present stage. We give here one out of the many examples which exist of games with *ordered symbolic combinations:*

> OBS. 88. J., at 4 ; 7 (3), was carrying a long stone to represent the jug of milk brought by Honorine every morning: " *I'm Honorine's sister, because Honorine is ill. She's got whooping-cough. She coughs and spits too sometimes. It would be a pity if the little girl* (J. herself) *caught it* (she said all this with a local accent, rolling her r's, and it was all made up). *Do you want some milk, madam?*—No, thank you.—*Oh, I came too late. There's Honorine coming* (J. changed her role and coughed). *I won't come near the little girl, so as not to give her whooping-cough* (she made the gesture of pouring out milk). *I don't think I can give the milk whooping-cough.* (J. then became herself taking the milk). *I want a lot, you know. Marécage* (obs. 25) *told me that she would bring back Julie, Claudine, Augustine and Philomène from Arolla* (where J.'s mother had gone that day). *All those children* (who were imaginary) *need a lot of milk for supper,"* etc.

It is clear that these ordered scenes show an advance on those concerning the " aseau," etc., in obs. 83 and earlier.

Obs. 88 is a good example of *exact imitation of reality* from the point of view of the role mimed by the player. But what is more interesting is the increasing attention to exact detail in the material constructions which accompany these games: houses, cots, tables, kitchens, drawings and models. At this level there are two kinds of interesting inter-

[1] *La Représentation de l'Espace chez l'Enfant,* Presses Universitaires de France. Paris, 1948.

connections. On the one hand, the constructions co-ordinate more closely with the symbol intellectual and sensory-motor ludic exercise (83): for instance, a doll's house made of wood and cardboard, with a straw roof and painted shutters, etc., which the child takes days to complete, is both sensory-motor practice and symbolic combination. On the other hand this very fact means that the symbolic assimilation is less and less distorting, and therefore nearer to mere imitative reproduction. In other words, the ludic symbol is evolving towards a straightforward copy of reality, only the general themes remaining symbolic, while the detail of the scenes and of the constructions tends towards exact accommodation and frequently even towards properly intelligent adaptation.

OBS. 89. From about 5 ; 6 onwards, J. spent her time organising scenes dealing with families, education, weddings, etc., with her dolls, but also making houses, gardens and often furniture. At 6 ; 5 (12), using interlocking bricks and rods she built a big house, a stable and a woodshed, surrounded by a garden, with paths and avenues. Her dolls continually walked about and held conversations but she also took care that the material constructions should be exact and true to life.

Later, it was a whole village, " *Ventichon* " that gradually grew up. J.'s whole life was connected with this place and its inhabitants. Reproduction of reality was the main interest, but elements of compensation could be observed (" *At Ventichon they drink a whole glass of water* " and not just a little in the bottom of a glass), and also protective transpositions: the inhabitants had a special costume (a veil over the face to protect them from adult indiscretions) and certain passwords: " *Ye tenn*," when going into a house (they were kept out if they pronounced it badly), " *to-to-to* " when going up certain stairs, etc.

At 6 ; 7 (4) J. made a bear-pit (at Ventichon) with great attention to detail. The bottom was covered with flat pebbles and the sides lined with wood. The grating at the entrance was made of crossed sticks. L. (4 ; 2) imitated it but was concerned with a more imaginative symbolism: gates prevented the dogs from coming and frightening the bears, etc.

At 6 ; 7 (5) she made a stable out of tiles placed one on top of another, with timber-work, doors, etc., and laid out a pond at the side. The cows were coloured stones, and the goats little pebbles. Altogether it made a very consistent picture. At 6 ; 7 (17) she imitated in detail work in the fields, scything, raking, etc., with the help of her dolls, dividing the work between them as she was used to seeing it done in the locality. She had a series of thin sticks representing scythes, curved sticks representing rakes, and so on.

At 7 ; 0 (7) she made a cemetery for her village, with straw crosses, walls made of stones, and cypresses of fir twigs, altogether a very satisfactory reproduction. The following days there was a medical scene: a boil being lanced, etc.

The words and actions which accompanied these varied constructions were copied from real life (*cf.* obs. 88) but with imaginary transpositions (the whooping-cough of obs. 88), and they were continued from one day to the next. J., and later L., ended by playing permanent parts as mothers of families, with numerous children, grandparents, cousins, visitors, etc., the husbands being rather in the background. " *Mrs. Odar* " and " *Mrs. Anonzo*," etc., thus became the starting point of new cycles, analogous to those of the preceding stages, but much closer to reality, always true to life and with scenery and buildings which became more and more elaborate.

The third characteristic, *collective symbolism*, has already shown itself in the previous stages when the child played with one or more companions, but then, although the players borrowed ideas from one another or imitated each other sometimes in detail it is difficult to note any change in the structure of the symbols. At first play is no more socialised than children's language in the case of " collective monologues." After the age of four, however, roles are differentiated and become complementary.

OBS. 90. At 2 ; 7 (2) J. was playing with a boy of five, who was " Mr. Durand " and was arranging a dinner for two. At first J. copied him slavishly and laughed gaily when she succeeded, but then she played an independent role (" *I'm washing the stairs* ") and went on with it, ignoring the other child, although he suggested that they should be " husband and wife." When her playmate, who had grown impatient, asked her after some time if she had finished washing her stairs, J. replied that she was " *washing Cousin Andrée*," which was quite unintelligible to the young husband, since he was unfamiliar with the cycles of obs. 81.

Again, at 3 ; 3 (27), J., who spent hours with three boys of 3 ; 6, 4 ; 6, and 6 ; 0, meekly took the parts she was given (they made her be the engine, pushing her by the shoulders), but merely went through the actions without really co-operating.

At 3 ; 11 (26) J. seemed to be trying to arrange a shop game with L. " *What do you want, Madam? Hold out your little hand* (L., who was only 1 ; 7 didn't understand and got restless). *Do you want some bags of flour? I am selling flour to Cousin Sazoulet*, etc." As L. then went away, J. said: " *That's the lady who has gone to the loft.*" Thus there were really no complementary roles, and J. merely included L. in her game as she would a doll. At 4 ; 3 J. was still playing a passive part like this with a boy scarcely older than herself.

When, however, it was a question of both playing the same part, collaboration was possible earlier. At 3 ; 9 (2) J. said to L.: " *Let's be two sisters reading a book, shall we?* " and both of them sat down (L. was 1 ; 4) and each looked at her book. At 4 ; 2 (13) there was the same agreement about flying aeroplanes, etc. (L. was 1 ; 9), but identical roles did not lead to any continuous development.

It was only at 4 ; 5 (13) that J. arranged parts without treating L. merely as she would a doll. J. decided that she would be " Joseph " and L. " Thérèse " (two of their friends in the neighbourhood), and as L. seemed to accept her part (she imitated Thérèse without becoming her), J. adapted herself to the leads given by her younger sister. A moment later, J. reversed the roles and the play went on more or less satisfactorily (meal-time scenes, errands, etc.). At 4 ; 7 (12) J. did her utmost to stage a scene with a car ride. L., who was 2 ; 2 (18) was in process of constructing a bed, and said " *Brr* " to show that she was taking part in the movement of the ear, but did not stop her own game. What followed was for L. a confused medley of the two games, while J. perseveringly arranged the parts. J. came off victorious, and made L. the wife of a doll, " *You're the wife of this husband.—Yes*," and herself another lady: (J) " *We're two ladies in a car.—*(L) *Are you in a car, madam?—*(J.) *Yes, and I'm throwing your husband and your child through the window* (she threw the doll away)." But L. went and got it and forgot the game.

At 4 ; 7 (23), when J. was playing with a girl of ten, she adapted herself perfectly to all her games of meals, families, etc., thus showing that she would have been quite capable of developing the complementary roles of the preceding games if her playmate had been her own age. L., who profited by J.'s examples, acquired the ability to do so at about 3 ; 8 or 3 ; 9.

It is obvious that this organised collective symbolism implies the progress in order and coherence which we observed to be the first characteristic of stage II. But it could equally well be maintained that coherence of thought comes from progress in socialisation. It is clear that they are two aspects of the same development, and it is interesting to find this interaction of social and mental acquisitions in the field of ludic symbolism in addition to finding it continually in that of adapted representation. In both cases there is a transition from initial egocentrism to reciprocity, as a result of a double coordination in inter-individual relationships and in representational correlation. But in the case of the ludic symbol we must note that progress in socialisation, instead of leading to an increase in symbolism, transforms it more or less rapidly into objective imitation of reality. At this second stage, when socialisation is still in its infancy (collective games are to individual symbols as socialised language is to egocentric language) it is already converging, as we saw in obs. 89, with a definite tendency to objectivation of the symbols in the direction of exact imitation of reality. In the third stage, which we shall now study, the decisive turning point at the age of seven or eight leads to a very definite modification of ludic symbolism as well as to the general socialisation whose effects on thought we have so frequently stressed.

STAGE III. This last period, which we place between the age of seven or eight and eleven or twelve, is characterised by a definite decline in symbolism and the rise of either games with rules, or symbolic constructions which are progressively less distorting and more nearly related to adapted work.

In an earlier research on the game of marbles (*The Moral Judgment of the Child*, Chap. I) we saw the seven-year-old child substituting for the egocentric play of his earlier years a game involving rules and the team spirit. The same thing happens in the case of collective symbolic games, in which we find, from the age of seven to ten or eleven, an ever-increasing co-ordination of roles and an expansion of the socialisation begun at the previous level. We observed this in the case of J., L., and T. when they played at families, with dolls, and we shall see it again in the dramatic scenes of obs. 91.

Parallel with this progressive social adaptation we must notice the development of constructions, handwork, and drawing, increasingly better adapted to reality and indicating the final stage of ludic symbolism. It was T. (obs. 92) who gave us the best example of the final stage of symbolic play, which seems to end with childhood, whereas games with rules, which are unknown to the small child, continue up to the adult stage.

OBS. 91. With regard to collective symbolism, we shall confine ourselves to noting how J. and L., after seven or eight years of systematic collaboration in their games with dolls and families, reached the stage of continually organising for themselves and for T. (and later with T.) plays or theatrical performances. At first everything was improvised, and the play was merely a collective symbolic game with an audience. Later on the theme was decided beforehand, and its general outline discussed (sometimes there was even detailed preparation of the first part). But once the part that had been prepared was played there was always a wide margin for improvisation. In particular, the end was never definitely planned.

These behaviours give us a first example of the transition from symbolic games to the spontaneous creation or free activity which characterise later childhood, and which have been so widely used in activity methods of teaching.

OBS. 92. After playing symbolic games with J. and L., in which each of them had her own village, then her own country (called Two Balls, Three Balls, etc.), T. made himself a country called " Six-Twenty Balls, which began in the same way as the cycles of stage II (obs. 82–83 and 89). But from the age of seven onwards, T., after drawing the various aspects of Six-Twenty Balls, began to make maps of the country. Its name became Siwimbal, and it had in it towns called Bergai, Mir, Blanker, Sogar, etc. Numerous adventures took place there (journeys, animal stories) and T. peopled Bergai with schoolchildren like himself with whom he had imaginary relations.

After the age of eight T. eliminated the imaginary characters, but put increased care and ingenuity into the drawing of his maps, and into extending Siwimbal. He made his cartographic models with as much attention to detail as though they were the maps of real countries, in which he was beginning to be interested. At 8 ; 2 and 8 ; 3 he divided his time during an illness, between making the most complete planispheres, and drawing in detail districts of Siwimbal. In addition he distributed to his sisters and friends particular districts of the country which had varied climates (a bathing resort with a tropical climate to one, a piece of arctic territory to others, and so on), and gave detailed descriptions of them by transposition of those parts of the globe that he was then actually studying with intense interest.

Later on, at about the age of nine, their place was taken by real maps, though there were occasional returns to the imaginary ones. But a curious transitional stage occurred, in which his drawings were very exact from the point of view of physical geography, but in which frontiers were changed, e.g., Switzerland included part of northern Italy and a corridor running along the Rhone down to the Mediterranean. Germany was reduced to its simplest form, and so on.

Finally, at about the age of ten, the maps became quite objective, but symbolic play appeared again on another plane. T. was beginning to take a great interest in history, and amused himself by reconstructing the costumes, furniture, houses, etc., of very varying periods. He drew and made all the material himself with great skill, and dressed tiny bears and monkeys in the costumes of Rome, the Middle Ages, the Renaissance, the time of Louis XIV, the eighteenth century, the Empire, etc., and housed them appropriately! With tireless patience, he and a schoolfellow went through a whole literature on the subject so as to be able to show his characters as they had been century after century. Symbolism was here reduced to its simplest terms. Being merely a ludic pretext for work with a companion, it added enjoyment to sustained effort which was both intellectual and artistic. One needs to have seen a little monkey in a wig, a three-cornered hat, silk breeches and lace ruffles, in an eighteenth century setting made of cardboard, in order to understand the pleasure that two eleven-year-old boys can find in spending their leisure time in evoking the spirit of the past.

A comparison of this final form of symbolic play with its initial stages reveals the advance made. At its starting point, symbolic construction (the given object and the imitative actions to which it is assimilated) merely represents a situation and objects not directly related to it which are themselves assimilated to a system of subjective combinations: e.g., a basket is assimilated to a car, and the car is evoked for the purpose of an imaginary journey, etc. At its point of arrival, symbolic construction (e.g., the houses, furniture and costumes of the eighteenth century) has become merely imitative reproduction of the corresponding reality, this reality being evoked only as an aid to intelligent understanding. The symbol has become an image whose purpose is no longer assimilation to the ego but adaptation to reality, the little monkey (representing a human character) being the only point of contact between this objective adaptation and the ludic assimilation of reality to subjective fantasy.

§ 5. *Games with rules and evolution of children's games*

While mere practice play begins with the first months of life and symbolic play during the second year, games with rules rarely occur before stage II (age 4–7) and belong mainly to the third period (from 7–11). But in the adult stage, although examples of practice games (*e.g.*, playing with one's wireless set) and symbolic games (*e.g.*, telling oneself a story) are rare, games with rules remain, and even develop throughout life (sports, cards, chess, etc.). The explanation of this late appearance and protracted continuation of games with rules is very simple: they are the ludic activity of the socialised being. Just as the symbol replaces mere practice as soon as thought makes its appearance, so the rule replaces the symbol and integrates practice as soon as certain social relationships are formed, and the question is to discover these relationships.

We must first point out that the individual does not of his own accord give himself rules, except by analogy with those he has been given. We have never observed spontaneous rules in the case of an isolated child. J. at the age of three [1] when she was given marbles, either used them as symbolisers (eggs in a nest, etc.) or played at throwing them, etc. (mere practice), thus developing habits, *i.e.*, achieving spontaneous regularity (throwing from the same spot, the same distance, etc.). But in the rule, there is in addition to regularity an idea of obligation which presupposes at least two individuals.[2] The nearest approach to rules observed in the case of a child when alone is to be found in the sensory-motor ritualisations of which we saw examples in obs. 63 and 68, but these cannot be considered games with rules since they involve neither obligation nor prohibition. When J. said " I'm playing a game. I'm trying not to let the ferns touch me " (obs. 68), she could of course have gone further and given herself a rule " The ferns must not be touched " as she went through the copse. Children, and even adults, often decide as they walk along a pavement that they must not step on the lines between the paving-stones. There are two alternatives here: either it is a simple practice game with ritualisation, or the subject gives himself a rule because he

---

[1] *The Moral Judgment of the Child*, p. 25.

[2] K. Bühler's " Regelbewusstsein " is not therefore necessarily awareness of the rule in this strict sense.

knows other rules, and in so doing is interiorising a social behaviour (leaving aside the element of magic which may come into such games, as into all rituals).

As regards rules themselves, two categories can be distinguished: those which are handed down, and those which are spontaneous. In other words, there are games with rules which have become " institutional " in the sense that they are social realities which are passed on through the pressure of one generation on the next, and games with rules which are in the nature of a temporary agreement. The games of the first category imply action by the older children on the younger, imitation of the older children because of their prestige, etc., as, for example, in the game of marbles, which in Switzerland is not played after the end of childhood, and is therefore passed on purely through the social pressure of children. We have studied these games elsewhere, and shall not return to them. Spontaneous games with rules are more interesting to us here since they are the outcome of the socialisation either of mere practice games or sometimes of symbolic games, socialisation which, though it may involve relationships between older and younger children, is often only a matter of relationships between equals and contemporaries.

OBS. 93. After the happenings described in obs. 79, the game with the seat became general in the class, by imitation. The players jumped two by two on to a seat, one at each end, and ran along it towards one another, the collision when they met causing one to fall off and leave the way free for the victor. But while the little ones (who began the game) played almost without rules, the older children of seven or eight very soon began to observe certain norms. They started at the same moment from each end, sometimes standing at the same distance from the seat; moreover, the girls and boys played separately, but this may have been from choice, without previous decision.

Three five-year-old boys, playing at jumping one, two, three, or more steps of the school stairs reached a stage which was a beginning of rules. They had to jump as far as they could: anyone who fell lost, and the turn only counted if a boy jumped from the same step as the others. Obviously there is nothing very complex in these rules, but they are a beginning which is capable of extension.

OBS. 94. An interesting example of the transition from symbolic games to games with rules was provided by some little shepherd-boys of Valais who were amusing themselves by cutting hazel branches in a Y shape to represent cows. The two tips of the Y were the horns and the lower part was the body (there were no legs). The bark was loosened on the underside to represent the belly, and spotted on top to indicate the markings on the back. So far there was only symbolism, of the stage II type (imitative construction). But these cows fought one another, and here rules came in. The cows had to stand horn to horn and the players pushed them by the base of the Y: the one that fell on its back lost. These conditions had to be observed, the players had to push without jerking, etc., and the losing cow became the property of the winner.

No doubt it is in this way that games with policemen, burglars, black men, etc., which are at first symbolic (and remain so with little children) lose their representational content and become chasing games with rules.

Games with rules, then, are games with sensory-motor combinations (races, marbles, ball games, etc.), or intellectual combinations (cards, chess, etc.), in which there is competition between individuals (otherwise rules would be useless) and which are regulated either by a code handed down from earlier generations, or by temporary agreement. Games with rules may be the outcome of adult practices which have become obsolete (magico-religious in origin), or of sensory-motor practice games which have become collective (obs. 93) or lastly of symbolic games which have also become collective, but which in so doing have lost all or part of their imaginative content, *i.e.*, their symbolism (obs. 94).

These few indications suffice to enable us to conclude this chapter by sketching the broad outline of the evolution of children's play. We shall attempt to clarify the mutual interpenetration of the three successive systems: mere practice, symbolism and rules, as well as their various relationships with constructional or creative games.

While practice games are the first to appear, they are also the most labile, since they are vicarious: they appear with each new acquirement and disappear after saturation. But as in the course of development really new acquisitions become less and less numerous, mere practice games, having reached their climax during the first years of life, diminish in importance (absolutely and relatively) with age. Certain of them last rather longer because they are bound up with situations which recur over a longer period: *e.g.*, fighting games, which appear in all social situations involving competition and which we therefore find at various ages,[1] or jumping and climbing, etc., which reappear whenever occasion offers. But in general there is gradual disappearance of the mere practice game as a result of the three following kinds of transformations:—

In the first place, the child passes imperceptibly from mere practice to fortuitous and then to purposive combinations. As soon as his actions and manipulations are co-ordinated in relation to an aim, such as arranging bricks according to size, etc. (obs. 71), the child soon reaches the stage of setting himself definite tasks and the practice game becomes construction. But between ludic construction and

[1] P. Bovet. *L'instinct combatif, Delachaux et Niestlé,* 1937.

work in the strict sense there are all shades of transitions [1] and the first cause of the gradual disappearance of practice games is therefore to be found in the reintegration of play into adapted activity.

In the second place, mere practice may become symbolism or be coupled with symbolism, either when the sensory-motor schema is itself changed into a symbolic schema (obs. 64 and 65), or when the constructions which emerge from ludic combinations lead to symbolic imitation (obs. 71 and 89) instead of becoming adapted activity or work.

In the third place, the practice game, by becoming collective, may acquire rules and thus evolve into a game with rules (obs. 70 and 93), and we have here the last reason for the disappearance of practice games with age, quite apart from their spontaneous extinction as a result of saturation.

Symbolic games decline after the age of four, for reasons which it is important to discover, since they also explain why these games are so numerous earlier. In a general way it can be said that the more the child adapts himself to the natural and social world the less he indulges in symbolic distortions and transpositions, because instead of assimilating the external world to the ego he progressively subordinates the ego to reality. There are three essential reasons for the diminution of ludic symbolism with age.

The first is inherent in the content of the symbolism: in the cases in which this content indicates a need for expansion of the ego, for compensation, for liquidation or even a mere continuation of real life (dolls, etc.), the child finds, as he grows older, more and more opportunities of satisfying these needs in his own life, if it is normal, and recourse to symbolic make-believe assimilation becomes unnecessary. His social circle expands, and, more important, he becomes the equal (or the superior) of an increasing number of real persons. In many cases where hitherto play was indispensable, life itself then offers him the means of compensating, liquidating, etc.

The second reason is that as symbolic games involving more than one character may give rise to rules, so games of make-believe may become games with rules (obs. 94).

Finally, a third and more important reason explains the diminution not only of symbolic play but also of play in general. It is the extent to which the child attempts to adjust to reality rather than to assimilate which determines how far the distorting symbol is transformed into an imitative image, and how far imitation itself is incorporated into intelligent or effective adaptation. We have seen that at first the child becomes more and more exacting in his symbolism: from the age of four to seven he aims at exact reproduction and his symbols

---

[1] See Claparède, *Psychologie de l'enfant*, 8th ed., pp. 498–509.

therefore become more and more imitative (obs. 89).[1] For this very reason symbolic play incorporates sensory-motor or intellectual practice play and becomes to some extent constructional. In the transition from constructional games to work, all the intermediate stages are again to be found, largely owing to the fact that there is a similar relationship between the imaginative symbol and adapted imitation (obs. 91 and 92), and we have here the explanation of the decline of both symbolic play and play in general between the ages of eight and twelve.

It is only games with rules that are not subject to this law of involution and that increase in number, both absolutely and relatively, with age. They are almost the only ones that persist at the adult stage. Since these are socialised games, controlled by rules, the question arises whether there may not be one and the same explanation for both the decline of children's play in its specific forms of practice and symbolic make-believe, and the development of games with rules in so far as they are essentially social. If it is true that practice play results from the child's pleasure in exercising his newly acquired powers, and that ludic symbolism is primarily assimilation of reality to the ego and intensification of this same pleasure through fictitious control of the whole natural and social world, then the disappearance of the earlier games in favour of adapted construction on one hand, and the evolution of games with rules on the other, can be easily explained. In the next chapter we shall attempt to give this explanation.

[1] In the same way symbolic anticipation (obs. 87) becomes deduction.

CHAPTER VI

EXPLANATION OF PLAY

Having attempted to classify and describe games, we shall now endeavour to find an interpretation of them by an examination of their position in the general context of the child's thought. The task is not easy: the many theories of play expounded in the past are clear proof that the phenomenon is difficult to understand. But the reason for the difficulty lies perhaps in the fact that there has been a tendency to consider play as an isolated function (as has been the case with " imagination ") and therefore to seek particular solutions to the problem, whereas play is in reality one of the aspects of any activity (like imagination in respect to thought). The prevalence of play among children is therefore to be explained not by specific causes peculiar to the realm of play, but by the fact that the characteristics of all behaviours and all thought are less in equilibrium in the early stage of mental development than in the adult stage, which is, of course, obvious.

§ 1. *Criteria of Play*

An examination of the main criteria usually adopted to distinguish play from non-ludic activities shows clearly that play is not a behaviour *per se*, or one particular type of activity among others. It is determined by a certain orientation of the behaviour, or by a general " pole " of the activity, each particular action being characterised by its greater or less proximity to the pole and by the kind of equilibrium between the polarised tendencies. For instance, according to a well-known formula play is an end in itself, whereas work and other non-ludic behaviours involve an aim not contained in the activity as such. If this were so, play would be " disinterested," or as J. M. Baldwin says " autotelic." But this first criterion is at once seen to be lacking in precision. On the one hand, as P. Souriau has already emphasised in his *Esthétique du mouvement*, every game is in a sense profoundly " interested," since the player is certainly concerned with the result of his activity. In the case of practice games the result is materially identical with that of the corresponding " serious " activity. If, then, the distinction is between " autotelism " and " heterotelism," it can only be made in relation to the kind of equilibrium that exists between the specific behaviour and the set of other behaviours. In " heterotelic " activities the direction of the behaviours is outwards, in so far as there is subordination of the schemas to reality, whereas in " autotelic " activities the direction is inwards, in so far as the child, while using the same schemas, enjoys exercising his powers and being aware of himself as the cause of the activity. On the other hand, almost all the activities of the first year of life seem to be autotelic, and yet they are not always ludic. The true meaning of this first criterion is therefore to be found in the opposition between assimilation of objects to the child's activity and accommodation of the child's activity to objects. When assimilation and accommodation are not differentiated, as at the beginning of the first year, there seems to be autotelism without there being play in the strict sense, but as assimilation gains on accommodation play is divorced from the corresponding non-ludic activities. The too sharp theoretical distinction between autotelism and heterotelism thus becomes rather a difference of degree, with the whole series of transitions it involves between behaviours in which assimilation and accommodation are still in equilibrium and those in which assimilation predominates in varying degrees.

A second criterion frequently used is that of the spontaneity of play, as opposed to the compulsion of work and real adaptation. But are the primitive intellectual investigations of the child, and even those of pure science, not equally " spontaneous " ? If what is intended is a more precise distinction between the " superior " games, science and art, and games which are not " superior " but just games, all that can be done is once again to distinguish two poles, the one truly spontaneous, since it is uncontrolled, the other controlled by society or by reality. But viewed in this way, this second criterion amounts to the same as the first: play is assimilation of reality to the ego, as distinct from " serious " thought, in which the assimilating process is in equilibrium with accommodation to other persons and things.

A third criterion often applied is that of pleasure. Play is an activity " for pleasure," while serious activity is directed towards a useful result irrespective of its pleasurable character. This might be expressed as autotelism and heterotelism translated into affective terms. But it confuses the issue even more, for much " work " properly so-called has no other subjective end than satisfaction or pleasure and yet it is not play. Can we agree with Claparède that play is an immediate realisation of desires or needs while work is a mediate realisation? But it is more than a question of degree of complexity. The action of grasping for the sake of grasping may be a non-ludic exercise although there may be immediate satisfaction, and on the other hand a game may involve all kinds of complicated intermediaries. Freud has expressed the exact shade of difference, in similar terms, in contrasting the " Lustprinzip " and the " Realitätsprinzip " : on one side immediate satisfaction by way of non-compliance with the laws of reality, and on the other adaptation to reality in which there is an element of satisfaction, which is, however, subordinated to a kind of compliance, or respect for objective data. But one difficulty still remains. Certain games (which we called symbolic games of liquidation) are symbolic reproductions of painful occurences with the sole aim of digesting and assimilating them (obs. 86). In such games we have situations analogous to those described, on another plane, by Freud himself as being beyond the pleasure principle: "Jenseits des Lustprinzips." These cases show that mere assimilation, in the form of repetition of an experienced event, even when such experience was painful, is the primary factor in play and is more widespread than the pursuit of pleasure for its own sake. Once this is understood, the difficulty disappears, for it is clear that although play sometimes takes the form of repetition of painful states of mind, it does so not in order that the pain shall be preserved, but so that it may become bearable, and even pleasurable, through assimilation to the whole activity of the ego. In a word, it is possible to reduce play to pleasure-seeking, but with the proviso that the pursuit of pleasure is conceived as subordinated to the assimilation of reality to the ego. Ludic pleasure then becomes the affective expression of this assimilation.

A fourth criterion which is sometimes applied, particularly by American writers, is the relative lack of organisation in play. Play is considered to be devoid of organised structure and contrasted with serious thought, which is always ordered. Here, again, one of Freud's remarks has bearing on the criterion. In his view, symbolic thought (in the Freudian sense of unconscious symbolism) is not "directed," in contrast to logical thought which is systematically directed. But this criterion also can be reduced to that of assimilation. Why is it that a day-dream or a symbolic game is not "directed," unless because reality is being assimilated to the whims of the ego instead of being thought in accordance with rules?

A fifth criterion, which is of interest to us, is freedom from conflicts. Conflicts are foreign to play, or, if they do occur, it is so that the ego may be freed from them by compensation or liquidation, whereas serious activity has to grapple with conflicts which are inescapable. There is no doubt that this criterion is on the whole sound. The conflict between obedience and individual liberty is, for example, the affliction of childhood, and in real life the only solutions to this conflict are submission, revolt, or co-operation which involves some measure of compromise. In play, however, the conflicts are transposed in such a way that the ego is revenged, either by supression of the problem or by giving it an acceptable solution. But what this criterion does is to stress only one aspect of ludic assimilation in general. It is an important aspect, but nevertheless it is only part of the whole picture. It is because the ego dominates the whole universe in play that it is freed from conflicts, and not the converse, unless when we speak of conflicts we mean any limitation of the ego by reality.

Finally, there is the interesting criterion suggested by Mrs. Curti: overmotivation.[1] For instance, sweeping a floor is not a game, but the fact of describing a figure as one sweeps gives it a ludic character (*cf.* the child cutting his spinach into little squares as he eats it, or taking " one spoonful for mummy," " one for daddy," etc.). Judged by this criterion, play would begin when incentives not contained in the initial action are included, and additional incentives would be characteristic of all play. But it then becomes a question of determining the nature of these ludic incentives, for it cannot be asserted that every behaviour which has successive polyvalent incentives is thereby play. In each particular case, the incentives depend on the pleasure gained through unrestricted combinations, or through symbolic imagination. But since this is so, we come back once again to the fact that an activity becomes ludic merely through a process used by the ego to integrate a reality which was independent of it and which sometimes required painful accommodation. Overmotivation thus becomes merely another way of expressing the predominance of assimilation.

To sum up, it is clear that all the criteria suggested in order to define play in relationship to non-ludic activity result, not in making a clear distinction between the two, but rather in stressing the fact that the tonality of an activity is ludic in proportion as it has a certain orientation. This amounts to saying that play is distinguishable by a modification, varying in degree, of the conditions of equilibrium between reality and the ego. We can therefore say that if adapted activity and thought constitute an equilibrium between assimilation and accommodation, play begins as soon as there is predominance of assimilation. This criterion seems to be generally applicable, from the merely functional assimilation characteristic of practice games, to the varied forms of assimilation of reality to thought found in symbolic games. Since all thought involves assimilation, and ludic assimilation is only distinctive in that it subordinates accommodation instead of being in equilibrium with it, play is to be conceived as being both related to adapted thought by a continuous sequence of intermediaries, and bound up with thought as a whole, of which it is only one pole, more or less differentiated. This is what we shall now find in an examination of the three main theories of play.

§ 2.   *The Theory of Pre-exercise*

The importance of the ideas which as long ago as 1896 K. Groos

[1] Curti, M. W.   *Child Psychology.*   Longmans Green, 1930.

opposed to the accepted views on play cannot be exaggerated. In spite of the prophetic visions of the great educationists, play has always been considered, in traditional education, as a kind of mental waste-matter, or at least as a pseudo-activity, without functional significance, and even harmful to children, keeping them from their homework. For its part, common-sense, imbued with the adulto-centrism which has been the great obstacle in genetic research, saw in play only a relaxation, or a drain for superfluous energy, without enquiring why children play in one way rather than in another. Groos's great merit is to have understood that a phenomenon which is so general, common to the higher animals and man, cannot be explained outside the laws of psycho-physiological maturation. In other words, K. Groos saw in play a phenomenon of growth, growth of thought and of activity, and he was the first to ask why the various forms of play exist. Moreover, being an æsthetician as well as a psychologist, Groos was interested in play in relation to art, and it was the mechanism of imagination in particular that he sought to explain. K. Groos's doctrine has therefore two quite distinct aspects: a general theory of play as pre-exercise, and a special theory of symbolic imagination. It is true that the originality of his theory lies precisely in his interpretation of " make-believe " as pre-exercise. This makes it all the more necessary to distinguish the two parts of his thesis, for although we have no difficulty in accepting the essentials of the first as far as practice games are concerned, the second seems to us unsatisfactory when we consider symbolic games.

Play, according to Groos, is " pre-exercise " and not merely exercise, because it contributes to the development of functions whose maturity is reached only at the end of childhood: general functions such as intelligence, etc., to which games of trial and error are related, and special functions or particular instincts. (The spring of activity is for Groos instinctive in character.) But instinct comes into play at its own time and requires preparation beforehand. The preparatory exercise necessary for its maturation, and which therefore must take place before maturation is achieved, is the specific occupation of childhood, and that is play. Groos had previously said in *The Games of Animals* " animals are young so that they may be able to play." The pleasure which accompanies the stimulation of any instinctive tendency, and the joy inherent in any successful action, the well-known " joy of being the cause," are the affective concomitants of this pre-exercise. From them consciousness of make-believe will be derived. " The joy of being the cause " involves consciousness of an aim. Far from being purposeless activity, play can only be conceived as the pursuit of specific ends. But the simplest aim is immanent in pre-exercise: the puppy which seizes another by the scruff of the neck is only stimulating his fighting instinct, and the joy of success is a sufficient explanation of his activity, without assuming him to be conscious of make-believe. But from the day when he can bite, and when in his pretended fights he imposes a certain limitation on his instinct, then, according to Groos, there is awareness of make-believe: symbolism is born of this pre-exercise. In short, if all play, objectively speaking, is pseudo-activity, awareness of make-believe is the consciousness of this pseudo-activity, and follows from it sooner or later.

Awareness of make-believe is extended into "imagination," *i.e.*, "the faculty of considering mere representations as real." In dreams and delirium, we are deceived by imagination, because we then have "an illusion not imbibed by the ego; in play and art, on the contrary, there is deliberate, conscious illusion." Konrad Lange's idea of deliberate illusion is thus used by Groos to describe what he calls a kind of "duplication of consciousness," imagination representing the ludic aim as real, while the pleasure of being the cause reminds us that it is we who are creating the illusion. This is why play is accompanied by a feeling of freedom and is the herald of art, which is the full flowering of this spontaneous creation.

Leaving aside the reservations that might be made to this comparison between play and art, we shall show that, in spite of the ingenious efforts of K. Groos, symbolic imagination cannot merely be considered as the interiorised interpretation of the behaviours of pre-exercise, and therefore preparatory exercise and awareness of make-believe cannot be reduced to a simple unit. It is true that, about the beginning of the second year, symbolic imagination is added to the earlier sensory-motor practice games (obs. 65), but it is in the same way as conceptual representation continues the schemas of sensory-motor intelligence, and this in no way implies that the former is mere awareness of the latter. On the contrary, once it is constituted, the ludic symbol orientates play in new directions, further and further removed from simple practice.

Let us first consider the notion of pre-exercise, and ask ourselves whether it is indispensable in comparison with that of exercise and nothing more. In the first place, it is descriptive rather than explanatory. Wundt has already objected strongly to the finalism which in Groos's work sometimes takes the place of causal explanation. It is true that Groos refers to instincts, and if these exist, it is natural that they should be activated prior to their maturation, in which case the initial exercise could be called "pre-exercise" in contrast to the final activations. But without wishing to discuss here the role of training in the "instincts" of animals (see the work of Kuo on the predatory instinct in cats), we do not believe that the problem of the existence of instincts in man has been solved, apart from the two definite cases where the instinctive tendency corresponds to differentiated organs and therefore to innate techniques forming specific reflex systems (sexual and nutritive instincts). As for children's games, leaving aside the much more complex question of symbolic games and games with rules, can all practice games be considered to be " pre-exercise " of particular instincts or general functions? It would be an exaggeration to make such a statement, and we fail to see what the idea of " pre-exercise " adds to that of mere " exercise." What is exercised in play is any new acquirement, or anything in process of being acquired, and although this exercise, by developing the mechanism involved, obviously contributes to its consolidation, we should be guilty of unjustified finalism in explaining ludic exercise as preparation for future stages in which the mechanism being exercised will be integrated. For instance, when at about the age of one the child discovers free fall, he amuses himself by throwing everything to the ground. In this way he exercises his new power, which will one day be integrated in his knowledge of the laws of the physical world, but there is certainly no pre-exercise of his future understanding of physics. By the same reasoning, we are prepared to see in games of this kind exercise of existing intelligence, but not pre-exercise of future intelligence, unless the term pre-exercise be used in a purely temporal and not in a teleological sense.

Freed from its finalism, the idea of pre-exercise becomes that of functional assimilation.[1] Just as any organ assimilates (and therefore develops) by functioning, so any behaviour or mental mechanism is consolidated by active repetition. Baldwin's " circular reaction " has no other meaning, and all the child's early activity obeys the same principle. But although sensory-motor assimilation, *i.e.*, active repetition of behaviours and incorporation of external objects into this activity, thus constitutes one of the essential poles of psychic development, there is during the process of any adaptation, a second pole determined by the accommodation of schemas to the specific character of these same objects. Play begins when this accommodation becomes of secondary importance because it is subordinated more or less completely by assimilation. The attempt at accommodation is then replaced by action for its own sake, the " pleasure of being the cause " so well described by K. Groos. We must repeat, however, that this preponderant, ludic assimilation can only be exercise, and not pre-exercise.

A much more complex question arises with the appearance of make-believe and symbolic play. We agree with Groos that there is a relationship between symbolic and practice play, since we shall find in symbolism a product of the same assimilating process that explains exercise as such. In both our theses then, there is correspondence between symbol and exercise, but for Groos symbolic make-believe is only the interior interpretation of the objective fact of pre-exercise,

[1] It is in this sense that Carr considered play to be a stimulus to growth.

while for us symbolic play is mental assimilation, as practice play is sensory-motor assimilation, without the content of all symbolic play necessarily being practice play.

The main question, therefore, is this: does exercise as such lead *ipso facto* to symbolic make-believe? For us, a negative answer seems imperative, and this for two reasons. In the first place, the young child during its whole first year, as well as all the animal species which play (except the chimpanzees), seems to know nothing of make-believe, although he is able to play practice games. It is a definite anthropomorphic abuse on the part of Groos to assume that the puppy which bites another puppy in play is conscious of make-believe, when the mechanism of opposite tendencies (liking and pleasure inhibiting combativeness) is an adequate explanation of this " self-restraint " without there being any question of representation. In the second place it is impossible to prove that all the symbolic games of children prepare them for a specific activity, or even for general activity. Once the symbol is constituted, it goes far beyond practice, and even if we confine ourselves to saying that it trains thought as a whole we then have to explain why there is any need for symbols and make-believe, and not just exercise of conceptual thought as such. Why, indeed, does the child play at being a shopkeeper, a driver, a doctor? If it is suggested that such games are pre-exercise, by analogy with the games of little goats capering or kittens running after a ball of wool, we then ask why L. (obs. 80) played at being a church, imitating the rigidity of the steeple and the sound of the bells, and why J. (obs. 86) lay motionless like the dead duck she had seen on a table. Far from being preparatory exercises, most of the games we have given as examples either reproduce what has struck the child, evoke what has pleased him or enable him to be more fully part of his environment. In a word they form a vast network of devices which allow the ego to assimilate the whole of reality, *i.e.*, to integrate it in order to re-live it, to dominate it or to compensate for it. Even games with dolls, which might lend themselves to a special interpretation, are much less pre-exercise of the maternal instinct than an infinitely varied symbolic system which provides the child with all the means of assimilation it needs in order to rethink past experiences.

In his commentary on K. Groos, Claparède, who was clearly aware of this fundamental difficulty, tries to compromise in this way: " In saying that the child exercises activities which will be useful to him in the future, we mean exercise of mental activities, psychic functions such as observation, manipulation, association with companions, etc." [1] This is clear, but why then have recourse to symbolism? In order to think of a church steeple or a dead duck, or to re-live a

[1] Claparède, *Psychologie de l'enfant*, 8th ed., p. 436.

scene which took place because one wouldn't eat one's soup, would it not suffice to use interior speech, *i.e.*, verbal and conceptual thought? Why imitate the church steeple, lie motionless to mime a duck, make one's doll drink imaginary soup, scolding or encouraging it the while? The answer is obvious: the child's interior thought is not as yet sufficiently precise and mobile, his logico-verbal thought is still too inadequate and too vague, while the symbol concretises and animates everything. But this means that the symbol is not to be explained by pre-exercise: it is the very structure of the child's thought.

Furthermore, while verbal and conceptual thought is collective thought and therefore inadequate to express individual experience, ludic symbolism, on the contrary, is created by the child for his own use, and the egocentrism of the signifier is thus exactly suited to the nature of what is signified. Far from being used as pre-exercise, the symbol is essentially the expression of the child's present reality. True pre-exercise, in the field of initiation to adult life, is to be found not in imaginative play, but in questions, spontaneous remarks, drawings of things observed, in a word in all "serious" activity in the making, which gives rise to exercises comparable to sensory-motor practice.

Is it true, as some parts of Groos's theory would have us believe, that symbolic games at least train imagination as such? Since symbolism does not contribute to the training of thought as a whole, being orientated in the opposite direction to logical and conceptual thought, is it a preparation for imaginative aptitudes? No doubt it is, provided that we make certain distinctions. Imagination is not a faculty, despite Groos. It is one of the two poles of all thought, that of free combination and mutual assimilation of schemas. In this sense, symbolic assimilation is a source of creative imagination, *i.e.*, of spontaneous constructive activity, as distinct from accommodation to reality and from both logical and experimental verification. It was in this sense that Baldwin had previously seen in play the beginning of deduction, *i.e.*, free construction of thought. But we must again emphasise that symbolic play will only achieve its final form of creative imagination provided that it is as it were reintegrated in thought as a whole. Since it is the outcome of assimilation, symbolism first expands this assimilation in an egocentric direction, and then, with the double progress of interiorisation of the symbol towards representational construction, and expansion of thought towards conceptualisation, symbolic assimilation is reintegrated in thought in the form of creative imagination.

To sum up, after discovering that elementary games are for exercise, K. Groos failed to find the explanation for symbolic fiction because he attempted to explain it by the content of the tendencies exercised. In his opinion the child makes do with make-believe fights or imaginary characters because he cannot really fight or nurse real babies. Like Groos, Freud also failed to understand the cause of the unconscious symbols which he himself discovered, and for the same reason, that he sought to explain them by their content. For Freud, there is symbolism because the content of the symbols has been repressed, while for Groos there is symbolic fiction because the content of the ludic symbols is still beyond the child's reach. But in both cases the formation of the symbol is not due to its content, but to the very structure of the child's thought. Wherever there is symbolism, in dreams, in the images of the half-sleeping state or in children's play, it is because thought, in its states of low psychological tension or in its elementary stages, proceeds by egocentric assimilation, and not by logical concepts.

§ 3. *The Recapitulation Theory*

While Groos's interpretation of make-believe in play reminds us in some respects of Freud's interpretation of dream symbolism, both explaining the symbol by the forbidden character of its content, Stanley Hall's famous theory is in line with that of C. G. Jung in that both these authors have recourse to heredity. This curious parallelism makes it necessary for us to say something about the theory of re-capitulation, although nowadays this conception of the ludic function is considered antiquated. Just as Jung's hypothesis of heredity of unconscious archetypes led him into a very wide investigation into the generality of the elementary symbols of humanity, so the somewhat strange ideas of Stanley Hall led his disciples and his adversaries to discover important statistical facts as to the spread and evolution of children's games. It not infrequently happens that a false theory does valuable service to science through the work of verification it involves.

The three essential points in Stanley Hall's thesis are well-known: games follow one another at relatively constant age stages, determined by the content of the ludic activities: the content corresponds to ancestral activities which have followed one another in the same order in the course of human evolution: the function of children's play is to liberate the species from these residues, at the same time hastening its development towards higher stages (hence the famous comparison between play and the tadpole's tail).

We shall not stop to enquire whether play really does " purge " the individual of his troublesome or useless tendencies. Do tin soldiers rid the child of his bellicosity, or do they " pre-exercise " him to become a good soldier? Other writers have maintained that such games compensate, or free the ego, etc. It seems to us that such questions have no significance, or rather that any explanation might be the right one in any particular case. If symbolic play is a form of thought which assimilates reality to the ego, it may fulfil any of the possible functions, just as the interior thought of the adult may purge, liquidate, or compensate as easily as it may prepare, develop or do anything else.

For us the interesting question in Stanley Hall's theory is the first one, that of regular age stages related to the content of play. On this point the facts are in direct contradiction to the theory. This does not mean that there is no regular succession in the evolution of games with age (we recognised this fact in Chaps. IV and V), but a distinction must be made between the content of play and its structure. The content consists of the particular ludic interests linked with this or that object (dolls, animals, buildings, machines, etc.), while the structure is the form of mental organisation: exercises, symbols, rules and their various varieties. In Stanley Hall's view it is the content which is inherited, and which gives rise to laws of succession analogous to embryological laws. On this point, all the statistics of Hall's school have led nowhere. It is now generally agreed, mainly as a result of the work of Lehmann and Witty,[1] that the content of games varies with the child's natural and social environment. The invention of cars, for instance, has upset the order of the stages, and even very young children who have had some experience of cars now play at pretending to change gear and start a car, games which obviously do not correspond to any biogenetic heredity. In 1929 Miss Whitley repeated Burke's well-known investigation into children's collections (1900), using children with the same American background and of the same age. The difference was remarkable. As far as the content is concerned, therefore, all the indications are that play is rather a matter of participation in the environment than of hereditary resurrection.

As to the structure, it would not be impossible to find in the development of children's games a sequence analogous to that of the behaviours of the race,[2] but it was not with this aspect of the question that Hall's school was concerned. Practice play appears long before symbolic play, just as in animals sensory-motor intelligence comes much earlier than representation, which is the prerogative of the higher apes, and even then only exists to a very rudimentary degree. Games with rules follow symbolic play just as articulate speech (necessary for the transmission of codes and therefore for their construction) follows the stage of imaged representation.

If we admit that there is a certain parallelism between children's behaviours and primitive behaviours, or those of phylogenetic development, problems of interpretation arise which raise new difficulties for Stanley Hall's theory. Either there is heredity, which is restricted

---

[1] Lehmann and Witty. *The Psychology of Play Activities*. Barnes, 1927.
[2] *Cf.* C. Gattegno. *Etude sur le Jeu*. Bulletin de l'Institut d'Egypte, Cairo, 1945. [*Tr. Note.*]

to very general functions, or else there is detailed similarity, in which case there is no question of heredity but merely of resemblances due to the fact that the same causes produce the same results. For instance, even if the capacity for constructing symbols is the result of hereditary mechanisms, it does not follow that some symbols have been inherited from the " primitives." As we know that no speech has ever become hereditary (whereas the ability to acquire articulate speech is certainly inherited), we are compelled to seek a more simple explanation than that of acquired characteristics for any similarities there may be between primitive man and the child. There is no need to seek very far, since the so-called " primitives," and even the true paleolithic or tertiary primitives, were themselves children before becoming adults. In order to explain symbolism, let us confine ourselves then to the field of the child's psychology, and we shall be more likely to discover the general phenomena than by resorting to heredity, either of content or structures.

It is none the less true that certain games with rules may have their origin in the distant past. Attempts have been made to show that games such as spillikins, and even marbles, derive from magic and divinatory practices, but in this case it is a question of social transmission and not of heredity. Moreover, nothing in adult origins of what has become ludic for the child explains the present function of these games, any more than the origin of a word explains linguistically its later position in the system of the language at any given moment.

§ 4.   F. J. J. Buytendijk's theory of " infantile dynamics "

In addition to the classic explanations of K. Groos and S. Hall there are many other interpretations of play, but it would be useless to discuss them in detail since they are rather functional descriptions than causal explanations. In this field, all the authors are right since, as we have constantly seen, play can serve all purposes. Carr sees in play a " catharsis " which not only eliminates dangerous tendencies but makes them acceptable through canalisation and sublimation. The compensating function of play was stressed by Carr, and more recently by Reaney (1916) and Robinson (1920–23). For K. Lange, the main aim of play is to complete the ego (*Ergänzungstheorie*, 1901). For W. S. Taylor and Mrs. Curti (1930) it is " free satisfaction." Delacroix, in his *Psychologie de l'Art*, supports a similar view and contrasts the primitive practice play which precedes the separation of play from work, with free creative play in which " the personality of the child is expressed as he feels inclined (p. 7). Claparède, in his *Psychology of the Child*, suggests an eclectic and flexible definition, that of " derivation through make-believe ": " The function of play is to allow the child to express his ego, to display his personality, to pursue momentarily the line of his greatest interest in cases when he cannot do so through serious activities."

All these writers agree in stating, in various ways, that play is essentially the assimilation of reality to the ego. " In play," says Claparède (*Arch. Psychol.*, Vol. XXIV, p. 363), " the ego aspires to its full expansion, and reality is only taken into account in so far as it provides the pretext. In non-ludic activity, reality is considered for its own sake." We are, however, still left with the causal problem of understanding the reason for this structure of play, and more especially symbolic fiction.

One of the few writers who has attempted to solve the structural problem is F. J. J. Buytendijk,[1] in a book in which he seeks to reduce play not to a single function but to the general characteristics of " infantile dynamics." To Groos's formula that the higher animals have a childhood in order to be able to play, Buytendijk replies that the child plays because he is a child, *i.e.*, because the essential characteristics of his " dynamics " prevent him from doing anything else but play. To the hypothesis of pre-exercise it can be objected that animals such as birds, which do not play, have instincts as perfect as those of other animals, that the part played in development by exercise is much less important than that of internal maturation, and that true pre-exercise is not play but " serious " training (this last point being completely in agreement with what we said earlier).

What, then, is the nature of " infantile dynamics "? Buytendijk ascribes to them four main characteristics capable of explaining play: sensory-motor or mental lack of coherence, impulsiveness, a " pathic " attitude as opposed to a " gnostic " attitude (*i.e.*, a need for sympathetic understanding rather than for objective knowledge), and a certain " shyness with respect to things " which keeps the child from using them, leaving him vacillating between attraction and withdrawal. From these dynamics which govern the relationship between the child and his environment, play emerges as a privileged interaction between the child, or player, and his active partner, the external object which he views as a plaything. From this point of view play is essentially ambivalent. It is a liberation by virtue of the incoherence, the impulsiveness and one of the two aspects of the shyness with respect to reality, but it is at the same time communion with the environment by virtue of the pathic attitude and the other aspect of the " shy " attitude. In its organisation, play is essentially rhythmic, from the early motor manifestations up to the dualism of tension-relaxation which Buytendijk considers to be the essential structure of play as well as the manifestation of its ambivalence. Finally, and most important, there is the role of the image, which Buytendijk understands in a very wide sense, since for him animals

[1] *Wesen und Sinn des Spiels*, Berlin (K. Wolff), 1934.

and man play only with images: the image is the actual expression of the child's " pathic " attitude to reality, it is essentially fiction, spontaneous combination and symbol.

As far as " infantile dynamics " are concerned we cannot but agree in the main with these theses, especially as Buytendijk's view, although it is expressed quite differently and with more insistence on the motor and affective aspects of the child's mind, seems to tally more than is at first apparent with our analysis of children's thought. The lack of coherence and the impulsiveness are obvious. As to the " pathic attitude " which creates an intuitive communion with the physical and social environment, and is a source of " images " which animate reality, as well as of imitation and suggestibility, it seems to us, in spite of the terms used, to correspond approximately to what we called the child's egocentrism, *i.e.*, the confusion of his own point of view with that of others. In particular, the relationship which is assumed between the pathic attitude and the " image " seems to us to be very characteristic of the intuitive and pre-operational thought peculiar to the egocentric mentality, which is proof against any objective or gnostic discipline.

But given that this is so with regard to the general mentality of the child, in our opinion Buytendijk has not made clear the details of the ludic mechanisms involved in the transition from these dynamics to play. The chief merit of his thesis lies in his statement that play essentially derives from the child's mental structure, and can only be explained by that structure. We go so far as to agree with Buytendijk that all the characteristics of these " dynamics " are to be found in play, but the great difficulty is to know where to stop. By explaining too much, Buytendijk is in danger of failing to understand the origin of play itself, as a particular case of infantile dynamics. Play is but a part of the whole infantile dynamics, and although we agree that it derives from them, the question to be answered is in what conditions it does so, and why it does not always do so. In his analysis of Buytendijk's work, Claparède rightly stressed this point: all the manifestations of infantile dynamics are not play. On the plane of thought, especially, what we called the child's animism or magic, artificialism, etc., are typical products of this egocentric or " pathic " mentality, but they are not play. The logical incoherence and imaged character of all the young child's intuitive thought is the result of this same mental structure, but it is not play. How is play, as a particular function, dissociated from this general structure? Why is it that the " image," whose scope is much wider than that of play, becomes in certain cases a make-believe or ludic symbol? In our view, we are still in the dark as to the crux of the problem, perhaps because Buytendijk failed to see clearly that a " pathic " mentality, as distinct from one that is " gnostic," is essentially egocentric, although it co-operates with the environment, and that egocentrism implies an assimilation of reality to the ego capable of being detached in varying degrees from the process of adaptation and directed towards make-believe and symbolic imagery.

§ 5. *An attempt to interpret play through the structure of the child's thought*

A baby sucks his thumb sometimes as early as the second month, grasps objects at about four or five months, shakes them, swings them, rubs them, and finally learns to throw them and retrieve them. Such behaviours involve two poles: a pole of accommodation, since there must be adjustment of movements and perceptions to the objects, but also a pole of assimilation of things to the child's own activity, since he has no interest in the things as such, but only in so far as he finds them useful for a behaviour learnt earlier or for one he is in process of acquiring. This assimilation of reality to sensory-motor schemas has two complementary aspects. On the one hand it is active repetition and consolidation (hence the " circular reaction " described by Baldwin), and in this sense it is essentially functional or reproductive assimilation, *i.e.*, growth through functioning. On the other hand, it is mental digestion, *i.e.*, perception or conception of the object in so far as it is incorporated into real or possible action. Each object is assimilated as something " to be sucked," " to be grasped," " to be shaken," etc., and is at first that and nothing more (and if it is " to be looked at " it is still being assimilated to the various focusings and movements of the eyes and acquires the " shapes " which perceptive assimilation gives it). It is obvious that in the actual activity these two functions of assimilation become one, for it is by repeating his behaviours through reproductive assimilation that the child assimilates objects to actions and that these thus become schemas. These schemas constitute the functional equivalent of concepts and of the logical relationships of later development. At all stages of the development of intelligence we find both accommodation and assimilation, but they are increasingly differentiated, and consequently more and more complementary in their increasing equilibrium. In scientific thinking, for instance, accommodation to reality is nothing but experiment, while assimilation is deduction, or incorporation of objects into logical or mathematical schemas. But there are two important differences between this rational assimilation and the initial sensory-motor assimilation. In the first place, rational assimilation is not centred in the individual, the mental activity in this case being only an assimilation of things one to another,[1] while the initial assimilation is centred in the individual, and is therefore non-opera-

---

[1] It is, of course, real activity, and the assimilation of things one to another therefore amounts to assimilating them to " operations," *i.e.*, to active schemas constructed by the mind.

tional, *i.e.*, it is egocentric or distorting. In the second place, and this second difference explains the first, rational assimilation is complementary to accommodation to things, and therefore in almost permanent equilibrium with experience, while sensory-motor assimilation is as yet undifferentiated from accommodation and gives rise to a fresh " displacement of equilibrium " with every new differentiation. Phenomenism and egocentrism are the two undissociated aspects of elementary consciousness as distinct from experimental objectivity and rational deduction.

This being so, children's play is merely the expression of one of the phases of this progressive differentiation: it occurs when assimilation is dissociated from accommodation but is not yet reintegrated in the forms of permanent equilibrium in which, at the level of operational and rational thought, the two will be complementary. In this sense, play constitutes the extreme pole of assimilation of reality to the ego, while at the same time it has something of the creative imagination which will be the motor of all future thought and even of reason.

Play begins, then, with the first dissociation between assimilation and accommodation. After learning to grasp, swing, throw, etc., which involve both an effort of accommodation to new situations, and an effort of repetition, reproduction and generalisation, which are the elements of assimilation, the child sooner or later (often even during the learning period) grasps for the pleasure of grasping, swings for the sake of swinging, etc. In a word, he repeats his behaviour not in any further effort to learn or to investigate, but for the mere joy of mastering it and of showing off to himself his own power of subduing reality. Assimilation is dissociated from accommodation by subordinating it and tending to function by itself, and from then on practice play occurs. Since it requires neither thought nor social life, practice play can be explained as the direct result of the primacy of assimilation. The " functional pleasure " and pleasure of being the cause, which accompany this type of play, raise no particular problem, since the first comes from the *sui generis* character of this assimilation for the sake of assimilation, with no need for new accommodation, and the second from the fact that when the child has overcome the difficulties inherent in the corresponding " serious " action, the assimilation is more concentrated on his own activity.

The appearance of symbolism, on the other hand, is the crucial point in all the interpretations of the ludic function. Why is it that play becomes symbolic, instead of continuing to be mere sensory-motor exercise or intellectual experiment, and why should the enjoyment of movement, or activity for the fun of activity, which constitute a kind of practical make-believe, be completed at a given moment by imaginative make-believe? The reason is that among the attributes of assimilation for assimilation's sake is that of distortion, and therefore to the extent to which it is dissociated from immediate accommodation it is a source of symbolic make-believe. This explains why there is symbolism as soon as we leave the sensory-motor level for that of representational thought.

Although the distinction between practice play and symbolic play is greater than is generally thought (even Buytendijk supports Groos's ideas on this point), since their respective origins are to be found on two quite different levels of behaviour, there is still an undeniable relationship between them: *symbolic play is to practice play as representational intelligence is to sensory-motor intelligence.* And to this correspondence at two different levels must be added one at the same level: *symbolic play is to representational intelligence what practice play is to sensory-motor intelligence, i.e.,* a deviation in the direction of pure assimilation.

Representative thought, as distinct from sensory-motor activity, begins as soon as the " signifier " is differentiated from the " signified " in the system of significations which constitutes the whole intelligence and indeed the whole consciousness. In the process of adaptation through sensory-motor schemas there are already " signifiers." They are the " indices " which enable the child to recognise objects and relationships, to assimilate consciously and even to imitate. But the index is only one aspect of the object or of the situation, and is therefore not a " signifier " which is differentiated from the " signified." Language, on the other hand, provides the prototype of a system of distinct signifiers, since in verbal behaviour the signifier is the collective " signs " or words, while the signified is the meaning of the words, *i.e.,* the concepts which at this new level take the place of the pre-verbal sensory-motor schemas. Verbal, properly conceptual intelligence occupies this privileged position in representational thought by virtue of the fact that verbal signs are social, and that through their use the system of concepts attains sooner or later (later than is usually supposed) a high degree of socialisation. But between the index and the sign, or between the sensory-motor schema and the logical concept, the symbolic image and imaged or pre-conceptual representation have their place. As we have seen, the image is interiorised imitation, *i.e.,* the positive of accommodation, which is the negative of the imitated object. The image is therefore a schema which has already been accommodated and is now used in present assimilations, which are also interiorised, as " signifier " for these " signified." The image is therefore a differentiated signifier, more so than the index since it is detached from the perceived object, but less so than the sign, since it is still imitation of the object, and therefore is a " motivated " sign, as distinct from verbal signs which are " arbitrary." Moreover, the image is a signifier which is within the scope of individual thought, while the pure sign is always social. For this reason there is in all verbal and conceptual thought a stratum of imaged representation which enables the individual to assimilate for himself the general idea common to all, and for this reason also, the nearer we get to early childhood the more important is the role of imaged representation and intuitive thought. Each image has a corresponding object (*i.e.*, the concept of this object) which, even in the adult, serves as a representative or example of the general class of which it is a part, and which in the child is a partial substitute for the general class which is not yet constructed.

This then being the mechanism of adapted thought, which is the equilibrium between assimilation and accommodation, we can understand the role of the symbol in play, where accommodation is subordinated to assimilation. The ludic symbol also is an image, and therefore imitation, and therefore accommodation. But the relationship between assimilation and accommodation in play differs from that in cognitive or adapted representation precisely because play is the predominance of assimilation and no longer an equilibrium between the two functions. (1) In the case of the adapted image there is exact imitation, or at least imitation which aims at exactness, *i.e.*, a one-one correspondence with the object signified. For instance, the representation of a triangle can be obtained by a real imitation (a drawing, or an indication of the figure by movement of a finger), or by a purely mental imitation (an interior image or " intuition " of a triangle), but there is then correspondence between the parts of the drawing, those of the image and those of the object represented. But when in play one thing is symbolised by another, *e.g.*, a cat walking on a wall by a shell moved with the hand along a cardboard box, there is a whole series of signifiers, related one to another, but further and further removed from the real situation. First there is the shell representing the cat and the box representing the wall ; then there is imitation through gesture, *i.e.*, the movement of the hand representing the cat walking ; finally there is presumably the mental image of the cat on the wall, an image which may be vague and undifferentiated since it is supported by motor imitation and the symbol-object. (2) The representation of a triangle is adequate and exact in so far as the triangle raises a problem, *i.e.*, gives rise to a need for adaptation to reality, with accommodation to the object and assimilation of the object to a system of relationships not centred in the ego, while the evocation of the cat on the wall has no other purpose than temporary satisfaction of the ego : it is a " pathic " and not a " gnostic " attitude, to use Buytendijk's terms, but it is at the same time egocentric and not objective. We have here the explanation of the difference seen in (1). (3) In cognitive representation the mental or material image represents a particular object whose concept (the particular class) serves as a single representative or example of the general class of which it is a part. For instance, the triangle which is drawn represents all triangles, or at least all triangles of that class. But in play, the symbol-object is not only the representative of the signified, but also its substitute (the shell becomes for the moment a cat), whether the signified is general (any cat) or particular (a definite cat). In cognitive representation, therefore, there is adaptation to the signified (*i.e.*, equilibrium between assimilation and accommodation), while the signifier consists of images, which are exactly accommodated or imitated, and whose corresponding object is only one representative of a general class. In the symbolic representation of play, on the contrary, the signified is merely assimilated to the ego, *i.e.*, it is evoked for temporary interest or for immediate satisfaction, and the signifier is then less exact mental imitation than imitation by means of material pictures in which the objects are themselves assimilated to the signified as substitutes, by reason of resemblances which may be extremely vague and subjective. In a word, while in cognitive representation there is a permanent equilibrium between assimilation and accommodation, in ludic symbolism there is a predominance of assimilation in the relationship between the child and the signified, and even in the construction of the signifier.

This being so, the connection between symbolic assimilation, which is the source of make-believe play, and functional assimilation, which is the source of practice play, is at once obvious. Both symbol and concept already exist, in a sense, in sensory-motor assimilation. When the baby who has learnt to swing an object swings other objects, this generalised schema is the functional equivalent of the concept, because each particular case belongs to the general class of things " to be swung " of which it has become a representative or example. The same applies in the case of things " to be sucked," etc. But when the baby wants to go on sucking after his meal is over, and finds compensation in sucking his thumb, the thumb is more than a representative example. It becomes a substitute, and could even be considered a symbol if it were possible for the baby to evoke his mother's breast at the same time. But in spite of the Freudians, for whom such symbols exist as early as the age of two months, and in spite of K. Groos, who sees make-believe in all practice play, in our opinion there cannot be symbolism, consciousness of make-believe, before there is representation, which begins and gradually develops at the beginning of the second year, when sensory-motor assimilation becomes mental assimilation through differentiation between signifier and signified. When J. pretended to be asleep, holding a corner of the sheet and bending her head, the sensory-motor schema thus set in motion resulted in more than mere exercise, since it served to evoke a past situation, and the corner of the sheet became a conscious substitute for the absent pillow. With the projection of such

" symbolic schemas " on to other objects, the way is clear for the assimilation of any one object to another, since any object can be a make-believe substitute for any other.

The causality of symbolic play now becomes clear, since it derives essentially from the structure of the child's thought. Symbolic play represents in thought the pole of assimilation, and freely assimilates reality to the ego. As we said earlier, it is therefore to practice play what adapted thought is to sensory-motor intelligence, and it is to adapted thought what practice play is to sensory-motor intelligence, *i.e.*, the assimilating pole. But why is there assimilation of reality to the ego instead of immediate assimilation of the universe to experimental and logical thought? It is simply because in early childhood this thought has not yet been constructed, and during its development it is inadequate to supply the needs of daily life. Moreover, the most adapted and most logical thought of which the young child is capable is still pre-logical and egocentric, its structure being intermediate between the symbolic thought of play and adult thought.[1]

To sum up what has already been said, symbolic play is merely egocentric thought in its pure state. The essential condition for objectivity of thought is that assimilation of reality to the system of adapted notions shall be in permanent equilibrium with accommodation of these same notions to things and to the thought of others. It is obvious that it is only by the constitution of systems of logical operations (reversibility of transformations of thought), of moral operations (preservation of values) and spatio-temporal operations (reversible organisation of elementary physical notions), that such an equilibrium can be achieved, for it is only through operational reversibility that thought becomes capable of preserving its notions despite the fluctuations of reality and incessant contact with the unexpected. The reversible operation is at the same time an expression of the modifications of reality and the regulated transformations of thought, and is therefore both accommodation and assimilation. As elementary operations only begin to be " grouped " towards the end of early childhood it is natural that in the preceding stages the child's mind should be in a constant state of flux between three states: temporary equilibrium (liable to continual " displacements ") between assimilation and accommodation, intermittent accommodation displacing the previous equilibrium, and assimilation of reality to the ego, *i.e.*, to that aspect of thought which is still centred on itself because correlative accommodation is lacking. It follows that for the child assimilation of reality to the ego is a vital condition for continuity and development, precisely because of the lack of equilibrium in his thought, and symbolic play satisfies this condition both as regards signifier and signified.

[1] See our article, 1923. La pensée symbolique et la pensée de l'enfant, *Arch. de Psych.*, Vol. XVIII, p. 273.

From the point of view of the signified, play enables the child to re-live his past experiences and makes for the satisfaction of the ego rather than for its subordination to reality. From the point of view of the signifier, symbolism provides the child with the live, dynamic, individual language indispensable for the expression of his subjective feelings, for which collective language alone is inadequate. The symbol-object, being a real substitute for the signified, makes it actually present in a way that the verbal sign can never achieve. Since the child's whole thought is still egocentric and intuitive even in its states of maximal adaptation, and is thus linked at every inter-mediate stage with symbolic play, this form of play can be considered to be one of the poles of thought as a whole : the pole at which assimilation is dissociated from accommodation, or in other words, from egocentric thought in its pure state.

Symbolic play, then, is only one form of thought, linked to all the others by its mechanism, but having as its sole aim satisfaction of the ego, *i.e.*, individual truth as opposed to collective and impersonal truth, but we are still faced by the question of why the use of the symbol as opposed to the verbal concept results in make-believe and not in belief. The natural attitude of the mind is belief, and doubt or hypothesis are complex, derived behaviours whose development can be traced between the ages of seven and eleven up to the level of formal operations, at which there is a real distinction between thought and spontaneous acceptance. But although none of the conditions for this hypothetical-deductive thought obtain in the play of very young children, they make statements for the sake of stating, without believing in the game they are playing. It is a commonplace that children make the distinction between pretence and reality very early. How, then, is pretence to be explained, and why is it that ludic symbolism is divorced from belief, in contrast to the symbolism of dreams and delirium and the religious symbolism of primitive tribes? It is a complicated question, for as Janet has shown, there are various types of belief. At the level of early childhood there are two con-trasting types, the one connected with social, and more particularly adult behaviours, the other with spontaneous and egocentric indi-vidual behaviours. The first is Janet's " promise-belief " an accept-ance of others and of the adult, and therefore adherence to the reality which is generally approved. The second is Janet's " assertive belief," which precedes the distinction between what is certain and what is doubtful, and is linked with any impact of reality on the mind. At a later stage there is " reflective belief," associated with the mechanism of intellectual and affective operations, as for example, belief as a result of a deduction, or a deliberate, considered decision. When the child plays, he certainly does not believe, in the sense of socialised belief, in the content of his symbolism, but precisely because symbolism is egocentric thought we have no reason to suppose that he does not believe *in his own way* anything he chooses. From this point of view the " deliberate illusion " which Lange and Groos see in play is merely the child's refusal to allow the world of adults or of ordinary reality to interfere with play, so as to enjoy a private reality of his own. But this reality is believed in spontaneously, without effort, merely because it is the universe of the ego, and the function of play is to protect this universe against forced accommodation to ordinary reality. There is no question, therefore, in the early stages of symbolic play, of consciousness of make-believe like that of drama or poetry.[1] The two- to four-year-old child does not consider whether his ludic symbols are real or not. He is aware in a sense that they are not so for others, and makes no serious effort to persuade the adult that they are. But for him it is a question which does not arise, because symbolic play is direct satisfaction of the ego and has its own kind of belief, which is a subjective reality. Moreover, as the symbol-object is a substitute for the reality it signifies, there develops, during the first stages, a kind of co-operation between the two, analogous to that between the image and the object it represents.

The question then is whether collective symbolic games result in the strengthening or weakening of belief, and the answer depends on age. In the case of very young children, collective play either has no effect on the egocentric symbolism or, when there is imitation, it enhances it. In the case of older children, in whose play the symbols are replaced by rules, it is obvious that the effect of social life is to weaken ludic belief, at least in its specifically symbolic form.

Games with rules remain to be considered in the light of what has been said above. We have seen that they mark the decline of children's games and the transition to adult play, which ceases to be a vital function of the mind when the individual is socialised. In games with rules there is a subtle equilibrium between assimilation to the ego—the principle of all play—and social life. There is still sensory-motor or intellectual satisfaction, and there is also the chance of individual victory over others, but these satisfactions are as it were made " legitimate " by the rules of the game, through which competition is controlled by a collective discipline, with a code of honour and fair play. This third and last type of play is therefore not inconsistent with the idea of assimilation of reality to the ego, while at the same time it reconciles this ludic assimilation with the demands of social reciprocity.

---

[1] It is only after the age of seven that play really becomes make-believe in contrast to " reflective belief."

CHAPTER VII

SECONDARY SYMBOLISM IN PLAY, DREAMS, AND " UNCONSCIOUS " SYMBOLISM

ALTHOUGH make-believe play is the most important manifestation of " symbolic thought " in the child, it is not identical with it, and in order to have a complete picture of the development of the symbol and the mental image we must examine the question of the " unconscious " symbol, *i.e.*, the child's dreams, and also a certain ludic symbolism which is less conscious than that of ordinary make-believe and which we shall call " secondary symbolism." A whole volume would be needed to deal fully with these vast problems, which involve the whole question of psycho-analysis. We shall confine ourselves here to a few indications only, those which are necessary for the achievement of the theoretical aim of this book.

Symbolic play raises the question of " symbolic thought " in general, in contrast to rational thought whose instrument is the sign. A sign, as conceived by the school of de Saussure, is an " arbitrary " signifier, related to its signified by a social convention and not by any resemblance between them. Such are words, or verbal signs, and mathematical symbols (which are not symbols in the sense in which we use the word here). Since it is social, and therefore liable to generalisation and abstraction in contrast to individual experience, the system of signs makes possible the formation of rational thought. The symbol, according to the same linguistic school, is a " motivated " signifier, *i.e.*, there is a resemblance of some kind between it and its signified. A metaphor, for instance, is a symbol because there is a relationship between the image used and the object to which it refers, a relationship which is not due to a social convention but directly experienced by the mind of the individual. The symbol will therefore be used in " affective language," to express feelings and concrete experiences, rather than in " intellectual language " to express impersonal thoughts.

It is interesting to note that the word " symbol " as defined by the school of de Saussure is identical in meaning with that used by the various psycho-analytic schools: an image which has a meaning distinct from its immediate content, and in which there is a more or less direct resemblance between signifier and signified. But to the conscious symbol, *i.e.*, one which has a clear meaning for the subject himself (*e.g.*, a symbolic cartoon used by a newspaper to evade government censorship) Freud adds the unconscious symbol, whose meaning is hidden from the subject. As the English psycho-analysts have said, there are therefore two kinds of symbols: " metaphors " and " crypto-phors." Symbolic thought for Freud, Jung and many others is a form of thought independent of verbal signs, and even opposed by its structure and function to rational thought which uses signs. It is a form of thought whose individual and even intimate nature has been emphasised in contrast to socialised thought, since it is mainly found in dreams and day dreams: hence the idea of " autism." It is a form of thought whose roots are essentially " unconscious."

But the very existence of imaginative or make-believe play, which plays so important a part in the child's thought, proves that symbolic thought extends beyond the unconscious, and that is why we have called this form of ludic activity " symbolic play." There is, no doubt, evidence in the field of children's play of a more hidden symbolism, indicating in the child anxieties of which he may be unaware. The specialists in child analysis (M. Klein, Anna Freud, Löwenfeld, and others), have evolved a whole technique of psycho-analysis of play, based on the study of these " unconscious " ludic symbols. The problem is to discover whether a clear line of demarca-tion exists between the child's conscious symbolism and the hidden symbolism. We shall begin this chapter with a few remarks on secondary symbolism in the play and dreams of the child, in order to prove that there is no such separation and that symbolic thought forms a single whole.

In 1922, at the International Conference on Psychoanalysis in Berlin, we presented a short paper, in which Freud had been interested, on " Symbolic thought and the thought of the child." [1] In it we tried to show that the whole thought of the child, being syncretic and pre-logical, offers analogies with " unconscious " symbolic thought, and even appears to be intermediate between it and rational thought. But there are two possible derivations for such a relationship. Either dreams, the vast " chaos of the unconscious," are the first to exist and from them the child's thought and then logical thought emerge, or else the child's conscious thought is the first datum, first in the form of sensory-motor activity and intelligence, then as thought which is semi-socialised but still preconceptual and imaged, and whose higher intuitive activities, aided by social life, produce the operations of reason. Parallel with this development (and according as it is accom-modation which predominates over assimilation, or the reverse), appear either imitation, the simple image, etc., or play and dreams with " unconscious " symbolism as the extreme pole (the symbolism being unconscious to the extent to which egocentrism, which is at its maximum in dreams, leads to the suppression of the ego's conscious-ness of itself). It therefore seems to us essential to examine in this

[1] *Arch. de Psychol.*, Vol. XVIII, p. 273.

chapter the problems of unconscious symbolism and the main psycho-analytic interpretations. These questions are vital to our subject, and an examination of them will give us the best proof of the relationship between the formation of the image and the ludic symbol in the child, and the mechanism of symbolism in general.

§ 1. *Secondary symbolism in play and children's dreams*

When in play a child assimilates one object to another, it can usually be said that this assimilation is conscious. For instance, when J. at 1 ; 10 used a shell on a box to represent a cat on a wall, she was perfectly conscious of the meaning of the symbol since she said: " cat on the wall " (obs. 77). We shall call such cases conscious or primary symbols (primary symbols, and not primary assimilations, because there are much more elementary assimilations, *e.g.*, assimilation of the thumb to the mother's breast, which are not symbolic since there is no representation). But in many games we find symbols whose significance is not understood by the child himself. For instance, a child who has been made jealous by the birth of a younger brother and happens to be playing with two dolls of unequal size, will make the smaller one go away on a journey, while the bigger one stays with its mother. Assuming that the child is unaware that he is thinking of his younger brother and himself, we shall call a case of this kind secondary or unconscious symbolism.

Although this distinction is obvious in extreme cases, it is very relative, and in two ways, first because there are all the intermediary stages between conscious and unconscious symbolic assimilation, and then because all symbols are conscious from one angle and unconscious from another, since all thought, even the most rational, is both conscious and unconscious.

Let us first consider the intermediary stages between conscious and unconscious symbolism. They are to be found most commonly in the field of liquidating or compensating games, *i.e.*, those which, in addition to satisfying the ego in general, fulfil a definite affective function. For instance, when J. (obs. 86) liquidated a hurt I had unintentionally done her by reproducing the scene with inverted roles, she knew very well what she was doing, and the symbolism was primary. But when a child who has been frightened by a dog or a plane plays symbolically with " nice dogs " or planes that do not frighten the dolls, it is quite possible that the child has no recollection of the real scenes which are symbolised, and the symbols may be secondary. It is therefore among the affective symbols that secondary assimilations will occur, and the more intense the affectivity, the more frequent will be the assimilations, but it is, of course, a question of degree and not of water-tight compartments, since all symbolism implies interest and affective significance, as does all thought.

The distinction is relative also because every symbol is at the same time conscious and unconscious. Obviously it is always conscious in its result. As to the assimilation which makes the symbol, it probably never results in complete awareness, either affective or intellectual. In the example of the shell assimilated to a cat, why did the child choose to evoke a cat rather than anything else? He certainly had no idea. The shell may have symbolised only the cat seen earlier on the wall, but it may have symbolised other cats, other animals, other moving bodies, in fact, a whole possible series of related schemas, the mechanism of which would explain both why this particular cat was chosen and also the structure of symbolism in general. We must observe at this point, to avoid losing ourselves in a mythology of the unconscious, that what has just been said is true of all thought, rational as well as symbolic, and that while the result of all mental work is conscious, its mechanism remains hidden. The unconscious is not a separate region of the mind, since in every psychic process there is a continual and continuous coming and going from the unconscious to consciousness.[1] While accommodation of thought is generally conscious, because external or internal obstacles call forth consciousness, assimilation, even when rational, is usually unconscious. In intentional generalisation (*cf.* Newtonian attraction applied to molecular affinity) it is conscious because of the demands of accommodation, but in the underlying preparation of the original ideas it is not conscious (in Aristotle's physics there was unconscious assimilation of the physical facts of force, movement, position, etc., to schemas of bodily origin). Viewed thus, the nesting of schemas as seen in symbolic thought is no more mysterious than that to be found in any work of the intelligence. The unconscious is everywhere, and there is an intellectual as well as an affective unconscious. This means that it does not exist as a " region," and that the difference between consciousness and the unconscious is only a matter of gradation or degree of reflection.

It must be clearly understood, then, that symbols cannot be classified once and for all as either primary or secondary. Every symbol is, or may be, both, *i.e.*, it may have, in addition to its immediate meaning which is understood by the subject, more remote meanings, in exactly the same way that an idea, in addition to what is consciously involved in the reasoning of the moment, may contain a set of implications of which the subject is temporarily unaware, or of which he has long or even always been unaware. This being so, the primary symbols analysed in Chap. V might also be secondary symbols, and there are other cases in which there is almost no doubt that they contain more

[1] In his research on the act of intelligence, Binet came to the profound conclusion that " thought is an unconscious process of the mind " and Claparède, in his search for the origin of hypotheses in intellectual discovery, came to a similar conclusion.

than the child consciously puts into them, and which are therefore secondary.

Among the latter there are three groups of ludic symbols: those related to interests connected with the child's own body (suction, excretion), those related to elementary family feelings (love, jealousy, aggression) and those related to anxieties centred on the birth of babies. It is well-known how regularly these motives occur in the character troubles of the children who frequent child guidance clinics, and how many traces of them are to be found in the fantasies and dreams of adults undergoing psycho-analytic treatment. Moreover, direct observation shows that when these interests are present in the ludic symbols the child usually shows evidence of a state of slight excitement (a special way of laughing, etc.) or sometimes embarrassment at being heard, which in themselves indicate the existence of a content which is something more than that of the primary symbol.

Here are a few examples illustrative of the three categories:

OBS. 95. At 2 ; 6 (3), and on the following days, X. pretended to suck at his mother's breast after seeing a baby being suckled. This game was repeated at about 2 ; 9.

As early as 1 ; 4 (15) X., after simulating certain needs, burst into laughter, thus showing the first signs of symbolic play similar to that of J. who at 1 ; 3 (12) made a pretence of being asleep. At 1 ; 9 (29) X. put an open box on top of another and said: "*Sitting on pot.*" At 2 ; 1 (9) her dolls dirtied themselves: "*But must ask for pot.*" Scenes connected with the toilet were frequently reproduced during the following weeks. At 2 ; 7 (9) she laughed at an adult with a biscuit sticking out of his mouth and indulged in pleasantries it would be difficult to quote. On the other hand, at 3 ; 6 (10), her faeces were compared to a finger, a mouse, a rabbit, etc., or were even personified and given ladies' names.

From about 2 ; 6 to 3 ; 6 these games were associated with all kinds of symbolic fantasies and games in which all sorts of objects had excretory organs, not only animal toys, but little cars, planes, cups, sticks, etc. At about 3 ; 6 there were questions about the morphological differences between the sexes, and remarks which were sometimes serious and sometimes playful as to the possibility of making anatomical characteristics uniform (" masculine protest ") At 3 ; 6 (2): "*I think the mountain hanging here grows and turns into a little long thing with a hole at the end for water to come out, like boys have.*" And at 5 ; 8 (0): "*Why do boys need a long thing for that? They could do it through their navel. Zoubab* (an imaginary character) *makes water through her navel.*" And at 5 ; 8 (1), after saying that boys could do it through a gate, X. played at nursing Zoubab who was ill: "*I'm making her make water through the bars.*"

Y., at 3 ; 3 (12), looking at two male statues: "*It's a good thing they've got two things for water to come out; if they hadn't they'd quarrel.*"

OBS. 96. We must now give examples of all the games connected with family relations in which the affective tendencies which give rise to them are to some extent outside the child's consciousness. At 2 ; 0 (4) X. reproduced meal-time scenes with her dolls, in the course of which she exerted more maternal authority over her children than she herself was accustomed to experience. At 2 ; 7 (27) she played at being the mother of her younger brother, born a short time before. At 2 ; 8 (0) she identified herself with this baby brother, and imitated his attitudes and voice. Subsequently, from 3 ; 6 to 5 ; 0, she reproduced whole scenes of family life, playing all the roles in turn. At 5 ; 9 (16) she played at being in bed for a confinement, then declared that a certain doll was hers " *because it came out of my inside.*"

At 5 ; 8 (5), being for the moment on bad terms with her father, X. charged one of her imaginary characters with the task of avenging her: " *Zoubab cut off her daddy's head. But she has some very strong glue and partly stuck it on again. But it's not very firm now.*"

After 3 ; 3 Y. often played at being a boy. At 4 ; 2 (11) she made up a story of a little boy " *who laughed when his father died. But after he was buried, he cried and they had to comfort him. I wouldn't have had to be comforted because I'm a big girl. Afterwards he became a father. He became a father all of a sudden, without noticing. He didn't know he had. He was sleeping in a bed, as small as that, by his mummy, and then in the morning his mummy said to him:* " *Your bed is much too small for you.*" *His legs were much too long and fat. He was big all over. He had become a father suddenly during the night, because his mummy had given him a spoonful of potato. And then he had a little sister who became a mummy too, suddenly, without noticing it.*"

OBS. 97. The part played by games dealing with birth is particularly noteworthy. We have already seen X.'s game at 5 ; 9 (14). At 3 ; 3 (28) Y. said of her doll Nicholas, " *When he was born he stayed for a long time inside me; he had sharp pointed teeth and afterwards they became smooth.*" At 3 ; 6 (2) she pretended that her son Nicholas's head was in her head, etc. At 3 ; 9 (13) someone was arguing with her: " *No, don't do that. You know I have a little baby inside me and it hurts him.*" Then, when the person had gone: " *You know, when my little baby is born, he'll kick him and knock him down.*" At 3 ; 10 (17) she explained to her doll which wanted to be inside her again: " *No, you're too big now, you can't.*" In contrast to this, at 3 ; 10 (24), Y., who wanted to become a boy, said to her father: " *I want to go back inside you, and then when I come out I'll be a little baby again. I'll be called Y.* (the masculine form of her name) *because I'll be a boy.*"

We must now consider what it is that is peculiar to these symbols, and why we can assume that they have fuller and more hidden meanings than do ordinary ludic symbols, remembering that there is a whole series of intermediary stages between the two extremes. The general difference lies in the fact that the content of these symbols is more directly related to the child's ego, and involves relatively permanent affective schemas. When the child pretends that a shell is a car or a cat, or that he himself is a steeple or a dead duck, he is expressing what interests him, in the widest sense of the word, and there is certainly assimilation of reality to the ego. But these interests are only temporary, they are on the surface of the ego, while in the case of secondary symbols it is a matter of intimate, permanent concerns, of secret and often inexpressible desires.

Why, for instance, does a child who has been weaned for a long time find pleasure in pretending that he is a baby again and is being suckled? The Freudians who ascribe to the baby (if not to the embryo) a memory like that of the adult, reply that the child is still clinging to the memory of his mother's breast, especially if the process of weaning was clumsily handled. Quite apart from the question of memory, there is probably something to be said for this idea, since the schema of sucking the breast is for so long of primary importance to the child. There is, moreover, the fact that the child easily becomes jealous of the attention given to a new baby, and may pretend to be a baby himself in order to be given the same affection.

There is no need for us to emphasise that the excretory functions give rise to an interest disapproved of by adults, or that questions are asked about differences in the sex organs, or that little girls show a desire to be like boys (" masculine protest " complex). It is therefore perfectly normal that these tendencies should be found in play, and even if the child is partially conscious of them when the ludic symbol is constructed, it is obvious that they go deeper than this relative consciousness.

As to the child's relations to parents, brothers and sisters, a comparison of all the games in which they are symbolised clearly shows how revealing the detail of the symbolism is of tendencies and feelings many of which the child is not clearly aware of, for the simple reason that he never questions them. The first to appear are identifications with the mother (having a husband, children, bringing them up, etc.), the father, and with older or younger brothers and sisters. Although at first sight these may seem to be merely a reproduction of the child's environment, they reveal a mass of contradictory feelings, affection or resistance, acceptance or revolt, attraction or jealousy, a desire to be grown up, to live elsewhere, etc. We must beware of interpreting too closely, since verification of details is not an easy matter, and we shall confine ourselves to a consideration of the story of Zoubab who cut off her father's head and " partly " stuck it on again. Here the situation is clear. The child who is feeling rebellious will frequently play at being an orphan, but it is much rarer to find a pretence of decapitation such as this in the case of the mother. But the father is the object of ambivalent feelings: he is loved, but he is often a nuisance and his removal is not too serious a matter, while rebellion against the mother is much more disturbing. It is interesting to note how skilfully a balance can be achieved in symbolism between aggressiveness and its opposite, and how frequently in play the attitude to the father varies according as the parents are together or the father is alone. In a word, all those with whom the child lives give rise to a kind of " affective schema," a summary or blending of the various feelings aroused by them, and it is these schemas which determine the main secondary symbols, as they often determine later on certain attractions or antipathies for which it is difficult to find an explanation except in unconscious assimilation with earlier modes of behaviour.

A third and interesting source of secondary symbols is to be found in the anxiety resulting from the absurd education which refuses to give children a true explanation when babies are born, an anxiety which goes deeper than the child himself realises. But even in the case of children like those whose remarks we have given as examples, and who never had occasion to feel that any question was " taboo," we have found that interest in birth gives rise to a whole ludic symbolism. Before discovering the explanation, children symbolise various imaginary possibilities, and after discovering it, they play at being pregnant but often add new fantasies or readapt the earlier ones, showing in both cases how much wider their interest in this field is than the mere problem of causal understanding.

We shall now proceed to a study of the various dreams of the same children during the same periods, and we shall see to what extent children's dreams are as it were a continuation of symbolic play, both in its primary and secondary forms. The analogy between the two phenomena has often been observed, but what is important for our immediate purpose is that the technique of child psycho-analysis is based on it M. Klein, S. Isaacs, Searl and many others do not merely analyse the dreams of their young patients. They give them various toys, big and little dolls (parents and children, brothers and sisters, babies, etc.), big and small houses and trains, etc., and the symbolism spontaneously produced by the child with the help of these toys proves to be as revealing as that of dreams, and often shows finer shades of meaning. On the other hand, the few dreams we have been able to collect bear a remarkable resemblance to symbolic games. It is true that as the child tells his dream he arranges it in his own way and makes it more like a story with the element of play, but the whole dream is not made up, and in the case of nightmares in particular, enough of the spontaneous content remains to make the comparison legitimate.

It is very difficult to say at what point in the child's development dreams appear, since before the stage of language only behaviours can be analysed. It is often assumed that all mammals dream, but a dog which growls in its sleep is not necessarily evoking mental images, and its " dream " can be interpreted in terms of mere sensory-motor automatisms. Chimpanzees, too, dream, and in their case it is possible that there are images since they have a rudimentary symbolic power. In the case of children, we have been unable to find evidence of authentic dreams before the appearance of language. At about the age of ten months, J. used regularly to smile in her sleep when I went close to her face and laughed, but it is unlikely that there was any mental image because the phenomenon, instead of becoming more frequent, gradually ceased. The first definite proof of dreams in the children we have observed came between the age of 1 ; 9 and 2, when the children talked in their sleep and gave an account of the dreams when they woke.

But the question we asked ourselves in collecting these dreams does not depend on the date of their first appearance. Is there in children's dreams a symbolism comparable to that of their games at the corresponding age, or do they from the start present the same intricate character as most adult dreams? We know that Freud, who saw in every dream wish fulfilment, put forward the hypothesis (which he later modified) that the first dreams of children are direct realisations of desires through a simple, straightforward evocation of reality (*e.g.*, dreams about sweets or soup when the child is on a diet). The question, then, is whether the symbolism becomes more complicated with development, as in play, or whether there is any connection between the two manifestations of symbolic thought.

Here are a few examples, X.'s dreams before the age of six, and Y.'s first dreams:

OBS. 98. At 2 ; 2 (23) X. woke up crying: " *Poupette has come back.*" Poupette was a little girl she had met the day before and who had obviously worried her by unceremoniously taking possession of all her toys. At 2 ; 8 (4) she was wakened by a cock crowing, and said, still half asleep: " *I'm afraid of the lady who's singing. She's singing very loud. She's scolding me.*" At 2 ; 8 (11) X. woke with a loud scream: " *It was all dark, and I saw a lady over there* (pointing to her bed). *That's why I screamed.*" Then she explained that it was a horrid lady who stood with her legs apart and played with her fæces. At 3 ; 7 (1) she was dreaming and talking in her sleep: " *Mumcat and Babcat* (the mother cat and kitten belonging to the house), *they're granny and mummy.*" At 3 ; 7 (21), when she was trying to overcome a tendency to bite her nails, she said when she woke, but was still half asleep: " *When I was little, a dog bit my fingers,*" and showed the finger she most often put in her mouth, as she had probably been doing in her sleep. At 4 ; 9 (2) she dreamt about chimney-sweeps and at 5 ; 1 (19) about a little worm. At 5 ; 4 (19): " *I dreamt that a cat had eaten the baby guinea-pigs* "; and at 5 ; 8 (1): " *All the guinea-pigs were dead and there were lots of cats in the hen-house* (where the guinea-pigs were). *They ran away when we came, like the guinea-pigs when we give them dandelions. One of the cats was ginger. It was mine.*" As a matter of fact X. had for a long time been wanting cats instead of the guinea-pigs.

At 5 ; 8 (6): " *I dreamt that mummy laid a lot of eggs and a little baby came out of them.*" At 5 ; 8 (22): " *I dreamt there was a tiny little man like that* (four inches) *with a very big head. He ran after me to hurt me.*" The day before she had been interested in a picture of Humpty-Dumpty. At 5 ; 9 (21): " *I dreamt I was pouring water out of a watering-can in the garden, and I've wetted my bed.*"

At 5 ; 9 (23) she dreamt " *that there was a big owl in the garden. I was afraid and went and hid in granny's skirt.*" At 5 ; 9 (24): " *I dreamt I was going to school all by myself in the tram* (she laughed with pleasure at this idea). *But I missed the tram and walked, all alone* (more laughter). *I was late, and the mistress sent me away, and I walked home all by myself.*"

At 5 ; 9 (26): " *I dreamt that Dr. M. fired a gun at a man who was high up in the air. The man was very ill and was going to die so he killed him. He was very small, and then when he fell he was big: he got bigger and bigger; he had a fat tummy like you; he was just like you!* " (she laughed).

At 5 ; 9 (27): " *I dreamt I was eating a big pebble. Then granny said: don't eat it, it will give you a pain. So I stopped, and Y. went on eating it.*" X. had had a pain in her stomach when she woke that morning. At 5 ; 10 (7): " *I dreamt that N. and M. lent me all their toys.*" At 5 ; 10 (11) she dreamt she ate two eggs. At this time she was not allowed to have eggs, and was constantly asking for them. At 5 ; 10 (13) she dreamt that her mother, who was ill, was better and admired one of her games.

At 5 ; 9 (28): " *Mummy made a big, green statue out of leaves. A fox came and knocked it over by pushing its head into the leaves. I was frightened of the fox and went back into mummy's inside to hide. Then he couldn't catch me.*" At 5 ; 10 (10) she dreamt that a cousin who had just been married " *got fatter and fatter and his wife got thinner and thinner.*" The day before X. had been fitting a nest of little men one into the other and had asked whether fathers could have babies inside them.

obs. 99. At 1 ; 9 (28) Y. called out in the middle of the night " *Malar* " (her friend Bernard). At 1 ; 11 (5) and the following nights she said several times: " *Coucou baou* " (pussy's hiding), " *Ropa* " (her friend R.) and " *Malar.*" At 2 ; 6 (2) she dreamt about a lady she was very fond of. At 3 ; 2 (19) she dreamt her mother was sleeping in her little bed (which she was always wanting her to do).

These dreams were all pleasant, but at 3 ; 5 (6) she had her first nightmare (when she had indigestion). She dreamt of tractors (she was afraid of those in the fields near the garden). At 3 ; 8 (3) there was another pleasant dream: " *I dreamt there was some wood under the beds and the kitten went and lay on it.*" At 3 ; 10 (2): " *I dreamt we had a new maid. We were her nieces and her hair was done rather like mine.*" But at 3 ; 8 (4): "*A.* (her doll) *cried because a horrid lady told him he was a baby.*" The horrid lady was an imaginary being who was the cause of all evils. The same day "*Laocoon* (another doll) *wetted himself. It was the horrid lady's fault.*" At 3 ; 8 (5) she dreamt about a nest of pots (like the nest of little wooden men).

At 3 ; 9 (9) she dreamt that the whole house disappeared into the ground. At 3 ; 10 (13) she dreamt that her parents had gone away and she was alone in the house with her sister.

At 3 ; 10 (17): "*The horrid lady didn't make the beds or tidy the room and she broke a chair.*" In a symbolic game on one of the following days Y. played at eating the horrid lady "*except her mouth, which was nasty.*" Moreover, the " horrid lady " was the cause of all misdemeanours and unkindness, from wetting oneself to scolding: "*I dreamt that N. was crying because they said he was a baby. It was the horrid lady who said so.*"

OBS. 100. We have had brought to our notice the case of a boy U. who for several months in succession, beginning at the age of six, dreamt that there was a basin on a stand in his bedroom: "*In the basin I saw a bean that was so big that it quite filled it. It got bigger and bigger all the time. I was standing by the door. I was frightened. I wanted to scream and run away, but I couldn't. I got more and more frightened, and it went on until I woke up.*"

It would be difficult, in our opinion, not to recognise the analogy between these dreams and the games of the same children, the one difference being that in dream symbolism there are nightmares, while in ludic symbolism fear is still enjoyed. In other words, matters are settled more easily in play than in dreams. But as play is more easily controlled than dreams, this difference is natural enough, and the resemblances are all the more striking.

In the first place it is clear that there are dreams which fulfil wishes, by the mere evocation of the desired result, without any apparent secondary symbolism. Thus X. dreamt that a cat had eaten the guinea-pigs and that there were cats in the hen-house in their place, because that was what she actually wanted to happen. Similarly, Y. wanted her mother to sleep in her bed, as do all small children. Or again, X. dreamt she was eating eggs because she had not been allowed to have any for two months.

In the second place, we find dreams in which, just as in the primary symbolism of play, certain objects are consciously represented by others. For instance, Granny and Mummy are " Mumcat " and " Babcat," *i.e.*, mummy cat and baby cat. Are such dreams to be considered as wish fulfilment, in accordance with Freud's theory? Possibly, but with the proviso that a very wide meaning is given to the word " wish," that of assimilation of reality to the ego such as we find

in play.   Granny and Mummy are beings the child loves, and so are
Mumcat and Babcat, and the child enjoys identifying the two pairs
in dream as in play.   Since the dream may not be complete, it is
possible that this explanation is inadequate.

In the third place, there are dreams in which a painful happening
is recalled, but given a happy ending, as in play.   For instance, X.
dreamt of owls in the garden (the owls really were there and frightened
her), but hid in her grandmother's skirt to be safe from them.   We
can see here the function of " guardian of sleep " which Freud ascribes
to dreams, more particularly as the child might actually have heard
the owls hooting in her sleep.

But in a fourth category there are real nightmares, such as being
pursued by Humpty-Dumpty, being afraid of chimney-sweeps, seeing
Poupette come back (to take possession of all the toys).   How are these
to be interpreted?   In psycho-analysis nightmares are considered to
be disguised wishes, the more frightening the more they are disguised.
Being pursued by mischievous little men or by chimney-sweeps might
therefore represent for a little girl a real desire, despite the alarming
character of these persons, and even because of it.   As to Poupette's
return, it is impossible to tell what attraction is hidden beneath antipathies.   But as a matter of fact, we fail to see why desires should not
be found in everything, and even if a nightmare were the result of the
involuntary reappearance of anxieties, these anxieties would obviously
be accompanied by the desire for liquidation of them.   The only
point of interest to us here is the difference from play.   In play as in
nightmares we can find both fears which are deliberately recalled and
which are a source of pleasure proportionate to the anxiety, and also
involuntary unhappiness with the desire for liquidation, but in play
there is always more or less conscious control, while in dreams control
is more difficult, because the situation is assimilated to more deeply-
seated schemas, i.e., to a more remote past.

In a fifth category are the dreams of punishment or auto-punish-
ment.   X., who had bitten one of her nails as she went to sleep
announced when she woke that a little dog had bitten her fingers
when she was small.   Freud and his followers have often found
examples of animal phobias in children who ascribed the power of
punishment to them, but it is possible that the threats or foolish tales
of parents are sometimes at the root of such symbols.   This could
not have been so in the case given above.

A sixth and final category is that of dreams which are a straightforward symbolic translation of an immediate organic stimulus, e.g.,
the dream of the watering-can, connected with urination, or that of
eating a pebble, connected with a pain in the stomach.   In the case
of boys there are frequent examples of dreams of erection, such as
U.'s dream of a long bean growing to a fantastic size in a basin.

The dreams of this sixth category bring us to the question of the secondary symbols of which we spoke in connection with play. We notice at once that between the first and the sixth categories the symbolism, which was at first primary, becomes complicated by secondary interferences of varying strengths, and it is of interest to find that the three kinds of secondary symbols we noted in the children we observed are strikingly present also in their dreams, but often surrounded by a haze of slight anxiety, which characterises the difference between the ludic and oneiric planes.

The difference is clear, for instance, in the dream of the indecent lady (obs. 98). She really only did what X. pretended to make her dolls or other fictitious characters do, and yet this kind of interest, which easily becomes a joke in play, is accompanied in dreams by considerable anxiety.

The dream of the doctor killing a man in the air, and the dream about the statue made of leaves, with the return to the mother's womb, which took place within three days of one another, provide us with excellent examples of the " oedipus " symbols which the Freudians have shown to be so common. These dreams belonged to a period when X. showed a decided preference for her mother and a kind of periodic hostility for her father, alternating with affection (*cf.* the game in which Zoubab cut off her father's head and partly stuck it on again, a game which shortly preceded these dreams). The doctor who had just been giving X. some injections (which she was afraid would kill her) was identified with the men who used to shoot birds near her home, and he killed a little man who, as she said to her father, " had a big tummy like you ; he was like you." There is no need for far-fetched interpretations in order to see the analogy between the play symbolism of Zoubab and that of this dream. In the case of the dream about the statue, X. had asked shortly before how a statue of greenish bronze had been made, and she was also afraid that the foxes in the neighbourhood might kill the animals she was rearing. But whatever the assimilations may be which would explain these images, the fact remains that X., when frightened by the fox coming to destroy the statue, felt in her dream that the safest thing for her to do was to return to her mother's womb.

This brings us to dreams about birth, of which the one about the mother laying eggs is an almost ludic example. The dream about the cousin who got fatter and his wife who got thinner belongs, in our opinion, to the same category (though it is less conscious), because on the previous days X. had been anxious to know whether fathers also could have children. Moreover, when her mother pointed out to her how like her father she was, she answered: " Then was I inside Daddy and not inside you? "

To sum up what we have said, in their symbolic structure as well as in their content, children's dreams seem to be closely related to symbolic play. It is unnecessary to stress the differences—they are obvious. The dreamer believes what he dreams, while belief in the pretence of play is always very relative. The construction of games is much more deliberately controlled, while that of dreams carries the subject far beyond the point his conscious would wish. Most important of all, in play, material substitutes of all kinds which make it easier to imagine the object are used as symbols, while in dreams the object must be represented by a mental image or by another image symbolising the same object. Thus in one of the dreams quoted above, the image of a watering-can symbolises urination, while in the corresponding game a real watering-can would have been used. How is the formation of these oneiric symbols to be explained? We shall now proceed to examine the question, having already emphasised that there is a double continuity, between the primary and secondary ludic symbols, and between these symbols and the primary and secondary symbols of children's dreams. Are dreams entirely symbolic, or do automatism and chance play some part in them? It is a difficult question, since the further we pursue our analysis the more we give the child the opportunity of finding assimilations in retrospect. What is important is that oneiric symbolism exists, and that there is a whole series of intermediary stages between the simple, primary symbols, such as X. dreaming about eggs of which she had been deprived, and the secondary or unconscious symbols which become more and more complicated. It is this fundamental fact, of which the work of the psycho-analysts has made us aware, which compels us to complete our study of symbolic play by a study of the assimilations peculiar to unconscious symbolic thought.

§ 2. *The Freudian explanation of symbolic thought*

Freud's theory is too well known to require a lengthy restatement before we proceed to examine how far it can serve as an explanation of unconscious symbolism. It must be emphasised that Freud's contribution is essentially a new technique, and that although his theoretical conceptions now require a general overhaul, this technique continues to be the only systematic method so far discovered of exploring the " unconscious " schemas. While in the case of the child the existence and importance of these " unconscious " schemas can be discovered by watching him play, and by listening to his spontaneous remarks, noting the connections he himself makes, the principle of the technique of adult analysis consists in bringing about in the patient a " non-polarised " state of mind and then following his thought without intervening. Lying in a comfortable position, with eyes closed, the patient is asked to say, over a period of an hour daily, everything that comes into his mind, without trying to think and without excluding any thought which comes. Usually nothing very interesting occurs during the first week or fortnight. The patient merely learns not to conceal any intimate thoughts which may emerge, not to be afraid of appearing to be completely devoid of intelligence, and to tell the analyst frankly what he thinks both of him and of this absurd situation. Then, encouraged, his shyness and pride over-come, feeling confidence in the analyst whom he now looks on as a mere recorder and discreet confidant, the patient reaches the stage at which he enjoys talking unrestrainedly for an hour, and following with interest the thread of his spontaneous ideas. It is then that reactions occur which it is difficult to imagine clearly without having had the experience First there is a gradual relaxation of " direction " of thought, *i.e.*, the patient goes, without noticing it, from one evoca-tion to another, as if he were day-dreaming. At the same time there is a noticeable tendency to visualise rather than to reason. A series of pictures appears, which he watches and describes, which interest, move or disgust him, since they are recollections, but which he looks at like a spectator at a film. Then two things of capital importance take place. First his mind gradually goes back to the past. Among the recent and almost present recollections he evokes, more and more remote memories find their way to the surface, and he is surprised to find that he has spent the greater part of the hour in re-living scenes of his childhood and recalling his parents as they then were. In the second place, recollections of dreams creep into the context, forgotten dreams which come back to him and mingle with memories of real events. As the patient is asked to note every morning the dreams he has just had and to give an exact account of them, these too interfere with his free associations.

Such is the essence of the technique. An analysis of the dreams is undertaken if it seems useful, but it is often superfluous, because certain dreams acquire immediate significance through the connection the patient makes spontaneously (often without noticing that he does so) with his memories. If an analysis is necessary, the analyst reads out the written account of the dream, sentence by sentence, and at each one the patient says what comes to his mind (again without making any deliberate effort).

It was from this two-fold technique that Freud drew his hypotheses as to symbolism in general. Dreams are always wish-fulfilment, but their apparent content conceals a " latent content " of which it is merely the symbolic " transposition." This transposition is due to censorship coming from the subject's consciousness and from his super-ego, or interiorisation of parental action. The latent content is censored because it consists of repressed tendencies, so that the dream becomes the symbolic realisation of a repressed desire. Moreover, as each new experience of the subject is fitted into earlier situations, any recent repressed desires are necessarily bound up with the set of earlier repressed tendencies. This means that we are determined by the whole of our past, especially by the hierarchy of infantile tendencies, arranged according to the stages of " sexual " development: the oral stage, the anal stage, narcissism, then choice of another object of affection (towards the end of the first year) and œdipus tendencies, and finally transfer of affectivity to an ever-increasing number of new persons. A symbol is therefore never simple and there is always " poly-symbolism " owing to the fact that this intrication of tendencies and conflicts gives rise to a variety of meanings. The most elementary symbols are the product of a blending of images, which may be independent of censorship and may be due merely to factors of economy of thought. But there is also " displacement " of affective stress from one image to another, and this results from censorship. Symbolism is produced by identifications, projections, contrasts, coupling, etc., and is diametrically opposed to logic, since it only obeys the " Lust-prinzip " and its function is to mislead consciousness. The imaged character of dreams can be explained as follows. In any normal action, perception is associated with a set of memories in the unconscious and the result is expressed in a dynamic pattern (consciousness itself has no memory and is only a kind of internal " sense organ " which throws light on to memories which it finds useful, and refrains from bringing to light those which it finds unprofitable, i.e., it " censors " them). But when, on the contrary, a tendency is repressed, it cannot be translated into action and is projected in the direction of the sensory organs, hence the almost hallucinatory character of dreams. Moreover, this projection is in its turn associated with memory-images, which are selected so as to be acceptable to consciousness, and we get symbolism, whose connection with censorship becomes clear.

It is not easy to judge this interpretation impartially. This mass of incisive observations is expressed in language very remote from that of contemporary experimental psychology, and we should like to be able to separate theory from facts and reinterpret the facts in the light of present-day knowledge. The difficulty is that Freud and the psycho-analysts, who were for so long ignored and whose views were distorted by the laboratory psychologists, formed an organisation of their own, doing great practical service but showing the danger of crystallising and keeping sacrosanct an esoteric truth. But the time has come to forget both official prejudice and parochial attitudes, and to incorporate the living part of Freudian psychology, i.e., the method and the facts, in psychology as a whole. The facts are indisputable, and to be aware of them, all that is necessary is to undergo oneself a " training analysis." This is an essential condition for an understanding of the facts, and without it one is in the position of the philosophers who

talk of perception without ever having been in a laboratory to learn
to measure it! There is no doubt that for the psychologist who has
himself undergone the experience, and has to some extent tried the
method on others, by way of proof, the difficulty of the Freudian
doctrine does not lie in the facts of affectivity as such, but in the
general framework which the theory claims in the field of general
psychology: the nature of memory, the role of association, the conception of a lighting-consciousness of which intelligence is not the
active nucleus, the relationship between the conscious and the unconscious, the preservation of feelings, to quote only the most important.
All these are questions which call for reconsideration before we can
hope to find any adequate theory of symbolism.

The two fundamental facts discovered by Freud and his school are:
firstly that infantile affectivity passes through well-defined stages, and
secondly that there is an underlying continuity, *i.e.*, that at each level
the child unconsciously assimilates present affective situations to earlier
ones, even to those most remote. These facts are all the more interesting from our point of view in that they are completely in line with
those of intellectual development. Intelligence also passes through
stages which correspond in the main with those of emotional development. For instance, sucking plays as important a part in the
organisation of the primitive sensory-motor schemas (buccal space,
etc.) as in the baby's affectivity. " Narcissism " (in the sense of
narcissism without Narcissus, *i.e.*, without consciousness of the ego)
corresponds to the complete ego-centrism of the first year, during
which the universe and the ego are one, because there are no
permanent external objects. Corresponding to the affective level
of " object choice " there is construction of substantial objects and
organisation of external space, while the beginning of socialisation
of thought corresponds to the level of transfer of affectivity to others.
Moreover, the whole genetic analysis of thought shows continuous
assimilation of present data to earlier schemas and to those of the
child's present activity, the progress of intelligence consisting in the
progressive decentration of this assimilation, while its errors take the
form of unconscious fixation on what may be called repressed
intellectual " complexes."

In order to explain simultaneously this gradual elaboration of
affectivity (closely connected with intellectual development) and the
continuity of the unconscious assimilations of the present to the past,
a nice balance must be kept between the ideas of development and
permanence. In spite of appearances, Freud is much less of a gene-
ticist than he is usually considered to be, and he too often sacrifices
development to permanence, to the extent of ascribing to the baby
at the breast the attributes characteristic of the final stage of development: memory, consciousness of the ego, etc. What is needed,

therefore, is a genetic transposition of the Freudian doctrine through the elimination of those elements which make it too much a science of the permanent.

The first difficulty lies in the Freudian idea of instinct, which is neither the biological idea of a stable mechanism, nor the psycho-sociological idea, which uses the term " social transformation of feelings " to indicate the construction of new feelings as a result of new intercourse in social life, feelings which are bound up with instincts and integrate them. For Freud, instinct is a kind of per-manent energy, preserved throughout the whole development and merely transferred from one object to another (the child's own body, his parents, etc.). It is these affective " loads " which determine the various particular feelings, while the continuity of the general current explains " identifications " and transfers. As extremely little is known of the preservation of the total affective energy, and only the existence of rhythms and regulations is proved, it seems to us that this substantialist language is out of place here, and that it would be more profitable to consider how we can arrive at a more relativistic view nearer to reality. When there is transfer of feeling from one object to another, we must recognise that in addition to continuity there is construction of a new feeling through the integration of the old feeling in a new schema different from the previous one, and that affective continuity merely results from mutual assimilation of the two schemas. Thus the " loads " are relative to the general organisa-tion of the schemas and express its regulation (which is always dependent on a corresponding intellectual structure). For this reason it is dangerous to postulate preservation of a feeling in the unconscious during these periods of intermittency. Let us consider, for example, an aggressive tendency like the one directed against the father in the play and dreams quoted in § 1. Clearly such a " propulsion " (which alternates in consciousness with the opposite feelings of tender-ness and love), although it may appear periodically, does not neces-sarily persist in the unconscious between one manifestation and another. It is equally justifiable to assume that the things which do persist are modes of action and reaction, schemas of behaviour, and consequently certain permanent relationships between the reactions of the father and those of the child. It is these relationships which may give rise periodically to demonstrations of aggressiveness or affection. Perhaps after all there is no great difference between the two explanations. When the mind ceases to be consciously aware of a feeling which will reappear later on, it is the seat of a virtual feeling, and a virtual feeling is nothing else than a schema of action or reaction. But in expressing the situation in this second way, we avoid ascribing to the unconscious the power of feeling of its own accord, as though it were a second consciousness. In our opinion, if feelings are preserved in the unconscious, it is no longer as feelings. The unconscious is essentially dynamic, and it must be described in terms of reactions if the pitfalls of substantialist language are to be avoided. The explanation of why the subject can be unaware of certain hidden tendencies then becomes much simpler. It is much more difficult to become conscious of a schema of reaction and its intricate implications than of feelings which are already formed and ready to emerge.

This brings us to the central problem of memory, which raises exactly the same difficulties, but this time on the representative plane. For Freud, the whole of the past is preserved in the unconscious. Consciousness, having no memory, can only throw light on the memory-images which lie immediately below the surface of the unconscious. This theory of Freud's is in line with those of many other writers, and except for the theory of association, Freudian memory is not very different from that of Bergson. At various times, however, another conception of memory has been opposed to it, that of reconstruction-memory. It is, of course, impossible to know what becomes of a memory in the intervals between its disappearance and recall. We can only experiment with conscious memories, and when a forgotten memory is evoked the process may be either reconstruction or extraction. Moreover, all the recent work on memory shows that factors which involve the active organisation of memories: judgments, logical relationships, etc., intervene. From Janet, for whom memory is a behaviour of the " narrative " type, to the Gestalt psychologists who see general structures in the reconstruction of memories, a considerable body of facts has been amassed in support of the thesis of partial or total reconstitution. On being asked what I did at seven o'clock this morning, I am obliged to deduce the answer, and it is unlikely that it was noted (on a record always kept up to date) in my unconscious.

In accordance with their hypothesis, the Freudians make the beginnings of memory coincide with those of mental life. Why is it that we have no memories of our first years, and more particularly of our first months, which are so rich in affective experiences? The Freudians reply that there has been repression. But the theory of reconstruction-memory provides us with a much simpler explanation. There are no memories of early childhood for the excellent reason that at that stage there was no evocative mechanism capable of organising them. Recognition memory in no way implies a capacity for evocation, which presupposes mental images, interiorised language, and the beginnings of conceptual intelligence. The memory of the two or three year old child is still a medley of made-up stories and exact but chaotic reconstructions, organised memory developing only with the progress of intelligence as a whole.[1]

[1] There is also the question of memories which depend on other people. For instance, one of my first memories would date, if it were true, from my second

But then what becomes of the unconscious continuity between the present and the past which ensures the preservation of both affective and intellectual experiences? What, generally speaking, are the tracks which make recognition memory possible, and the assimilations on which the reconstructions of evocative memory are based? Here again it can only be a case of schemas of action and not of representative images deposited as such in the unconscious (which would again amount to making it a second consciousness). The baby recognises an object or a person in so far as he is able to react to them as he has done in the past, and it is these sensory-motor schemas which become memory-images, in the same way as the combination of signifying and signified schemas produces the mental image. But this transposition of active recognition into representative evocation presupposes the complete organisation of interiorised intelligence, and only gives rise to organised memory when speech and the system of concepts exist.

A comparison of this criticism of memory with that of unconscious feelings makes it clear that a theoretical readjustment is necessary for the understanding of the part played by infantile affective experiences in the whole life of the individual. The facts lose nothing of their clarity by being expressed in terms of schemas and their mutual assimilation, rather than of unconscious memories. The Freudians talk, for instance, as though the image formed of the father and mother at the stage of choice of first affective objects persisted throughout life, and as though an indefinite number of persons were later unconsciously " identified " with these first images. It is true that the individual frequently generalises his first ways of giving and withholding himself, of clinging or rebelling, and that there is sometimes a striking continuity between the first family reactions and subsequent social, religious and æsthetic reactions. Neither unconscious memory nor preservation of feelings as such are, however, necessary to account for these facts. Just as there are motor schemas and intellectual schemas, so there are affective schemas (which are the same schemas,

year. I can still see, most clearly, the following scene, in which I believed until I was about fifteen. I was sitting in my pram, which my nurse was pushing in the Champs Elysées, when a man tried to kidnap me. I was held in by the strap fastened round me while my nurse bravely tried to stand between me and the thief. She received various scratches, and I can still see vaguely those on her face. Then a crowd gathered, a policeman with a short cloak and a white baton came up, and the man took to his heels. I can still see the whole scene, and can even place it near the tube station. When I was about fifteen, my parents received a letter from my former nurse saying that she had been converted to the Salvation Army. She wanted to confess her past faults, and in particular to return the watch she had been given as a reward on this occasion. She had made up the whole story, faking the scratches. I therefore must have heard, as a child, the account of this story, which my parents believed, and projected it into the past in the form of a visual memory, which was a memory of a memory, but false. Many real memories are doubtless of the same order.

or at least indissociable aspects of the same realities) and it is the organised set of these schemas which constitutes the " character " of each individual, *i.e.*, his permanent modes of behaviour. When an individual has rebelled inwardly against excessive paternal authority, and subsequently adopts the same attitude to his teachers or to any constraint, it does not follow that he is unconsciously identifying each of these persons with the image of his father. What has happened is merely that in his relations with his father he has acquired a mode of feeling and reacting (an affective schema) which he generalises in situations that are subjectively analogous. Similarly, though he may have acquired the schema of free fall by dropping a ball from his cot, it does not follow that he subsequently identifies all falling bodies with that ball. It is true that sometimes in his dreams, some person with whom he has quarrelled will appear in situations taken from his childhood, and will be symbolised by characteristics belonging to his father. Moreover, if his dream were .to be analysed he would easily see the close inter-relation of past and present situations. But this raises the problem of symbolic thought, to which we shall return, and proves no more than that affective schemas are less susceptible to generalisation and abstraction than intellectual schemas. There is no need for a doubtful theory of memory or of preservation of feelings to account for the fact that affective situations are assimilated one to another.

There is a third general question which requires to be examined anew if psycho-analysis is to be adjusted to the essential ideas of contemporary psychology. Freud was trained in an atmosphere of classic associationism, and although the technique he invented was such as to make a restatement of the idea of association possible, he remained much too dependent on it. We even find in him traces of Taine's famous theory of perception as being true hallucination (*cf.* his explanation of the quasi-hallucinatory character of dreams). For Freud, consciousness is a mere lighting-up, an " internal sense organ," whose only role is to throw light on existing associations resulting from resemblances and contiguities between unconscious memories. This means that he denies to conscious activity what for most contemporary authors is its essential characteristic, *i.e.*, the constitution of thought, which is a real constructive activity. Freudism does not consider the problem of intelligence, which is a great pity, for consideration of the question of awareness in the act of comprehension and of the relationship between unconscious intellectual schemas and conscious " reflection " would certainly have simplified the theory of the affective unconscious.

In any case, since for Freud association is the paramount mental activity, he attempts to discover those associations which are the most spontaneous, in order to penetrate into the mysteries of the unconscious.

Hence his double technique of general analysis through the use of non-directed thought, and dream analysis through free associations.

We now know that association, far from being a primary fact, is always the result of a judgment, or at least of active assimilation.[1] There is therefore complete continuity between unconscious association and intelligent activity, and this naturally calls for a more functional and less topographical interpretation of the relationship between consciousness and the unconscious. With regard to the spontaneous, non-directed thought which is freed by the technique of psychoanalysis, it is obvious that what are called " associations " are assimilations. These are affective rather than logical, but are none the less active, which means that construction does take place. This in no way makes it less interesting, rather the contrary. In practice it involves no change, since the construction emanates from the subject and therefore reveals his unconscious schematism. But from the theoretical point of view it leads to the essential conclusion that, in the analysis of a dream, the " free associations " of the subject are not confined to the reproduction of those which gave rise to the dream. Of necessity they go beyond the dream and form a new system of assimilations which merely integrate the earlier ones. This new system, as we said before, reveals the subject's hidden tendencies, but it is not now confined to the field of dreams. Instead of a dream, any news item from a paper could be taken as the starting point for " associations." The spontaneous assimilations of the subject would then make him give a symbolic meaning to every detail, as though he were dealing with one of his own dreams. This in itself would provide further information about the patient's complexes, but the experiment would definitely prove that it is a question of active assimilations, and not of an automatic associative mechanism making contact with the one that gave rise to the dream.

This brings us to the problem of unconscious symbolism. After all that has been said on the general questions, are we to accept without demur the Freudian explanation of the symbol as being an image linked with one or more meanings through unconscious associations which elude censorship? In other words, the object of the symbol (the signified) is associated in the unconscious with various images, but since this object is censored, consciousness only accepts associations with those images which do not recall it too obviously. These images are therefore symbolic to the extent to which they outwit censorship, and the role of free associations becomes that of discovering the unconscious associations which were censored when the symbol was formed.

Such an interpretation seems to us to raise two essential difficulties,

[1] The Gestalt theory even denies the existence of any association, since it always seems to involve general structurisation.

related to what was said earlier. The first is that both the mechanism and even the very existence of this censorship are difficult to grasp. The second is that symbolism, and more particularly unconscious symbolism, extends far beyond the field of what can be censored or repressed, and rather than being a disguise or a camouflage, seems to constitute the elementary form of consciousness of active assimilation.

In fact, while Freud's idea of repression is clear and important (and immediately received general acceptance), his idea of censorship, linked with his conception of a passive consciousness, is obscure. Consciousness censors, we are told, when it wishes to remain unaware of a repression. But how can consciousness be the cause of ignorance, *i.e.*, of unconsciousness? Such a state of affairs is only comprehensible if consciousness is compared to a searchlight, lighting up certain points and avoiding others at the will of its manipulator. If consciousness is activity and intelligence, however, it is completely incomprehensible, the more so since a difficult repression usually requires the collaboration of consciousness for its completion. It is, of course, true that consciousness frequently wishes to remain unaware of what it dislikes, but there is no question of it being duped. When, for instance, we are tempted, and up to the last moment " shut our eyes " to the nature of the tendency to which we finally yield, we are really well aware of what the outcome will be, and consciousness is an accessory from the start. Is symbolism to be explained by such mechanisms? In view of the prevalence of symbolism, such an explanation would be quite inadequate. To talk of " censorship " of dreams is merely to use a redundant expression to indicate their unconsciousness, and what is meant is either repression, or the fact that the dreamer is incapable of clear awareness of all the tendencies which disturb him.

The essential point is that the field of unconscious symbolism is wider than that of repression, and consequently of what can be censored. The question that then arises is whether its unconscious character, *i.e.*, the subject's ignorance of its meaning, does not merely result from the fact that he is incapable of direct and complete consciousness of it. For Freud, censorship is a product of consciousness, and symbolism a product of unconscious associations which elude censorship. In our opinion, it is worth considering whether these two terms might not be reversed, censorship being merely the expression of the unconscious, uncomprehended character of the symbol, and the symbol itself being the result of a beginning of conscious assimilation, *i.e.*, an attempt at comprehension.

As a matter of fact, Freud gave two successive explanations of symbolism, a fact which is particularly interesting to us because the role of censorship was involved. The first explanation makes all the symbolic mechanisms depend on censorship, the symbol being no more than the idea of disguise.   Later on, however, probably under the influence of Silberer, Adler and particularly Jung, Freud recognised that symbolism also constituted a primitive language, but maintained that it was disguise as well as language.   In that case the mechanism of " condensation " is to be explained by factors of economy of thought, but " displacement " is still considered to be the result of censorship.

In reality, " displacement " and " condensation " are inseparable, since it is impossible to combine in a single image features borrowed from several objects, without displacing the affective stress.   Moreover, the whole set of mechanisms which constitute the unconscious symbol can easily function in cases where the content of the symbol is neither repressed nor censored, since it corresponds to thoughts or desires which are perfectly conscious and which the subject recognises when he is awake.   Examples of two types can be given in this connection: transparent dreams, i.e., dreams which are symbolic but whose symbolism is immediately comprehended on waking, and the images of the half-sleeping state, to which the impressive names of hypnogogical and hypnopompical hallucinations were formerly given.

Here are some examples of transparent dreams.   A young man wished his parents to separate, because his somewhat tyrannical mother was spoiling his father's life.   She was a Parisian and he had a southern French name.   In his dream the son was leaving the station at Avignon and was struck by the unusually tidy and clean appearance of the streets.   He was then told: " Everything is better than it used to be, now that the south of France has become an independent republic."   Here there is clearly symbolism, almost comparable to that of an imaginative game, but it is difficult to see where censorship comes in, since the meaning is obvious.   It might perhaps be objected that the separation of parents is always a delicate matter for a child, and that underlying these symbols there may be hidden complexes and a deeper meaning of which we are unaware.   Let us take another example.   A student of philosophy had to hand in to his professor, the day after the dream, a review of Goblot's *Traité de Logique* which had just been published.   He intended to be very critical of the work, but knew that the professor held a very different view, and therefore expected to find himself in difficulties.   Here is the dream: it was time for the lecture on logic to begin.   The professor came in accompanied by an elderly man, who began to lecture, while the professor stood leaning against the wall, his arms folded, and an enigmatical expression on his face.   The elderly man began quite well, but gradually digressed further and further from his subject. The student went out, irritated, but he was hardly outside when he heard the audience whistling and stamping, and went back, delighted. The lecturer stopped speaking and slowly went away, while the professor, still motionless, watched him go out.   He then gazed for a long time at the audience, and finally said, almost convinced: "After all, you were right to get rid of him. What he was saying was worthless." When he woke up, the student immediately recognised the elderly man as someone he had seen in the National Library sitting next to a reader who bore some physical likeness to Goblot. Moreover, he immediately remembered a lecture given by Goblot, which had annoyed him because of its digressions into a field remote from the subject. The meaning of the desire expressed by the dream is therefore obvious: to convince the professor by getting the audience to agree with him. But in that case why should there be such childish symbolism, instead of merely dreaming the desired result, which could be imagined just as easily? Why was Goblot himself not represented, and why was he symbolised not by the man who resembled him, but by his neighbour, as though there had been very strict censorship?

Freudians will perhaps again say that there was some father complex hidden away which would explain the camouflage. In order to convince them, we shall therefore not choose transparent dreams for our study of the formation of symbols, but the images of the half-sleeping state, and in particular those which are the symbolic expression of the last thoughts of the subject before going to sleep. We come to these now, in the work of H. Silberer.

§ 3. *Symbolism according to Silberer, Adler and Jung*

H. Silberer, a disciple of Freud, made a special study of symbolism in mystical thought. Being of a critical and experimental turn of mind, he tried to develop the theory of the symbol by analysing the images of the half-sleeping state using an original and very fruitful method. It is difficult to understand the silence with which the Freudians greeted his work (unlike Adler and Jung, Silberer did not form a dissenting school of thought), because it is of real interest, and had it been developed would have contributed towards reconciling psycho-analysis with current psychology. In his analysis of the formation of symbols [1] Silberer attempts to discover the exact point at which, in the half-sleeping state, thought abandons its coherent, logical structure for imaged symbolism. Having observed that the first images to appear are often a continuation and symbolic transposition of the last conscious idea, Silberer tries to reproduce the phenomenon experimentally by forcing himself to fix his thought on a chosen problem and to wake up and note the images which appeared after he had fallen asleep while meditating. For instance, before falling asleep, Silberer decides to compare the ideas of time developed by Kant and Schopenhauer. There comes a moment when his thought can no longer consider simultaneously the two systems, and

[1] H. Silberer, *Ueber Symbolbildung, Jahrb. Psychoan. Ges.*

then, almost asleep, he sees himself in a public office, trying to contact two officials at different counters, and missing one after the other. By this method, Silberer not only discovers a symbolism which is obviously independent of repression or censorship, but also succeeds in finding a distinction in the unconscious symbols. Alongside the " material " symbols representing particular objects or events, he suggests the idea of " functional " symbols, to indicate those which show the actual functioning of thought. In the example of Kant and Schopenhauer, for instance, the failure of thought in the half-sleeping state to maintain contact with the two systems is symbolised by the two counters between which the dreamer comes and goes. Moreover, Silberer, using the Freudian ideas of poly-symbolism and nesting of situations, as well as his own distinction between material and functional symbols, discovers that a single dream sometimes symbolises simultaneously infantile desires and serious present thought. He therefore suggests, in addition to the retrospective interpretation which delves deeper and deeper into the past, the possibility of an " anagogic " interpretation in the opposite direction.

Freud denied the existence of functional symbols, and found no justification for anagogic analysis. The question arises, however, whether the analyst is not prejudiced, by his methodological axioms, in favour of retrospective orientation as being the only possibility. Silberer seems to us more cautious in recognising the merits of the two points of view. Symbolism merely indicates continuity between past and present, but it may represent either evocation of the past for the purpose of present adaptation, or assimilation of the present to the past. As for functional symbols, their classification is unimportant, but the facts collected by Silberer are in themselves sufficient to prove that symbolism is independent of repression and censorship.

The reasons for which Adler adopted the idea of anagogic analysis are well known. In contrast to Freud, for whom sexuality is of primary importance, Adler finds everywhere the instinct of self-preservation and the desire for power. Even love is for the individual mainly a means of playing a part and asserting the ego. As for recollections, the patient creates them, again with the same end in view, rather than being affected by them. The real problem of affective development, for Adler, is therefore the gradual compensation for the feelings of inferiority characteristic of childhood. It is the realisation by the individual of the plan of life resulting from this need for compensation. It is the adjustment of " overcompensations," which give rise to disturbances as well as to super-normal aptitudes, and it is the elimination of residual feelings of insecurity and inferiority. In this perspective, symbolism seems to Adler to have no relation to disguise, but to be a mere reflection, either direct or " allegorical," of the subject's desire for expansion or his feelings of insecurity.

Children's play is a typical example. Symbolic make-believe is found in neuropaths who, by way of compensation, invent stories to justify themselves, and by way of overcompensation set themselves unattainable ideals. Dreams then are a concise, allegorical reflection of the dreamer's present attitudes, in which Adler has tried to find symbols representing tendencies to expansion or to inferiority, such as, for instance, images suggesting " top " and " bottom."

It is not our purpose here to discuss the respective roles of the instinct of self-preservation and the sexual instinct in the unconscious. Adler has not developed any theory of the origin of symbols, and has concentrated his attention on practical applications, the interest and variety of which are well known.[1]

In the case of C. G. Jung, however, we are faced with a whole new theory of symbolic thought, related to a new conception of the unconscious. Jung reproaches Freud with narrowing down the unconscious by restricting it to the field of past conscious experiences which have been repressed. Alongside this " individual unconscious " there is a considerable number of elements which have never been conscious, and which cannot be so because they are not yet adapted to reality. In contrast to the individual unconscious, which is made up of memories varying from one individual to another, these elements which are prior to all consciousness are common to all individuals, and therefore constitute a " collective unconscious " (collective in the sense of general, not social). These elements are characterised by the main innate, ancestral tendencies which govern the essential behaviours of the human race, from its most primitive vital instincts to its highest and most permanent mystical tendencies. Symbolic thought then appears to be primitive awareness of these inner realities. Underlying the variable and superficial individual symbolism, there is for Jung a collective symbolism which is the real language of the human soul. Inspired by these wide hypotheses, Jung embarked on a vast enquiry into the prevalence of symbols, collecting normal dreams, pathological day-dreams (his work on schizophrenia is well known), mystical symbols, the innumerable symbolic manifestations in the myths, rituals and religious rites of primitive and oriental peoples, in a word, pursuing with indefatigable patience and erudition the dream of reconstituting the original symbols of the human race. Collective symbolic thought corresponds, then, for Jung, to an initial phase of human thought, to a time when civilisation was not yet concerned with the conquest of the external world and was turned inwards, seeking to express in myth the psychic discoveries resulting from this introversion. The main general symbols are therefore hereditary. Jung used to call them " pre-existent forms of archaic types of apper-

[1] See Madeleine Ganz, *La psychologie d'Alfred Adler et le développement de l'enfant.* Delachaux and Niestlé.

ception," " congenital conditions of intuition," " *a priori* determinants of all experience." He now calls them the expression of " archetypes," *i.e.*, the affective and representational systems constituting the " paleopsyche." [1] This conception provides a new solution to the problem of the nature and prevalence of myths. Instead of viewing them, like Max Muller, as a " disease of language " with a single indo-germanic centre of diffusion, or like Andrew Lang, as the remains of primitive social institutions common to all societies, Jung considers their prevalence to be due to the fact that they constitute the convergent awareness of the same archetypes inherent in a single collective unconscious which is innate in humanity.

Jung has an amazing capacity for construction, but a certain contempt for logic and rational activity, which he contracted through daily contact with mythological and symbolic thought, has made him inclined to be content with too little in the way of proof. The better to understand the realities of which he speaks, he adopts an anti-rationalist attitude, and the surprising comparisons of which he has the secret cannot fail sometimes to disturb the critical reader.

Of Jung's contribution, the part that will endure is his conception of the relative generality of symbols and of symbolism as primitive language and thought. But if we wish to confine ourselves to what is susceptible of proof, a careful distinction must be made between the fact of the generality of symbolic thought and the hypothesis that it is hereditary or innate. When this is done, the general " primitive " character of symbolic thought can be interpreted in two quite distinct ways, as either congenital or merely infantile. Jung himself considerably modified his theory of hereditary symbolism when he stated, in reply to his critics: " I make no claim that these representations are inherited, but I believe we inherit the possibility of such representations, which is not the same thing." [2] If this reply were taken literally it would not only amount to the statement that it is only the possibility of thought that is innate (which is universally accepted), but it would also mean that the explanation of the special mechanisms of thought must be sought in the laws of its development in childhood.

What, in fact, do we find in the general symbols discovered or recognised by Jung? First there is a series of mystic symbols (the cross, etc.) whose content might well be collective in the social rather than the general sense. For a sociologist, there would be many reservations to be made in the field of myths, and it might be that the " collective consciousness " of Durkheim would include part of the " collective unconscious " of Jung. It might be said in answer to

[1] See C. G. Jung, *L'Homme à la découverte de son âme*, Trad. Cahen-Salabelle, Genève (*Coll. Action et Pensée*), 1944, and Yolan Jacobi, *Die Psychologie von C. G. Jung*, Rascher (Zurich), 1940, p. 57.

[2] Quoted by Raymond de Saussure, *La méthode psychanalytique*, p. 28.

this that symbolism as a general structure of thought is inherent in the individual before he is socialised, and to some extent we would agree. This, however, brings us back to the infantile interpretation, since it is only the child who is prior to any form of social life.

A second category of general symbols contains those which are common to the thought of the child, to dreams and to the various symbolic forms of adult thought. A good example is that of water, which is connected with the idea of " original environment," and therefore with the idea of birth and rebirth in a large number of representations. It is frequently found in oneiric symbols. In many myths, men or gods come out of water. In various baptismal rites the use of water combines the two ideas of rebirth and purification. In the stories made up by children to account for the origin of things —stories which are intermediary between ludic invention and serious thought—water again plays a part which, although there may be adult influence, has an original character. In an earlier work (*Representation of the World*) we quoted the case of a boy who explained the origin of man by saying that little worms came out of bubbles at the bottom of a big lake which covered everything. These little worms were thrown up on the shore, grew arms, feet and teeth, became babies who developed into the first men, and were divided into Swiss, French and Germans.

Even if we assume that such general symbols are not due to far-fetched comparisons, are we to conclude that hereditary factors intervene? Two explanations are possible. Either there is an innate, unconscious tendency common to all men, which actuates the child of to-day as it determined the representations of our ancestors, or else it is a question of mere imaged representation due to the symbolic assimilation which characterises the child's thought and which can be general in so far as the products of infantile thought influence " primitive " forms of thought.

In order to decide between these two possibilities, it seems to us essential, since on principle we are not prepared to isolate the question of symbolic thought from that of thought in general, to compare these possible convergences with those to be found between the true conceptual thought of the child and that of primitive or ancient societies. There are more points of similarity than might be thought. We shall not consider infantile magic, " participations " in the sense of Levy-Bruhl, or myths of origin, since they are intermediary between symbolic and conceptual thought, and therefore raise the same problem. We can, however, refer to the striking resemblances between the beginnings of rational thought in the child of from seven to ten and in the Greeks. We find, for example, explanation by identification of substances (stars which are produced by air or clouds, air and earth coming from water, etc.), by atomism resulting from this identification and the use of the ideas of condensation and rarefaction, and even the exact explanation of certain movements by reaction of the air (ἀντιπερίστασις) used by Aristotle. Are we then to conclude that the archetypes which inspired the beginnings of Greek physics are inherited by the child? In our opinion it is infinitely simpler merely to assume that the same genetic mechanisms which account for the development of the thought of the child of to-day were in action also in the minds of those who, like the pre-Socratics, were just emerging from mythological and pre-logical thought. As for the schema of " reaction of the air," it seems to have been borrowed by Aristotle from current representations, which may have been as widespread in a civilisation prior to mechanisation as they are among the children of to-day.

To sum up, where there is convergence between the thought of the child and historical representations, it is much easier to explain the latter by the general laws of infantile mentality than by reference to a mysterious heredity. However far back we go into history or prehistory, the child has always preceded the adult, and it can be assumed that the more primitive a society, the more lasting the influence of the child's thought on the individual's development, since such a society is not as yet capable of transmitting or forming a scientific culture.

If this is true of thought in general, there is no reason why it should not be true also of symbolic thought in particular. We shall therefore adopt Jung's central idea of primitive symbolic thought, independent of the mechanisms of repression and censorship. But in order to explain it, we must come back to the child's visible and analysable psycho-genetic development. We are indebted to Freud for confining the problem of unconscious symbolism to the field of individual evolution. Once the idea of disguise is removed, symbolism can, thanks to the truly primitive character of the mechanisms of the child's thought, acquire the same degree of generality that Jung found in his hypothesis of a " collective unconscious."

§ 4. *An attempt to explain unconscious symbolism*

Unconscious symbolism, *i.e.*, symbolism whose significance is not immediately recognised by the subject himself, is a particular case of symbolism in general and must be considered as such. The conscious symbolism of the adult (images, concrete comparisons, etc.) is very far removed from his unconscious symbolism (dreams, etc.). In the case of the child, however, we find all the intermediaries between these two extremes, since in imaginative or symbolic play there are symbols of every shade, from those analogous to the symbols of dreams to those which are deliberately constructed and completely comprehensible to the subject. It can even be said that between the ages of two and four it is the symbols half-way between the two extremes, *i.e.*, partly conscious and partly unconscious, which are the most common.

If this is so, it is clear that an explanation which is valid for symbolic play must *ipso facto* be valid also for unconscious symbolism, provided that this explanation is capable of generalisation in the new dimension of the unconscious, *i.e.*, is able to account for the fact that the subject fails to understand his own symbolism. If symbolic play is merely the expression of assimilation of reality to the ego, *i.e.*, assimilation dissociated from the corresponding accommodation, the unconscious symbol is even more so. The unconscious character of the symbol can be explained by the complete egocentrism of dreams (in so far as there is loss of contact with reality), and of repressed tendencies (in so far as they are opposed to actual reality). In a state of radical egocentrism there is complete lack of differentiation between the ego and the external world, and consequently a state of non-consciousness of the ego, or projection of internal impressions into the forms provided by the external world, which is the same thing. The origin of the unconscious symbol is to be found in the suppression of consciousness of the ego by complete absorption in, and identification with, the external world, and it therefore constitutes merely a limit case of assimilation of reality to the ego, *i.e.*, of ludic symbolism.

In attempting to prove our point, we shall distinguish three questions: that of anatomical symbols, in which part of the subject's body is represented by an external object, that of non-anatomical symbols independent of repression, and that of the relationship between symbolism and repression. Anatomical symbols may or may not be accompanied by repressions. Moreover, they may be formed at any age, and are not necessarily the most primitive. But they are particularly instructive because of their paradoxical character, and are often among the most unconscious, and we therefore think it useful to consider them first.

In § 1 we saw two examples of these anatomical symbols: a dream accompanying urination and representing a watering-can being emptied, and a dream of erection representing a bean which swelled. Numerous examples dealing with the masculine and feminine organs have been collected by the Freudians. In all these cases, it is obvious that there may have been repression, at least during the dream. It is important to note, however, that anatomical symbols are also to be found in the images of the half-sleeping state, symbols which involve parts of the body which do not give rise to repression.

An adult frequently went to sleep with his hand resting against the angle of his lower jaw, and could feel the blood pumping in the carotid artery. At widely separated times this position gave rise to the following images: (1) A stream bubbling against the corner of a rock, with a rhythm exactly corresponding to that of the heart beats (as the subject was able to verify when he woke up). (2) A horse galloping with the same rhythm. (3) The curves described in the water by the *Gordius Aquaticus*, a worm more than a yard long and as thin as a piece of string. Here again the intervals between the curves corresponded to the heart beats. (4) The pressure of the head on the open hand sometimes produced a numbness of the fingers which seemed, in the half-sleeping state, to swell to a ridiculous size. The subject then saw a number of long bags of cement, arranged fan-wise (this symbol recurred several times). (6) Half-wakened by cramp in a bent leg, the subject stretched it out, and just as he stood up he saw a frog with its legs moving from a state of flexion to an upright position. He had the feeling that he was still dreaming, and was himself the frog. (6) The dentist had left a small pad of cotton wool between two molars. The subject saw a mass of wet moss in between two rocks just when, in his half-sleeping state, he was feeling this foreign body with his tongue.

We are aware that in cases 1–5 there is the possibility that other internal sensations may have interfered with the main cause of the production of the image. In 6, however, these possible factors seem to be excluded, and even if they intervene in 1–5, which is a gratuitous assumption, the essential content of the symbol is still obviously the result of the sensations we have described.

If we consider the mechanism of the formation of the image in the very young child, we find a very simple explanation of the anatomical symbol. The semi-consciousness of the dreamer is indeed comparable to the state of complete egocentrism characteristic of the baby's consciousness. In both cases there is complete lack of differentiation between the ego and the external world, and assimilation of objects to the activity of the subject. These two aspects of elementary consciousness are interdependent, and for the following reason. The ego is unconscious of itself to the extent to which it incorporates external reality, since consciousness of the ego is relative to the resist-ance of objects and of other persons.[1] This being so, one of the essential tasks of primitive assimilation consists in the co-ordination of the heterogenous worlds, visual, tactile, kinæsthetic, etc. In the baby, the acquisition of the power to grasp marks the first stage of the mutual assimilation of visual and tactilo-kinæsthetic schemas, and this co-ordination takes place relatively early, because the hand can be simultaneously a visual object and a source of tactilo-kinæsthetic impressions. On the other hand, the whole problem of the imitation of movements related to the face is characterised by new difficulties

[1] Freud has already compared the " narcissism of dreams " with what he calls the " narcissism " of the baby. But we must insist that the essence of this narcissism is the absence of consciousness of the ego, and this alone explains the powers which the subject's own activity then acquires.

of co-ordination, which are very instructive for the understanding of the anatomical symbolism of a later stage. As the baby has only a partial knowledge of his physical self, and possesses no visual image of his face, but only a set of tactile, gustative or kinæsthetic impressions, he is obliged to use his perception of the bodies of others in learning to translate these schemas into visual schemas. He sometimes makes very significant mistakes. For instance, on seeing someone else's eyes close and open again, he will open and close his mouth, thus wrongly assimilating the visual schema of the model's eyes to the tactilo-kinæsthetic schema of his own mouth. It is clear that the sleeper, having lost consciousness of his ego, is by that very circumstance, and apart from any question of repression, in the same situation as the baby. He also must translate (but inversely) his physical impressions into visual images, and he will be liable to make the same mistakes.

There are, however, two essential differences between the dreamer and the baby learning to co-ordinate the tactilo-kinæsthetic and the visual. Firstly, the dreamer is capable of forming mental images, since as he already knows how to imitate and use his earlier accommodations, he can construct these images even in dreams. Secondly, while the baby is trying to adapt himself to reality, the dreamer cuts off all communication with reality and merely assimilates it in imagination, making use only of earlier accommodations on which the images used are based. It is precisely because there is no immediate accommodation that there is complete dissociation of the inner activity from the external world. As the external world is represented solely by images, it is assimilated without resistance to the unconscious ego, and it is in this respect that oneiric symbolism is a continuation of ludic symbolism.

It follows, firstly, that all impressions which are internal or related to the body (whether it be stimulation of organs or sensations resulting from action of the blood, from fingers or legs which are numb, from a foreign body in a tooth, etc.) are felt but not connected with the body of the subject, since there is no consciousness of the ego. They therefore become external images. The sleeper is still conscious of something, since he is dreaming, but he is not conscious of the ego, since he is not aware that he is asleep nor that he is dreaming. Even when he himself is part of his dream, it is through a kind of projection similar to that of children who talk about themselves in the third person. It is not consciousness of his present subjective activity, but an imaged story in which he is one of the characters. It is extremely difficult to put oneself in the position of a consciousness which is capable of perceiving a bodily impression without being able to connect it to an ego. Observation of a three- or four-months-old baby, whose hand is being held outside its field of vision, will, however, provide an example of a subject who is very conscious of experiencing a tactile and kinæsthetic sensation (since he struggles), but who looks all round him, and not at himself, to find the visual situation corresponding to the impression. The sleeper is in the same situation. The impression he feels, seeks as it were a visual correspondence, and then, since he can see nothing and is even unaware that he is involved, but is capable of constructing images, he has recourse to any external image which offers some point of resemblance.

This brings us to the second point. This resemblance implies assimilation of the imagined reality to the internal bodily impression. This assimilation raises no new problem. It is the assimilation which takes place in symbolic play, *i.e.*, in a situation in which present assimilation is dominated by assimilation to the subject's activity. Unconscious symbolism here continues ludic symbolism, but the continuation extends to the point at which, since there is no present accommodation, egocentric assimilation becomes imaginary absorption of the external world and suppression of consciousness of the ego. Dreams are therefore comparable to symbolic play, but play which, by lack of consciousness of the ego, is itself analogous to the lack of co-ordination between the visual and the motor, characteristic of the first year of life.

Since this is so in the case of anatomical symbols, there remains no difficulty in finding an explanation of any symbolism, when there is no apparent repression involved. Generally speaking, we can assume that dreams are a continuation of symbolic play, but such that the closer the connection between the ego and the desires involved, the more these desires are projected into external images. Moreover, it is clear that in dreams the absence of consciousness of the ego entails the kind of immediate belief that is prior even to the possibility of doubt, while in play this belief gradually gives way to the feeling of make-believe, for reasons that we have seen.

It is this factor of the degree of subjectivity of desires which accounts for those dreams of very young children which Freud calls non-symbolic because they translate wish-fulfilment into direct images whose meaning is obvious. Such, for instance, are the dreams of eating eggs, or of kittens replacing guinea-pigs, which we quoted earlier. But in the case of adult dreams, such as those related to the separation of parents or the criticism of Goblot (see § 2), the fact that the wish is more subtle explains why in the dream its realisation is projected into external images. The same thing is obviously true in the case of nightmares, irrespective of the question of possible repressions. In a general way, the fact that symbolism becomes more complex in the course of mental development (which is broadly speaking true) can therefore easily be explained by the increasing complexity and individualisation of desires, which are responsible both for the gradual elaboration of play and the progressive unconsciousness of oneiric assimilations.

To come finally to the effects of repression, it becomes possible to include them in what has been said, but as a particular case and not as a general factor. The inability of the subject to understand a symbol, and therefore its unconscious character, is accounted for by the fact that egocentric assimilation is carried to the point at which all present accommodation, *i.e.*, all contact with present reality, is suppressed, involving at the same time suppression of consciousness of the ego. A repressed tendency is one which the subject refuses to accept, and to which he therefore denies all accommodation to reality. It is consequently driven out of his consciousness, and there is no need to have recourse to " censorship " to account for its disguised character, since repression makes it incapable of awareness by refusing it any possibility of accommodation. This being the case, the fact that a repressed tendency is satisfied symbolically (*e.g.*, the dream of the doctor killing a fat man, obs. 98) can be explained in exactly the same way as the symbolic translation of any desires or bodily impressions when they are not related to consciousness of the ego. A repressed tendency is by definition deprived of accommodation, and therefore dissociated from the conscious ego. If, in spite of this, it seeks support, it can only be by way of egocentric and unconscious assimilation, *i.e.*, by means of a symbolic substitute. In our opinion therefore, to talk of " disguise " even in this case is to give a false picture. There is a symbolic substitute because there is no possibility of direct realisation of the desire, since it is repressed, and this symbolic assimilation remains unconscious just because it is only assimilation, without accommodation to reality.

That there is no question of disguise in the symbolism related to repressed tendencies, is proved by the fact that it remains unconscious even in cases where the repression itself is symbolised, as in the symbols of self-punishment. It sometimes happens that, instead of a symbolic substitute being used to express the realisation of a desire, the dream symbolises the result of the repression, and particularly the means of punishment. This symbolism is itself unconscious, whereas if there were censorship it would certainly be concerned to make the punishment known and even give it all the publicity of full consciousness. We have seen the dream of a dog biting fingers (obs. 98), and we might quote the many well-known dreams of castration to be found among adolescents. Here are a few examples:

A young man who was sometimes addicted to masturbation regularly punished himself during the following night in dreams of which we give three examples: (1) He saw an Eiffel Tower, reduced in size, and cut off at the level of the second storey (the upper part having disappeared). (2) He saw himself striking with all his might, with an enormous axe, at a python which was rearing itself in a bedroom. The head of the snake was already almost cut off, and hung bleeding. The subject's mother was hidden in the shadow of the room. (3) He saw himself with a broken leg surrounded by a white bandage, but he was terrified by splashes of blood which prevented him from undoing it.

The meaning of these dreams is obvious, and yet their symbolism is incomprehensible to the sleeper, the first being for him a kind of childish game, while the two others have a nightmare quality. In this particular case, there would seem to be no reason for disguise, since the object of the dreams is not to provide symbolic satisfaction for the repressed desire, but for the repression itself, or the desire for self-punishment. A simpler explanation must therefore be found for the unconsciousness of such symbols (which represent particular tendencies of a large class whose field extends far beyond that of dreams). There is no need to go very far for this explanation. These symbols are not understood by the subject because repression is itself an automatic or spontaneous regulation resulting from the interaction of affective schemas whose roots elude consciousness. The process is the same in the field of intuitive intelligence which precedes operational reflection. Having adopted a certain system of ideas, the person will, without knowing why, take up a position against an explanation or a hypothesis in a field which does not involve inter-individual affectivity. He will need to exert much effort and thought to find reasons for this incompatibility, because the intellectual schemas he uses are only conscious in their results, and not in their initial assimilations. There is no reason for affective schemas to be more conscious than intellectual schemas, far from it, nor for repression [1] to be more conscious than the elementary understanding of incompatibilities which characterises intuitive as distinct from reflective intelligence. In the most frequent cases of self-punishment, the inhibiting or repressing schemas is that of the super-ego. Its roots elude the subject's thought in the same way as do the remote, forgotten roots of the notions of cause, physical laws, etc., although in both cases the product of them (certain moral or natural laws) is known to consciousness.

Moreover, as in dreams the ego itself is no longer conscious, it is impossible to conceive that the repressed tendencies or the regulations of the repression should be so either. In this connection we must point out that the same symbolic satisfactions of repressed tendencies are sometimes more transparent in play than in dreams. Let us take, for example, the story of Zoubab cutting off her father's head (obs. 37). X. was entertained by what she made up because she knew that her aggressiveness was not very serious and was aware of the

[1] Repression being the blocking of inhibition for a tendency incompatible with others stronger than itself because they are organised in stable assimilating schemas.

opposite feelings which counterbalanced it. In the dream about the doctor killing a man in the air, on the other hand, everything was less conscious both because of the represssions and the absence of all control by the ego. In the case of play, there is assimilation superseding accommodation, and therefore relative consciousness of the symbolism even when there is repression. In the case of dreams, however, purely affective assimilation eliminates consciousness of the ego, and the assimilating mechanisms of the schemas of which repression is the expression, resist any awareness. We have here two reasons, similar in kind but distinct and complementary, which explain the unconsciousness of the symbol without having recourse to disguise.

To sum up, the unconscious symbol is an image whose content is assimilated to the desires or impressions of the subject, and whose meaning he fails to understand. The image is explained by earlier accommodations of the subject. Assimilation of reality to the ego superseding immediate accommodation is common to oneiric and ludic symbolism. The unconscious character of the symbol derives entirely from this primacy of assimilation, which in its extreme form eliminates all accommodation, thereby excluding consciousness of the ego and awareness of the assimilating mechanisms. Repression, being a result of the inter-regulation of schemas of affective assimilation, raises no special problem as far as symbolism is concerned. In the cases where it is present, it merely strengthens the general reasons for unconsciousness.

§ 5. *Unconscious symbolism and affective schemas*

Such, then, are the conclusions we reach when we compare unconscious symbolism with the processes of the child's thought, and it now remains to place unconscious symbolic thought within the framework of mental equilibrium. Since it is not disguise, its positive significance must be discovered and related to that of symbolic play and conscious symbolism.

We have seen that symbolic play is free assimilation of reality to the ego, assimilation which is essential because the young child's thought is not adapted to reality. The more the child progresses in adaptation, the more play is reintegrated into general intelligence, and the conscious symbol is replaced by constructions and creative imagination.

There is an exact correspondence in the case of the relationships which determine unconscious symbolism. Affective life, like intellectual life, is a continual adaptation, and the two are not only parallel but interdependent, since feelings express the interest and the value given to actions of which intelligence provides the structure. Since affective life is adaptation, it also implies continual assimilation of present situations to earlier ones—assimilation which gives rise to affective schemas or relatively stable modes of feeling or reacting—and continual accommodation of these schemas to the present situation. It is in so far as this equilibrium between affective assimilation and accommodation is achieved that there is the possibility of conscious regulation of feelings, and of the standards of values constituted by moral sentiments, under the direction of the will. But when this equilibrium is not achieved, assimilation of present to past continues to be a vital necessity, and it is this primacy of assimilation over accommodation which is expressed by unconscious symbolism, in complete continuity with conscious symbolism.

The function of unconscious symbolism is therefore closely linked with that of the affective schemas. The relationship is not however exclusive, for although affectivity intervenes almost constantly in play as well as in intelligence, intellectual schemas also interfere in dreams with affective schemas. Agassiz's dream about fossilized fish, and that of Kékulé about the benzine formula are well-known examples of symbolic solution of problems by means of images which later lead to real discoveries. There is, however, naturally a preponderance of affective schemas.

A system of affective schemas may be compared to schemas of sensory-motor and intuitive intelligence (as distinct from operational intelligence which corresponds to feelings of standards and moral values). For instance, when at about the end of his first year the child, playing with some toy, discovers the possibility of finding it again when it is behind or underneath another toy, he will apply to all kinds of other objects this capacity for existence outside the limits of the field of vision. In this way the schema of permanent objects independent of the child's activity is constructed through sensory-motor generalisation, which is partly conscious, but largely unconscious and spontaneous. Similarly, a little later, having discovered intuitively the usual proportion between the weight and volume of objects, the child will generalise it in a partially correct schema, which will for a long time resist the more precise idea of variable density of bodies, and will even give rise to perceptive illusions like the well-known illusion of weight. These sensory-motor or intuitive schemas naturally involve some intellectual activity, but affectivity is by no means absent. Interests, pleasures and difficulties, joy at success and disappointment at failure, all the " basic feelings " of Janet intervene here, as regulations of the action constructed by intelligence. As Claparède (in the case of interest) and Janet have shown, affectivity thus regulates the energetics of the action while intelligence provides the technique.

In the same way, the persons on whom the child acts and who act on him give rise to certain general schemas. At first, before the affective " object-choice " these schemas differ little from those we have just considered. Persons are merely particularly interesting and unpredictable sources of action, capable of dispensing special pleasures, as at meal-times or of giving rise to exceptionally amusing sensory-motor exchanges. As soon as the schema of substantial and permanent objects is acquired, and especially at the level of intuitive intelligence, persons become other " egos " at the same time as the ego itself is being constituted and becoming a person. Then the schemas related to persons are enriched with new feelings, which are inter-individual and no longer impersonal, resulting partly from the projection and transfer of feelings hitherto connected only with the child's own body (narcissism) and his own activity, but of which an essential part consists of new constructions.

Day to day observation and psycho-analytic experience show that the first personal schemas are afterwards generalised and applied to many other people. According as the first inter-individual experiences of the child who is just learning to speak are connected with a father who is understanding or dominating, loving or cruel, etc., the child will tend (even throughout life if these relationships have influenced his whole youth) to assimilate all other individuals to this father schema. On the other hand, the type of feelings he has for his mother will tend to make him love in a certain way, sometimes all through his life, because here again he partially assimilates his successive loves to this first love which shapes his innermost feelings and behaviours.

It must be pointed out first of all that this generalised application of initial affective schemas raises no particular problems with regard to the mechanism of assimilation which is necessarily involved. It is the same as that of sensory-motor or intuitive assimilation. Actions related to others are like other actions. They tend to be reproduced (reproductive assimilation), to find nutriment to sustain them (recognitive assimilation), and to discover new ones (generalising assimilation), whether it be a case of an affection, an aggressive tendency, or any other. It is the same assimilation, because personal schemas, like all others, are both intellectual and affective. We do not love without seeking to understand, and we do not even hate without a subtle use of judgment. Thus when we speak of " affective schemas " it must be understood that what is meant is merely the affective aspect of schemas which are also intellectual. The essential line of demarcation is the one which separates " personal schemas " from schemas connected with objects (inter-individual feelings and intuitive intelligence socialised by language, as distinct from a blending of interest and intelligence). But affective schemas extend in some measure beyond the personal sphere (primitive buccal schemas) and they are all both affective and cognitive.

A second point to notice is that normally the assimilation by which all schemas of whatever kind constantly incorporate new objects is accompanied by accommodation which is increasingly differentiated. A normal individual may find in his emotional life all kinds of traces of infantile behaviours connected with his relation to his mother. He will, however, add to them and anyone who marries with a mother fixation runs the risk of considerable complications in his married life. Similarly, the man who continues throughout his life to be dominated by an idealised image of his father, or who on the other hand pursues the dream of a freedom he never acquired in his youth must of necessity have diminished powers. Equilibrium consists in preserving the living aspects of the past by continual accommodation to the manifold and irreducible present.

If this conception of schemas is correct, the theories of the unconscious and of symbolic thought become much simpler, or at least they cease to form a realm apart and become part of the dynamism common to the development of thought in general and that of affectivity.

Why, in fact, is it that affective schemas, at least in their essence, remain unconscious ? Merely because all assimilation which does not combine with accommodation to form an equilibrium, *i.e.*, which does not result in purposive generalisation, takes place unconsciously both in the intellectual and the affective field. A sensory-motor transfer, which enables the subject to apply to a new problem schemas acquired earlier, is almost entirely unconscious. When in the field of reflective and even scientific thought a new problem is approached by way of uncritical transposition of habits of mind and ideas used in other fields, the assimilation is still largely unconscious. Even in the case of new, creative generalisation the origin of the new relationships which appear eludes the subject. As we recalled earlier, for Binet " thought is an unconscious activity of the mind." We see then that even when intelligence is at its most lucid the inner mechanism of assimilation is outside awareness, which first grasps only results and then by recurrent and ever incomplete reflection works back from the outside to a centre which it never reaches. It is therefore clear that the affective unconscious, *i.e.*, the affective aspect of the activity of assimilating schemas is in no way peculiar in its unconsciousness. It is only the veil of mystery which surrounds the personal element which has deceived psychologists on this point.

This being so there is no need to ascribe a representative memory to this unconscious in order to explain the continuity between past and present, since the schemas ensure the motor or dynamic aspect of this continuity. There is still less need to imagine a censorship to account for the fact that the subject fails to understand his hidden mechanisms. One might as well explain every case in which thought is ignorant of its own functioning as being due to censorship of intelligence. On the other hand, repression and its effects are as we have seen an essential element in the functioning of the schemas. These tend to assimilate one another wholly or in part, hence the total or partial transfers which constitute the equivalent of implications in the field of intelligence. Where assimilation is impossible, they tend to exclude one another, and correspond to incompatibilities in the intellectual field. The repression of one affective schema by another is therefore the very condition of the general organisation of the schemas.

But since we thus find all the transitional stages between unconscious assimilation and conscious adaptation, according as the assimilating mechanism is more or less in equilibrium with accommodation to new realities, there follows a series of consequences as regards affective thought, *i.e.*, the way in which the individual envisages both his own feelings and his relations with others. In so far as there is adaptation, *i.e.*, in so far as equilibrium is achieved, ordinary conceptual thought throws light on affective thought both in its intuitive form and in its operational or normative form. This thought never reaches the full mechanism of assimilation, of course, but the same is true in the intellectual field. On the other hand, when assimilation predominates over accommodation or is dissociated from it, the subject has only at his disposal for the understanding of his own reactions a mode of thought based on assimilation as such. This is symbolic thought.

In the child this primacy of assimilation constantly occurs, as we saw in considering play, both as regards intelligence and feelings. But in the adult, even when his intelligence is normally adapted, there is at least one kind of situation in which this primacy continues from the affective point of view, quite apart from the pathological states in which there is general regression. This is in dreams, during which affective life goes on, but without the possibility of accommodation to reality. It is for this reason that in dreams there is constant recurrence of symbolic thought analogous to that of children's play. They thus provide interesting indications as to the working of unconscious assimilations and the organisation of the subject's affective schemas. It must, however, be remembered that just because of their total lack of accommodation dreams reveal this organisation only partially, or in a relaxed form which in a state of real adaptation would be subject to other controls. Similarly, the state of half-dreaming and free assimilation in which non-directed thought is given free rein, during psycho-analytic treatment, breaks the equilibrium (although to a lesser degree) in favour of pure assimilation, and thus sometimes constitutes a partial return to symbolic thought. But here, again, this state is only partially revealing of an organisation which in a state of adaptation regains its right tension.

Symbolic thought is then the only possibility of awareness of the assimilation which takes place in affective schemas. This awareness is incomplete, and therefore distorting, since by the very nature of the situation the mechanisms which symbolic thought expresses are incapable of accommodation. It is, however, only awareness and not disguise. For this reason, while the schemas are translated into images and not into concepts and relationships as when there is adaptation through equilibrium with accommodation, symbolic thought is shaped by the organisation or reciprocal assimilation of these schemas, as we shall now show.

A system of affective schemas is comparable to a system of intellectual schemas, if it is true that they are complementary aspects of a single total reality, the system of schemas of real or virtual actions. It has not been sufficiently emphasised that, in spite of its apparent lack of coherence, symbolic thought contains an element of logic, a pre-logic of a level comparable to intuitive pre-logic except that there is free assimilation and no adaptation. Thus two basic processes " condensation " and " displacement," which according to Freud are constituents of the unconscious symbol, represent on this plane the functional equivalents of the generalisation and abstraction involved in concepts. It is true that there is no operational regulation, since symbolic thought is pre-logical, and like intuitive thought requires only regulations analogous to perceptive regulations because there is no operational reversibility. But condensation, like generalisation, involves giving a common meaning to a number of distinct objects, thus making it possible to give expression to a nest of affective schemas assimilating to one another various situations which are often widely separated in time. Take for example the case of a student of natural science dreaming of two birds and wondering whether they were two quite distinct species or merely two varieties of the same species. The presence in the dream of someone who disagreed with his conclusion showed that his preoccupation arose from an earlier situation in which a college friend maintained that the only difference between physical and ideal love is one of degree, while he supported the opposite view. The " condensation " of the symbol therefore expresses the assimilation of situations and is thus a kind of generalisation. Just as there can be no generalisation without abstraction, so in the symbol there cannot be condensation without displacement, since in the realm of images and affective assimilations displacement corresponds to abstraction in the realm of thought. In the conscious symbolism of play, we find all the intermediary stages between the initial condensations and displacements and the corresponding logical processes which make their appearance as the symbol tends towards conceptualisation.

In the same way the " projections " and " identifications " found in symbolism are merely pre-conceptual assimilations, as it were participations involving elementary thought. Images in which a part represents the whole or a thing represents its opposite are also evidence of pre-logical activity whose relationship with certain linguistic questions was pointed out by Freud. The doublets (two distinct images for the same signified), logical contradictions and lacunæ in symbolism are clear evidence of its inadequacy as compared with the coherence and synthesis of conceptual thought, but the same is true of the child's pre-logical and intuitive thought.

To sum up, symbolic thought, which is a pre-logical and not an anti-logical form of thought is the primitive expression of the assimila-of affective schemas. Is it an adequate representation ? The first point to note is that affective schemas do not achieve the same degree of generalisation and abstraction as logical schemas, except in the one case when they are regulated by reversible operations of reciprocity, etc., *i.e.*, when they thereby become moral schemas. Even in that case it is not merely a question of unconscious submission to the super-ego, but of an autonomous normative system parallel with the rational systems. At the level of spontaneous, non-regulated feelings, affective schemas can only correspond to intuitive intellectual schemas, which means that they do not achieve logical or moral generalisation and abstraction. An intuitive thought is intermediary between the image and the concept. It represents only by imagining, in contrast to logic, which represents by deducing relationships. In what is imagined, the general is always replaced by a particular case, sub-stituted for it not only as an example, but as a participation, or, in the strict sense, as a " substitute." Thus, for example, the schema of affective reactions assimilated to feelings connected with the father is more closely related to the particular schema of this father than is a logical concept to the object which gave rise to it. " Identification " with a father, to use the psycho-analysts' expression, is therefore nearer to a kind of pre-logical participation than to abstract con-ceptual assimilation, although, as we have already stressed, there is always a schema and not merely reduction to unconscious memories. But " unconscious " symbolic thought belongs to a much lower level than that of these intuitive schemas, since instead of representative examples being directly imagined, they are assimilated to imaged signifiers of some kind, of whose meaning the subject is unaware. At this point, however, we must remember that unconscious symbolic thought is by no means a permanent expression of the organisation of affective schemas. It operates only in certain exceptional situa-tions, such as children's play, the dreams of both children and adults, and sometimes in states of completely relaxed thought. All these are situations in which assimilation either takes precedence over accom-modation or even entirely supplants it. Only then does secondary symbolism intervene, because radical egocentrism makes conscious-ness of the ego impossible, and the only means by which the affective assimilations can then have any consciousness of themselves is by incorporating images as a support. The assimilation of these substitutes then continues the assimilation of the schemas, the former serving as signifiers, and the latter constituting their unconscious meaning.

On the whole, unconscious symbolic thought follows the same laws as thought in general, of which it is merely an extreme form, being an extension of symbolic play in the direction of pure assimilation. This functional coherence of the various manifestations of thought is all the more striking when, after seeing symbolism in its various forms in action, we find that it is implied in the beginnings of all the child's conceptual thought.

PART III

COGNITIVE REPRESENTATION

In the first part of this work we saw that imitation, which begins as a mere " positive " replica of accommodation, is continued in the form of representative images which serve as signifiers in play and in adapted thought, while the higher reflective forms of imitation proper are integrated in intelligence.   In the second part, on the other hand, we saw that play, which is at first merely a special form of functional sensory-motor assimilation, later becomes symbolic and is continued in this new form as unconscious symbolism, whereas the ludic symbol itself is integrated in intelligent activity to the extent to which the symbolism is a preparation for the construction of representation and free assimilation becomes creative imagination.

Broadly speaking, it can therefore be said that in the course of mental development, imitative accommodation and ludic assimilation, from being differentiated, gradually become more and more closely co-ordinated.   At the sensory-motor level they separate ; in symbolic play, earlier imitative images provide the " signifiers " and ludic assimilation provides the significations ; and finally, when they are integrated in adapted thought the image and the assimilation involve the same objects, imitative accommodation determining the signifiers for which free assimilation (which is no longer ludic precisely because of this co-ordination) provides the significations.   But obviously this progressive integration of imitative accommodation and constructive assimilation in intelligence only results from a gradual broadening of this intelligence which is responsible for the diminution of imitation and play, and from the start there is an essential nucleus of co-ordination between assimilation and accommodation which constitutes sensory-motor adaptation in general and intelligence itself. On the plan of sensory-motor intelligence it is a matter of simple co-ordination.   Either the two tendencies are in equilibrium and there is intelligence, or there is primacy of accommodation over assimilation and we have imitation, or there is the converse and we have play.   It is when the level of representation has been reached that varying gradations appear, owing to the greater number of possible combinations between assimilation on the one hand and on the other accommodations which are no longer only actual, as on the sensory-motor plane, but both actual (accommodation proper) and past (images).

In this last section we therefore have to attempt to determine the connection between the imitative image, ludic symbolism and representative intelligence, *i.e.*, between cognitive representation and the representation of imitation and play. This very complex problem is still further complicated by the intervention of language, collective verbal signs coming to interfere with the symbols we have already analysed, in order to make possible the construction of concepts. It will therefore be necessary to separate the various factors, and we shall begin by doing this in the case of the first conceptual schemas and the first reasonings, and then in the case of the formation of representative categories.

CHAPTER VIII

FOR some authors the explanation of the transition from sensory-motor intelligence to conceptual intelligence is to be found in social life and in the logical representative forms provided by the system of collective representations and signs. Thus for Wallon there is a radical opposition between " intelligence of situations," which acts on reality without the use of thought, and representation, which is due to the influence of language, myths, rituals, and collective life in general. This attitude is entirely justifiable if we adopt the viewpoint and speak the language which are those of the sociologist, but the psychologist cannot leap straight from neurology to sociology. What has to be discovered is not only an explanation of representation in general, but an explanation covering the detail of the representative mechanisms, as, for example, the many forms of spatial intuitions (order, position, displacement, distance, etc., up to simple geometrical operations). To take only the example of space, it is certainly impossible to interpret psychologically the most evolved representative structures without recognising that there is a certain continuity with sensory-motor space. As for the social element which obviously intervenes sooner or later in all representation, the problem is to discover by what processes it does so. For the psychologist, " social life " can only be considered to have value as a cause on condition that the kinds of social relationships in question are exactly defined. " Socialised " or common space, for example, comprises the most varied relationships, from rational co-ordination of perspectives to the most irrational mythical space. Our task is therefore to follow step by step the transformation of the sensory-motor schema into concept, and to consider the socialisation and verbalisation of the schemas as only one of the dimensions of this general transformation. In this way, the stages noted in the social dimension will be clarified by the phases of the internal evolutionary process which leads from sensory-motor to conceptual intelligence, and the various relationships of this multi-dimensional table will be seen to be only interdependent aspects of one and the same reality.

§ 1. *First verbal schemas*

In order to see how slowly the process of transformation of sensory-motor schemas into true concepts takes place, it is sufficient to observe the use made by the child of the first verbal signs and to analyse the types of assimilation to which they correspond.

Here are some examples of such schemas linked with semi-verbal signs, contemporaneous with stage VI of sensory-motor intelligence.

OBS. 101 (a). At 1 ; 1 (0) J. used the conventional onomatopœic sound " *tch tch* " to indicate a train passing her window, and repeated it each time a train passed, probably after the suggestion had first been made to her. But she afterwards said " *tch tch* " in two quite distinct types of situation. On the one hand, she used it indiscriminately for any vehicles she saw out of another window, cars, carriages and even a man walking, at 1 ; 1 (4). At about 1 ; 1 (6) and on the following days any noise from the street, as well as trains, produced *tch tch*. But on the other hand, when I played bo-peep, appearing and disappearing without speaking, J. at 1 ; 1 (4) also said " *tch tch* " probably by analogy with the sudden appearance and disappearance of the trains.

At about 1 ; 1 (20) she said " *bow-wow* " to indicate dogs. At 1 ; 1 (29) she pointed from her balcony at the landlord's dog in the garden and said " *bow-wow*." The same day, a few hours later, she made the same sound as she pointed to the geometrical pattern on a rug (a horizontal line crossed by three vertical lines). At 1 ; 2 (1), on seeing a horse from her balcony, she looked at it attentively and finally said " *bow-wow*." Same reaction an hour later at the sight of two horses. At 1 ; 2 (3) an open pram which a woman was pushing and in which the baby was clearly visible, produced " *bow-wow* " (this too was seen from her balcony). At 1 ; 2 (4) she said " *bow-wow* " at the sight of hens, and at 1 ; 2 (8) at the sight of dogs, horses, prams and cyclists, " *tch tch* " being apparently reserved for cars and trains. At 1 ; 2 (12) " *bow-wow* " referred to everything seen from her balcony: animals, cars, the owner of the house (whose dog had first been called " *bow-wow* ") and people in general. At 1 ; 2 (15) the term was applied to the trucks railway porters were pulling, a long way from the house. At 1 ; 3 (7) it again referred to the pattern on the rug. Finally, after 1 ; 4, " *bow-wow* " seemed to be definitely reserved for dogs.

At 1 ; 2 (4) J. was in her mother's arms and said " *daddy* " to a man and then a moment later " *mummy* " to a strange woman. For some weeks " *daddy* " was applied indiscriminately to all sorts of men, while the use of " *mummy* " was more restricted, although it was applied two or three times to women who had not got children with them.

At about 1 ; 6 J. was becoming more and more skilful in using adults in order to obtain what she wanted, and always grizzled when they refused or pretended not to hear. One of her grand-fathers was the person she found most accommodating, with the result that at 1 ; 6 (13) she began to use the term " *panana* " not only to call her grandfather but also to indicate that she wanted something, even when he was not present. She would indicate what she wanted by saying its name, give a definite grizzle and add " *panana*." At 1 ; 6 (9) she even said " *panene* " when she was finding it boring to be washed ; " *panene* " was merely an indication that she wanted something to amuse her.

Also at about 1 ; 6 the word " *papeu* " was used to mean " gone away " and was applied to people going out of the room, vehicles going away, matches that were blown out. At 1 ; 6 (11) she even used it of her own tongue which she had put out and then put in again.

OBS. 101 (*b*). L., at 1 ; 3 (4), said " *ha* " to a real cat and then to a toy elephant, but not to a hen or a horse. But at 1 ; 3 (19) " *ha* " was applied to the horse as well as to her toys. At 1 ; 6 (25) " *ha* " had become " *hehe* " and referred to all animals except the cat and the rabbit, to all kinds of people and even to her sister. The rabbit was " *hin* " and became identified with the cat, for which the same term was therefore used.

At 1 ; 3 (14) L. said " *no* " not only when she was refusing something but when she failed to find something she was feeling for. The transition between the two senses was the " no " applied to a forbidden object. Similarly the word " *avoua* " a corruption of *au revoir*, referred to people going away, herself going out of a room, touching a door or merely getting up from her seat.

OBS. 102. T., at 1 ; 0 (0), said " *tata* " for all successful actions, *e.g.*, getting hold of a toy with a string on it, or finding an adequate response to an attempt at imitation.

At 1 ; 2 (22) he cried " *Mummy!* " when his mother, who had been with him for more than an hour, began to swing to and fro. This was therefore an exclamatory appreciation of unsuspected powers on the part of his mother. At 1 ; 2 (23) he said " *daddy* " to J. who held out her arms to him like his father. The same day he used " *daddy* " in reference to a male visitor and to a peasant who was lighting his pipe (though he never referred to him thus in the usual way). For several weeks after 1 ; 3 (2) " *mummy* " was used, like " *panene* " in the case of J., to indicate that he wanted something. At 1 ; 4 (4), for example, he said " *mummy* " as he pointed to what he wanted, even when he was referring to his father or to some other person. Also at 1 ; 6 (23) he said " *mummy* " to his father as he pointed to a lamp that he wanted him to light and put out (although it was only his father who ever played this game with him). At 1 ; 4 (10), however, he said " *mummy* " when he gave his mother a piece of paper and also when he saw her clothes in a cupboard. Similarly, he said " *daddy* " at 1 ; 4 (23) when he saw his father shaving, also a few days later, when his father was swinging him, and then when he saw his father's rucksack. At 1 ; 4 (29), when one of my friends was there, and I asked him " Who is it? " he replied " *daddy*," pointing to him. At 1 ; 5 (19) " *daddy* " referred to any man who was from fifteen to twenty yards away, and at 1 ; 5 (25) to men in general.

At 1 ; 2 (24) he said " *bow-wow* " to a dog (as he had already done during the preceding days), but also to a hen, a cow-bell, cows themselves, guinea-pigs and a cat. At 1 ; 3 (5) he even said " *bow-wow* " to anything moving, from an ant to a tractor in a field. At 1 ; 3 (13), however, there was a differentiation: the cows, a deer's head and a stag's antlers became " *moo* " (although sometimes the antlers were still " *bow-wow* "), the cat became " *pussy* " and pigs wandering about were either " *moo* " or " *pussy*."

At 1 ; 4 (22) *ali* (the pillow) became an expression of achievement (like *tata* at 1 ; 0). At 1 ; 4 (23) he said " *nono* " while closing his eyes in an effort to make a lamp go out and come on again, but at 1 ; 5 (30) " *nono* " was used in reference to all his dolls (who slept when he was not playing).

At 1 ; 5 (19) " *no more* " meant going away, then throwing something on the ground, and was then used of something that was overturned (without disappearing). He thus said " *no more* " to his blocks. Later " *no more* " merely meant that something was at a distance from him (outside his field of prehension), and then it referred to the game of holding out an object for someone to throw it back to him. At 1 ; 6 (23) he even said " *no more* " when he wanted something someone was holding. Finally, at 1 ; 7 " *no more* " became synonymous with " begin again."

In spite of their trivial character, these examples are deserving of careful examination. At this stage, they are, with respect to purely sensory-motor schemas, in the same relation as the first symbolic schemas are to practice play, and the first forms of deferred imitation to immediate imitation. In other words, these first verbal schemas are intermediary between the schemas of sensory-motor intelligence and conceptual schemas, just as symbolic schemas are intermediary between practice play and ludic symbols abstracted from the child's own activity, and as deferred imitation is intermediary between sensory-motor imitation and representative imitation. Moreover, the words applied by the child to these schemas are themselves intermediary between symbolic or imitative signifiers and true signs.

Can these first verbal schemas be in fact compared to true concepts ? At the level of concrete logical operations (*i.e.*, as early as the age of seven or eight), concepts are either systems of classes, sets of objects grouped according to relations between wholes and parts, or systems of particular relations grouped according to their symetrical or asymetrical nature. But in all cases, the relations in question are determined by the qualities of the objects composing the groups, whether or no the child himself and his own activity are also involved. Now, whereas in the observations relating to later levels we shall see the beginning of the elaboration of such concepts, it is clear that the schemas described in obs. 101 and 102 do not correspond to this structure. On the contrary, they are characterised by the fact that the principle for grouping of objects under one heading is only partially determined by direct assimilation of the objects one to another owing to their objective qualities, and involves also assimilation of the objects to the point of view of the subject (this often being the predominating element) : *e.g.*, the spatial situation in which the child finds himself, or the repercussion of the objects on his own actions. Thus for J. the semi-verbal sign " tch tch " was applied to anything that appeared and disappeared when she was looking out of a window (trains, cars, etc.) as well as to her father playing bo-peep with her. The sign " bow-wow " referred not only to dogs and similar animals, but to anything she saw from the balcony from which she had seen the original dog. " Panana " (a corruption of grandpa) referred to her grandfather but was also used to express a desire for something her grandfather would have given her had he been present. As for the words " mummy " and " daddy," which are often considered to be the first words used by children, their complexity is obvious. We are all familiar with the generalisation of " daddy " to apply to all men. In the case of J., " mummy " was also applied, though more rarely, to all kinds of women. But these terms are most frequently used to refer to particular actions which interest the child or are connected with him in some way. For T., " daddy " was anyone who lit a pipe or who stretched out his arms as his father did (in this particular instance it was his sister J.), and " mummy " became a term expressing a desire for something and a word of command to get his father to do something. Generalisation may also occur from the point of view of the child himself. Thus one day T. used " daddy " to refer to any men who were fifteen to twenty yards away and who were walking (as distinct from those who were motionless) and only later included all men like his father in this class. Moreover, " mummy " and " daddy " may be used to emphasise some action done in an unusual way by the parents. It is clear that these words, far from denoting merely singular classes and being proper names, as the statistics of Mrs. Buhler (*Kindheit u. Jugend*, pp. 149–150) suggest, really represent complex schemas of actions, either related to the subject or partly objective. Similarly, the zoological classifications of L. (" ha " and " hin ") and of T. (" bow-wow," " moo " and " pussy ") indicate, by their uncertainty, that they referred much more to systems of possible actions than to objects. Schemas such as " papeu " (*i.e.*, gone) in the case of J., " no more " in the case of T., and " avoua " and " no " in the case of L., as well as " tata," " ali " and " nono " are evidently only schemas of actions which are as much subjective as they are objectively classified.

Thus these first verbal schemas are merely sensory-motor schemas in process of becoming concepts ; they are neither purely sensory-motor schemas nor clear concepts. They are still essentially sensory-motor, in that they are modes of action capable of generalisation and of application to an increasing number of objects, but they partake of the concept in that there is already a partial dissociation from the child's own activity. Moreover, since they are expressed by verbal phonemes through which they are related to the actions of others, they involve the element of communication characteristic of the concept.

Although these verbal schemas are an indication of development in the direction of the concept, it must be noted, even from this second point of view and irrespective of their character as schemas of action, that two peculiarities still considerably restrict their evolution in this direction and remind us once again of the sensory-motor schematism of stage VI, but this time on the new plane of concepts in process of formation. Firstly, the concept implies a fixed definition, corresponding to a stable convention which gives the verbal sign its meaning. The meanings of words do not constantly change, because the classes and the relations they denote involve a conceptual definition determined once for all by the social group. But the meaning of a term such as " bow-wow " in the case of J. changed in a few days from dogs to cars and even to men. The method by which one object is related to another is therefore different in the case of the true concept from that of the intermediary schema of this level. In the case of the concept, there is inclusion of an object in a class and of one class in another, whereas in a schema such as " bow-wow " and the others, there is merely a subjective feeling of kinship between the related objects, a kinship which is the forerunner of the " participations " which we shall show to be characteristic of the preconcepts of the next stage. Secondly, the first words used, " bow-wow," " daddy," precede " signs " properly so called, i.e., the inter-related elements of an already organised language. They are still intermediary between the individual symbol or imitative image and the sign which is properly social. They still have, indeed, the imitative character of the symbol, either because they are onomatopœic (imitation of the object indicated), or because they are an imitation of words used in adult language, but which are abstracted from it and imitated in isolation. But more especially as we have just seen, they still have the disconcerting mobility of the symbol, as distinct from the fixity of the sign.

Hence we find all the intermediaries between these semi-concepts expressed by semi-signs and ludic symbols. For instance, when a child denotes a design on a rug by the term " bow-wow " (J. in obs. 101), is it a case of conceptual classification by means of a sign, or of construction of a ludic symbol merely accompanied by language ? Here are some examples of the transition between symbols in the strict sense and the semi-concepts of obs. 101 and 102.

OBS. 103.   At 1 ; 6 (10) J. thought she saw a fish (*cf.* her celluloid gold-fish) in the marks on the wooden ceiling, and she said "*frog*" when looking at a mark on the wall.   At 1 ; 8 (20), seeing similar marks in the woodwork of a chalet, she pointed to a mule, a boy, a dog and a cat, and almost every time she added "*gone*," either because she was playing, or because she stopped seeing them, or even perhaps because she wanted to indicate that they were not real.   Similarly, at 1 ; 9 (0) she saw a "*pussy*" in the pattern of a dress and then said "*gone*."   At 1 ; 10 (1), on seeing the moon, she spontaneously said "*lady*," without laughing and without the comparison ever having been suggested to her either by words or pictures.   Moreover, she added "*bell*," referring to the one that hung over the door of the chalet.

At 2 ; 0 (26), however, when she was watching her food being diluted with milk in a bowl, and said, "*look, dog, bird,*" etc., she definitely laughed.

It is clearly almost impossible to determine whether these identifications are purely ludic symbols, as they tend to be at the age of 2 ; 0, simple comparative judgments based on imitative images, or judgments of conceptual assimilation.   Probably they cannot be classified, precisely because they are intermediary between these three terms. Being at one and the same time symbolic, imitative and conceptual, they enable us to understand in retrospect the nature of the identifications of obs. 101 and 102, which also, though their proportions are different, represent intermediate stages between the symbol and the concept.

§ 2.   "*Preconcepts*"

This being the position towards the end of the development of sensory-motor intelligence, how will the first verbal schemas, which as we have seen are half-way between sensory-motor schemas (adapted, imitative or symbolic in varying degrees) and conceptual schemas, evolve in the direction of the latter ?   Obviously, since conceptual schemas are related to the system of organised verbal signs, progress in conceptual representation will go hand in hand with that of language. Once he is in possession of the semi-signs described in obs. 101 and 102, the child will quickly learn to speak, his progress following the lines with which Stern's investigations have made us familiar, word-sentences, sentences of two words, and complete sentences which soon come to be linked one with another.   This brings us to the second phase of the development of representation, corresponding to stages I and II of Chapter V.   But there still remains the problem of discovering in what way language makes possible the construction of concepts, for the relationship is naturally reciprocal and the capacity for constructing conceptual representations is one of the conditions necessary for the acquisition of language.

The first use of language is mainly in the form of orders and expressions of desire. As we have seen in the preceding examples, the act of giving a name to an object is not merely that and nothing more, but the statement of a possible action. At this level, the word does little more than translate the organisation of sensory-motor schemas to which it is not indispensable. The first question is to discover how the child proceeds, from this language which is coupled on to an immediate, present action, to the construction of true verbal representations, *i.e.*, to recognition-judgments and not merely to judgments of action. Recounting, which according to P. Janet is the beginning of memory, seems to be an essential intermediary here, since it is a means both of evocation and of reconstruction, and it is worthy of note that the child begins to recount precisely at the border-line between the preceding stage and the phase we are now analysing, and that his accounts are given to himself as well as to others.

OBS. 104. The first time we had verbal evidence of recall in the case of J. she was talking to herself. At 1 ; 7 (13) she was in bed in the evening when it was quite dark, and was sitting up talking to herself, unaware that I was listening. "*Look, look, uncle G., aunt A., uncle G.*" Then she stopped and lay down, saying to herself "*Nono.*" After that she sat up and began again: "*Look, mummy, daddy, grandma, uncle G.*, etc.", going on for fully ten minutes. At 1 ; 7 (14), while she was having her nap (and again thought she was alone), she went through the list of food she had just had, then moved the forefinger of her right hand an inch or so away from her thumb and said: "*Little Istine,*" an allusion to a cousin who had just been born.

At 1 ; 7 (28) J. told her mother about a grasshopper she had just seen in the garden: "*Hopper, hopper jump boy,*" meaning that the grasshopper jumped as a boy had made her jump. A boy cousin had in fact made her jump two days earlier. At 1 ; 11 (11), after she had been on a visit she said to me: "*Robert cry, duck swim in lake, gone away.*"

L., on the other hand, began giving an account of something to others and to herself on the same day. At 1 ; 11 (28), a few minutes after it had happened she said: "*Auntie Madaine in car, gone in car.*" Then, an hour later, when she was alone in the garden, she said to herself: "*Mummy gone, Jacqueline gone with mummy.*"

These behaviours are an illustration of the turning point at which language in process of construction ceases to be merely an accompaniment to an action in progress, and is used for the reconstitution of a past action, thus providing a beginning of representation. The word then begins to function as a sign, that is to say, it is no longer merely a part of the action, but evokes it. Then and then only is the verbal schema detached from the sensory-motor schema and acquires, as the imitative schemas of the same level have already done, the function of re-presentation, *i.e.*, of new presentation. Moreover, whereas imitation can only reproduce the action as such, either externally by miming or internally by the image, in the verbal account there is in addition a particular kind of objectivation peculiar to it and connected with the communication or socialisation of thought itself. But the verbal account is still only the reconstitution of an action. A further step is taken in the transition from expression of actions to recognition in the strict sense, when the verbal account is continued into the present, brought up to date as it were. It then still accompanies the action in progress, as did the original language, but it describes the action instead of being an integral part of it. Description thus becomes present representation, since it is at the same time present perception and perception with respect to the past. The best indication of progress in conceptualisation is therefore the appearance of the question " what is it ? " which involves both the name of the object and the concept (the class to which it belongs).

OBS. 105. At about 1 ; 9 and 2 ; 0 J. felt the need to introduce things and people by name to anyone who came into the room: " *Daddy, mummy, nose* (of her doll), *mouth,* etc." She would often bring a doll to her parents and say " *little man*," or bring some object, calling it by its name, " *stone* " for instance, as if she wanted to share her knowledge. Then she would bring anyone who was there into what she was doing, pointing things out, and saying what she was doing while she was doing it. But she behaved in exactly the same way when she was alone, and oddly enough it was during one of her monologues that we observed her first " *What's that?* " At 1 ; 9 (24), for example, I heard her say to herself: " *What's that, Jacqueline, what's that? . . . There* (knocking down a block). *What's falling? A block* (then touching a necklace). *Not cold,*" etc.

It is obvious that this kind of verbal account, with its denominations and descriptions, necessarily involves a split in the sensory-motor schema, since to the schema inherent in the action there is added a representative schema which translates it into a kind of concept. But it must not be forgotten that both in the field of deferred and representative imitation and of symbolic play a similar split has already occurred without the resulting representations thereby becoming concepts. How then are we to be sure that the nouns used in obs. 105 really represent concepts and not still merely internal images, more individual than a class and with a greater load of individual symbolism than an objective notion ? The concept is general and communicable, the image is singular and egocentric. Now the language of the child at this level is still, in fact, half-way between communication with others and the egocentric monologue:

verbal accounts, descriptions and even questions are addressed by the child to himself as much as to others.[1]   Socialisation at this stage therefore amounts to no more than lack of differentiation between the ego and others and is not yet an exchange based on clear differentiation.   May it not therefore be that the conceptualisation corresponding to this egocentric language is also intermediary and undifferentiated, and that the first apparent concepts, or " preconcepts," partake both of the sensory-motor schemas which give rise to them and of the imitative images or ludic symbols to which they are akin in that they are only partially socialised representations?

Let us now consider from this point of view the use made between the ages of two and four of the verbal schemas which seem to be nearest to what the concepts of a later stage will be, *i.e.*, operational. We find one constant characteristic of the " preconcepts " of this age which seems to be decisive: the child at this stage achieves neither true generality nor true individuality, the notions he uses fluctuating incessantly between the two extremes—which also happened in the structure of sensory-motor schemas and of the imitative or ludic symbols to which they gave rise.

OBS. 106 (*a*).   At 2 ; 2 (12) J. was in the garden walking on the landlord's flower-beds.   Her mother stopped her from doing so and J. at once replied: " *Me spoil uncle Alfred's garden*," *i.e.*, she was identifying this situation with another, very similar, but which she had experienced in another town and in the garden of an uncle who had no connection with the landlord in question.

At 1 ; 11 (0), on coming in from a walk, J. said that she was going to see: " *Daddy, Odette and Jacqueline in the glass* " as if " Jacqueline in the glass " was someone other than herself (although she could recognise herself very well in a mirror).   Again at 2 ; 7 (12), seeing L. in a new bathing suit, with a cap, J. asked: " *What's the baby's name?* "   Her mother explained that it was a bathing costume, but J. pointed to L. herself and said: " *But what's the name of that?* (indicating L.'s face) and repeated the question several times.   But as soon as L. had her dress on again, J. exclaimed very seriously: " *It's Lucienne again*," as if her sister had changed her identity in changing her clothes.

At 2 ; 11 (13) J. saw a photograph of herself asleep on my back and leaning against my shoulder (during a mountain walk).   She asked anxiously: " *Oh, what's that?* (pointing to herself).   *I'm afraid of it*.—But who is it?   Can't you see?—*Yes, It's me.   Jacqueline's doing this* (imitating the action).   *So she's not afraid* (projection on to the photograph)."   An hour later she saw the photograph again: " *I'm still a little bit afraid*.—But who is it?—*It's me.   It's Jacqueline doing this* (imitating)."   The next day, when she woke up, J. asked:

---

[1] Charlotte Buhler (*Kindheit und Jugend*, p. 163) objects to this view, but like many other authors who disagree with us on this point she uses the term " egocentrism " in quite a different sense from ours.

" *Can Nonette* (L.) *shut her eyes?*—Of course.—*So when Nonette is big* ' *Jacqueline doing this* ' (pointing to the photo) *she'll be able to shut her eyes.*" In other words " J. doing this " was a person that one became when going through a certain stage and that L. would become in her turn. Similarly, when I showed J. another photograph of herself she said: " *It's Jacqueline.*—Is it you or not?—*Yes, it's me, but what has the Jacqueline in the photo got on her head?* "

OBS. 106 (*b*). On the other hand, L. at 2 ; 4 (28) was looking at a photograph of J. when she was younger. " *Who is it?*—It's J. when she was small.—*No, it isn't.*—Isn't it J. when she was small?— *Yes, when she was Lucienne.*"

As an illustration of the reality attributed to pictures, L., at 2 ; 8 (14), said spontaneously: " *It's very heavy* (a picture book) *because there's a little girl in it.*"

At 3 ; 2 (20) we passed a man: " *Is that man a daddy?*—What is a daddy?—*It's a man. He has lots of Luciennes and lots of Jacquelines.*— What are Luciennes?—*They're little girls and Jacquelines are big girls.*"

At 4 ; 2 (20) L. thought the mists forming over our heads in an Alpine valley were those of quite another place where she had been six months earlier. At 4 ; 3 (0) also, seeing a mountain stream in a village: " *It's the same one we bathe in* (in another village).—But where does it come from? Look! (we could see it coming down from the mountain) *—From the stream we bathe in.*—And the stream we bathe in?—*From that one.*"

OBS. 107. J. at 2 ; 6 (3): " *That's not a bee, it's a bumble bee. Is it an animal?* But also at about 2 ; 6 she used the term " *the slug* " for the slugs we went to see every morning along a certain road. At 2 ; 7 (2) she cried: " *There it is!* " on seeing one, and when we saw another ten yards further on she said: " *There's the slug again.*" I answered: " But isn't it another one?" J. then went back to see the first one. " Is it the same one?—*Yes*—another slug?—*Yes.*— Another or the same?—. . . " The question obviously had no meaning for J.

At 3 ; 3 (0) J. was playing with a red insect, which disappeared. A quarter of an hour later when we were out for a walk we tried to look at a lizard, which darted away. Ten minutes afterwards we found another red insect. " *It's the red animal again.*—Do you think so?—*Where's the lizard then?* "

At 3 ; 3 (27): " *Are little worms animals?* "

OBS. 108. J. at 3 ; 2 (23) could not understand that Lausanne was " all the houses together " because for her it was her grandmother's house " Le Crêt " that was " *the Lausanne house.*" For instance, talking about a lizard climbing up the wall she said: " *It's climbing up the Lausanne house.*" The next day I wanted to see if my explanation had been understood. " What is Lausanne? —*It's all these houses* (pointing to all the houses round). *All these houses are Le Crêt.*—What's Le Crêt?—*It's granny's house, it's Lausanne.*'

" All these houses " thus constituted a complex object depending on one of its elements which was seen as representing the whole.

Similarly, at 4 ; 2 (8), L. did not understand that some pennies removed from a group of pennies formed part of the whole.

These are very characteristic examples of pre-conceptual structures between the ages of two and four, and they link up with many of the observations we had made earlier of children from four to four and a half.[1]

On the one hand, the particular objects involved in the child's thought have less individuality, i.e., they are less identical with themselves, than in the later stages. For instance (obs. 106), a particular garden was identified with another: J. refused to accept the identity of her sister L. when she was wearing a bathing-suit and then said, " it's Lucienne again," when she was wearing her dress again; J. separated herself, according to the images she saw of herself, into " J. in the glass," " J. doing that," and " J. in the photo." In a word, the same individual can be composed of distinct persons, according to the clothes worn or the images presented in a mirror or a photograph. In the same way, L. (obs. 106 (b)) thought that her elder sister J. had been a Lucienne, and that little girls were Luciennes before becoming Jacquelines. The essential character of these beings is thus not their identity through time, but the distinct successive stages through which they pass in changing character.[2]

But on the other hand, classes are less comprehensive than they will be later, a class being a kind of typical individual reproduced in several copies. Slugs (obs. 107) are all " the slug " reappearing in various forms, and the same is true of " the red animal," with the interesting addition that once it had been connected with the lizard it was expected to be accompanied by the lizard when it reappeared.

These two characteristics, absence of individual identity and of general class, are in reality one and the same. It is because a stable general class does not exist, that the individual elements, not being assembled within the framework of a real whole, partake directly of one another without permanent individuality, and it is the lack of individuality in the parts which prevents the whole from becoming an inclusive class. Thus, as it is still half-way between the individual and the general, the child's preconcept constitutes a kind of " participation " (in the sense of Lévy-Bruhl), this relationship being defined as follows: absence of inclusion of the elements in a whole, and direct identification of the partial elements one with another, without the

[1] See in *The Child's Representation of the World* the explanations of shadow and air; in *Judgment and Reasoning in the Child* and *La genèse du nombre chez l'enfant* the development of the notion of a part.

[2] We have here a further illustration of our earlier observations of the systematic lack of comprehension of the notion of time in young children (see *La genèse de la notion du temps chez l'enfant*).

intermediary of the whole. To take an example from earlier observations we made, a shadow thrown on a table was thought to come directly from the shadow of trees, without going through the general class of shadows which is defined by their law of formation.

Hence the importance of questions dealing with wholes and parts, *i.e.*, with the notion of inclusion, which gives rise to true concepts, questions, for instance, such as whether bumble bees and little worms are " animals " (obs. 107). For the child to be able to decide such a question, he would have to be able to unite the parts in a whole according to a reversible mode of composition, but the examples in obs. 108 are evidence of the difficulties he still experiences in establishing this kind of connection, even when he is dealing with a set of elements he can grasp spatially.

We shall now see how closely these preconceptual structures, without general classes or individual identities, are related, on the plane of cognitive representation or intelligent adaptation, to the symbolic structures of the ludic plane. What is, in fact, the difference between the act of taking one garden for another, or separating oneself into several characters, or reducing several slugs to one, and that of identifying in play one object with another and oneself with other people? Is it not merely that in one case there is belief and an effort at adaptation, and in the other there is only pretence and assimilation to the ego? Apart from this functional distinction, the preconcept and the ludic symbol both proceed by direct assimilation, without true identity or true generality, by prelogical " participation " and not by operations.

We find, moreover, between the ludic symbol, the imitative image and the preconcept, all kinds of gradations which are a continuation during this stage of the examples in obs. 103 and which fluctuate between " active analogy " and simple concrete comparison:

OBS. 109. At 3 ; 6 J. saw some little waves on a beach by the lake pushing little ridges of sand forwards and backwards, and exclaimed: " *It's like a little girl's hair being combed.*"

Again, at 4 ; 7 (26) she asked if syrup made with barberries was " *prickly syrup,*" an example of " active " analogy. The same day, looking at the sunset: " *I'd like to go for a ride in the rays and go to bed in sheets made of clouds,*" an example of a mere image. At 4 ; 7 (22) a thin piece of grass that had been slipped into a wider stalk gave rise to imitative images that were partly ludic and partly analogical. " *Look, it's spectacles in a spectacle case,*" then " *It's an insect in its case* " (a reference to a caddis-fly she had seen in a stream), etc. A bent twig: " *It's like a machine for putting in petrol.*" A few days later, during a quarrel: " *Well, we'll leave one another then. Here's a wall that separates us* " (making a gesture with her hand to indicate an imaginary limit). Then: " *So I'm going back into the shell of that snail* " (though she did not know the expression " to retire into one's shell "). The winding of a river: " *It's like a snake*," etc., etc.

This facility for thinking in images, together with the structural relationship we have just noted between the identifications of the ludic symbol and the preconcept, leads us to enquire whether there is not in the preconcept more of the imaged schema than of the true concept, which will be completely freed when it reaches the operational level. In the case of the ludic symbol, the given object is identified with various realities, thanks to the imitative images which serve as signifiers. In the case of the preconcept, the given object is also identified with others through a kind of direct participation. Now if a general class existed, this conceptual identification of objects one with another would merely consist in considering them as equivalents by reason of the fact that they were included in the same class, in which case the general class itself would serve as an operational schema of assimilation. The word or verbal sign would be the " signifier " of this schema and the imitative image would then be no more than an individual symbol supporting from within the collective sign. The image would thus remain quite distinct from the concept, since it would be reduced to the rank of mere signifier, in contrast to the signified content. But since, at this level, general classes functioning as operational schemas do not yet exist, and since there is direct assimilation of one object to another through these half-general, half-individual schemas which constitute preconcepts, the word or collective sign is still inadequate to the content of these egocentric assimilations. Therefore, although the image naturally already plays its part as signifier, it still keeps a function derived from its imitative origin (a function already noted in the case of the ludic symbol): it constitutes a partial substitute for the thing signified, through a kind of " adherence to the sign " typical of all primitive symbols. In fact, just because objects are directly assimilated one to another, the assimilating object becomes a kind of selected sample with respect to the object assimilated. Thus " the slug " is the prototype or representative of all slugs, while in a general concept all slugs are equivalent through their common abstract characteristics. Hence the particular image to which " the slug " corresponds keeps a much higher value, with respect to other slugs, than the equally particular image which serves as individual symbol to a child thinking in terms of the general class of slugs. Each of these two images consists of an individualised schema, *i.e.*, a schema accommodated to a particular object, but whereas in the case of the general class it is no more than a mere signifier, its relationship to the preconcept is much closer, since the preconcept itself is only a schema half-way between the individual and the general, depending on the existence of an individual prototype. In so far as the image is a signifier with respect to the preconcept, it represents the typical individual and not just any object. In its two-fold quality as representative of the typical individual and as individualised schema, like the preconcept itself to some extent, the image is therefore more than a mere signifier of the preconcept. It is the representative of the object which serves as a substitute for all the others, and is thus itself a substitute of the second order.

In this sense, the preconcepts of this level can be considered to be still half-way between the symbol and the concept proper. Like the ludic symbol, the preconcept involves the image and is partially determined by it, whereas the concept, precisely because of its generality, breaks away from the image and uses it only as an illustration. To put it more exactly, since the operational concept achieves permanent equilibrium between assimilation of objects one to another and accommodation to each of them, accommodation is not continued as image, and the image itself, when it does come in, remains on a lower plane (as in the case of direct perception). Since in the case of the preconcept, on the contrary, there is assimilation to a selected object without generalised accommodation to all, accommodation to this specific object is necessarily continued as image when the child's thought is projected on to the others. The image intervenes as essential aid to assimilation, and therefore as privileged signifier, and to some extent as substitute.

During stage II, from the ages of four or five to six or eight, however, the various characteristics of the preconcept tend towards the operational concept, through the construction of a hierarchy of nestings, by means of which assimilation becomes mediate and generality is gradually achieved. Complete generality is only reached when operations become reversible, as we have shown elsewhere, but between the preconcept and the system of operationally connected concepts a gradual articulation of intuitive thought takes place. These articulated intuitions result in partial constructions, which are still linked with the perceptual configuration and with the image, but which are already logical within this restricted field. Here are some examples of cases of spontaneous inclusions, which contrast with the preconceptual structures, although they cannot be qualified, without further detailed examination, as articulated intuitions or as systems of operations.

OBS. 110. J. at 6 ; 7 (8) said: " *They're all called mushrooms, aren't they? Are fuzz-balls* (which we were looking for in fields) *mushrooms?* "

The same day, referring to a hamlet of four or five houses: " *Is that a village?*—No. It's still La Sage.—*Then it's part of La Sage?* " (*cf.* obs. 108).

At 6 ; 7 (9): " *The crows are afraid of us. They are flying away.*—Yes.—*But the blackbirds aren't afraid.*—No.—*They're the same family,*

blackbirds and crows, so why are they afraid if they're the same family?—
But in our family you are never afraid now and L. is often afraid.—
—I'm not talking about J. and L. but about blackbirds and crows (*cf.*
resistance to simple analogical comparison in contrast to obs. 109).

We find in the above questions the use of the part-whole relation,
either in connection with a collective object such as a village, or with
abstract inclusions such as zoological classes. (N.B.—The characteristic use of the word " all " in " they're all called.") Hence
implicit reasoning through inductive generalisation, in the example
of the frightened crows, which brings us to the analysis of reasoning.

§ 3. *First reasonings: preconceptual reasoning (transductions) and symbolic
reasoning*

It is interesting to discover that all the characteristics we have
seen in the first concepts, from absence of generality to quasi-symbolic
structure, are also to be found in the first reasonings. When it is a
case of adapted investigation, we find simple, disinterested " transductions," while in the case of a social situation in which a desired
action may involve distortion of reality, we find reasoning which is
interested or tendentious (but not lacking in guile), or even symbolic
reasoning, in which the combinations of images corresponding to the
desires take strange forms.

We shall first give a set of examples, and then discuss them category
by category:

OBS. 111 (*a*). The first examples of verbal reasoning [1] observed
in the case of J. were of the following type.

At 2 ; 0 (7) J. had no inclination to go to sleep in the evening
and called to her parents for a light and for someone to talk to. We
went to her once to tell her to be quiet and warned her that we should
not come again. She managed, however, to get us to go to her a
second time, but understood that it was the last. After a long
silence piercing screams were heard, as though something dreadful
had happened. We rushed in and J. confessed that she had taken
a toy from the shelf above her bed (which she was forbidden to
touch at bed-time). She even looked really contrite, but everything was in its place and it was obvious that she had not touched
anything. She had thus preferred to pretend she had done wrong
and believe it, in order to get the light and the company she wanted,
rather than to stay alone in the dark and have nothing on her
conscience.

At 2 ; 0 (14) J. wanted for her doll a dress that was upstairs.
She said " *dress* " and when her mother refused it, " *Daddy get dress.*"

---

[1] It is very difficult to agree as to the earliest examples of reasoning. Co-ordination
of judgments passed with regard to the same situation, each of these judgments
corresponding merely to a perceptive reading of it, cannot be called reasoning.
Reasoning must involve judgments going beyond the field of immediate perception
and connected with it by a bond of necessary subordination.

As I also refused, she wanted to go herself " *to mummy's room.*"
After several repetitions of this she was told it was too cold there.
There was a long silence, and then: " *Not too cold.—Where?—In
the room.*—Why isn't it too cold?—*Get dress.*"   Thus the judgment
" not too cold," made to meet the need of the situation, was subordinated to the practical end in view.   This is another example of
what we called elsewhere sensory-motor reasoning (co-ordination
of schemas for a definite end), but with the inclusion of representation which transformed reality and served as a means to
attaining the end.

It should be pointed out that at this stage the child cannot yet
rely on the promises of others, for the simple reason that it is still
incapable of co-ordinating or even of conserving the representations
involved.   For example, at 2 ; 0 (13) J. was grizzling in her bath.
I told her I would get her duck and she was pleased at the suggestion.
But as I went out to get it she began to grizzle even more, as if she
could not keep in mind the promise I had given her.   In the case
of the dress that was upstairs, however, the representations were
kept in mind, because they had been arranged by the child herself
to satisfy her need and without reference to reality.

OBS. 111 (*b*).   At 2 ; 10 (8) J. had a temperature and wanted
oranges.   It was too early in the season for oranges to be in the
shops and we tried to explain to her that they were not yet ripe.
" They're still green.   We can't eat them.   They haven't yet got
their lovely yellow colour."   J. seemed to accept this, but a moment
later, as she was drinking her camomile tea, she said: " *Camomile
isn't green, it's yellow already. . . . Give me some oranges!* "   The reasoning
here is clear: if the camomile is already yellow, the oranges can
also be yellow—a case of " active " analogy or symbolic participation.

OBS. 112 (*a*).   We now have the first examples of recognitive
reasoning as distinct from teleological or practical reasoning.
At 2 ; 1 (13) J. wanted to go and see a little hunchbacked neighbour
whom she used to meet on her walks.   A few days earlier she had
asked why he had a hump, and after I had explained she said:
" *Poor boy, he's ill, he has a hump.*"   The day before J. had also
wanted to go and see him but he had influenza, which J. called
being " ill in bed."   We started out for our walk and on the way
J. said: " *Is he still ill in bed?*—No.   I saw him this morning, he
isn't in bed now.—*He hasn't a big hump now!* "

At 2 ; 4 (16): When I was called and did not reply J. concluded:
" *Daddy didn't hear.*"   At 2 ; 4 (27) in the bathroom: " *Daddy's
getting hot water, so he's going to shave.*"

At 2 ; 6 (24): " When you're big, we'll buy you a big bicycle.
—*No, a little one.*—Why a little one?—*Like me. . . . I'm not big.
You're big but I'm not big.*"

At 2 ; 6 (26) we went to look for " the slug " (see obs. 107):
" Shall we see it to-day?—*Yes.*—Why?—*Because it isn't sunny.*"
The next day: " Shall we see them?—*No, because it's sunny.*"

At 2 ; 9 (14): " *She hasn't got a name* (a little girl a year old).—
Why?—*Because she can't talk.*" At 3 ; 2 (26): " *Granny says it's the
sun that makes negroes black. Why aren't they brown then!*" (J. was sun-
bathing).

OBS. 112 (*b*). L. at 3 ; 1 (3): " *You're going to see mummy, so
you're not coming to see me.*" At 3 ; 3 (12): " *You must have another
little baby, then I'll have a little brother.*" At 3 ; 10 (24), looking at
three chairs: " *I think that one* (the medium size) *is big enough for J.,
so Cl. can sit on that one* (the big one)." At 4 ; 2 (15) she learnt that
an ornamented bodice formed part of the Bernese costume: " *Cl.'s
Bernese girl hasn't got that, so she isn't Bernese.*" At 4 ; 3 (14): " *Why
do people put on rubber suits when they go on motor-bikes?*—Because of the
dust.—*So if we had a motor-bike you would have rubber clothes, but we have
a car so you don't need rubber clothes.*" At 4 ; 3 (17), when she was on
a mule: " *Little girls who go on mules aren't afraid of motor-bikes.
They aren't afraid of anything* (to reassure her).—*No. When little
girls are on mules like the men who ride motor-bikes, then they're not afraid
of the motor-bike. But I didn't drive the mule. I was on daddy's knee,
so I was afraid of the motor-bikes.*" At 4 ; 10 (21), an afternoon when
she had not had her nap: " *I haven't had my nap so it isn't afternoon.*"

OBS. 113. Here we have J.'s reasoning between the ages of five
and seven. At 5 ; 7 (12): " *Is Mr. S. a grandfather?*—Why?—
Because A. and L. (his sons) *aren't big yet.*"

At 5 ; 8 (24): " *I've got two friends, Marécage and Julia. Marécage
has two friends, Julia and Jacqueline. Julia has two friends, Marécage
and Jacqueline. That makes three little friends.*" And at 5 ; 8 (6):
" *You'll be the granny of godfather's children because you're their daddy's
mummy.*" But at 6 ; 7 (13): " *Laurent has two sisters and a little
brother* (himself)."

At 6 ; 5 (11): " *Why does Laurent do that?* (a kind of hiccup, which
I imitated)—Just by chance.—*No, not by chance, because you did it
first and he did it after* (a false premiss but sound reasoning)."

At 6 ; 7 (8): " *Do blue butterflies like the wet?*—Yes.—*And the brown
ones? They like it to be dry.—Then why are there some here with the blue
ones?* "

At 6 ; 10 (0): " *The angel is like D., and D. is like T., so T. is like
the angel too.*" Similarly L. at 5 ; 3 (26): " *E. is as big as you, I'm
as big as you, so he's as big as both of us,*" but this was probably under
the influence of J. (7 ; 8) who indulged in this kind of reasoning.

OBS. 114. We give here the only examples observed up to the
age of seven of proofs or demonstrations:

J. at 2 ; 10 (4) showed me a postcard: " *It's a dog.*—I think it's a
cat.—*No, it's a dog.*—Is it? Why? . . . Why do you say it's a
dog? . . . Why do you think it's a dog? *It's grey.*" *Cf.* this conversation at 2 ; 11 (7): " *Is your doll's dress new?*—*No, it's yellow.*—
Is it an old one you've altered or a new one?—*It's new but it's
yellow.*"

At 3 ; 11 (25): " *It's a horse, because it has a mane.*—Haven't mules got manes?—*Yes.*—Well then?—. . ."

At 4 ; 4 (2), looking at an iron bar: " *What's that stick, is it iron?*—Yes.—*Oh, yes, because it's cold, because it makes music* (hitting the ground with it)."

At 5 ; 7 (24): " Look what that ant is pulling. It's heavy.—*No, it isn't heavy.*—Oh, yes it is, for an ant.—*No, it's light. It's quite little and it's a bit of wood.*"

At 6 ; 3 (12) she thought her stuffed duck had lost one of its legs merely because she had put it on the ground. She tried the experiment for herself and saw that it did not lose its other leg: " *Then somebody must have trodden on it.*"

The first of these reasonings are very informative both as regards the connections between perconceptual and sensory-motor schemas, and the relations between preconceptual reasoning, or transduction, and symbolic or ludic co-ordinations. The reasonings of obs. 111 (*a*) are obviously closely related to the co-ordination of schemas of action that characterises sensory-motor reasoning. " If I do something silly, they will come and light the lamp and talk to me," and " if the room upstairs isn't cold, I shall be able to get the dress that daddy and mummy won't bring me," are the inferences. In one sense, they are a continuation, in a slightly more complicated form, of the practical co-ordinations of the baby of twelve to sixteen months, *e.g.*, rolling a watch-chain into a ball to make it go into a box, etc. In both cases, it is merely a question of achieving an aim and of finding adequate means for so doing. But on the other hand, there are two distinct differences between these reasonings which are both practical and verbal, and purely practical co-ordinations. In the first place, the child does not now confine himself to " reasoning by action " on what he sees and manipulates, but uses images and words to evoke the end in view and the means to be used. In the second place, and just because representation enables him to go beyond the perceptual field, he can distort the reality represented to suit his wishes, and subordinate it to the aim he wants to achieve. Although it is in its origin practical and teleological, like the simple sensory-motor co-ordinations, the child's first reasoning contains from the start the possibility of distortion, which also characterises symbolic or imaginative play. The interested auto-accusation of J. is in this respect an excellent example of both intelligent combination and what Stern has called " pseudo-lying " (Scheinlüge), *i.e.*, a made-up story which deceives the subject himself. P. Janet was accustomed to say that the discovery of lying marked one of the turning points in the intellectual development of humanity, and it is clear from what we have said that distortion of reality is a direct result of the first deductive constructions, and that it is as characteristic of the dawn of reasoning as of ludic pretence and symbolic play, except for the degree of belief.

The relationship between these first reasonings and the symbolic thought at work in imagination is evident, not only in these semi-practical deductions, in which reality is distorted as in a game, but also in cases such as obs. 111 (b), where the child refutes an objection. It is assumed that the yellow colour of the camomile tea should entail the ripeness of the desired oranges, in the same way as there can be pretence that one object is another, except that here again it is not a question of pretence, but of belief.

Let us now consider the recognitive reasoning of obs. 112 (a) and (b). The reasoning of 111 (a) and (b) is influenced by desire, hence the continuity with practical sensory-motor reasoning and the relationship with symbolic or ludic thought. But what of reasonings of a recognitive or reflective character, which consist in relating recognition judgments one with another and drawing a conclusion not desired in advance? Careful distinction between the external or empirical truth of the conclusions and the internal or logical truth of the co-ordinations as such, shows that these recognitive reasonings, which will eventually become rational, operational connection, are at first only " mental experiences," a continuation, on the representational plane, of practical co-ordinations, and more particularly, that they remain for a long time intermediary between symbolic and logical thought, by reason of their preconceptual or transductive character.

It is well known that Stern described the first reasonings of the child as being inferences which proceed neither from the particular to the general nor from the general to the particular, but from the particular to the particular—in which case " transduction " would precede induction and deduction. As we have seen (§ 2), at the lowest levels of thinking, the child is equally incapable of attributing permanent individuality to particular elements and of constituting really inclusive classes. On the other hand, the classic definitions of induction and deduction are inadequate, since it is possible to have reasonings which follow a complete deductive pattern and yet only proceed from the particular to the particular (e.g., the reasonings of the type $A = B$; $B = C$ therefore $A = C$ in obs. 113). Nevertheless, in the main, Stern's thesis holds good if we define transduction as an inference that is non-regulated (non-necessary) because it bears on schemas which are still half-way between the individual and the general. In other words, transduction is reasoning without reversible nestings of a hierarchy of classes and relations. Since it is a system of co-ordinations without nestings, through direct connection between semi-particular schemas, transduction will thus be a kind of mental experi-ence continuing the co-ordinations of sensory-motor schemas on the representational plane. As the representations do not as yet constitute general concepts, but simply mentally evoked schemas of action, they will remain half-way between the imaged symbol and the concept proper.

This explains why in some cases transduction leads to correct conclusions, while in others the reasoning is false and incomplete. When the reasoning does not involve any reflective, intentional nesting, but merely practical schemas, *i.e.*, schemas generalised through previous actions and bearing on individual objects, transduction gives a right result, whereas when nestings of classes or compositions of relations are required, transduction fails, for want of a reversible operational mechanism.

Thus, in the following cases (obs. 112 (*a*) and two examples in 113), the reasons for the mistake are clear. The hunchback cured of his influenza no longer had a hump because the child identified the illnesses one with another, instead of distinguishing, in the general class of illnesses, the one that produced the hump and other possible ones. The bicycle that J. would have later on must be small, as if future heights were conditioned by her present height. The baby who could not speak had no name, through lack of dissociation between the point of view of the subject and that of the object. The father whose sons were little must be a grandfather, as if ages cor˙e-sponded univocally to heights. T. had two sisters and a little brother who was himself, through lack of dissociation between the po˙nt ˙f view of T. and that of J. herself. And in L.'s reasoning (112 (*b*)), an afternoon without a nap was not an afternoon, and a baby could only be a little brother. In each of these cases there is imɟroper assimilation, either of the general class to one of its members, or of one point of view to another. And the reason why there is this assimilation of the particular to the particular, and not generalisation or reciprocity is obvious. The elements ignored in the reasoning (*e.g.*, the influenza in the case of the hunchback, the future height in the case of the bicycle, etc.), are assimilated to the elements " centred " by the child's thought (the illness which caused the hump, J.'s present height, etc.) merely because it is the latter which are the object of the child's interest, attention and activity, or because they characterise his present point of view, in a word, precisely because they are " centred." Thus the assimilation of the particular to the particular, characteristic of transduction, is distorting and irreversible in so far as it is centred, and will become logical and give rise to a hierarchy of nestings and reciprocities in so far as its decentration makes it reversible. When the element B is illegitimately reduced to the element A because A is centred, and the assimilation is therefore irreversible, we have transduction. When the elements A and B are assimilated one to the other in reversible fashion, and their reciprocal decentration leads to the formation of a class A + B which contains them both, we have logical construction. The processes that constitute transduction are thus only a particular case of the general mechanism which characterise the whole development of the cognitive functions: the passage from centration of perception to decentration, and from egocentrism of thought to logical reciprocity.

In those cases where transduction leads to a correct conclusion, it is easy to see that this is due to the fact that the reasoning does not require new nestings (reflective and intentional), either because it is merely the application of a practical schema already generalised through earlier action, or because the simplicity or the nature of the compositions in question compels decentration. Thus when J. concluded that because there was no response " Daddy can't hear," or that a jug of hot water meant " he's going to shave," or when T. said " You're going to mummy, so you're not coming to me," etc., there is obviously no need for these judgments to imply general propositions which would be the implicit premisses of a formal deduction. They are merely practical schemas applied by mental experience. It thus often happens that the reasoning has all the appearance, verbally, of a logical deduction, with integration of particular cases in general classes or propositions, whereas in reality the generalisations in question are in no sense operational, being due merely to the empirical bringing together by the action itself of earlier experiences. For instance, the reasoning about the slugs which did not come out in the sun and did come out in the rain, belongs, in spite of its precision, to the same category as the ones we have already quoted, as is proved by what was said in § 2 about " the slug " as opposed to the conceptual class of slugs. In the same way, the seriation of the three chairs, which were made to correspond to the three little girls, of whom L. was one (obs. 112 (b)), was clearly practical and intuitive, since all the elements were visible and there were only three pairs. On the other hand, the reasoning about the Bernese girl, the motor-cycle, and more especially the mule (obs. 112 (b)), were perfectly logical, and depended on compositions that were new at the particular moment. But in the case of the first two of these, their very simplicity leaves little room for distorting centration, and in the case of the subtle reasoning about the mule, although L.'s fine distinction between the driver who was not afraid and the person driven who was, certainly does imply decentration between her point of view and mine, this decentration was unavoidable, since L. was replying to me and defending her point of view against my statement, in which the distinction had not been made.

The best confirmation of the part played in thought by centration and decentration, the one resulting in distorting assimilation and the other in coherent generalisation, and of their two-fold aspect, noetic (centration or decentration of interest and attention) and social (egocentrism and reciprocity), is to be found in the difficulty experienced by the child in finding a proof or demonstration of his remarks, *i.e.*, in justifying to others what seems obvious to him (obs. 114). Thus J. thought that an animal was a dog and not a cat because it was grey, as if that colour could not also apply to a cat ; or that a mane was an indication of a horse and not of a mule, or that " yellow " was the opposite of " new," or that a piece of wood was light for an ant because it was light for her, etc. And yet, when it was a case of proving to herself that a pole was made of iron, she managed to find much better reasons.

To sum up, it is clear that transduction, which is co-ordination without a hierarchy of nestings, remains half-way between practical reasoning, which is a continuation of sensory-motor co-ordinations, and truly logical reasoning. The schemas it uses are the product of assimilation that is direct and distorting because it is centred on the individual elements which interest the subject. It is this egocentric assimilation that is continued in the form of the ludic symbol, whereas the mental experience which constitutes the accommodation characteristic of transductive reasoning has as its signifiers the imitative images representing the elements centred by thought. Transduction is thus the result of an incomplete equilibrium between distorting assimilation and partial accommodation.

But between the ages of 4 ; 6 and 7 ; 0 (stage II) this equilibrium tends to be completed through relative decentration of assimilation and extension of accommodation. Thus we see in obs. 113 the appearance of co-ordinations some of which are still transductive, but which are tending towards reciprocity or towards seriation of relationships (*e.g.*, the reasoning about the three friends, the grandmother and the resemblances between three individuals), as well as towards construction of general classes and propositions. At the same time the need for verification becomes more definite, as can be seen in obs. 114 (at 6 ; 5). These various forms of progress influence and transform the ludic symbol and imitation, but between the ages of five and seven, it is still impossible to speak of operations properly so called, for lack of general " groupings " to stabilise and generalise these first connections, which are no more than the result of articulated intuitions and mark the transition from transduction to operational thought.

§ 4. *From sensory-motor intelligence to cognitive representation*

The facts we have just analysed show clearly that logical thought is not at once superimposed on sensory-motor intelligence with the appearance of language. We must therefore attempt to discover the links between the prelogical thought of early childhood and intelligence prior to language, as we did in the case of those between

symbolic play and sensory-motor practice play, and between representative imitation and sensory-motor imitation.

We have tried to show elsewhere that the schemas of sensory-
motor intelligence constitute the functional equivalent of concepts
and relations, and that sensory-motor assimilation is a kind of practical
judgment, the co-ordination of schemas one with another being thus
equivalent to sensory-motor reasoning. But obviously it is only a
question of functional equivalence, which in no way entails structural
identity. Between sensory-motor intelligence and conceptual intelligence, there are, in fact, four fundamental differences, which indicate
how far the former falls short of being logical thought. 1. The connections established by sensory-motor intelligence link only successive
perceptions and movements, without an overall representation
dominating the states, distinct in time, of the actions thus organised,
and placing them simultaneously in a complete table. For instance,
the system of displacements involved in a behaviour such as the search
for a lost object may be co-ordinated in a kind of experimental
" group," but the only relationship is between successive movements
and there is no representation of the system as a whole. Sensory-
motor intelligence thus functions like a slow motion film, representing
one static image after another instead of achieving a fusion of the
images. 2. Consequently, sensory-motor intelligence aims at success
and not at truth; it finds its satisfaction in the achievement of the
practical aim pursued, and not in recognition (classification or seriation) or explanation. It is an intelligence which is only " lived "
(an intelligence of situations, to use Wallon's expression) and not
thought. 3. As its field is defined by the use of perceptual and motor
tools, it acts only on real objects as such, on their perceptual indices
and motor signals, and not on the signs, symbols and schemas related
to them (concepts and representative schemas). 4. It is thus essentially individual, and lacks the social dimensions resulting from the
use of signs.

If we accept the functional continuity between sensory-motor
intelligence and conceptual thought, and also their structural dissimilarity, as defined by these four differences, four conditions, capable
of being fulfilled simultaneously, would seem to suffice for the transition
from one of these forms of intelligence to the other. 1. A general
acceleration of movements, successive actions being merged into a
mobile epitome of the action as a whole—the speeded-up film of the
behaviour thus becoming interior representation, the draft or preliminary schema of the action. 2. An awareness of this abridged
draft, a conscious unwinding of the film in both directions—the mere
pursuit of a practical aim thus being replaced by recognition and
explanation based on graded classification and seriation of relationships. 3. The addition of a system of signs to actions—construction

of the general concepts necessary for this classification and seriation thus becoming possible. 4. The socialisation that goes with the use of these signs—individual thought thus being integrated in a common, objective reality.

These conditions can even be reduced to two: (A) a system of operations transposing exterior actions into mobile, reversible mental actions (conditions 1 and 2); (B) an inter-individual co-ordination of these operations ensuring both general reciprocity of points of view, and correspondence between the detail of the operations and their results (conditions 3 and 4). As to whether it is the construction of the operations, *i.e.*, their " grouping," which determines social co-ordination, or the converse, it is clear that the two processes are interdependent. A system of operations cannot be general unless these correspond term for term with those of others, but also socialisation of operations presupposes the possibility of their " grouping."

Having seen the functional continuity and structural dissimilarity of sensory-motor and conceptual intelligence, we can now examine by what means the child who speaks, imitates and plays will succeed in realising the conditions we have just defined. Will he do this all at once, as a result of " representation " being suddenly superimposed on " intelligence of situations "? Or will it be necessary for him, in spite of the functional continuity dominating all stages, to go through a new, slow structural evolution, corresponding on the new plane of representations to the one he has just completed at the sensory-motor level?

As a result of increased co-ordination of sensory-motor schemas—and hence of acceleration of movements and interiorisation of actions in the form of anticipatory drafts—the child is already capable, at stage VI, of representations, when there is equilibrium between assimilation and accommodation, of deferred imitation when there is primacy of assimilation. It is at this point that the acquisition of language becomes possible, and that words, or collective signs, enable the child to evoke schemas which have hitherto been merely practical. But is this evocation sufficient for the sudden, miraculous production of operations proper, the motor nucleus of reflective intelligence?

The preceding facts provide a decisive answer to this question. The first words are no more than a beginning of conceptualisation of sensory-motor schemas; they in no way complete it. Like the schema of action, the concept implies a complex interplay of assimilations and accommodations (conceptual assimilation being the judgment, and accommodation its application to experience). But in addition to accommodation to immediate, perceptual data, it obviously also implies a two-fold supplementary accommodation: (*a*) accommodation to all the data to which it refers outside the immediate perceptual field, or the field of immediate anticipations and reconstitutions which affect the action in progress; (*b*) accommodation to the thought of others and to their individual experiences. Moreover, in addition to assimilating perceptual and motor data (both of which are essential as a basis for operations), the concept must assimilate: (*a*) all other concepts in coherent systems (classifications and seriation); (*b*) the corresponding concepts of others. It is therefore merely a question of whether, as a result of language, sensory-motor assimilation and accommodation will automatically become operational assimilation and accommodation, thereby forming logical systems. These extensions of assimilation and accommodation, all of which are essential for the realisation of the four conditions for the development of conceptual intelligence, presuppose permanent equilibrium between the assimilating and accommodating processes. What, in fact, constitutes an operation such as uniting or separating, placing or displacing, arranging or disarranging, etc.? It is, on the one hand, imitation of possible transformations of reality [1] and therefore continuous, stable accommodation to experimental data. But on the other hand it is an action of the subject, an action which integrates the data to which it is applied, this assimilation having the peculiar feature of being reversible, *i.e.*, of linking objects one with another in such a way that movement in either direction is possible, instead of distorting them by reducing them to the activity of the subject. Now this reversibility is nothing else than the expression of the attainment of permanent equilibrium between generalised accommodation, and assimilation which has thereby become non-distorting. Reversibility is, in fact, the possibility of retrieving an earlier state of the data, which is not inconsistent with its present state (assimilation) and is as real or as realisable as that present state (accommodation). It is this mobile, reversible equilibrium that ensures the conservation of concepts and judgments, and that governs both the correspondence of operations between individuals (social exchange of thought) and the interior conceptual system of the individual himself. It thus becomes clear that there is some way to go between sensory-motor assimilation and accommodation and the operational processes that ensure both reversibility of individual thought and intellectual reciprocity between individuals. Indeed, assimilation and accommodation, which had arrived at a temporary equilibrium at stage VI of sensory-motor intelligence, are again dissociated on the plane of representation and language, owing to the intervention of new elements, extra-perceptual and social in character, which still remain to be assimilated and investigated. Before equilibrium can be restored on the representative plane, a road similar to the one just ended must thus once more be travelled.

[1] It was in this sense that F. Gonseth called logic a " physics of the arbitrary object."

This is, in fact, precisely what we can observe taking place throughout the second period (1 ; 6 to 7–8), but principally up to about 4 ; 0 or 4 ; 6 (stage I). Generally speaking, before the age of seven, we do not find any system of reversible, grouped operations, and only when there is " grouping " is there evidence of permanent equilibrium between assimilation and accommodation. Between the ages of four and seven (stage II), we find only a few intuitions capable of articulation (simple inclusions and intuitive co-ordinations of familiar relations) but without generalisation or reversibility. As for the period from 1 ; 6 to 4 ; 6 (stage I) which we have just studied in the preceding paragraphs, it is a striking fact that thought never achieves permanent equilibrium between assimilation and accommodation, but presents a sequence of partial, unstable equilibria, whose range explains the set of schemas varying from the ludic symbol and the imitative image to the preconcept, and also explains transduction.

The fundamental difference between sensory-motor equilibrium and representative equilibrium is that in the former, assimilation and accommodation are always in the present, whereas in the latter, earlier assimilations and accommodations interfere with those of the present. It is true that the sensory-motor schema itself is the past acting on the present, but the action is not localised in the past in the same way as, for instance, an evoked memory as distinct from a habit. What characterises representation, on the other hand, is that earlier accommodations persist in the present as " signifiers," and earlier assimilations as " signified." Thus the mental image, the continuation of earlier accommodations, intervenes as symboliser in both ludic and conceptual activity, thanks to which (and of course to the verbal, collective signs which accompany it in individual thought), present data can be assimilated to non-perceived, merely evoked objects, *i.e.*, objects that have taken on meanings provided by earlier assimilations. On the representative plane, accommodations are therefore two-fold: present (simple accommodations), and past (representative imitations and images), and the same is true of assimilations, which are present (incorporation of data in adequate schemas) and past (connections established between these schemas and others whose meanings are merely evoked, and not provoked by present perception).

In view of these differentiations, it is obvious that on the representative plane equilibrium cannot be immediately attained, and that the ground already covered on the sensory-motor plane must be covered again at the new level before complete co-ordination of the various differentiated processes takes place. Just as the assimilation of the sensory-motor stages begins by being centred on the child's own activity, and is gradually decentred during the course of this first period of development, so representative assimilation begins as a process of centration, of which we saw examples in dealing with the preconcept and transduction, and which explains the initial irreversibility of thought. Confronted by various objects which he compares in order to arrange them in classes, discover their relationships, and combine the two in reasonings, the child who is on the threshold of the representative realm is incapable of putting at the same level present data and the earlier data to which he assimilates them. According to his interests and the object that drew his attention at the starting point of his actions, he centres this or some other element and assimilates the others to it. It is this irreversible assimilation which, as we have seen, explains the " participation " of preconcepts, which are neither truly individual nor truly general, and it also explains reasoning by transduction. Reversible assimilation, on the other hand, leads to the formation of real classes, *i.e.*, classes that are both general and based on the stable individuality of the elements, and to inductive and deductive reasonings. Moreover, precisely because one of the elements is centred as a prototype or representative sample of the set, the schema of this set, instead of achieving the abstract state that characterises a concept, continues to be linked to the representation of this typical individual, *i.e.*, to an image. Thus, corresponding to the irreversible and therefore incomplete assimilation of the preconceptual schema, there is accommodation which is also incomplete, being centred on one object of which it constitutes the image as " signifier " of the schema. Consequently, present assimilation continues to be distorting, and present accommodation inadequate, since they involve new objects and not the prototype; hence the instability of their equilibrium. The preconcept is thus related by a series of intermediary terms to the ludic symbol, in which present assimilation predominates over accommodation, and by another series of intermediate terms to representative imitation, in which accommodation predominates over assimilation. A similar relationship exists between transduction and symbolic reasoning or the coordinations of pretence on the one hand, and between transduction and mental experience or reproduction of an empirical development through the image, on the other. It is, moreover, unnecessary to emphasise that this irreversible centration of the first conceptual representations is mainly expressed socially as egocentrism of thought, since a concept centred on typical elements corresponding to the " lived " experience of the individual and symbolised by an image rather than by language, could neither be a general notion nor be capable of being fully communicated.

This then being the starting point of representative thought, it is clear that the initial processes can only find their equilibrium in the direction of decentration. A thought centred on one object to which it assimilates others cannot be in equilibrium, whereas by assigning an equal value to each in turn, the reciprocal assimilation born of decentration leads to stable equilibrium between present and past data. Accommodation to all the elements (present as well as past), which results from this same decentration, then ensures their individuality, and the reciprocal assimilation which unites them leads to the elaboration of general, abstract schemas, *i.e.*, of concepts, in the form of classes and relations. Decentration thus results in equilibrium between assimilation and accommodation, an equilibrium which of necessity tends towards a reversible structure.

It is not difficult to see, however, that between preconceptual thought on the one hand, and operational thought on the other, there is room for a certain number of intermediary terms, according to the degree of reversibility attained by the reasoning. It was these intermediaries that we described, between the ages of four and seven, as intuitive thought [1] which in its higher forms is reasoning that appears to be operational, but which is bound up with a given perceptive configuration. We saw, for instance [obs. 112 (*b*)], that L. was capable of assessing mentally the correspondence between three chairs of unequal size and three little girls of different heights. Between the ages of five and seven, the child is even capable of finding a one-one correspondence between sets of from six to ten elements, but in the case of these numbers, the correspondence requires the support of a figure or an imaged representation. Once the figure is destroyed (*e.g.*, two rows corresponding optically) the child ceases to believe that the two sets are equivalent, in spite of the fact that he has just recognised visually that they correspond term for term.

It is evident that in these articulated intuitions, the higher forms of intuitive thought, assimilation is still insufficiently decentred. As for accommodation, it is no longer linked to the image of an individual object, as in the preconceptual schemas, but it continues to be a source of images. As the general schema is not yet sufficiently abstract to acquire the reversible mobility of an operation, it does not give rise to accommodation that is the same for all possible situations, and therefore remains linked to a " configuration." But a configuration, which is by definition a structure involving a set of elements linked by a single total form, is still an image. It is therefore no longer the image of an object, but the image of a schema, an image which in intuitive thought is as essential to the existence of the schema as is the image of the typical individual object to the existence of the preconcept. Thus in intuitive seriations and inclusions, in the various cardinal and ordinal forms of intuitive correspondences, etc., either perception or the image of the configuration is indispensable to the thought. They are the last remains of the symbolic, imaged character

[1] *La genèse du nombre chez l'enfant* and *Le développement des quantités chez l'enfant*. Delachaux and Niestlé.

that we have found in all the initial forms of representative thought.[1]

It is, then, at the level of operational thought, and only at that level (period III), that assimilation becomes completely reversible, by reason of the fact that accommodation is completely generalised and is no longer translated into images. The image does of course persist, but merely as symbol of the operational schema, and no longer as an integral part of it. Thus a system of inclusions can be intuited by means of Euler's circles, or a series of numbers by means of a spatial figure, but there is free choice of representations, and the operation is independent of any particular figure of the chosen system, since it is essentially the expression of the transformation from one state to another, and no longer of the state as such. The figure is then no more than an illustration, which may or may not accompany the operational schema, which can only be adequately expressed by means of properly defined collective signs (language, or mathematical and logistic signs).

It is only at this point that the four conditions, described at the beginning of this section as being essential to the transition from sensory-motor intelligence to logical thought, are fulfilled. Operations are possible actions reduced to an anticipatory schema by which they are speeded up and become capable of a two-way movement; they are actions expressed by signs instead of being actually performed, and finally they are a guarantee of correspondence between individual points of view, which can acquire objectivity only through co-ordination.

[1] A special place must be reserved for geometrical intuition, to which we shall return in Chap. IX, § 6.

CHAPTER IX

HAVING examined the general evolution of thought from the sensory-motor schema to the concept, we shall now analyse this development with reference to the essential categories of causality, the object, space and time.

Once language has become instrumental, these categories evolve according to two distinct though more or less continuously related processes. On the one hand, they continue to develop in the field of practical manipulations, particularly in relation to the interaction of solids and liquids, and thus give rise to spatio-temporal constructions permeated at first with a variety of subjective elements (muscular force, personal perspective, etc.), but gradually becoming more and more objective. But on the other hand, the various causal and spatio-temporal connections extend beyond the field of action (distant space, effects of air and wind, etc.) and give rise, mainly under the influence of the " whys " and the questions as to origins, which become possible with language, to a multiplicity of spatial and temporal representations, and of apparently satisfying myths. These are questions that we studied in the past in *The Child's Representation of the World* and *Physical Causality in the Child*. It may be of interest to consider the problem in the light of spontaneous examples of the same kind observed in the case of our own children, and to relate it to the question of symbolic thought.

§ 1. *Myths of origin and artificialism*

It is noticeable that before the age at which the child can profitably be questioned (none of the children in the works quoted above was younger than four), numerous spontaneous myths make their appearance, myths that are half-way between ludic or imaginative symbolism and the investigation proper to intelligence.

OBS. 115. We have seen (obs. 101 and 102) the adult becoming an instrument for obtaining what the subject wants (" panana " in the case of J. and " mummy " in that of T.). In connection with this tendency we have evidence that natural phenomena are very early related by the child to adult activity.

At 1 ; 8 (12) J. was looking through the window at the mist forming on the mountain (200 yards away) and cried: " *Mist daddy smoke*," alluding to the smoke of my pipe. The next day, in the same situation, she merely said: " *Mist daddy*." At 1 ; 8 (14), when she was in her bath, she pointed to the steam and said: " *Mist smoke.*" From 1 ; 9 to 1 ; 10 she constantly said: " *Clouds daddy* " or " *Mist daddy* " whenever she saw mist.

At 1 ; 10 (19), 20 yards away from a stationary tram she asked me: " *Please go,*" wanting me to make it go, and without wanting to go herself. Same reaction in the case of trams we saw later, as if I had intervened in the movement of the earlier ones. At 2 ; 0 (1) she expressed herself in terms that can easily be imagined when she saw water spurting from a fountain. The same thing occurred in the case of water-spouts, mountain torrents (2 ; 7), etc.

At 2 ; 1 (4) she woke in the dark and asked for a light, but there was a breakdown in the electricity supply. An hour later there was a most beautiful sunrise over the mountains opposite: " *Light not broken now!* " At 2 ; 7 (30) I was blowing on her bare feet: " *The wind's cold.—Which* wind?—*The smoke wind.*—Which smoke?—*In your mouth.*" At 2 ; 11 (19): " *Daddy, if we walk at the edge of the lake, can we get the sunrise down?*—What do you think?— *I think so.*" At 2 ; 11 (17) she woke very early and wanted to be dressed. We refused. Shortly after, she found it was light enough and said: " *Now they've put the light on outside.*"

OBS. 116. At 3 ; 3 (10) J. asked her first question about birth in the shape of a query as to where L. came from (L. was 1 ; 8): " *Daddy, where did you find the little baby in a cradle?*—Which baby?— *Nonette (i.e., L.).*" My reply was simply that mummy and daddy had given her a little sister. At 3 ; 6 (13) she touched her grand-mother's eyes, nose, etc., and said to her: " *Is that how grannies are made? Did you make yourself?* " And later: " *Did she make herself? What made her?* " The same evening, when looking at L.: " *Why do they have little hands, little teeth, little eyes, a little mouth?* " The next day she exclaimed spontaneously: " *Oh, no, I don't think granny made herself.*" At 3 ; 7 (11): " *How are babies made?* " and two days later: " *How are plums made?*" then " *and cherries?* " At 3 ; 7 (18): " *Where did that little baby come from (i.e., L.)?*—What do you think? *I don't know. Out of the wood* (troubled). *There wasn't a little baby before.*" The next day: " *She came out of the wood. A long way away in the trees.*[1] *It was mummy who brought her out of the wood*". At 3 ; 8 (1) when we were in the wood we passed a woman with two small children: " *She's been looking for little babies.*" At 3 ; 11 (12): " *That little baby was bought. They found her in a shop and bought her. Before that she was in the wood, and before that in a shop. I don't know all the rest.*" At 4 ; 1 (0) she came " *out of the wood* " and " *out of a shop.*" At 4 ; 3 (2): " *It was daddy who went to fetch her. He found her at the edge of the water in the wood.*" At 4 ; 10 (18) babies came " *from the clinic. There's a mother in the clinic. All the babies in the clinic have the same mummy and then they change their mummy. This mummy gets them ready and then they grow. They have teeth and a tongue put in them.*" At 5 ; 3 (0) J. discovered some kittens behind the

---

[1] She was very fond of walking in the woods. There was naturally no adult suggestion in this idea.

wood-pile: " *How did they come?*—What do you think?—*I think the mummy went to fetch them.*" At 5 ; 3 (21): " *The babies were bought in a factory.*" At 5 ; 3 (23), referring to the guinea-pigs she had just been given to help her to discover the true solution: " *Where do little guinea-pigs come from?*—What do you think?—*From a factory.*" At 5 ; 4 (17): " *What are you before you're born?*—Do you know?—*An ant. Lots of little ants* (laughing)." At 5 ; 4 (19): " *Are you dust before you're born? Are you nothing at all, are you air?* " At 5 ; 5 (7) the young of the pair of guinea-pigs that had been given to J. were born during the night in a box in a little hen-house which was securely fastened and in which there were no other animals: " *The mother guinea-pig went to fetch them.*—How did she get out?—*Oh, the hen-house is locked. Then she made them!*—Yes, that's it.—*But where were they before?*—That's easy.—*In the mummy guinea-pig! Inside her! In her tummy!* " At 5 ; 5 (8): " *Were the little guinea-pigs inside their mother? I think they were.*" But two days later: " *They come from the factory.*" Her mother replied: " You know they don't," whereupon J. at once said: " *Where do babies come from?* —What do you think?—*From inside you!* " At 5 ; 6 (20): " *How do babies make themselves?*—. . . *They're bubbles of air. They're very tiny. They get bigger and bigger and when they're big enough they come out from inside the mother's tummy.*" At 5 ; 6 (22): " *Babies are air at first, aren't they? They're so very small. So they must be air at first. But there must be something in the air that babies are made of: a tiny little bit like that* (pointing to some dust). See the continuation of this conversation in obs. 127, also at 5 ; 6 (22).

OBS. 117. Closely related to her interest in birth and her discovery of a solution, was J.'s change-over from the diffused artificialism of obs. 115 to a mythical artificialism, of which we now give the chief manifestations (beginning with an example of ludic artificialism and a case in which there is a trace of diffused artificialism).

At 4 ; 3 (28) J. was playing at making a seed out of soil: " *This is where they make seeds!* " At 4 ; 6 (15): " *Why are there big stones like those, on the Salève?*—Do you know?—*Because they go and get them to make houses.*"

At 5 ; 5 (20): " *Why is there a sun? Why is there a red ball for the sun?*—Do you know?—*I think it's the moon. I think it's the sky that makes the moon.*" The same day: " *Are stones born in the lake?* " At 5 ; 5 (26): " *How are the ponds in the wood made?* " At 5 ; 5 (27): " *Why is there a moon?*—. . .—*It's the sky that makes it. When the clouds come up it gets big.*"

At 5 ; 6 (20): " *Mummy, how do they make water? How was it made?*—What do you think?—*Does it come from the sky?*—Yes, that's right.—*But how does it get into the taps?* " The same day: " *What did they do to fill the lake?*—Do you know?—*Yes, they use watering-cans.*" The same day: " *I think the rain's made with the sky: I think it opens and then the water comes out. Does the light come from the sky too, all the light that comes here?*—Yes.—*How is it made? Does it make itself? No, it's daddy's student* (the object of J.'s admiration at the moment) *who made everything, the sky and the water and the light and everything* (quite seriously). The next day: " *Does daddy's student make the clouds* (laughing)? "

At 5 ; 5 (22): " *Babies don't make themselves, they're air. Egg-shells make themselves in hens. I think they're air too. Baby guinea-pigs make themselves in the mummy.*—What things make themselves?—*Pipes, trees, egg-shells, clouds, the door. They don't make themselves, they have to be made. I think trees make themselves, and suns too. In the sky they can easily make themselves.*" At 5 ; 7 (11): " *I think the water's clouds. It's rain. It runs into the lake. There's a big hole and the water runs in. It's the sky that makes the clouds.*" The same day: " *How is the sky made? I think they cut it out. It's been painted.*" At 5 ; 7 (12): " *How do they make stones? How do they hold together? How are they made?—. . .—I think it's with cement.*" At 5 ; 7 (22), on seeing the sun set behind a mountain ridge: " *So the sun moves too, does it? Like the moon? Somebody makes it moves, somebody behind the mountain, a giant, I think.*"

OBS. 118. L. at 3 ; 2 (18): " *I think the sky's a man who goes up in a balloon and makes the clouds and everything.*" This remark was no doubt inspired by J., who was then 5 ; 7. As early as 3 ; 3 birth was no longer a problem for L. who got the solution from J. At 3 ; 3 (7), when L. was told of the birth of a cousin, she at once replied: " *Well, my Christian* (her doll) *came out through my foot.*" At 3 ; 4 (0) L. said spontaneously: " *The sun was up there, and now it's there* (almost set). *It makes the sun too sad when there's water.*— What water (it was a fine day)?—*The water in the sky.*—Is there water in the sky?—*Yes, when it's put there. They put it on the blue varnish.*" At 3 ; 10 (2) L. was in bed in the evening and it was still light: " *Put the light out, please.*—But the sky isn't lit, look (I switched the electric light on and off).—*Yes, it is, it isn't dark.*—Look outside: it's daylight.—*Then put the light out.*—But I can't put out the light outside.—*Yes you can, you can make it dark.*—How?—*Turn it out very hard.*—But it's outside that it's light.—*Yes.*—Well then?—*You must turn it out very hard. It'll be dark and there'll be little lights everywhere* (stars)."

At 4 ; 0 (0) during a walk: " *What are those balls* (boulders on the Salève)?—What do you think?—*To make it pretty.*" At 4 ; 2 (8): " *The sun doesn't like the rain. When it rains, it goes away and hides behind a blanket* (mist) *and it's all white.*" At 4 ; 2 (11) on the Salève: " *They put those rocks there. Some very strong people put them there.*—Could I have done it?—*No, not you, some very strong people. They* (the rocks) *were little at first and then they got big.*" At 4 ; 3 (16): " *Mountains are little stones that have got very big. They stayed little for a long time and then they got bigger and bigger. Perhaps somebody threw a little stone here and it turned into the Solève* (L. called it Solève. See obs. 123). At 4 ; 3 (26): " *Why are there two Solèves?* [1]—Do you know?—*For fun.*"

[1] *Cf. Language and Thought in the Child*, the same question put by Del at the age of six and the replies.

At 4 ; 2 (26): The water of the rivers (in the mountains) " *comes from the lake* (Geneva)." At 4 ; 3 (0) also, but the same day, referring to the house on the bank of the river, L. said: " *It's older, because it's much harder to make streams and rivers and the lake. They made houses first and then the lake.*" And at 4 ; 3 (22): " *Rivers flow because they're made to flow. The beach* (the bed) *makes them flow, They flow faster and faster because they come from a spring.*" At 4 ; 10 (4). talking about Sion and looking at the Rhône valley: " *They made a big hole, they dug and dug, and then they made the houses.*"

At 5 ; 10 (6): " *The moon's the sun, because it doesn't always have its rays: we don't need the sun at night because we're asleep.*"

It is interesting to compare these spontaneous reactions of J. and L. with those we obtained many years ago through questioning, and to analyse them from the point of view of the symbolic and preconceptual mechanisms of thought.

What is first noticeable is that although we again find a general tendency to artificialism, which begins by being diffused, and in its evolution becomes first mythical and then immanent, the ages of J. and L. at the time of the reactions did not correspond either with one another or with those of many other subjects. The reason for these divergences is clear. Firstly, questions as to origins being connected with curiosity about birth (a connection which is complex and probably bilateral), their evolution will largely depend on the education of the child, which may either encourage adaptation to reality or make for the continuance of mythical explanations. Then also, older children influence the younger ones. Thus L. tackled these problems earlier than J. and in particular knew about birth as early as 3 ; 3, whereas J. only solved the problem for herself at 5 ; 5. Clearly thereforefore the stages of artificialism lack the regularity which characterises the stages of acquisition of number, quantities, etc., and operational development in general.

But this is not all. It is evident that although in the case of J. and L. there is a certain continuity in the questions and preoccupations, there is no systematisation in their statements, which contradict one another from day to day and even from hour to hour. In this field, truth is of quite a different order from that of logical, numerical and spatial intuitions, which are related to manipulation and perceptual verification. It is verbal, and not intuitive causality. What is particularly interesting for our present purpose is that we find all the intermediary stages between play properly so-called and " serious " belief. It is obvious, for example, that when J. attributes the creation of the sky and the earth to a student of mine of whom she is very fond, her words contain a large dose of ludic imagination, whereas the child who merely says that " they " made mountains and lakes has much more belief in her statement. There is every indication that assimilation of natural processes to the activity of the subject or of some other human being gives rise to a whole series of states ranging from symbolic play to real belief, according to the degree of accommodation (to objects and to the thought of others) by which it is accompanied.

What then are the processes of thought involved in the construction of artificialism? There is, above all, continuous assimilation of natural processes to human activity. But this assimilation takes place in the same way as that of the preconcept, *i.e.*, through direct participation and without general classes, and thus allows of continuity with the ludic symbol, in which there is the same type of assimilation, though with a lesser degree of accommodation.

Thus J. differentiates between " being made " and " making oneself." The sky, for example, " is made " and the sun " makes itself." For her the *vis fabricatrix naturæ* proceeds in exactly the same way as human activity. The sun " makes itself " because " someone " made the sky and the process continues of itself, in the same way as " someone " puts babies into the world and they then grow by themselves.

Underlying this assimilation there is the myth, or symbolic narrative. The artificialist myth is therefore a good example of preconceptual structure, which remains close to the imaged schema because it lacks both the true generality and the individual identity characteristic of concepts and their elements. Thus the child talks of the water, the light, the rain, but of the suns (obs. 117). There are at the same time several suns and several moons, and yet there is identity (in the sense of a participation) between the sun (which is thus semi-individual and semi-generic) and the moon. This artificialist thought is therefore still far from being operational, since it is assimilatory in the egocentric sense of the term, and since it is imaged, its accommodation being inadequate to attain the generality of the conceptual schema. It will become operational, however, when the assimilation peculiar to immanent artificialism (*i.e.*, artificialism attributed to nature itself), becomes identification of natural bodies one with another. Spatiotemporal composition will then lead simultaneously to the idea of atomistic partition and to the preservation of wholes. But this type of comprehension is not possible before the age of about seven, after a phase of intuitive thought linking the preconcept with the operation.

§ 2a. *Animism*

Reactions such as the following can be observed contemporaneously with artificialism, to which they are closely related, since they also have reference to ideas about birth and human development.

OBS. 119. At 1 ; 11 (20) J. said " *no, no-o* " to her blocks in tones varying between vexation and entreaty, as if to people who were opposing her wishes. At 2 ; 1 (0) she said: " *Moon running* " when walking in the evening along the lake (illusion of being followed by the moon). At 2 ; 5 (8): " *You can hear the wind singing. How does it do it?* and " *There aren't any boats on the lake; they're asleep.*" At 2 ; 7 (11), talking to her rolling ball: " *Come on, darling, I'd like you.*" At 2 ; 7 (20) she was looking for her lost spade and asked seriously: " *Shall I call it?* " At 2 ; 10 (13): " *Do they like dancing* (dead leaves)? At 3 ; 3 (11): " *Why do clouds move?*—Do you know?—*To hide the sun.*" The next day: " *It's funny, the sun moves. Why has it gone? To go and bathe in the lake? Why is it hiding?* "

At 3 ; 5 (29), in a field, when the grass was swaying in the wind: " *Is the grass real? It's moving!* [1]—What do you mean by ' real '?—*Real.*—Is Radou (her cat) real?—*Of course, he walks.*" At 3 ; 7 (19), watching some oil dropping from a car engine: " *It's the car's milk.*" At 4 ; 0 (3): " *The moon moves, it moves because it's alive.*" Similarly, at 4 ; 0 (9). At 4 ; 6 (2): " *The clouds go very slowly because they haven't any paws or legs; they stretch out like worms and caterpillars, that's why they go slowly.*" At 5 ; 6 (23): " *The moon's hiding in the clouds again. It's cold.*" And: " *Why must it hide in the mountain?* "

At 5 ; 7 (11): " *A huge stone would stay on the water because they're very old. Old ladies are lighter than little children.*" The same day: " *Look at the trees over there: they're alive, because they're moving.*" Also the same day I heard her say to L.: " *My car's more alive than yours.*— (L.) What does that mean?—(J.) *It means that they go when they're alive.*" At 5 ; 8 (0), watching the mist rising in a valley and then hanging in mid-air: " *Oh! how well it can stay in the air! What a long time it can stay in the same place!* " (no doubt connected with the child's belief that gliding explains floating). At 5 ; 9 (25): " *Why don't stones die like insects when you put them in a box?* "

At about 6 ; 0 there was little evidence of animism, except in affective reactions. For example, at 6 ; 5 (21) she screamed with fright when the door of the hen-house, blown by the wind, hit her in the back. Then, crying, she said: " *The wind's horrid, it frightens us.*"—But not on purpose?—*Yes, on purpose. It's horrid, it said we were naughty.*—But does the wind know what it does?—*It knows it blows.*"

At 6 ; 7 (8) I questioned J. about her earlier remarks. Nothing was then alive except people and animals. Even the sun and the moon did not feel or know anything. At 6 ; 7 (18), however, I told her that L. had just said that the sun knew when it was fine: " *Yes, she's right, because it's the sun that makes it fine. That's what I told you the other day* (having said the opposite !)—And does a stone know it's rolling?—*Oh, no, it's the person who throws it that knows.*" After this there was no further trace of animism.

OBS. 120. L., after a series of remarks between 2 ; 6 and 3 ; 4, analogous to those of J. at the same age (*e.g.*, " the sun goes to bed because it's sad," etc.) began at 3 ; 4 (3), like J. at 3 ; 5 (29), to ask explicit questions about the life of bodies. She watched a

---

[1] *cf.* " Are leaves alive? They move in the wind."

cloud moving: " *Is the cloud an animal?—An* animal?—*Yes, it's moving.*" At 3 ; 7 (14) we missed a train: " *Doesn't the train know we aren't in it?* " The same day: " *The stairs are horrid, they hit me.*" At 4 ; 3 she thought that stones grew (see obs. 118). At 4 ; 3 (18), seeing the moon appearing from behind the Salève: " *I think it has little paws that you can't see.*" Similarly, at 4 ; 3 (22): " *Oh, the sun's moving. It's walking like us. Yes, it has little paws and we can't see them.—Where* is it walking?—*Why, on the sky. The sky's hard. It's made of clouds (cf.,* obs. 130). Then she discovered that it was following us: " *It's doing that for fun, to play a joke on us, like you when you smoke your pipe and play tricks on us.—Why* like me?—*Like grown-ups.—Not* like children?—*No, it's having a joke like grown-ups.—But* does it know we're here?—*Of course it does, it can see us!* "

At 4 ; 3 (23) when I was having some difficulty in driving through a herd of cows : " *The blue car knows what it has to do. It knows how to do everything now. It didn't know before. It's been taught.*" And after a mistake at a crossroads: " *You see, the car's helping you.*"

At 4 ; 3 (26): " *The clouds move by themselves, because they're alive.*" At 4 ; 10 (0): " *The clouds move because it's cold.—How?—By themselves. They come when it's cold. When it's sunny they aren't there. When it's cold they come back.* How?—*They know.*"

OBS. 121. Connected with these animist reactions are the notions of causality and of force based on the child's own physical, psychic and even moral activity. At 1 ; 10 (21), for example, J. used indiscriminately " *heavy,*" " *difficult* " and " *not allowed* " to describe the physical resistance she experienced in moving a table, pulling a rug, etc., even when there had never been any question of being forbidden to do these things. When trying to undo a button which would not come undone she said: " *Too heavy.*" At 2 ; 11 (9), talking about two big objects (a brush and a carpet-beater) which were light, but which she found awkward to carry: " *There, I'm bringing some very strong things.*"

Similarly, L., at 3 ; 6 (12), when looking at the Arve: " *You see, the water's flowing very hard.—It's because of the stones. The stones make the water move. That makes the lake flow* (the Arve).—How?—*Yes, the stones help it. The water comes out of this hole* (an eddy behind the stone). *Then it goes very fast.*" We can see again here the theory of the two motive powers we noted earlier in the child [1] (*Physical Causality*), another example of which is the explanation of things floating on water or in the air. At 4 ; 5 (1), for example, L. was with me in a small boat, and we had not moved for several minutes: " *Row, daddy, row fast, the boat's going to fall.—Why?—Because when you don't row it falls to the bottom.—And* what about that boat (in front of us, motionless) ?—*Because it's a boat on the lake.*

---

[1] It is also noteworthy in this connection that between the ages of one and two, when the child throws an object to the ground he does so as if it would not fall by itself. On the other hand, a ball is placed on the ground as if it would roll of its own accord. As late as 2 ; 0 (0) J threw a box of matches in the air, but without letting go of it, as if it would go by itself.

Boats have to float.—What about ours then?—*It doesn't fall because of the oars. We can stop for a minute because of the oars* (source of movement)." Then L. pressed her feet against the bottom of the boat: " *I'm putting my foot so that it doesn't fall.*" And at 5 ; 0 (o): " *The boat stays on the water because the man rows.*—And when there isn't a man? *It goes to the bottom.*—And what about those over there?—*But they aren't new. New boats go to the bottom, and when the man's in them they don't go to the bottom any more because the man gives the direction.*—And when the man gets out?—*The direction stays in the boat.*—Where?—*At the bottom, you can't see it. It's the man that gives it, but you can't see it.*"

These examples bear a striking resemblance to those we collected many years ago (*Child's Representation of the World*, Chaps. V–VII, and *Physical Causality in the Child*, Chaps. III–IV). They illustrate an animism that is the result of assimilation of physical movements to intentional activity, particularly those which appear to be spontaneous. They contain (1) the notion of an active force resulting from assimilation of external resistances to schemas of muscular effort, (2) a moral causality assimilating physical laws to obligatory rules (boats " must " float, etc.), and (3) a conception of movement reminiscent of the two motors of Aristotle, resulting from assimilation of the interaction of physical bodies to that of living bodies.

From the point of view of causality, it would be interesting to study the detail of these reactions, but we are here concerned merely with the form of this thought. Not only do we again find the quasi-symbolic structure of the preconcept, already noted in connection with artificialism, but this fusion of the assimilating schema with the exterior image is even more complete and calls to mind the mechanisms of the unconscious symbol (*cf.* Chap. VII). Indeed, the question which faces us is how interior impressions (feeling of effort, consciousness of intention, etc.) can be projected on to inert objects or physical movements and thus form schemas of assimilation that distort the external data. The problem ceases to exist if the egocentric assimilation characteristic of preconceptual structures is continuous with the symbolic assimilation characteristic of ludic and even of oneiric symbols. It becomes merely a special case of the general mechanism of symbolic thought. We saw earlier that the unconscious anatomic symbol results from fusion between a muscular or kinesthetic impression and the visual image of some object which might correspond to it— this object being chosen from the external world because consciousness of the ego is inadequate to localise the internal impression during dreams or in the half-sleeping state. In general, the unconscious or secondary symbol is produced, in play or dreams, through assimilation of the external to the internal, for lack of equilibrium with accommodation, *i.e.*, for lack of adequate consciousness of the ego. Now in the case of animism there is a very similar phenomenon. Since the child is unaware of the subjectivity of his thought, his intentions, his effort, etc., these internal elements are attributed to any external situation capable of corresponding to his movements and his activity, by an analogy which is immediate and not conceptual. This lack of subjective awareness will be obvious in the examples quoted in § 3, but before considering them, we must examine the evolution of animism and artificialism towards the end of early childhood, when these egocentric assimilations begin to disappear.

§ 2*b*. *Decline of artificialism and animism*

Between preconceptual thought, which gives rise to animism and artificialism, and operational thought, which leads to causality through spatio-temporal composition, there is a phase of intuitive thinking which preserves the imaged character of the former, and is a precursor of the latter by its successive articulations. In the field with which we are concerned here, we find forms of explanation obtained through identification of substances, but still preserving the notion of a kind of biological evolution.

OBS. 122. At 5 ; 7 (17) J., having asked three days earlier if clouds were made with cement, put the question in a new way: " *What are clouds made of?*—Do you know?—*Liquid.*—That's right.— *It's water, evaporated water.*" At 5 ; 7 (20): " *The clouds are very small at first, then very big. Then they burst . . . look at that one. What are they made of?*—But you know.—*Air* (it was beginning to rain). *Oh! the cloud's melting.*" The next day: " *Now the moon's undone!* (a crescent). *We said the other day* (the day before) *that the moon was made of air, like the clouds* (she had said it only of the latter). *Then how does it stay in the sky? Like balloons?* " At 5 ; 7 (22): " *Well then, does the moon move? Tell me what makes it move.*—You can find that out yourself.—*It's the air. I think the moon's made of air, air that gets golden at night. It's air that undoes itself like that* (the crescent) *and then makes itself again.*" The same day: " *Where does the dark come from? I think it comes from the lake, or from all the little streams, because they come from the stones. You've seen the dark that stays under the stones. That's why stones are black sometimes. The dark is dirty water that evaporates.*" At 5 ; 7 (2): " *How is air made?* " then: " *Ah! I see* (as some mist moved), *clouds are air that's all white.*" The same day: " *The light comes from the sky, no, it comes from the stars: they're always light. The stars stay in the air because they're air too, like the moon.*" At 5 ; 7 (23): " *How do they make water? No, they don't make it: it comes from the clouds.*" At 5 ; 11 (16): " *Snow is cloud-water with a bit of cloud round it.*" At 6 ; 3 (4): " *Can you say that the sun is a big cloud?* " At 6 ; 7 (9): " *Why is the sun made of fire? Is it lightning that makes the sun?*—That's an idea.—*Is it right?*— We'll think about it." At 6 ; 7 (14): " *Clouds are the sky breaking up because it's bad weather. Rain is snow that's melting and snow is little bits of cloud. The sky is air, but it's blue because it's a long way away and we see it from very far away* (see obs. 127). *And rain falls into the ground: it makes the mountain streams and the clouds and the lakes."* At 6 ; 7 (15): " *Wind and clouds are the same thing. That's why clouds move. Earth is very fine wet sand. Sand is what comes out of the water of the lake. The lake is the water from the streams and the streams are rain-water."* The same day: " *The sun and the moon are fire like lightning* " and " *Lightning is storms when there are a lot of clouds, it depends on the colour of the clouds."* The next day we found some gypsum. J. exclaimed: " *It's powder from the sky, dust. It's what makes the rocks. Stone is a bundle of sand. Sand is very little stones and when they're pressed together it's a pebble. Mountains are very big rocks."* At 6 ; 7 (28), same explanation, then: " *Sand came out of water. Water made it."* At 6 ; 8 (4): " *Daddy, will this rock grow when it rains?* " At 6 ; 8 (23): " *Fire came from the sky. It's lightning. It comes from the moon and the sun."*

It is clear from these examples that animism, and artificialism that has become immanent in nature are reduced to a kind of evolution of bodies still considered to be living and active. This transformation of the elements (soil being made out of water, water out of air, etc.) thus leads to causality through identification, which, with the addition of the schemas of compression and separation (sand pressed together forming pebbles, and pulverised pebbles becoming sand), is the forerunner of composition through atomistic partition. Between the preconceptual, symbolic myth and operational composition, intuitive thought thus ensures all the intermediary stages, thanks to a progressive balancing of assimilation with generalised accommodation, the former thus ceasing to be direct, and the latter to be imaged, and both tending towards the general, reversible schema.[1]

§ 3. *Names, dreams and thought*

The following examples of spontaneous reactions illustrate the evolution leading to the child's awareness of his own activity and of the subjectivity of mental tools—an evolution which is in conformity with the findings of our earlier works.

obs. 123. At 3 ; 6 (7), when J. was sitting on the grass, she asked me the names of some flowers, spiders, etc. I merely said: " Do you like me to tell you the names of things?—*Yes, I like it when you tell me the names* . . . (silence) *Where are the names of things?*— What do you think?—*Here* (pointing round us).—And the name of that spider?—*In its hole."*

At 5 ; 9 (0), looking at the Dent Blanche: " *How did they find*

[1] As for the ages of J and L, compared with those of the children quoted in *The Child's Representation of the World*, they show that although the sequence of stages is the same, the average age naturally depends on environment. This same factor also explains the lag between the ages observed by American authors (Dennis, Deutsche, etc.) and those of the lower class children we questioned many years ago.

out the name of the Dent Blanche?—Do you know?—*No, I don't. It's too difficult.*—Could it have been called something else?—*No, everything must have its own name.*"

At 6 ; 9 (15), however, when her sister L. insisted that she could see that the Salève was called Solève, as she had always pronounced it, and not Salève, J. said: " *It isn't true, is it? It's just because everybody has called it Salève for a very long time that it's called that, but they didn't see it.*—But what about at the beginning?—*Someone called it that and said it to other people, but they never saw it.*—Yes, but L. is very small, she doesn't know. When you were small, you thought things like that, too. You used to ask where the names of things were, spiders, for example, do you remember?—(Laughing) *No, I don't remember. I don't think the name of the Salève is anywhere: you can't see it, you know it.*"

And here we have L. at 4 ; 3 (16): " *Why do you say Salève for the Solève?*—But it is Salève, and not Solève.—*But its real name is Solève.*—No, it's Salève.—*But I saw it.*—What did you see?—*I saw it was the Solève.*—What?—*I looked at that peak. It's the top of the Solève and I saw it was the Solève and not the Salève.*—But there's nothing to see.—*Well, I had that idea.*—How?—*Because I saw it was the Solève.*"

OBS. 124. At 2 ; 9 (11) J. screamed in the middle of the night: " *It was all dark and I saw a lady on there* (pointing to her bed)." She had also seen a little man in the room and still believed in him once she was awake.

After the age of three, she admitted that dreams were not real, but she thought they existed in the room as visible pictures. At 6 ; 7 (21) she still believed in this external quality of dreams and then discovered that they were " *in her head.*"

L. at 3 ; 10 (8): " *I didn't have any dreams last night, because it was quite light. It has to be very dark to have them. Dreams are in the dark.*" And at 3 ; 11 (24): " *The dark's lovely. You can take everything you want in the dark, and put it back afterwards.*—Did you dream last night? —*Yes, I dreamt a boat was flying. I saw it in the dark. It came with the light. I took it for a minute and then I put it back. It went away with the dark.*" It was at about the age of six that L. also discovered that dreams were in one's head.[1]

OBS. 125. At 6 ; 7 (4) J. was looking for her doll and could not find it: " You've no idea where you put it?—*No, I've no more ideas in my tummy. My mouth will have to give me a new idea.*—Why your mouth?—*Yes, it's my mouth that gives me ideas.*—How?—*It's when I talk, my mouth helps me to think.*" The same day we freed a goat whose rope had got tied up round a tree-trunk: " You see it never thought of walking round the tree itself.—*No, because it's an animal.*—But don't animals have thoughts?—*No. Only parrots a little bit, because they talk a little. But not the others, and not goats.*" At 6 ; 7 (26),

[1] It is obvious that these examples are analogous to those we gave in *The Child's Representation of the World*, although we refrained from questioning J. and L. in order not to influence them.

however: "*You still have ideas when your mouth is shut, but you can't say them.*—So then you haven't any ideas?—*Yes, you have, it's your tongue.*"

It is clear from these examples that names begin by being localised in objects, dreams in the bedroom, and thought in the voice, and that it is only at the age of about seven that mental activity is grasped as being internal. It is at the age when symbolism is at its height that names and dreams are projected into external reality, and it is when symbolism is declining, and when true concepts are taking the place of imaged preconcepts, that thought leads to an awareness sufficient to allow of relative, internal localisation. Obviously this two-fold correlation is not fortuitous. The symbol is the expression of the compulsion felt by the mind to project its content on to objects, for lack of consciousness of itself, while the progress of operations is essentially linked with the reflective development that leads to this consciousness and thus dissociates what is subjective from external reality.

§ 4. *Magic-phenomenism, reactions related to air, and co-ordination of view-points*

It remains to show how co-ordination of view-points influences the structure of concepts by freeing the child from his symbolic ego-centrism and leading him to socialisation of his thought. One of our examples is particularly helpful in this connection: that observed in the case of J. with respect to air, and showing the transition from certain magic-phenomenist notions to adapted cognitive representations. It provides evidence of a remarkable continuity between the egocentric preconcept and logical, or at least intuitive, co-ordination.

OBS. 126. We first give some examples of magic-phenomenist behaviours observed during the last sensory-motor stages, in which they are merely a continuation of the initial forms of causality. At 1 ; 7 (28) J. was playing in a room where I was lying with a cape over my legs. She put her head on the hump made by my feet. I gave a little shake, and she raised her head, then put it back, and so on. Finally I stopped. She then confined her gaze to the spot where my feet were and moved her head, as if this procedure acted directly on the hump! At 1 ; 10 (16), similarly, J. banged a key on the bottom of a basket behind the bed where I was lying. I said " Oh . . ." and she laughed and did it again. This was repeated six or seven times. When I finally stopped saying " Oh . . .", she took the key out of the basket, which she pushed a few inches away with her other hand, put it straight, and banged again louder than before. She was thus behaving as if my exclamation had depended merely on the material arrangement of the basket and the key.

At 3 ; 2 (20), *i.e.*, a considerable time after the preceding stage,

L. heard a waggon on a road at right angles to the one on which we were, and was frightened: "*I don't want it to come here. I want it to go over there.*" The waggon went by, as she wished: "*You see, it's going over there because I didn't want it to come here.*"

At 4 ; 6 (2) J. was afraid of chimney-sweeps. One day when she fell down on the stairs as she was running away, it was the sweep himself who comforted her. Although she was very touched, she did not lose her fear, but at 4 ; 6 (4) I found her running round and round a vertical metal pole: "*I'm going round like this to learn to like sweeps. This little music* (rubbing her hand on the metal) *tells me that they're nice.*" At 4 ; 6 (6) she was running at top speed round a little flower-bed: "*I'm running round the grass so as not to be afraid of sweeps any more.*" But she continually thought they were there, in the cellars, under the roof, in spite of our assurances to the contrary, and then she ran round again to reassure herself.

At 4 ; 6 (20) she was afraid when she saw me going off on a friend's motor-cycle. She put her fingers to her mouth in a special way, which was new, and said to her mother: "*I'm putting my fingers like that so that daddy'll come back.*" At the same period she stamped her foot in her room, saying: "*I'm stamping, because if I don't the soup isn't good enough. If I do, the soup's good.*" Obviously nothing in these behaviours could have been suggested by the adults with whom J. lived. For instance, neither her parents nor her nurse were accustomed to stamp their feet!

When J. was 5 ; 6 (11) I overheard a conversation between her and L. in bed. L. was afraid of the dark and J. was reassuring her. L. then asked: "Where does the dark come from?—*From water, because when it's daylight, the night goes into the lake.*" But at 5 ; 6 (22) I heard J. alone in the garden saying: "*I'm making the daylight come up, I'm making it come up* (making a gesture of raising something from the ground). *Now I'm making it go away* (gesture of pushing something away) *and now the night's coming. I make the night come up when I go to the edge of the lake: the man* (walking outside the garden) *still has a bit on his coat. I'm making the light come up.*" After this, she amused herself the rest of the day in "*making light*" with a stick (making the gesture of pulling it towards her and throwing it away). This brings us to the ideas connected with air and to the story of the "amain" (see the following observation, from 5 ; 7 onwards).

OBS. 127. Both J. and L. began at the age of two to be interested in the wind and air. At 2 ; 0 (3) L. saw the leaves of a tree moving and said: "*Wind.*—Where?—*In the leaves.*" At 3 ; 10 (17) she connected shadow with the wind (see obs. 132). At 4 ; 2 (12) she saw a big cloud coming up: "*It's the wood that brought it.*—The wood?—*Yes, the wind from the trees.*"

Similarly, J., at 2 ; 11 (14), saw from her bed some mist on the trees at the edge of the lake: "*The clouds are moving.*—Yes.—*They're going a long way away into the trees, because the trees are moving; there are some winds.*" An hour later she told her mother what she had seen:

" *The clouds were moving because the trees were moving.*" The next day she noticed the waves and said: " *I understand everything. I understand the waves: it's because there's a tree at the edge of the lake. You see that white thing in the tree* (pointing in the distance either to the white trunk of a birch or to the foam on the waves seen through the foliage), *it's the waves. It's the tree that makes the waves: trees make wind.*"

But at 4 ; 6 (15) the age at which we have already seen her behaviours in relation to sweeps and the motor-cycle (obs. 126), J. saw the moon rising over the Salève at about 9 p.m.: " *Oh! a moon over the Salève! It's moving because there's some wind. It's gliding with the sky. All the sky is gliding.*" J. then tried with her hand to make a draught in the opposite direction, then she blew twice and exclaimed in delight: " *It was quite flat. Now it's big. It's with the air. It's blown up now!* "

At 5 ; 6 (6): " *What makes the clouds move? I think it's the sky. Tell me, now that I've told you!*—What in the sky?—*The wind* (then spontaneously): " *Can you get hold of air?* (grasping with her hand)."

At 5 ; 6 (21) she was turning round on herself: " *This moves the grass.*—I don't see how.—*It's because I'm turning: then it turns too.*"

At 5 ; 6 (2), in connection with " the air of babies " (see the latter part of obs. 116, also at 5 ; 6 (22): " babies are air at first," etc.), J. added: " *There's air in my mouth, isn't there? I make it come out when I do that* (blowing). *I think the north wind comes from the very big trees.*" The remark " *I'm making the daylight come up . . . etc.*" was also made at 5 ; 6 (22) (see end of obs. 126).

At 5 ; 7 (11): " *Can air be made?*— . . . —*Can you make air?* " The same day: " *The air in the sky is blue, but the air by the house isn't blue.*—That's right.—*Then how do they make air?*—I don't really know." The same evening: " *But tell me really how they make air.*" At 5 ; 7 (20) she blew into a glass and turned it upside down: " *I'm shutting in air, aren't I?* "

At 5 ; 7 (22) she was by herself in a room, walking up and down and clapping her hands. Then she went into the next room, still clapping, and came up to me, saying: " *I'm making fresh air.*"

At 5 ; 8 (24) J. turned round faster and faster until she was giddy and then said to me: " *Can you feel it turning?*—Why?—*Because I turned. Why don't we feel when somebody else turns?*—What do you think?—*Oh, I really can't find that out* (pause). *It's ' hand.'*—What? When I turn, it's ' hand ' that makes the air turn, and when you turn very fast, it flies, everything flies, ' hand ' flies into the air. You see, when I do that* (gesture of moving the air with her hand), *the air comes, and when I do that* (pushing away), *it goes away. ' Hand ' makes the air rise.*—Then why do you say that it doesn't turn for me when you turn?—*It's blue ' hand,' it's your ' hand.'*—What does that mean?— . . . " A moment later, spontaneously: " *I know what blue ' hand ' and white ' hand ' are. ' Hand ' is when it moves. Blue ' hand ' is when it doesn't move. When I do that with my hand* (moving it), *I'm doing white ' hand,' and that moves the trees and the clouds and all the air, and* *when I do that* (gesture of raising something from the ground), *it raises the air and then it's all blue.*—And what is it that we can see now, blue ' hand ' or white ' hand '?—(Looking at the sky) *It's white ' hand,' it's full of clouds. It's the air that has gone up, that's moving. And when you raise it, it's all blue and it doesn't move any more.''* Then she began to run, without speaking, turned round and said: '' *Look at my hand* (beating the air), *I'm doing white ' hand,' it makes me run very fast. You're not moving, that's blue ' hand.' There* (pointing to my motionless arm), *you can't see anything. Now, look* (running and then stopping), *that's blue ' hand,' I'm not running now.*

Just after this we were out for a walk and she told me that she understood why I did not see things turning when she herself turned: '' *You see, it's like this: when I do that* (beginning to turn), *it's white ' hand,' and when I do this* (gesture of lifting up), *it drives the air away, there's no more white air in the sky, and it's blue ' hand.'* Thus, when she turned, she thought she made things move objectively through the draught she caused, while I who was motionless and higher up than she was, was in '' blue hand '' and could not see anything going round. I decided to wait for a verification of this interpretation or to ask her one day in the future for a résumé. As there was no further reference to '' hand,'' I therefore merely said to her at 5 ; 11 (2): '' Do you remember what you once told me about ' hand '? I've forgotten.—*Yes, white ' hand ' is when you push the air* (gesture). *' Hand ' is white when it's down below, and up above there's blue ' hand.' ''*

OBS. 128. Here we have the last phase of J.'s ideas about air. At 5 ; 9 (25): '' *The Arve is flowing fast. It's when there's a lot of wind.*'' At 5 ; 10 (21) she was watching me balance a walking-stick on my finger: '' *Why does it stand up? I think it's because there's air all round it.*''

At 6 ; 3 (10) J. was whirling round as in the preceding observation but she no longer believed in its objective results: '' *You can feel it going round, but things aren't really turning.*''

At 6 ; 7 (8): '' *It's the air that makes trees move, because air is moving all the time, and the trees make the wind when they move. That's why clouds move. The air makes the trees move and then the air moves by itself. That's what makes the clouds move.*'' This was almost '' environmental reaction,'' but with the circle as yet incomplete. The evening of the same day: '' *It's the air that makes the clouds move. Air moves by itself. No, it's the trees. But when there aren't any trees, I don't understand it.*''

At 6 ; 7 (11): '' *Wind and clouds are the same thing. That's why the clouds move. Yes, because they're air, and when they move, it's because of their wind.*'' And at 6 ; 7 (12): '' *It's the air, I think, that makes the moon move along.*''

Then, at 6 ; 7 (15): '' *The wind is air that's moving. It's the leaves and the grass and the air that make the wind, and then up above it's the air and the clouds.—What?—Yes, it's the air that makes the clouds move.—* Yes, that's true.—*But it is. The clouds make the air move: the air pushes them and then they make the wind. They both help one another.—* What does that mean?—*That the cloud helps the wind, it makes it blow, and the wind helps the cloud to move.—*But who begins?—*The wind pushes the cloud a bit and then the cloud moves and makes wind.—*And when there isn't any wind?—*But the cloud moves a bit by itself, because it's air. And then it makes wind.—*And what about the grass?—*The wind pushes it and then it makes more wind."*

At 6 ; 9 (1): " *Air comes from the leaves and the leaves move in the wind, that's what it is!* " And at 6 ; 9 (17): " *Clouds are the sky breaking up, they're air that's made into clouds, and the cloud makes wind when it moves."*

These examples are interesting both from the point of view of the structure of thought and also because of their content. The continuity between the beginnings of magic-phenomenist causality, appearing as early as the sensory-motor levels (belief in the effect of a gesture on reality), and the facts concerned with the production of light at the end of obs. 126, is obvious. The first examples given in this observation are merely remains of sensory-motor causality. Then come semi-serious, semi-ludic combinations of the same order, and finally the action of the hand on air, an action which is incomprehensible to the child for whom air is not a substance when it is motionless. It exists only when it is set in motion, *i.e.*, when it " is made." This causal connection, resulting both from experience of the phenomenon and from the child's own activity, is immediately generalised by J. into a kind of " action at a distance " exerted on darkness, wind, and the various celestial movements (clouds, moon, etc.). An excellent illustration of this is to be found in the episode of " hand," or air produced by the hand, in which the child goes so far as to believe that he makes everything round him turn as a result of his own turning movement that produces wind (obs. 127). From the point of view of the structure of thought, it is clear that this causality, based on egocentric assimilation, is translated into a preconcept in which the part played by the imitative image is evident, and of which the logical structure is still that of participation. Moreover, we find all the gradations between the ludic symbol and cognitive representation, according to the degree of belief at various stages.

The child gradually abandons these egocentric preconcepts and arrives at objective notions, or at least at a degree of objectivity comparable to that of the idea of " environmental reaction " used in Greek physics. Probably he begins, as early as the age of two or three, by noticing that there is a connection between wind and the movements of trees and clouds, but for him these remain preconceptual notions, since wind is a substance directly produced by objects endowed with spontaneous living activity. In the case of " hand," on the contrary, in spite of the initial egocentrism of this preconcept, J.

gradually succeeds in dissociating two distinct points of view as her thought begins to be socialised. She becomes aware of her own point of view, *i.e.*, that of the subject whirling round and thus producing " white hand " (involving the movement of objects situated within its range) and the point of view of the adult observer, *i.e.*, of the motionless subject who is in " blue hand," and who consequently cannot see anything turning. This co-ordination of view-points later enables her to abandon her subjective belief in the reality of movements provoked by her own activity. She then tries to relate objects one to another (obs. 128) and finally arrives at the intuitive notion of " environmental reaction " according to which bodies in motion are moved by the stream of air produced by their displacement. In this schema we again find the original magic-phenomenist idea of air produced by movement, but here air is beginning to acquire the status of a substance capable of preservation. Thus here, as always, intuitive thought is the transitional stage between imaged, pre-conceptual schemas and truly operational concepts, as we shall see more clearly later on.

§ 5. *Objects, spatial perspective and time*

We come finally to the investigation of the evolution of the notions of objects, space, and time, beginning from sensory-motor schemas, passing through the stage of preconceptual and then intuitive schemas, and finally reaching schemas capable of operational manipulation. The later stages of this evolution must of course be dealt with separately elsewhere.

It is in relation to these three notions that both the continuity and the opposition between sensory-motor schemas and representation are most clearly visible. As we saw in *La Construction du Réel Chez l'Enfant*, a vast spatio-temporal construction takes place in the mind of the child between birth and the last stage in the development of sensory-motor intelligence, *i.e.*, during the first eighteen months. Starting from a world containing neither objects nor permanent substances, with various sensorial spaces centred on the child's own body, a world in which there is no time other than the moment being experienced by the child, the construction results in a universe of permanent objects constituting a single practical space that is relatively decentred (in that it includes the child's own body as one element among many), and evolving in temporal series that allow of practical reconstitution and anticipation. But in order that the representative universe, which becomes possible with the co-ordination of images and verbal schemas, may be constructed, two new spheres of activity must be conquered: (1) the extension in time and space of the immediate practical universe, *i.e.*, the conquest of distant space and by-gone time, both of which demand a representation that goes beyond perception, and not merely direct movement or perceptual contact; (2) the co-ordination of the child's own universe with that of others, *i.e.*, the objectivation of the representative universe for the purpose of co-ordination of view-points.

The question then is to discover whether the intervention of representation involves a complete break with the past—as Wallon suggests, particularly with respect to space—or whether representation extends and co-ordinates the conquests of sensory-motor intelligence, reconstructing them on the new plane of representation, this reconstruction involving a shift from earlier constructions but not complete discontinuity. The evidence on the subject leaves no room for doubt. If there were discontinuity, either the whole construction would have to be begun again, and representation would in its turn start with a world without objects, without single space, etc., or else the new construction would be from the start quite distinct from the sensory-motor construction, which it would, however, integrate in itself. What we do in fact find, is, on the contrary, that there is partial reconstitution and progressive extension of the sensory-motor schemas, and that the phases of this reconstitution and extension are analogous to those observable in the development of sensory-motor activity.

OBS. 129. At 2 ; 4 (3) L. heard water running in the bathroom upstairs. She was with me in the garden and said to me: " *That's daddy up there.*" At 2 ; 5 (0) L. went with her uncle to his car and saw him drive off along the road. She then went back into the house, and went straight to the drawing-room, where he had been earlier, and said: " *I want to see if uncle C. has gone.*" She went in, looked all round the room and said: " *Yes, he's gone.*" At 2 ; 5 (9) she had a visit from little B. in the drawing-room instead of on the verandah as usual. As soon as B. had gone, L., who had accompanied her to the garden gate, returned to the house, went to the verandah and said: " *I want to see if B. is here.*" The scene was repeated some days later.

On the same days, we observed that when L. was looking at pictures she behaved in the way pointed out by M. Luquet, and that we ourselves also studied many years ago.[1] Although she recognised the characters who reappeared in the various pictures illustrating a story, she took them to be several different ones: " *What's that little girl doing?* " etc., as if it was not the same little girl she had just seen in the preceding picture.

It would seem therefore that real persons in certain definite situations, and characters in pictures in all situations, constituted objects of which there were several copies, half identical with one another and yet distinct in so far as they were connected with different situations. It is the same phenomenon we noted above in relation to the sun and the moon, each of which was at the same

[1] *Archives de psychologie*, XIX (1925), pp. 211–239 and pp. 306–349.

time one and many, and also the one identical with the other (*cf.* also " the " slug of Chap. VIII).

OBS. 130. When J. was 3 ; 3 (1) we were walking along a road and kept to the right because of the cars. On the way back she kept to the left: " *This was the right.*—What is the right?—*It's the side where the hand is that holds the spoon.*" She maintained that there was an absolute right, however, as far as the road was concerned.

At 3 ; 7 (12) seeing the sun rise in the mountains at an unexpected place: " *Are there two suns then?* "

At 3 ; 11 (13) L. was in a car on a road at right angles to the Salève: " *Oh, the Solève* (she still said ' Solève,' *cf.* obs. 123) *is moving.* —Is it really, or does it just look like it (it did, in fact, appear to be receding as we went along)?—*It's really moving.*—Can that lady on the road see it moving?—*Of course, because it's the car that makes it move.*" A moment later: " *It's moving even more than before, because the car's going faster.*" When she was 3 ; 11 (20) we were driving along the same road, but in the opposite direction, and slowly: " *The mountain is moving again because we're moving.*—Is it really, or does it just look like it?—*It looks like it.*—So it isn't moving?—*No, because we aren't going fast enough.*—And the other day, it wasn't really moving either?—*Yes, it was, because we were going fast.*"

L., at 4 ; 3 (22): " *Oh! the sun's moving quickly. It's going for a walk like us. It's going the same way as we are. Soon it'll be on that grass.*" We turned back, and L. laughed hard when she saw the sun coming back too: " *It's doing that for a joke, to play tricks on us . . .* (*cf.* obs. 120)." An hour later: " *Oh! it's running with us.*" Then, as we were coming down: " *It'll come down now.*—Why?—*Because we're going down.*" We went through a gorge that was in shadow, and then came out into the sun: " *Ah! it's there again, and when we're in the car it'll be here again, and at home too: it always goes with us.*" At 4 ; 5 (1): " *Oh! the moon's moving along with us, because of the boat.*— But does it move by itself?—*No, not by itself. It's the boat, it's us.*" The same day L. was swinging with J. (6 ; 7) and a friend who was seven. L. thought the moon also was moving and swinging, but J. and the friend refused to accept this.

At 4 ; 6 (3) L. saw the Salève from Archamp instead of from the usual place: "*It's all changed.*—Has it really, or does it just look as if it had?—*It really has.*—Did it look like that to the people who were here yesterday? *No, different.*—But wasn't it like that here yesterday?—*It was different.*" A moment later, from the same spot: " *Why can't we see the Petit-Salève?*—What do you think?—*I don't know.*—Has it gone or is it hidden? By what?—*I don't know. It ought to be there* (pointing to a spot at the foot of the Salève." As we were coming back, by car: " *The Salève is following us.*" Then: " *It's losing its shape, like the sun when it goes into the clouds, and then afterwards it gets its shape again.*"

At 4 ; 11 (4), going up a hill at the foot of which there was a little lake, she said that the lake was " *bigger when we go up.*—Why?— *Because we're further away.*—And what about the houses?—*They're* *smaller.—*And the lake?—*It's bigger, because the water from the Rhone has come and made it bigger."*

OBS. 131. Between the ages of six and seven, J., who had up till then shared these misconceptions, gradually got rid of them. As early as 5 ; 11: " *You'd think the stars are moving, because we're walking,*" but she was not sure whether they really did or only seemed to do so.

At 6 ; 7 (8): " *Lausanne is much further than La Sage, and La Sage much further from Lausanne, isn't it?* (We measured distances between two points, in both directions).—*But that's what I meant: La Sage is as far from Lausanne as Lausanne is from La Sage."* She was thus expressing symmetry in terms of equal asymmetrical relations.

At 6 ; 9 (15), as she was going up the Salève, she saw clouds scudding across the summit: " *The Salève is moving, why?—* . . . — *Ah! No, it's the clouds that are moving. It's not the Salève."* The same day: " *The lake's bigger, because we're higher: so we can see deeper."* On the way down, it got smaller: " *It's because we're going down, so the barrier* (the part of the hill that screened it from us) *goes up."*

At 7 ; 3 (29), on the hill from which L. at 4 ; 11 (4) saw a little lake getting bigger (obs. 130): " *It's because it's uncovering itself."*

OBS. 132. It is interesting to add to these ideas of perspective the analysis of projective notions related to shadows, which also raise a problem connected with the object.

As early as 1 ; 6 (6), J. ran after her shadow, in the garden, pointing to it. At 1 : 7 (27) she did the same thing, but tried to catch it. She bent down, got up again and tried again a little further on, pointing to it from time to time and saying: " *Jacqueline."* At one moment she made a shadow with her hand and said: " *Hand."* In the afternoon, when she was sitting on my knee, she saw her shadow again, and again said: " *Jacqueline."* I replied: " Where is Jacqueline "? and then, instead of pointing to herself, she got off my knee, took a few steps towards her shadow, which moved with her, then bent down and pointed to it. Same obs. at 1 ; 9 (28), then, when I made a shadow with my hand, she said " *daddy,*" pointing to the shadow herself. At 2 ; 6 (5) she showed me the shadow of a tree and said: " *tree."*

After various similar reactions, there were no further developments of interest until about the age of five. (L., on the other hand, at 3 ; 10 (17) thought that " *shadow comes from the wind."*) At 5 ; 7 (21) J. asked with reference to a rock that was full in the sun: " *Why doesn't it make a shadow?* " Immediately afterwards, we saw the shadow of a single little cloud fall over a village below us: " Can you see that shadow?—*Yes, it's the shadow of the village.—* It's not the shadow of that cloud? (we could see it moving and going into the fields)?—*No, it isn't. It's the shadow of the village."* She still thought the dark " *comes from the clouds,*" as though it were a substance that emanated from them. At 5 ; 7 (22), in the evening, she saw that it was already dark at the bottom of the valley, while the mountains were still in sunshine: " *You see, the dark comes from down below. It is the water that makes the dark, it's the stream.*" Then: " *Where does the dark sleep?—* . . . —*In the lake, I think. So where it is, it's all dark.*" At 5 ; 8 (o): " *It's all black, this dark, it comes from the clouds.*"

At 5 ; 9 (o) she saw the shadow of some little clouds passing across the mountain: " *Is it the shadow of the clouds? Why do clouds make shadows too?* " Then: " *Is there shadow where the negroes live?—* Of course. What is shadow?—*It's things that run.*—Is there shadow at night?—*Oh, yes, lots.*"

At 5 ; 9 (20), at about sunset, she saw that the shadow of a post was longer than the post itself: " *But why is the shadow longer than the post?* " At 6 ; 3 (2), same question: " *Why is the shadow of the nine-pin longer than the nine-pin?* " We were sitting in a circle on the grass and J. was looking at my shadow, which was behind me. " And where will the shadow of L. (opposite me) be?—*On the other side because she has her shadow behind her, like you.* J. then turned round, and could not understand.

At 6 ; 7 (7), at sunset, when we were on a hillock about thirty feet high, J.'s shadow fell on another mound about eighteen feet high, separated from ours by a ditch which was naturally in shadow. J. noticed her shadow: " *It's such a long way away because we came up the hill and it stayed down below.*"

At 6 ; 7 (22), when the sun's last rays were lighting up the mountain-tops, she first said: " *There's still some sun there and the clouds are on the other side for the night.*" She then discovered that the rays passed over the ridge opposite and that the shadow of the valley was merely absence of light: " *It's that mountain that hides the sun, and the shadow is because the rays don't reach here any more.*"

OBS. 133. At 1 ; 11 (10) J. translated a temporal succession into words as she carried out the action: " *Soup first, prunes after.*" Similarly, between 2 and 2 ; 6 she understood the length of time indicated by: " in a minute," " just a moment," etc.

At 3 ; 10 L. asked, in reference to that day, which she had been told the day before would be " to-morrow ": " *Is it to-morrow in Pinchot* (our district) *or is it to-morrow everywhere?* J. at 5 ; 7 (11): " *Is it Sunday to-morrow?*—Yes.—*Is it Sunday where the real negroes are too?*—Yes.—*Why is it Sunday everywhere?* At 5 ; 9 (o): " *Is there a* ' *yesterday* ' *where the negroes are too?* " At 5 ; 9 (2): " *Are there times when there aren't any hours, or are there always, always hours?* "

At 4 ; 3 (o), talking of a river, she said it was: " *Older than a house.*—How do you know it's older?—*Because the river interests me more.*" At 5 ; 11 (o), when their old uncle had just got rid of a servant who was too old: " *P. left uncle A. because she was too old and tired, didn't she? So when E. (the new, young maid) is as old, she'll leave uncle A. and he'll get someone else.*" Thus uncle A. was considered to be an invariable system of reference. He himself did not grow older. At 6 ; 5 (9): " But T. may one day be bigger than you.— *Oh, yes, because he's a boy so he'll be older.*" T. was seventeen days old, and there was more than six years difference between J. and her little brother!

These facts leave no doubt as to the relation between representative objects, space and time on the one hand, and the corresponding sensory-motor schemas on the other. Generally speaking, it can be said that what has been acquired on the practical plane of sensory-motor intelligence (*i.e.*, permanence of form and substance of immediate objects, and structure of immediate space and time) does not demand a new apprenticeship on the representative plane, but can be directly integrated in representations, whereas all that is beyond immediate individual space and time requires a new construction. This new process is a construction in the strict sense of the term, and not immediate generalisation based on practical structures that are already familiar. It is extremely interesting to find that the general lines of this new construction are those followed by the construction already completed on the sensory-motor plane. It is the various stages of this development which characterise first the preconcept, then intuition and finally the operational mechanisms.

Let us take the notion of object as a typical example. As we showed elsewhere (*La Construction du Réel Chez l'Enfant*) the child's first behaviours indicate that his universe lacks permanent objects and is made up of pictures he can recognise, but which disappear and reappear without his co-ordinating the displacements either in space or time. Between about 0 ; 8 and 1 ; 0 the child begins to look for objects that vanish, *i.e.*, he attributes some measure of permanent substance to them, but without allowing for their visible displacement, as if they were linked with a particular situation. When he is between 1 ; 1 and 1 ; 6, however, objects come to have individual substance that is preserved in spite of displacement and makes their reappearance possible. In connection with this sensory-motor construction, two fundamental perceptual schemas are formed: a certain constancy of magnitude and a certain invariance of shape. As regards the first of these, the Gestalt school held that constancy of magnitude existed at all ages, but as has been shown [1] it is constructed very gradually during the first months of life. As to the experiments of H. Franck with babies of 0 ; 11, a repetition of them failed to confirm the constancy found by the author on the first occasion. Our own experiments, in collaboration with Lambercier, with children of school age,[2] confirmed that this notion is not completed earlier than from five to seven (in accordance with Beyrl, but not with Burlaff). We must therefore conclude, in view of the knowledge at

[1] Brunswik and Cruikshank, *Perceptual Size-constancy in Early Infancy*, *Psychol. Bull.*, 1937, **34,** 713-714.
[2] See *Archives de psychologie*, 1944-45: " *Recherches sur le développement des perceptions.*" See *Rech.*, III and VI-VIII.

present at our disposal, that towards the end of the first year there are only the beginnings of the notion of constancy of magnitude, closely connected with the construction of the object, and that in the case of greater distances the notion is only completed at the end of childhood.[1] With regard to the second perceptual schema of constancy of shape, its evolution is illustrated in the examples given in obs. 78 and 87 of the work quoted above.

The construction of the notion of object with constant shape and dimensions is then completed, as far as immediate space is concerned, at the age of about twelve to eighteen months. But what is the position between the ages of two and four or four and a half, the period illustrated in obs. 129 and 130? It is clear, first of all, that the intervention of language and representation in no way affects perception of immediate objects. What has already been acquired in this field through sensory-motor mechanisms automatically gives rise to correct judgments and representations. But it is a different matter when it is a case of distant objects, e.g., mountains, trees, and even people that disappear into the distance. Here a new construction of permanent objects, and of constant shapes and dimensions, becomes necessary and takes place through a striking repetition of the stages of the earlier sensory-motor construction related to immediate objects. Let us compare, for example, L.'s reactions at 4 ; 6 (3) on seeing the Salève from a new angle with those of T. at 0 ; 7 on being given his feeding-bottle the wrong way round (op. cit., obs. 78). In both cases the object was thought really to have changed its dimensions and shape: the Little Salève, hidden behind the Great Salève " ought to be there " in the same way as the rubber teat that T. sought at the wrong end of the bottle; the Salève was " losing its shape " like the sun when it seemed to sink into the clouds, and so on. In the same way, the child thought that the lake that seemed to get bigger as she climbed really did so. It is also interesting to see that even at 2 ; 5, when displacements and permanence of immediate objects were no longer a problem for her, L. expected, immediately after she had seen her uncle driving away, and a baby being wheeled away in its pram, to find them in the house, in the place where she had seen them earlier (obs. 129).

Notions related to the apparent movements of trees and mountains, which are considered to be real displacements up to the age of six or seven, reproduce the attitudes of the baby of a few months with regard to immediate movements, e.g., when he moves his head and is doubtful whether the perceived displacements of objects are apparent

[1] We can therefore no longer concur in the objection, very pertinent at the time, made by P. Guillaume (L'intelligence sensori-motrice selon J. Piaget, Journ. de Psychologie, 1942) that sensory-motor intelligence and perception constitute two quite distinct fields. The evidence with regard to perception justifying this point of view has since then been superseded.

or real. In both cases, the capacity for distinguishing real movements comes when the perceived displacements are organised to form a " group," *i.e.*, to allow of reversible composition (with the possibility of return to the original position through a movement either of the object or of the subject himself). Similarly, the behaviours related to shadows are in many respects reminiscent of the evolution of the sensory-motor behaviours in cases where screens were used, and they involve similar procedures.

Finally, we find the same mechanisms at work in connection with the notion of time. Practical sequences and estimates of duration of action are automatically transposed on to the plane of representation, whereas a new construction is necessary for sequences and duration involving distant time (time in distant space, *e.g.*, " where the negroes live " or time extending over a long period, as in the relative ages of two people). This new construction begins with the reproduction of the " subjective series " found at the first sensory-motor levels, and this later becomes exact, operational seriation corresponding to the objective practical series.

To sum up, we have seen that the representative categories of objects, space and time, which start from a nucleus formed by spatio-temporal sensory-motor schemas related to action on immediate objects, finally integrate these schemas in a new construction that embraces both immediate and distant space and time. We have also seen that this new construction goes through a series of phases analogous to those of sensory-motor development. In this respect, the stage of the preconcept, extending from the appearance of language to the age of four or four and a half, corresponds to the stage at which objects have not yet acquired permanent identity, and space and time have not yet been objectively organised. The stage of intuition constitutes the transition from this level to that of operations, in the same way as the intermediary sensory-motor stages constituted the transition to the practical co-ordinations of stage VI of sensory-motor intelligence. It now remains to examine briefly the reasons for these lags and correspondences.

§ 6. *Conclusions: preconcepts, intuition and operations*

We have seen elsewhere that, by the age of eighteen months, sensory-motor adaptation has provided the child with an immediate practical universe, through the gradual establishment of equilibrium between assimilation of objects to his schemas of action, and accommodation of these schemas to the data of experience. Representative adaptation exactly continues this process, but embraces greater spatio-temporal distances, this being possible since there is the possibility of evocation of objects and events outside the perceptual field, by means of symbolic images, signs and thought. In other words, in addition to adapting himself to immediate, perceptible objects, the child must also adapt himself to a universe distant in space and time, as well as to the universe of others.

In the case of real or spatio-temporal categories, this adaptation takes place by way of progressive extension of the sensory-motor schemas, *i.e.*, schemas of movement and perception. But the imitative accommodation characteristic of these schemas gives rise to the image, as we saw in Chap. III, and thus provides the individual signifiers necessary for representative assimilation. It is therefore natural that once they are disconnected from immediate reality, the schemas thus used, whether as signifiers or signified, lose, on entering the new field, the equilibrium that originally characterised them. It is no less natural that the procedure by which equilibrium between accommodation and assimilation is regained on the representative plane should follow the same general lines as the earlier sensory-motor construction.

The first stage (1; 6–2 to 4–4; 6) will therefore be characterised both by egocentric assimilation that reduces the data of distant space and time to those of the child's own immediate activity, and by imitative accommodation that symbolises reality by means of particular images for lack of ability to accommodate to the new transformations taking place. We recognise here the preconceptual structure that explains animism, artificialism, and magic-phenomenist participations ("hand," etc.), and that also explains the property attributed to distant objects of being both one and several according to the positions they occupy (*e.g.*, "the" slug, and the uncle and the baby who were sought in their usual place after they had gone). Space and time themselves are reduced to their perceptible qualities, and these are envisaged from the immediate practical angle, without any of the co-ordinations that will later allow of their being generalised.[1]

During the second stage (4–5 to 7–8) assimilation and accommodation tend towards equilibrium, but achieve it only within certain special configurations. For example, at 6 ; 7 (8) J. accepted the equality of two distances AB and BA when they were horizontal, but later observations have shown that there is doubt in the child's mind as to this equality when it is a case of vertical or oblique distances. Precisely because it is still bound up with perceptual structures, *i.e.*, with certain special perceptible states as opposed to general transformations, thought at this stage continues to be imaged and intuitive, and the equilibrium between assimilation and accommodation is not yet permanent. It is this intuitive thought, semi-reversible but without rigorous compositions, that constitutes the transition from preconcepts to concepts, in causality through identification of sub-

[1] *Cf. La notion du temps chez l'enfant, La notion de vitesse et de mouvement chez l'enfant,* Paris, 1947; *La representation de l'espace chez l'enfant,* Paris, 1948; *La géométrie spontanée de l'enfant,* Paris, 1949.

stances still envisaged as living, in the first co-ordinations of points of view (blue and white " hand ") and above all in the first correct articulations of distant space (obs. 131).

Equilibrium between representative assimilation and accommodation is finally reached when thought becomes completely reversible, *i.e.*, when operations are constituted (period III). But in the spatio-temporal field, with which we are concerned here, these operations, far from excluding imaged representation, even seem to require it. When we speak of geometrical " intuition " we use the term not only in contrast to reasoning with regard to space but frequently also in the sense of a faculty intermediary between perception and reasoning. This is a point of great importance in connection with the relations between the imaged schema and operations. As we have shown elsewhere, time and a given space can have the character of single objects without thereby being deprived of their operational nature, and without there being any need for the conception of " *a priori* forms of sensiblity." Intellectual operations are in fact of two kinds. Logico-arithmetical operations relate objects to one another in classes, relations and numbers, in accordance with the " groupings " or ' groups " that are applicable. Infra-logical or spatio-temporal operations relate not the objects themselves, but elements of those objects. In the infra-logical field, partition or inclusion of parts corresponds to inclusion of classes, operations of placing (order) and displacing correspond to asymmetrical relations, and measure corresponds to number. Thus although they constitute single objects, space and time are systems of operations, corresponding univocally to logico-arithmetical operations but differing in scale. Like all operations, these spatio-temporal operations are merely sensory-motor schemas that have become first intuitive and then reversible as the result of an evolution characterised by the gradual establishment of equilibrium between assimilation and accommodation. But in contrast to logico-arithmetical schemas, these schemas are related to individual objects and not to sets of objects. The relation between the images (produced by accommodation to these objects) and spatio-temporal operations is quite different from that which exists in the case of operations involving classes, logical relations and numbers. In the latter case, the image of an object is merely a symbol of the set of objects, a symbol that usurps the rank of substitute or special representative sample at the level of preconcepts or intuition, but which at the level of operational thought is reduced to the rank of mere symbol, inadequate though sometimes useful, its role being that of a mere assistant to the verbal sign. In the case of spatio-temporal operations, however, the image remains at the level of the operation, since the operation is concerned with the object itself. The image is then the expression of an accommodation whose equilibrium with assimilation constitutes the operation. This is why there exists a geometrical intuition almost adequate for operational reasoning in connection with space, whereas ordinary language is inadequate to express the detail. Nevertheless, we do not say more than " almost " adequate, for the image born of the sensory-motor schema is restricted within the perceptual framework, whereas the operation, once it has acquired its unlimited capacity for reversible composition, becomes capable of any generalisations. The great difference, therefore, between the naïve spatial intuition of the stage of intuitive or pre-operational thought, and properly geometrical intuition that persists at the level of infra-logical or spatio-temporal operations, is that the former is a substitute for reasoning, or at least determines it, whereas the latter is merely an accompaniment to operational thought and is always subordinated to it. It nevertheless remains true—and it is on this note that we shall end this chapter—that there is a remarkable unity in the development which leads from the sensory-motor schema to spatio-temporal representation by way of preconceptual and intuitive forms of thought.

CHAPTER X

THROUGHOUT our analysis we have considered the various forms of representative thought—imitation, symbolic play and cognitive representation—as being interrelated, and their evolution as being dependent on the gradual establishment of equilibrium between assimilation and accommodation. At an earlier stage, the development of sensory-motor intelligence is also determined by the equilibrium between these two functions—the two poles of any adaptation— but it is then only present assimilation and accommodation that are in question, as we showed in an earlier work. Representation, on the contrary, is characterised by the fact that it goes beyond the present, extending the field of adaptation both in space and time. In other words, it evokes what lies outside the immediate perceptual and active field. Representation is thus the union of a " signifier " that allows of recall, with a " signified " supplied by thought. In this respect, the collective institution of language is the main factor in both the formation and socialisation of representations, but the child's ability to use verbal signs is dependent on the progress of his own thought. Thus in addition to words, the beginnings of representation require the support of a system of usable " signifiers " at the disposal of the individual, and for this reason the child's thought is much more symbolic than that of the adult (in the sense in which the symbol is opposed to the sign). Now in our view—and this is the hypothesis underlying our whole study—this " signifier," common to all representation, is the product of an accommodation that is continued as imitation, and hence as images or interiorised imitations. Conversely, the " signified " is the product of assimilation, which, by integrating the object in earlier schemas, thereby provides it with a meaning. It follows that representation involves a double interplay of assimilations and accommodations, present and past, tending towards equilibrium. This process is of necessity a slow one, and occupies, in fact, the whole of early childhood—hence the evolution we have constantly pointed out. As long as equilibrium has not been achieved, either there is primacy of accommodation, resulting in representative imitation, or there is primacy of assimilation, resulting in symbolic play. When equilibrium is first achieved, there is cognitive representation, but thought only reaches the level of preconcepts or intuition, since both the assimilation and the accommodation are still incomplete, the former being direct, without hierarchies of nestings, and the latter still linked with particular images. When, however, with further development, the equilibrium becomes permanent, imitation and play are integrated in intelligence, the former becoming deliberate and the latter constructive, and cognitive representation then reaches the operational level, having acquired the reversibility characteristic of the equilibrium between generalised assimilation and accommodation.

In view of the variety of questions studied in the preceding chapters, it seems desirable, in order to emphasise the unity of our thesis, to summarise in conclusion the main results we have reached, grouping them according to the general trends of their common evolution.

I. *First Period: Sensory-motor activity*

We shall start from sensory-motor development, and more particularly from the existence of schemas of action, *i.e.*, co-ordinated systems of movements and perceptions, which constitute any elementary behaviour capable of being repeated and applied to new situations, *e.g.*, grasping, moving, shaking an object.

The use of such schemas implies on the part of the child movements that can be reproduced and that change the movements and positions of the objects affected by the action. Moreover, the movements and positions of the subject determine his particular " point of view " at any given moment, and the relations between this point of view and external movements and positions condition his perception and comprehension of them. It is this objective modification of external movements and positions by the movements of the subject, as well as the subjective modification resulting from the fact that perception or comprehension of these movements and positions essentially depends on the subject's point of view, that we call *assimilation*. The subjective modification thus always corresponds to a potential objective modification, which may or may not become actual. By virtue of the fact that the child's action is susceptible of being repeated and applied to new data, these data become interrelated. Thus assimilation of present data to the schema may be said also to entail their assimilation to the earlier data involved in the same action. This assimilation of present to past data will then be determined merely by the fact that the same action, *i.e.*, the same schema, is applied to both of them. Grasping, for instance, is an action which modifies the position and movements of external objects, both subjectively and objectively, and being an action susceptible of repetition and generalisation, it gives rise to a recognition that is visual, tactual, kinesthetic, etc., so that the object is perceived and understood not only as an object actually being grasped, but also as capable of being grasped. It is in all its senses combined (and they are of necessity interdependent) that we say that the object is assimilated to the schema of prehension, or that it is assimilated to objects to which the schema of prehension has been applied earlier.

Conversely, the movements and positions of the external objects to which the schema is applied react on the movements and point of view of the subject. For instance, according as the object to be grasped is more or less distant there is perception of this depth and a correlative displacement of the hand, and the hand and the eyes follow the movement of the object. It is this modification of the movements and point of view of the subject under the influence of the movements and positions of external objects that we call *accommodation*.

It must be borne in mind that the two notions of assimilation and accommodation are purely functional in character.[1] The structures to which they correspond, *i.e.*, the organs which perform these functions, can in principle be entirely arbitrary, since the two functional invariants are at work throughout the whole evolution from the reflex to sensory-motor intelligence.

This being so, a first possible relationship between assimilation and accommodation is that of being in *equilibrium*, in which case there is what we call *adaptation*, the higher forms of which result in intelligent activity. As, however, the two elements are present in every behaviour, the extent to which the accommodation to external data is complete and permanent must be determined. For the equilibrium to be stable, the assimilating activity of the subject must be in keeping with the movements or the specific causality of the objects it involves. For instance, if A is an occurrence entailing objectively the occurrences B, C, etc., and A' an action of the subject entailing the actions B', C', etc., we say that there is stable equilibrium if the series of actions A', B', C' . . . preserves the objective series A, B, C. . . . The simplest case is that of a perceptual process, when A, B, C . . . are the positions of elements of a figure and A', B', C', the movement of the eyes. But if in this case the schema of assimilation does not objectively modify the external data, the point of view of the subject may lead to distortion, as in the case of special centrations, and there is then distorting assimilation and imperfect equilibrium. In order that the equilibrium may be restored, there must be new centrations in order to correct the earlier ones, *i.e.*, there must be adequate co-ordination of the sequence of assimilating actions in order to decentre the point of view and guarantee the preservation of the external positions and movements. In short, the degree of equilibrium between assimilation and accommodation is determined by the degree of preservation of external sequences: the broader and more complex these sequences,

[1] They are borrowed from biology, in which " accommodation " is defined as individual variation under the influence of the environment.

the more stable the equilibrium of the schema that includes them. But from the most elementary perception to the most advanced thought, this preservation always presupposes co-ordination of the schemas, or in other words the reciprocal assimilation necessary for their decentration. A second possibility is *primacy of assimilation over accommodation* primacy which may show itself either in insufficient decentration of the child's action with respect to external sequences or in inadequacy between the schema of assimilation and external objects or movements. Every degree of this primacy is to be found, its extreme form being characteristic of *play*, and all the intermediary stages linking play with adaptation properly so-called.

Let us first consider the situation in which ludic action is objectively identical with adapted action, *e.g.*, grasping an object for fun, and grasping it either in order to learn to grasp, or in order to use the object. In all these cases the object is integrated in the same schema of assimilation but in the case of adaptation (learning to grasp) the position and movement of the object demand more advanced accommodation, *i.e.*, they modify the behaviour more radically (attention, effort, and other regulations of energy used with a view to consolidation), whereas the schema of assimilation is itself in process of construction. In the case of play, on the contrary, the accommodation is easy because it is automatic, and the action leads to a lack of balance in favour of assimilation, since the available energy is used up in the " pleasure at being the cause," *i.e.*, in practice of the schema for its own sake. In the case of prehension with a view to a definite aim, both assimilation and accommodation are automatic and thus equilibrium is restored.

Next there is the situation in which a given object is assimilated to a schema other than its usual one, or in which the schema of assimilation functions in the void, *e.g.*, swinging a spoon for fun, or, when a desired object is out of reach, outlining the gesture of grasping it. Obviously in such cases there is no longer equilibrium between assimilation and accommodation, either because only the former is at work, or because it ignores the significance of the object which is thus not brought into a causal series to which the child's action ought to accommodate. Moreover, in both cases the action the child has chosen to do is easier than the usual action. This second situation eventually leads to the situation in which the schema applied to the object is taken from a context alien to the action taking place, which gives it a symbolic character and brings us to the limit of the sensory-motor field.

Finally, there is a third general possibility, that of *primacy of accommodation over assimilation*. This primacy is characteristic of imitation, even as early as the level at which the child merely reproduces known sounds, or gestures he has already seen himself make in relation to his own body. For instance, a child who has discovered how to separate his hands and bring them together again will reproduce this action if it is suggested to him as a model, because he will assimilate this model to the known schema. But a comparison of this kind of assimilation with that which consists, for example, in sucking a thumb and a series of other objects, shows that the following difference exists. There is nothing in the nature of these objects to suggest that they are intended to be sucked, whereas the sight of someone else's hands moving is an inducement to the child to make the same movement with his own hands. In the one case assimilation is the incentive of the action, and the schema of assimilation is of necessity accommodated to its objective. In the other, it is accommodation of the schema to the model that is the incentive and that gives rise to recognitive and reproductive assimilation. When it is a case of imitation of new models, accommodation is all-important. Being new, the model affects the schema of assimilation, which means that the accommodation is now active, and no longer merely passive. This accommodating effort is directed not towards the utilitarian aim of assimilation to the child's own activity, but towards the production of a copy or an equivalent—another manifestation of the role of accommodation. Finally, with the deferred imitation of stage VI, accommodation begins to be interiorised and is continued as representation. In a word, in becoming dissociated from assimilation, accommodation constitutes as it were the " negative " of the object to which the schema of assimilation is applied, and this " negative," by subordinating reproductive assimilation, is continued as a " positive," which is imitation, either external or interiorised.

II. *Second Period: Egocentric representative activity*

Stage I: Preconceptual thought

Representation begins when sensory-motor data are assimilated not to elements that are actually perceptible but to those that are merely evoked. All assimilation, even at the sensory-motor level, consists in relating present to past data, but sensory-motor assimilation of a series of objects one to another does not involve evocation, since earlier objects affect present objects only implicitly, through the intermediary of a schema of action, *i.e.*, a motor repetition. In representative assimilation, on the contrary, objects not actually perceptible to which the perceived object is assimilated are evoked by means of " signifiers " that recall them to mind when they are not actually present.

Representation thus occurs as a result of the union of " signifiers " that allow of evocation of absent objects with a system of meanings by which they are related to present objects. This specific connection between " signifiers " and " signified " is typical of a new function that goes beyond sensory-motor activity and that can be characterised in a general way as the " symbolic function." It is this function that makes possible the acquisition of language or collective " signs," but its range is much wider, since it also embraces " symbols " as distinct from " signs," *i.e.*, the images that intervene in the development of imitation, play and even cognitive representations. It has in particular frequently been observed, in cases of aphasia and in the development of children, that there are certain connections between the use of language and spatial representation. The symbolic function is thus essential for the constitution of representative space as well as of the other " real " categories of thought.

But the symbolic function raises a psychological problem, the solution of which is to be found neither in social life (since the individual symbol has a wider meaning than the collective sign), nor in neurology (since a new behaviour, even when it requires the use of different nervous mechanisms, is always to some extent determined by earlier behaviours). It is the problem of differentiation between signifier and signified, and our attempt in this work to trace the history of the various initial forms of sensory-motor and mental accommodations and assimilations has been directed towards finding a solution. This differentiation between two kinds of schemas, " signifiers " and " signified," does in fact become possible precisely through the differentiation between accommodation and assimilation, *i.e.*, between imitation and the assimilating mechanisms of intelligence and play. During the sensory-motor period (except in stage VI when dissociation enters its final phase), " signifier " and " signified " are undifferentiated, the only " signifiers " consisting of " indices " or " signals " which are merely certain aspects of the object or of the schema of action. As soon, however, as imitation has become sufficiently flexible and reliable to function as a separate unit, it becomes capable of evoking absent models and consequently of supplying " signifiers " for the assimilating activity, provided that the latter is capable of connecting them with present data. Thus by the very fact of their differentiation, accommodation and assimilation acquire the capacity for being integrated in new systems that are more complex than sensory-motor actions, and are formed through extension of these actions to the non-perceptible field. Whereas sensory-motor activity involves accommodation only to present data, and assimilation only in the unconscious practical form of application of earlier schemas to present data, representative activity demands a two-fold interplay of assimilations and accommodations. In addition to accommodation to present data, it requires imitative accommodation to nonperceptible data, and thus involves, besides the meaning of the present object (provided by perceptual assimilation) the assimilating meanings of the signifiers. This complex mechanism is, of course, both simplified and made socially uniform by the use of collective signs (words), but the use of such signifiers presupposes that the child learns them. This he does precisely through imitation, by means of which he has become capable of representative thought. Moreover, the interior imitative images continue to serve as individual signifiers even when language comes to be used.

As we have shown, the beginnings of representation entail transformation in the field of imitation, of play and of intelligence. The two-fold system of assimilations and accommodations constituting representative thought may, in exactly the same way as the simple system of sensory-motor assimilations and accommodations, develop in any one of three ways, according as there is primacy of one or other of the processes or equilibrium between them.

In contrast to sensory-motor imitation, which requires the presence of the model, the *imitation* of this second period is representative, *i.e.*, it is not only deferred, but is based on a mental image of the model. Hence the situation is the reverse of that of the previous stage. In stage VI of the sensory-motor period, the action of imitating takes the place of representation. When, for example, L. opened her mouth in her efforts to get at the contents of a match-box (obs. 57), she was representing the enlargement she wanted in the visible opening of the box, her imitative gesture thus already being a representative " signifier." In truly representative imitation, on the other hand, the interior image precedes the exterior gesture, which is thus a copy of an " internal model " that guarantees the connection between the real, but absent model, and the imitative reproduction of it. But as we have frequently pointed out, the image does not make a sudden, miraculous appearance. What actually happens is that the accommodation of the sensory-motor schemas, which has hitherto been expressed in exterior imitations, becomes interiorised, and extends the sensory-motor activity which still controls perception and motivity. Hence the image is both interiorised sensory-motor imitation and the draft of representative imitations. The auditory image of a word, for instance, is both the interiorised result of sensory-motor imitation and at the same time the draft of its future production, *i.e.*, of representative imitation. Similarly, a visual image is the continuation of movements and perceptual activity [1] and at the same time a source of potential imitations. In a word, the image is not a foreign element that makes its appearance at a given moment in the development of imitation, but an integral part of the process of imitative accommodation. It is imitation that has been interiorised as a draft for future exterior imitation, and marks the junction-point between the sensory-motor and the representative.

While, however, imitation, with the help of images, provides the

[1] In contrast to perception as such, *cf.* Chap. III (3), accommodated to an object.

essential system of " signifiers " for the purpose of individual or egocentric representation, it also makes possible the acquisition of language,
the system of conventional or " arbitrary " social signs (" arbitrary "
in the sense of the linguists, and as distinct from the " motivation "
of the imaged symbol). Through this channel, imitation becomes the
instrument for the acquisition of an indefinite number of collective
signifiers which in their turn give rise to a whole series of socialised
representations. Verbal representations constitute, in fact, a new
type of representation, the conceptual, whose scope is much wider
than that of imitative representation. The early language of the
child does not, however, at once reach the conceptual level, being
essentially restricted to the consolidation of the representative capacity
so far acquired through imitation as such. The representations
evoked through language are thus either ludic (*i.e.*, based on a whole
symbolism that language merely accompanies and emphasises but
does not create), or perceptual (*i.e.*, giving rise to new representations
that foreshadow the concept but are still dependent on the sensory-
motor schema, thus being intermediary between the imaged symbol
and the concept proper).

Having seen that imitative accommodation accounts for the formation of the " signifiers " necessary for representative activity, let us
now review the way in which assimilation determines the meanings
expressed either by these images (individual imitative signifiers) or
by these signs (arbitrary socialised signifiers).

A possible situation, in imaged representation, is that of primacy of
assimilation over accommodation, *i.e.*, the image of the absent object
is not used as part of a system of assimilations which would adapt it
to present data, but merely for the purpose of subjective assimilations
of one sort or another. This constitutes *symbolic play*—the assimilation
of any object to any other by means of imitative images. What,
then, is the difference between the ludic symbol and the image that is
present in an act of representative imitation or of adapted intelligence,
and what precisely is the form in which equilibrium between the
assimilating and accommodating processes characteristic of symbolic
play is expressed?

The pure image is an interiorised imitation of the object to which
it is related, just as exterior imitation is a direct copy of the model
by means of the subject's own body or of actions that result in a material
reproduction of the model (drawing or construction). In the case
of the ludic symbol (*e.g.*, a shell on a box representing a cat on a wall),
there is the difference that the objective (the cat) is not directly
evoked either by any action of the subject's own body or by a material
reproduction (drawing, model, etc.), but through the intermediary
of an object vaguely comparable to it and to which the qualities of
the signified object are attributed. Again in this case there is either

exterior or interior imitation of the signified object. In so-called "imitative play" the child's own body is the signifier (*e.g.*, "I'm a church," obs. 80), but the only difference here is in the instrument used, and as we saw earlier, all symbolic play involves imitation. The position is the same in the case of secondary symbolism, except that the subject is unaware of the relation between signifier and signified, and the signifier may be reduced to a pure image.

In this complex situation we see again the two-fold system of assimilations and accommodations which we showed above to be characteristic of representation. On the one hand there is the assimilatory relationship of meaning between the perceived object and the evoked object, and on the other, the relationship between these two meanings and the two accommodations, one of which is direct (the given object) and the other imitative (the image signifying the evoked object). As for the relationship of the meanings, it is obvious that if the subject assimilates for instance a shell on a box to a cat on a wall, he is not at that particular moment interested in the shell as such, and subordinates it to his interest in the cat. Thus assimilation of the shell to the cat has primacy over accommodation to the shell and over direct perceptual assimilation of it. On the other hand, the child is not thinking of the cat on the wall in an effort at understanding and adaptation, but merely for the pleasure of combining these real objects to suit his whim, and of subordinating them to his activity. In so doing, he strengthens the primacy of assimilation and gives the objects a purely ludic significance. Here the image representing the signified is not purely imitative, since it integrates the given object as a signifier in support of the imitation, *i.e.*, as a symbolic substitute for the represented object (the shell representing the cat). In some cases, for instance in dreams where an external object represents a part of the body, it is a case of a mere image, but one which differs from the purely imitative image in that it presents the features both of what it represents directly and what it represents through unconscious symbolism. This use of a given object as a signifier to support the imitation of the signified object can be compared to the use of a drawing to illustrate reasoning, but in the latter case the mental image and the drawing, both of which are signifiers, correspond directly one to the other, and correspond directly also to the signified schema (*e.g.*, the mental image, the drawing and the notion of an equilateral triangle). In the case of the ludic symbol, on the contrary, the signifier is only more or less related to the object it signifies and also to the imitative schema through which this object is evoked, and yet it is this signifier and the imitative schema which together form the symbol. It is quite obvious that in such a structure there is primacy of assimilation over accommodation.

Assimilation predominates firstly in the signified schema, since it is evoked merely for the pleasure of the combination; secondly in the relation between signifier and signified, since the former is assimilated to the latter without objective correspondence ; and lastly, even within the signifier itself, since it is not purely imitative but depends on a substitute of some kind.

We come finally to the distinction between the system of ludic signifiers and signified and the corresponding system that determines imitative representation.   When the child imitates an absent model that he evokes through the image, the situation again involves a substitute object or signifier (in this case the body of the child), an evoked object (the model), and the imitative image of the model. But here, as in the case of adapted thought accompanied by both mental image and drawing, and in contrast to the case of the ludic symbol, the mental image, the signifier and the evoked object are in exact correspondence, and not merely subjectively analogical.   In representative imitation, however, the correspondence differs from that of intelligent adaptation in that there is primacy of accommodation over assimilation, since the whole system is moulded on the model-object and the assimilating activity is restricted to reproduction of the schemas thus accommodated.

Let us now come to the question of *cognitive representation*, which at this level takes the form of the " preconcept." It might be expected that with the beginnings of cognitive representation, characterised by equilibrium between assimilation and accommodation, and having the support of collective signifiers in the shape of verbal signs, the schemas of sensory-motor intelligence would be at once transformed into general concepts and their co-ordinations into operational reasoning.   What actually happens, on the contrary, is that at the level at which symbolic play and imitative representation are at their height, the highest adapted thought of which the child is capable still remains very close to one or other of these.   The elementary cognitive thought of the child, which, as we showed in our earlier works, is intermediary between symbolic and logical thought, must therefore be interpreted in relation to the development of representation as a whole, imitative, ludic and conceptual.

The preconcept, the first form of conceptual thought superimposed on the sensory-motor schemas as a result of language, is a conceptual framework, but one which achieves neither true generality (a hierarchy of nestings) nor true individuality (constancy of the object outside the immediate field of action).   Its essential mechanism consists in assimilation of a given or perceived object to objects evoked by representation, but not yet forming general classes or relations, and merely signified by the image and by semi-individual verbal expressions (" the " slug, etc.).   The two-fold system of assimilations and accommodations characteristic of all representation here shows a definite tendency towards equilibrium, and not to primacy of one or the other as in imitation and symbolic play. This equilibrium is, however, still unstable and incomplete, one of the perceived or evoked objects of the set being considered as a sample of the whole, and not as one individual among others, as in the case of conceptual schemas. Consequently the assimilation is centred, as in play, instead of being generalised, and accommodation to the typical sample continues to be imaged, as in imitation, instead of being extended to the whole set, thereby losing its imitative character. The co-ordination of preconcepts, *i.e.*, "transductive" reasoning, thus remains half-way between symbolic or imitative co-ordinations and deductive reasoning. It is at the same time a mere mental experience (a continuation of sensory-motor reasoning in the form of imitation of real sequences), and, like symbolic reasoning, a series of direct participations (without inclusions or hierarchies of nestings). These features of early cognitive representation are easily explainable if we consider them in the general context of representation at this level, and in the light of the forms taken by equilibrium between assimilation and accommodation at this stage.

The first question that arises is why, during this first phase of the development of representations, the part played by cognitive or conceptual representation is so restricted, whereas subsequently it becomes more and more predominant in representational activity as a whole. In other words, why is it that the young child devotes almost all his time to symbolic play or imitation, instead of to an effort at adaptation? The answer is not difficult. Adaptation to new realities, before achieving the relationships essential between subject and object, always starts from the surface, both of the ego (egocentrism) and of the objects (imitation). There cannot be immediate equilibrium between assimilation and accommodation when the child goes beyond the sphere of immediate, practical activity and finds himself confronted by physical reality extended both in space and time, and by social reality. The new universe which representation lays open to him thus compels him to repeat the evolution he has just completed on the sensory-motor plane. When understanding is not immediate (through assimilation and accommodation combined), he either assimilates reality to the ego without accommodating to it (symbolic play), or accommodates his activity or his representation to models without immediately assimilating them (imitation, drawing, etc.). The effort at adaptation, in which the two functions are combined, thus occupies only an intermediary position, restricted at first, but gradually extending until it includes the two extremes. The lack of equilibrium between assimilation and accommodation which characterises the beginnings of representative adaptation in general thus adequately accounts for the initial scarcity of truly cognitive representations.

The preconceptual and transductive structure of these representations is the direct result of this general lack of equilibrium, since, as we have just seen, it is the expression of incomplete and unstable equilibrium between the assimilating and accommodating processes. The preconcept is characterised by incomplete assimilation, since it is centred on the typical sample instead of including all the elements of the set, and by accommodation that is also incomplete in that it is limited to the imaged evocation of this typical individual instead of embracing all the individuals of the set. The incomplete character of these two components of adaptation is thus clearly due to the same cause as the primacy of one or other of them in play and imitation, namely a general lack of equilibrium. Stable equilibrium between the two processes presupposes a situation in which thought is no longer confined to static states but can grasp transformations, transformations that are not merely imitations of irreversible modifications of reality, but which owing to their reversibility can reproduce earlier states and guarantee the existence of constancies. Hence there is permanent equilibrium only when there is a system of operations, since an operation is both a potential modification of reality, each step of which can be followed by imitative accommodation, and an assimilating action whose reversibility is evidence of its efficacy. Before a system of operations can be formed, however, assimilation and accommodation must be in action together and continuously, not temporarily or alternately. Now the characteristic feature of the representations of this level is that they fluctuate between egocentric assimilation, of which the extreme form is play, and the phenomenist accommodation of the imitative image, and the characteristic feature of preconceptual thought is that the assimilations and accommodations that are in equilibrium are limited and incomplete, being static and centred on priveleged elements. Since preconceptual thought lacks the mobile, permanent equilibrium of operations, it remains intermediary between the symbol, the image and the concept. When imitative accommodation remains static and is not applied to the whole set of elements and transformations, preconceptual thought remains imaged and expresses only momentary situations or partial elements. When, on the other hand, the assimilation is incomplete and there is direct participation between objects, without inclusive classes or co-ordination of relations, preconceptual thought remains symbolic and fails to achieve operational generality. Hence it is clear that at this first level of representation there is mutual influence between the characteristic structures of preconceptual thought, play and imitation, and that they form a totality clearly defined by its general conditions of equilibrium.

III. *Second Period: Egocentric representative activity*

Stage II: Intuitive thought

Between the ages of four or five and seven, we again find the same interdependence between the various forms of representation (play, imitation and conceptual representation) as we have just seen in the earlier stage.

Egocentric thought is characterised by its " centrations," *i.e.*, instead of objective adaptation to reality there is assimilation of reality to the child's activity, the angle from which the child views this activity resulting in distortion of relationships.[1] It follows that there cannot be equilibrium between assimilation and accommodation, and that the evolution towards equilibrium will be the result of decentration. A first step forward in this direction is to be found in intuitive thought.

The gradual decentration of egocentric assimilation is already visible in the symbolic games of this second stage and in their connection with representative imitation. As it develops in the direction of multiple combinations and cycles properly so-called, play becomes as much an expression of reality as an affective modification of it. Moreover, as the symbol becomes gradually less distorting in its approach to imitative construction and the adequate image, the result is closer co-ordination between ludic assimilation and the signifiers supplied by imitation. We therefore find, between the ages of five and seven, an increasing number of intermediary stages between play and adapted investigation, with the result that in schools where free activity is practised it is very difficult to distinguish the boundary between play and work in the strict sense. This co-ordinated evolution of play and imitation marks the beginning of a process that will be completed during the following period, namely their progressive integration, or rather reintegration, in intelligence

[1] For us, egocentrism is on the one hand primacy of self-satisfaction over objective recognition (hence the nature of the early thought of the child, which is half-way between play and adaptation), and on the other, distortion of reality to satisfy the activity and point of view of the individual. In both cases it is unconscious, being essentially the result of failure to distinguish between the subjective and the objective. It may be that the choice of the term egocentrism, which we have always used in this sense, is unfortunate, but it has been used for want of a better. The idea itself has been criticised, particularly by Wallon, but we are of the opinion that on this fundamental question we are more in agreement than Wallon himself realises, since while rejecting the term he has kept the notion. In his study " Réactions au monde extérieur " (*Encycl. franc.*, 8, 3, D, 1938) in particular, he develops the idea that the child begins by conceiving things through activities of which they are the object, this accounting for the difficulty children experience in objectifying their spatio-temporal concepts. Moreover, in his well-found formula, " The child thinks in the optative rather than in the indicative," which might be the definition of egocentrism from the functional point of view, Wallon is again expressing the primacy of self-satisfaction. The fact that several times in this work we have had occasion to mention misunderstandings of our results in Wallon's interpretation of them, makes us the more happy to point out this agreement on the fundamentals of the question.

proper. In other words, it represents a movement towards equilibrium between assimilation and accommodation.

The corresponding transformations of adapted thought at the same level show that, between the ages of four or five and seven, intuitive thought is exactly intermediary between preconceptual and operational thought, as we saw at every point in our analysis in Chaps. VIII and IX. Let us consider again the example of correspondence between chairs and little girls (obs. 112 (b)) and the comparison suggested earlier (Chap. VIII) between serial correspondence and intuitive thought in general.[1] When a child is asked to make objects in one set correspond in order of magnitude with those of another set (e.g., chairs and people, sticks and dolls, etc.), or more simply, when a child tries to seriate the objects in a single set, three stages are apparent in the reactions between the ages of four and seven. In the first, in which thought is still to some extent preconceptual, the child only succeeds in making correspondence between pairs or small sets of objects, and there is no seriation or serial correspondence. In the second, he succeeds through trial and error in finding both the right order and the serial correspondence, but once his configuration is destroyed he is no longer sure either that the two sets are still equivalent in number, or even that it is possible to restore the one-one correspondence without adding or subtracting some terms. In the third, the correspondence is successfully made and equivalence is preserved whatever the modifications of the configuration. These three successive phases, which are typical of what occurs in all fields, are evidence of the part played by intuition in the transition from the imaged preconceptual thought of the early stages to the operational thought of the following period.

It is obvious that the first phase represents merely a continuation of preconceptual transduction, since the child is incapable of anticipating the whole figure of a single or double series, and is still at the level of semi-individual, semi-general relations, bringing them together by successive centrations without general assimilation and accommodation. The second phase, however, which develops almost imperceptibly from the first, marks definite progress in the direction of decentration and extension of the adaptive processes. On the one hand, the small sets of objects are no longer kept together but are assimilated one to another to construct the whole series. On the other hand, this assimilation is supported by the schema of the series or of the correspondence, which serves as a signifier, since the construction could not be achieved unless the child's imitative accommodation was adequate for him to anticipate it. Is it in this case still

[1] Our analysis of intuitive thought, in the logico-arithmetical and spatio-temporal fields, is mainly to be found in *La genèse du nombre chez l'enfant* and *Le développement des quantités chez l'enfant*.

an image that is involved, or already an operational schema? Experiments prove conclusively that there is no doubt as to this essential point, since even when the child has himself made the correspondence he ceases to believe in the equivalence of the two sets when the configuration is modified. It is therefore not an operational system, but a figure, a figure bound up with accommodation to the action, in contrast to the mobile symbol of a reversible operation capable of use at any time (and in particular after the destruction of the perceived configuration). The only difference between this intuitive figure and the image of the previous stage is that it is a complex structure, a configuration, and not merely a simple individual image. It is therefore clear that while this articulated intuition shows progress over preconceptual intuition, the stage of the operational schema has not as yet been reached. What is still lacking is complete freedom from the image, and accommodation of thought not only to static configurations but to their possible transformations. It is only during the third phase that this is achieved.

To sum up, the existence of intuitive thought, with which recent research has made us familiar, is an additional confirmation of the importance of imitative and imaged accommodation in the initial phases of conceptual representation, and it can be explained as an intermediary stage in the development from symbolic preconceptual thought to operational thought. Thus in this, as in the earlier stage, it is the general relationship between assimilation and accommodation that determines both the relationship between play, imitation and adapted thought, and also the specific forms taken by adapted thought when equilibrium has been achieved.

IV. *Third Period: Operational representative activity*

Adapted thought reaches a state of permanent equilibrium between assimilation and accommodation at about the age of seven or eight on the plane of concrete operations, and at about eleven or twelve on that of formal operations. Now it is precisely at the age of seven or eight that we can say that there is real reintegration of play and imitation in intelligence, and at about twelve that the last forms of symbolic play come to an end. It only remains for us to consider these final correlations and to see their place in the general development of representation.

During this third period, imitation becomes reflective, *i.e.*, it is subordinated to the ends pursued by intelligence, thus completing an evolution whose vicissitudes are noteworthy. As we have seen, at the sensory-motor levels at which it makes its first appearance, imitation is correlative to the development of intelligence. Since it is accommodation of assimilatory schemas, imitation in its initial stage, although gradually becoming more and more differentiated from assimilation, remains dependent on it, and is only one of the manifestations of sensory-motor intelligence. There is the maximum of differentiation when imitation becomes representative, at the level at which the child, suggestible and open to every influence, automatically reproduces all the models he notes, his choice being mainly determined by affective reasons. Only towards the end of the egocentric period does the child become capable of distinguishing between points of view, and thus of learning both to recognise his own (as distinct from other possible ones) and to resist suggestion. It is then that the progress of reflection embraces imitation, which is thus reintegrated in intelligence. Interior imitation, or reproductive imagination follows the same line of evolution. With the beginning of the representative period, it is dissociated from perceptual activity and becomes active for its own sake as well as to provide symbolic play and thought with signifiers that are gradually reintegrated in intelligence. This can easily be proved by an examination of the evolution of drawing. Younger children draw merely to represent objects, whereas older children include their drawings in systems of wider intellectual significance. This does not, of course, mean that with the development of thought in the direction of operations there is any diminution of imitation or accommodation. On the contrary, there is a continuous broadening of intelligence. This is easily understandable, since intelligent activity is equilibration of assimilation and accommodation, and imitation is a mere extension of accommodation. Hence the reintegration of imitation in intelligence merely means that accommodation, which, as we have seen, is not in equilibrium with assimilation at the beginning of the representative period, regains a state of equilibrium.

Play follows an exactly similar line of development. Just as imitation is gradually reintegrated in intelligence by being brought into equilibrium with assimilation, so the evolution of the ludic symbol shows a complementary and correlative reintegration of the assimilating activity in intelligence through progressive equilibration with accommodation. Whereas sensory-motor play is merely a continuation of what has been grasped through the development of intelligence, the symbolic play of the beginning of the representative period develops more and more independently throughout the whole of early childhood. At about the seventh or eighth year, when the first concrete operations appear, symbolic play tends towards progressive adequation of the symbols to the reality symbolised, i.e., towards reduction of the symbol to a mere image. This is particularly clear in the transformation of symbolic games into constructional games in which the object constructed symbolises the object it represents through direct correspondence analogous to that of drawing.

But although this reintegration of symbolic play in intelligence restricts the extension of the distorting aspect of the symbol, it in no way reduces its creative activity. Creative imagination, which is the assimilating activity in a state of spontaneity, does not diminish with age, but, as a result of the correlative progress of accommodation, is gradually reintegrated in intelligence, which is thereby correspondingly broadened.

This general extension of equilibrium between the assimilating and accommodating processes is naturally accompanied by a more stable and complete equilibrium in the field in which the mind attempts to assimilate and accommodate simultaneously, *i.e.*, in adapted thought and intelligent investigation. This progressive equilibrium leads both to the broadening of intelligence, through integration of imitation and ludic or spontaneous construction, and to its structuration as a permanent co-ordination between the assimilating and accommodating processes.

This co-ordination in permanent equilibrium constitutes operational thought. A system of operations such as the elementary operations of arithmetic or geometry and logical seriations and nestings, can equally well be considered as a set of objective transformations successively reproduced through mental experience (imitative accommodation) or as a system of combinations resulting from the assimilating activity of the subject. Moreover, the characteristic feature of operations is their reversibility, and reversibility can only be explained as the product of equilibrium between assimilation and accommodation. Accommodation by itself is essentially irreversible, since it depends on one-way modifications of external reality, and when there is accommodation without assimilation there can be no return journey by the same route. Assimilation by itself is also irreversible, for without correlative accommodation its object is distorted to suit the activity of the subject, this activity always being directed towards an aim and thus functioning in one direction only. When there is equilibrium between assimilation and accommodation, however, the former is decentred in accordance with the transformations of reality, while the latter has to take into account both earlier and later states. Equilibrium between the two tendencies thus ensures reversibility, and thereby produces the operation or reversible action.

The continuity between the operation and the intuition of the previous stage is clear. In intuitive thought, accommodation is still dependent on certain configurations, whereas operational accommodation is freed from the influence of any figure, being concerned with transformations as such and not with the image of isolated static states. Moreover, operational assimilation is a natural continuation of intuitive assimilation, itself a continuation of preconceptual assimilation. Thus the evolution of thought is shown to be the gradual achievement of equilibrium between assimilation and accommodation through successive stages, while play and imitation evolve correlatively towards their complementary reintegration.

*   *   *   *   *

In conclusion we shall relate this new aspect of mental development to the two other aspects with which we dealt in earlier works. The first of these was the egocentric character of the child's thought, a prelogical structure dependent on his individual points of view and schemas of activity, and we attempted to show that with the progressive socialisation of the child, this egocentrism gradually tends towards intercourse and co-operation. The second aspect we considered was the operational mechanism that characterises the internal processes of this evolution, and we showed that " grouping," which is reversible co-ordination of points of view, both within the thought of a single individual and among several observers, corresponds to logical socialised thought, whereas the irreversibility characteristic of intuition and perception corresponds to egocentric thought. And now, in this work, we have seen that thought evolves from symbolic and preconceptual imaged representation to operational conceptual representation, which suggests that thought which is egocentric and irreducible to " grouping " is essentially symbolic, intermediary between the image and the concept, while rational conceptual thought presupposes socialisation and " grouping."

These correlations are self-explanatory. Egocentrism must obviously be defined not only by primacy of assimilation over accommodation, but by lack of equilibrium between the two processes, one or other alternately predominating. In our earliest investigation (*Language and thought in the child*) we pointed out that on the social plane the child is most egocentric at the age at which he imitates most, egocentrism being failure to differentiate between the ego and the group, or confusion of the individual view-point with that of others. From the point of view of thought, we noted that phenomenism is at its maximum in the most egocentric forms of causality and representation, there being no more than superficial accommodation when assimilation distorts objects because only their most immediate attributes are involved in the action. (See Conclusions of *Physical Causality in the Child.*) This is one reason for the fact that in egocentric thought the accommodation is always imaged and the assimilation symbolic. Moreover, in so far as egocentric thought is preoperational and irreversible, it requires the support of the image and of perception. As for rational conceptual thought, its relation to logical " grouping " and to socialisation through co-operation or co-ordination of points of view, is too evident to need further detailed analysis. The important point is that the best proof of the functional continuity that we have so frequently stressed is to be found in the equilibrium which terminates the development.

Rational operations are, in fact, systems of aggregates, characterised by a definite mobile and reversible structure, which cannot be explained by neurology, sociology, or even psychology, save as forms of equilibrium towards which the whole development tends. In order to account for the fact that the successive structures (sensory-motor, symbolic or preconceptual, and intuitive) culminate in these general systems of action constituted by rational operations, it is essential to understand how each of these behaviours is continued in the one that follows, the direction being from a lower to a higher equilibrium. It is for this reason that in our view a static analysis of discontinuous, stratified levels is unacceptable, whereas the functional dynamism of assimilation and accommodation, while respecting structural variety, makes it possible to trace the evolution towards equilibrium and thus to grasp the specific role of mental life: the achievement of complete mobility and reversibility, which are unattainable on the organic plane.

INDEX

Words marked with an asterisk occur so frequently throughout the book that page references have not been given.